Displacements and Diasporas

Displacements and Diasporas

Asians in the Americas

EDITED BY
WANNI W. ANDERSON
ROBERT G. LEE

RUTGERS UNIVERSITY PRESS

NEW BRUNSWICK, NEW JERSEY, AND LONDON

LIBRARY OF CONGRESS CATALOGING-IN-PUBLICATION DATA

Displacements and diasporas : Asians in the Americas / edited by Wanni W. Anderson and Robert G. Lee.

    p.   cm.

Includes bibliographical references and index.

ISBN 0-8135-3610-3 (hardcover : alk. paper) — ISBN 0-8135-3611-1 (pbk. : alk. paper)

1. Asians—America—History. 2. Asians—America—Ethnic identity. 3. Asians—Migrations. 4. Refugees—America—History. 5. Immigrants—America—History. 6. Transnationalism. 7. America—Emigration and immigration. 8. Asia—Emigration and immigration. 9. America—Ethnic relations. I. Anderson, Wanni Wibulswasdi, 1937–II. Lee, Robert G., 1947–

E29.A75D57 2005

305.895'07—dc22

2004025322

A British Cataloging-in-Publication record for this book is available from the British Library

CONTENTS

ACKNOWLEDGMENTS

This volume would not be possible without the generous support of the Francis Wayland Collegium for Liberal Learning and the Thomas J. Watson Jr. Institute for International Studies, Brown University, for their grants in support of the Asian displacements and diasporas project and subsequent editing of the papers. In particular we are grateful to Professor Anne Fausto-Sterling, Senior Fellow of the Wayland Collegium, and Professor Abbot Gleason of the Watson Institute for their encouragement and support.

We would like to acknowledge the logistical assistance of Walter Harper, Aporn Ukrit, Karen Inouye, and Jim Gatewood at different points along the way. Paul White assisted in the copyediting of the final version of the manuscript. Professor William Simmons, Matthew Guterl, and our colleagues at the Center for the Study of Race and Ethnicity in America provided constructive comments for the first introductory chapter. And finally we would like to thank Melanie Halkias, editor at Rutgers University Press, and Professor Lane R. Hirabayashi for his careful reading and most thoughtful critique of the volume.

PART ONE

=========================

Frameworks

1

===

Asian American Displacements

WANNI W. ANDERSON AND ROBERT G. LEE

We arrived after the Statue of Liberty celebrated her 100th birthday and was polished to look new. We are people of the next century. We are many different peoples and most of us can be polished and made to look like new.

> −Quan Nguyen, in John Tenhula, *Voices from Southeast Asia*, 1991

My eyes hurt from straining under poor lighting; my throat hurt because of the chemical fumes from the fabric dyes. . . . My back never stopped hurting from bending over the sewing machine all day. . . .There was a sign in the shop that said, "No loud talking. You cannot go the bathroom.". . . Last year my employer closed his shop and left us holding bad paychecks. The twelve Chinese seamstresses including myself were so mad.

> −Fu Lee, Hong Kong immigrant, in Lisa Lowe, *Immigrant Acts*, 1996

Once we accept the actual configuration of literary experiences overlapping with one another and interdependent, despite national boundaries and coercively legislated national autonomies, history and geography are transfigured in new maps in new and far less stable entities, in new types of connections.

> −Edward Said, *Culture and Imperialism*, 1993

With an optimistic nod toward the new millennium, Quan Nguyen voices the hopes of a newly arrived Vietnamese, one of almost half a million refugees from the wars in Southeast Asia. Quan Nguyen and many other immigrants from Asia have imagined the Americas as the new "land of opportunity," the "Golden Mountains," or a "safe haven." As Mrs. Fu Lee, an immigrant seamstress from Hong Kong testifies, however, for large numbers of them the realities of life and work in America are harshly at odds with these dreams. Quan Nguyen and Fu Lee are among the millions of migrants who are part of the massive human displacement that has been a hallmark of the current wave of migration and globalization. Globalization is a contemporary dynamic that has generated mass migrations from Asia to the Americas in the past three decades and provides an impetus and context for the comparative study of the experience of Asians across the Americas. The long history of Asian migration to the Americas provides strong evidence that the current collapse of time and space that characterizes the contemporary moment is not unique but rather a stage in the trajectory of the modern world capitalist system.[1]

The landmass that is now Asia has been an epicenter of migration throughout history; among the oldest of these human movements have been those to the Americas. Millennia before Asia and America existed as geocultural categories, the initial peoples of North and South America came from Asia via the Bering land bridge. Later prehistoric migrations from Asia across the Pacific Ocean are still a matter of debate among anthropologists (Railey et al. 1971). Asian settlement in the Americas has been a more or less continuous feature of the modern world system at least since Columbus stumbled on the Americas in the course of his search for a route to the fabled wealth of India, China, and Southeast Asia. Indeed, the initial value of America to Europe was as a source of silver to pay for entry into the preexisting China-centered trading system (see, for example, Blaut 1993; Frank 1998). Trade in silver, commodities, labor, manufactures, and ideas have brought diverse peoples from across Asia to virtually every corner of the Western Hemisphere. Asians have come to the Americas as free and indentured laborers, miners and farmers, merchants and shopkeepers, craftsmen and artists, doctors and scientists, nurses and seamstresses, dissidents and refugees. As early as the sixteenth century, Filipino and Chinese sailors arrived in Mexico on Spanish galleons plying the Manila-Acapulco silver trade. Chinese traders and tradesmen were a prominent feature of early Spanish Mexico and Peru, and Filipinos established communities in what are now Louisiana and Texas (Espina 1988; Hu-DeHart, this volume). One of the first economic imperatives of the newly independent United States was to secure a foothold in the lucrative China market. By the end of the eighteenth century and the early decades of the nineteenth century, Chinese sailors, Japanese castaways, and Hawaiian schoolboys had arrived in New England. In the mid-nineteenth century, after the abolition of the African slave trade, European and American planters brought indentured Indian and Chinese to the Caribbean, Guyana, and Peru (and for some, thence to New York). The discovery of gold brought Chinese merchants, artisans, and miners to California, Alaska, and the Dakotas. From the late nineteenth century on, Japanese farmers and laborers came to the United States and Hawaii and, after the United States excluded Japanese immigrants in 1924, to Brazil.

The restructuring of global capitalism in the last three decades has generated a surge in migration from Asia (Castles 1998). Although Asians have established elaborate migration networks that span virtually the entire globe, the Americas continue to be a major site of this new settlement. The Asian population of the United States, for example, has doubled in each of the last four decades. Other countries in the Western hemisphere and elsewhere have also seen significant increases in immigration from Asian countries, with the result that older Asian communities such as the Japanese Bolivians have been rejuvenated, and new Asian communities in the Americas and elsewhere have emerged, such as the Korean Venezuelans, Vietnamese Australians, and Cambodian Swiss. There has also been considerable secondary migration of people of Asian descent from places other than Asia, such as Africa or Britain, to the Americas, and migration of Asians within the Americas, so that communities of second- and third-generation Indo-Guyanese, Mexican Chinese, and Ugandan Indians, for example, can be found in the United States. Scott Lucious's essay in this volume points to a significant stream of mixed-race Asian immigrants to the Americas. All of this calls into question the stability of the concept of "Asian" in the rubric "Asian American."

It is important to emphasize that these configurations of migration and settlement have always been extremely uneven across time and place. The political, social, and economic fortunes of Asian immigrants and their offspring have differed widely over time and from place to place across the Western Hemisphere. Linked to a variety of trade and labor markets, war and political upheaval around the world, Asian migration to the Americas has historically been a multiclass phenomenon. Certainly, labor immigration has dominated the nineteenth- and twentieth-century histories of Asians in the Americas, but entrepreneurs, artisans, farmers, intellectuals, and professionals have also played significant roles (Hu-DeHart, this volume; Cheng and Bonacich 1984; Look Lai 1993; Chen 2000; Lesser 1999). From deeply oppressed indentured labor in nineteenth-century Cuba, Jamaica, Trinidad, Guyana, and Peru, from "inassimilable alien" to "model minority" in the United States and Canada, to welcomed nation-building immigrants in Brazil, Asians in the Americas have had to negotiate a wide range of political, social, and cultural terrains.

Not unlike their predecessors in earlier centuries, Asian migrants of recent vintage have come for the widest variety of reasons and with the widest range of resources. Many have fled threats to their lives from war and revolution, others have been displaced by economic and social upheaval, and still others have been recruited to meet the demands of new labor markets or seek opportunities to invest their human or financial capital.

With regard to Asian immigration to the United States, several national and international factors have contributed to the increased flow of Asian immigrants since the early 1970s. Albeit inadvertently, the Immigration Reform Act of 1965 reversed eighty years of heavy restrictions of Asian immigration to the United States. The act favored scientific and medical personnel and entrepreneurs, as well as giving preference to family members of those already in the United States (Hing 1993). From the late 1960s onward, countries on the Pacific Rim produced a huge number of technical, medical, and managerial personnel whose training made them a desirable commodity in the American labor market. It is said that in one year in the late 1970s, the entire graduating class of Chiang Mai University Medical School, Thailand, boarded a single jetliner and headed to the United States, a massive brain drain from the Thai national healthcare perspective. From 1969 to 1985, these professionals made up the majority of Asian immigrants to the United States, filling a growing labor market eager for highly trained but relatively low-cost personnel. In addition, Asian capitalists—both small business entrepreneurs and large investors—have immigrated in significant numbers (Ong, Bonacich, and Cheng 1994). The changes to the social landscape are felt as far north as the Arctic Circle, where in Kotzebue, northwest Alaska, the business community, including the proprietors of the Pizza Hut, the beauty parlor, and video rental shop, are Korean immigrants; in the last two years, the more entrepreneurial of the two taxi companies in that city is run by three Thai men.

The end of the U.S. war in Indochina in 1975 opened a flow of displaced Vietnamese, Cambodians, Lowland Laotians, Iu-Miens, and Hmong to the United States, the country that accepted the largest number of refugees for resettlement. Eventually, close to 500,000 refugees from Southeast Asia made new homes in the United States (United Nations High Commissioner for Refugees 1995). Southeast Asian refugees are a diverse population with a wide range of financial and human capital. The first wave of refugees from Vietnam was principally military and government personnel and businessmen and their families, who arrived with relatively high levels of education, in some cases financial resources, and an urban culture. Subsequent groups of Southeast Asian refugees have arrived with considerably less education, less money, and less cosmopolitan backgrounds. In addition, for some, the trauma of genocide, of dehumanizing struggles for survival, and lengthy stays in the harsh conditions of refugee camps continue to shape their experiences in the Americas.

In the last two decades, the majority of Asian immigrants have again been working-class migrants. The restructuring of capitalism has left a jetsam of displaced and dislocated peoples, including millions drawn into a global labor market in the wake of neoliberal economic policies in China, India, and Southeast Asia. Women now make up the majority of these working-class immigrants. Hundreds of thousands of displaced Asian workers have been drawn into the U.S. economy as servers, cleaners, sex workers, low-wage assembly workers, data processors, and software engineers (Ong, Bonacich, and Cheng 1994; Portes 2000; San Juan Jr., this volume). Asian immigrants arrive daily in the United

States by the hundreds as smuggled labor, deeply indebted to transnational criminal gangs and completely unprotected from the worst sorts of exploitation (Kwong 1997).

The narratives of Asians in the Americas form an extraordinarily rich, complex, and contradictory tapestry of human experience. As the conflicting testimonies of Quan Nguyen and Fu Lee suggest, there are different realities among widely diverse Asian populations. This volume takes as its point of departure the radically different lived experiences of various Asian communities in the Americas and attempts to lay out a conceptual framework—displacement—as a comprehensive, contextualized, and critical route of inquiry into their contemporary realities.

Asian America and Asian American Studies

Asian America was conceived in the United States in the late 1960s and 1970s as an act of resistance to the dominant U.S. racial hierarchy (Espiritu 1992; Wei 1993; Gee et al. 1976). Deeply influenced by the Black Power movement in the United States and by revolutionary currents in the Third World, the Asian American movement was rooted in the support of community struggles against racial and class oppression (Omatsu 1994; Umemoto 1989). Asian American Studies developed as a corollary to the Asian American movement, and constitutes a direct challenge to the invisibility of Asian American communities in the U.S. academy. Over the past thirty years, Asian American Studies has mounted a radical critique of U.S. history, society, and culture.

The principal modality of Asian American Studies has been the construction of a "usable past" and critical voice through which to lay claim to full citizenship rights, social, cultural, and economic as well as political (Okihiro 1995; Aguilar-San Juan 1994; Lowe 1996). Rejecting the interpretation of the Asian experience in the United States as that of temporary sojourners (Siu 1987; Barth 1964), Asian Americanists have focused on the relationship between Asian settlement and the patterns of American history and society. Some Asian Americanists have focused on the roles played by Asian immigrant workers in shaping both the land and social terrain (for example, Chan 1986; Ichioka 1988; Friday 1994; Takaki 1983; Beechert 1985; Fujita-Rony 2003; Louie 2001), while others have emphasized the use of American legal and political institutions by Asian immigrants to defend themselves and expand the realm of their civil rights (for example, Chan 1991; Kim 1994; McClain 1994; Salyer 1995). It is no accident that Carlos Bulosan's searing portrait of the struggle of Filipino migrant workers in the United States and the hope that the working-class struggle holds for America remains central to the Asian American literary canon (Bulosan 1943; San Juan Jr. 1972). It has been a hallmark of Asian American Studies to approach the struggles of Asian communities in the United States as a part of the contested terrain of American history, with the power to expand and transform the U.S. national narrative itself (for example, Takaki 1993; Okihiro 2001). In the face of the perpetual racial designation of Asian Americans as indelibly alien, the Asian Americanist claim to an American history ought not to be dismissed as merely assimilationist, but may be understood as a radical assertion of subjectivity and transformative of the nation itself. It is a recognition of the nation-state as the primary interlocutor of the Asian body in America and is, to borrow Gayatri Spivak's term, a moment of "strategic essentialism" (Spivak 1987).

From its inception, Asian American Studies has recognized the connection between American imperialism and the trajectories of class, race, and gender in the United States (Tachiki, Wong, and Odo 1971; Gee et al. 1976). The structure of Asian immigrant communities was understood to be a product of internal colonialism in the United States (Liu 1976). Asian American Studies scholars interpreted Asian immigration to the United States in the nineteenth and early twentieth centuries as a feature of capitalist development in the United States and of the distortions in Asian societies brought about by imperialism (Cheng and Bonacich 1984). Some Asian Americanists have emphasized the strong, if sometimes contentious, political, economic, and kinship relationships between Asian immigrants and their respective countries of origin forged as consequence of their political disenfranchisement and social isolation in the United States (for example, Ichioka 1988; Jensen 1988; Ma 1990; Yu 1992; Chan and Wong 1998; Zhao 2002). Others have put emphasis on the colonial or neocolonial Asian context of the Asian immigrant experience (Fujita-Rony 2003; Choy 2003; Light and Bonacich 1982; Ableman and Lie 1995; Yuh 2002).

Asian America and the Diasporic Imagination

In recent years, the explosive growth of the Asian population and the arrival of a large number of Asian professionals in the United States have given Asian American communities a greater visibility in American society. This demographic revolution has, however, represented something of a crisis for Asian American Studies and, more broadly, for the very concept of a panethnic Asian American social formation. For some analysts, the plethora of ethnic identities, class contradictions, and subject positions underscores the contingent and unstable nature of "Asian America" and the structural difficulties in constructing a cross-class and panethnic Asian American politics (Espiritu 1992; Wei 1993; San Juan Jr., this volume).

The Asian American Studies project is confronted, moreover, with the reality that the majority of Asians in the United States do not articulate their experiences as Asian American. Asians in the United States, particularly immigrants, who once again make up the large majority, are apt instead to express their ethnic identities as Taiwanese-American, Hmong-American,

Indian-American, or Korean-American, leading some scholars and popular writers to refer to an Asian diaspora. This ethnonational self-definition, which ties the immigrant subject to a specific (if sometimes only imagined) national homeland rather than to a collective ethnic or racialized American history is deeply embedded in the discourse of diaspora. Historian Robin Cohen summarizes the diasporic imagination as a nostalgic trope: "Diaspora signified a collective trauma, a banishment, where one dreamed of home but lived in exile . . . all diasporic communities settled outside their natal (or imagined natal) territories, acknowledging the 'old country'—a notion often buried deep in language, religion, custom and folklore—always has some claim on their loyalty and emotion" (Cohen 1977, ix).

The contradiction between laying claim to America and the claims of diaspora has been a central tension in the development of an Asian American culture distinct from immigrant ethnic cultures. It has often been at the center of generational conflict between immigrant Asians who, until the late 1940s and 1950s, were ineligible for naturalization, and their American-born citizen children (for example, see Weglyn 1976). The conflict between Asian America and Asian diasporas is a central trope throughout Asian American literature (for example, Lowe 1943; Okada 1957; Kingston 1976; Chin et al. 1975; Hagedorn 1993, Maira and Srikanth 1996; Chuh and Shimakawa 2001).

In the case of Asians in the Americas, a discourse of diaspora that is deeply grounded in the notion of banishment, exile, and return to a real or imagined homeland must be juxtaposed with transnational practices in everyday life. The concept of transnationalism describes the practice among immigrants of establishing and maintaining kinship, economic, cultural, and political networks across national boundaries, and the creation of multiple sites of "home" (Glick Schiller, Basch, and Blanc-Szanton 1992; Basch, Glick Schiller, and Szanton Blanc 1994; Maira and Srikanth 1996; Anderson, this volume; C. Lee, this volume). Transnationalism has been commonly identified with the globalization of late-twentieth-century capitalism and the expansion of transportation, communications, and information networks, and in that respect it may be said to be a feature of postmodernity (Bammer 1994; Harvey 1989; Rouse 1996; Hu-DeHart 1999). Other scholars, however, have shown that transnational practices of family formation, economic enterprise, and political organization have been characteristic of Asian communities in the Americas since at least the nineteenth century (for example, Chen 1940; Jensen 1988; Lee 1996; Hsu 2000; Fujita-Rony 2003). Indeed, more recently some historians, reflecting an earlier tradition of Overseas Chinese Studies (*hua qiao shi*) have argued for understanding Chinese settlement in North America as an extension of a transnational Chinese social order (Chen 2000; McKeown 2001). Other scholars of contemporary patterns of Asian migration such as the anthropologist Aihwa Ong (1999) have emphasized the political and economic participation across national borders among highly mobile managerial and entrepreneurial elites in the globalized capitalist economy. In stark contrast, Peter Kwong (1997) shows how the dismantling of socialist institutions and social dislocations caused by the rapid introduction of market capitalism to China have generated a massive illegal trade in human bodies.

Christopher Lee, in his critique of diaspora theories in this volume, suggests that the rigors of the debates over diaspora have made it "an influential term" and have engaged scholars in diverse disciplines to rethink "Asian America" (for example, Palumbo-Liu 1999; Hu-DeHart 1999; Chuh and Shimakawa 2001), but he views the debates over diaspora and its research implications for Asian America as still evolving and as being "structured along methodological divides." Recently, for example, Linger (2003, 208) sees constraints of the diaspora concept as it is applied to the case of the returned migration of Brazilians of Japanese descent to Japan. These debates may lead to divergent views, approaches, and sites or subjects selected as the foci of critical inquiries. We remain mindful of the caveat that the deterritorialization of Asian America threatens to derail the commitment of Asian American Studies to a critique of actually existing local structures of race, class, and gender oppression. It should be noted that these structures of domination not only exist on the global level but also continue to be exercised through the nation-state (Wong 2000; Dirlik 1999; Ong 2003; San Juan Jr., this volume). For Asian populations in the Americas, ethnic and diasporic identities exist not simply in uneasy tension with each other but also as products of racialized citizenship often caught between nation-states and their agendas (for example, Wilson 2000; Wilson and Dissanayake 1996; Wilson and Dirlik 1995; Palumbo-Liu 1999).

Displacement

The key theoretical framework for this volume is displacement, which we find to be an analytically productive paradigm for understanding the Asian experience in the Americas historically and comparatively. Angelika Bammer offers a succinct definition of displacement as an analytical construct: "Displacement refers to the separation of people from their native culture, through physical dislocation (as refugees, immigrants, migrants, exiles, or expatriates) or the colonizing imposition of a foreign culture" (Bammer 1994, xi). We think that the relationship between the tropes of diaspora and transnational social practice can be understood best as two related but often contradictory aspects or subsets of displacement. Talking about diaspora or transnationalism without placing them in the broader context of displacement is to diminish the weight of exile, the notion of home, or conversely the act of recreating the new home place and thence the construction of new identities and community within the nation-state in which the group has resettled.

The dynamics of the displacement framework lies in the fact that, as a theoretical construct, displacement shares with diaspora the notions of physical dislocation, banishment, and exile, but emphatically draws attention to the cultural dimension; that is, how one's ancestral culture or the culture of the birthplace has been dislocated, transformed, rejected, or replaced by a new one, one of "cross-connections, not roots" (Bammer 1994, xv). In addition to considering immigrants, refugees, and exiles as displaced peoples, the displacement framework incorporates existing groups that are usually neglected in diaspora studies: migrant workers; expatriates who, by choice and by occupation, live in a different culture; as well as externally or internally colonized peoples. The trans-Pacific people known in Alaska as Iñupiat and in Siberia as Yupihat or Asian Eskimos are an example of an internal colonized people who are not physically dislocated and displaced but who have been culturally displaced through the political construction of national borders across their land, their incorporation into national political economies, and the imposition of new cultural elements (Anderson, forthcoming). Native Americans, Alaskan Natives, and Canadian Natives, by Bammer's definition, are displaced and disenfranchised peoples that the diaspora framework has neglected. The inclusion of migrant workers in the category of displaced population likewise allows us to account for new underclass groups such as the undocumented Chinese community in New York (Kwong 1997).

At beginning of the twenty-first century we identify four existing forms of displacement as the lived experienced of the immigrant, the refugee, the exile, the expatriate, and the migrant: physical/spatial displacement, cultural displacement, psychological/affective displacement, and intellectual displacement. Each form of displacement is not exclusive. A displaced group can experience one form or several forms, and one displaced person in a group can live a displaced life differently from others, depending on the relative degree of his or her estrangement. As Smadar Lavie and Ted Swedenberg (1996, 4) write, displacement "is not experienced in precisely the same way across time and space, and does not unfold in uniform fashion." In this volume, Chinese immigrants in Mexico, Cuba (Hu-DeHart), and the West Indies (Look Lai), and the Japanese in Brazil (Lesser) are both physically and culturally displaced. The physically displaced French-speaking Vietnamese refugees in Quebec (Dorais) are not as linguistically estranged in Quebec as Lao refugees (whose second language in Laos is French) are in Rhode Island (Anderson). Most of the Rhode Island Lao experience all the four forms of displacement, particularly those who held respected professional positions in Laos and found themselves intellectually displaced as blue-collar factory workers in America. Scott Lucious, in his chapter, shows how the displacements experienced by Vietnamese Afro-Amerasians are physical, cultural, and psychological.

Another new frame for displacement analysis that the studies in this book point to is that the specificity of the displacement of each group of peoples must be contextualized as a function of time, namely, the specific political and historic moments of the settlement. Each group's experience is configured as a function of place, that is, where the resettlement occurs. What is the population structure of the place? Who is the majority and who are the minorities? What are the dynamics of interracial or interethnic relations and racial politics within the new place? Whether one sees displacement as a "theoretical signifier, a textual strategy, or a lived experience" (Bammer 1994, xiii), displacement, like diaspora and citizenship, is inextricably intertwined with the sense of place. The sense of place has been understood to play a central role in the construction of individual and group identity. The philosopher Martin Heidegger (1993) maintains that people hold a "lived relationship with places and assign meanings to them." The anthropologist Keith Basso (1996, 53) sees one's experience as "irrevocably situated in time and space," and argues that "one's attachment to specific localities contributes fundamentally to personal and social identity."

Bammer (1994, xiv) insists that "place" needs to be put back into the displacement framework. How do "home" and "cultural identity" become sites of struggle over place? Karen Leonard (1999) sees the creation of new identities of the Japanese and the Panjabis in California as being linked to their evocations of familiar landscapes and resemblances to their "old homes." Making a place home, as noted pointedly by Olivia Cadaval (1991, 205) is a means for "asserting and negotiating one's culture and one's right to place and space." It involves the inevitable recreation of a new home place, a New York, another Lebanon, another Lao Vientiane, or another Cambodian Angkor Wat—all of which evoke the nostalgia or the cultural characteristic of there but take on a new character or new attributes of here. Vientiane and Angkor Wat are not only historic cities but also grocery stores in Rhode Island. Conversely, the name of a Vietnamese noodle shop in Boston, Chinatown's Pho Bolsa, references Bolsa Avenue in Orange County, California, the main drag of a new American Vietnam. Maira's chapter on the desi youth culture of second-generation South Asians in New York in this volume is another case in point. Obviously, the old South Asian cultures are not retained here in their entirety, but remixed to form a new South Asian American youth culture. Such a conceptualization of displacement is therefore linked to the construction of new identities and new cultural or ethnic communities within the new nation-state in which the group has resettled. In other words, in the creation of the new identity or a new community, what do displaced members maintain, reject, replace, or reinvent to create a new whole?

Incorporating the discourse on the sense of place as a key component of the displacement paradigm importantly extends and underscores the utility of displacement in broader debates around community and belonging, including the issue of national and/or transnational citizenship (Ong 1999, 2003).

Dorinne Kondo (1996, 97), rephrasing Spivak (1987), describes, "home" as "that which one cannot not want. It stands for a safe place, where there is no need to explain oneself to outsiders; it stands for community; more problematically, it can elicit a nostalgia for a past golden age that never was, a nostalgia that elides exclusion, power relations, and difference." "Home," Kondo reminds us, may mean radically different things to the abused spouse, rejected gay child, or the "homeless." For marginalized minorities such as Asians in the Americas, historically excluded from citizenship and nationality, "home" has always been a problematic and contested terrain.

Where is "home"? Is the birthplace over there "home," or is the place here where one currently resides "home"? While living and holding a citizenship "here," how should the relationship to "homeland" politics over there be defined? Home as a physical space, an economic space, a political space, a social space, or an emotional space has been experienced, challenged, and contested at different historical moments by different Asian groups in the Americas. Filipino American involvement in the struggle against the Marcos regime in the Philippines has shaped Filipino community politics in Honolulu, Seattle, and Los Angeles. For first-generation Vietnamese Americans, many of them from military and political elites in Vietnam, "homeland" politics and anti-Communist ideologies are central signifiers (Vô 2003, xiv). Similarly, the Korean immigrant generation in Los Angeles had held Korean "homeland" politics to be closer to their hearts than American politics until the Los Angeles riots in 1992 gave them a "rude awakening" and an awareness that their everyday lives and work were shaped by events "here" (Abelmann and Lie 1995). It propelled them toward a new identity and an attempt to define their Korean Americanness and their place in the American community. "Coming home" for the Japanese detainees in the relocation camps during the Second World War, on the other hand, did nor refer to going back to ancestral Japan but to the American home community they left behind because of imprisonment (Kondo 1996, 111). For another group of Japanese immigrants to the Americas, the Japanese Brazilians, "returning" to Japan awoke their sense of Brazilian and Nikkei identity, and of Brazil as a homeplace (Lesser 2003; Hirabayashi, Kikumura-Yano, and Hirabayashi 2002). At what particular moment the new place is cognitively internalized as "home," on the other hand, is differently timed and invoked by the Lao Americans in Rhode Island. Despite their eligibility for U.S. citizenship, it was not until they had fully internalized their additional identities as Americans that they applied for U.S. citizenship (Anderson, this volume).

The displacement framework of this volume does not treat all ties to the homeland as a product of volitional nostalgia. Many thousands of Asian migrants who belong to the transnational working class, the new hewers of wood and haulers of water in the global economy, are tied to "homelands" by debt, familial obligation, and statelessness. In all the chapters in this volume, regardless of geographical location and context, the sense of physical and cultural displacement, exile, marginality, and of being viewed as the "other" can be felt at different physical and affective spaces and at different analytical levels. Bammer (1994: xvii) sees the identity of the displaced as being constructed and lived out on the terrain between necessity and choice. Basso in *Senses of Place* (1996, 54) observes, "little is known of the ways in which culturally diverse people are alive in the world around them, of how they comprehend it (place) and of the different modes of awareness with which they take it (place) in and discover that it matters."

When one hears or reads about lived experiences of displaced individuals in the Americas and elsewhere, one finds again and again articulations of another dimension of displacement that cannot be overlooked—the affective dimension and the emotional template. Edward Said, who lived and died in exile away from the land of his birth in Palestine, sees the affective side of displacement as painfully significant. Cogently he expresses his feelings: "Exile is compelling to think about but terrible to experience. It is an unhealable rift forced between a human being and a native place, between the self and its true home; its essential sadness can never be surmounted. Even when an exile achieves success, his success is undermined by something lost forever" (Said 2000, 173). Said sees the displaced person living in exile as living between worlds. His view places the exiled in a marginalized location, neither "here" nor "there." To Said, the twentieth-century was the age of refugees, and he identifies a significant new genre of twentieth-century Western literature, a literature written by exiles and about exiles.

South Asians in America, like many other Asian immigrant communities, are affected by both the lived and the imagined notion of "home." For them, the present home, the United States, exists as a physical space; but in their affective, psychological state of mind and awareness, another home, South Asia, exists as an emotional space, tied to memories of their forebears (Maira and Srikanth 1996; Rangaswamy 2000; Khandelwal 2002; Shukla 2003). For a large number of Vietnamese refugees in Orange County, California, the incessant haunting of the past is of the death of loved ones and the pain of having left living relatives behind (Le 2004). Likewise, an emotional link to ancestors, including dead ancestors across the ocean in Laos, holds symbolic significance, as expressed in the Rhode Island Lao wedding ritual (Anderson, this volume). In another case study, the Vietnamese Afro-Amerasians (Lucious, this volume) suffered severe discrimination in Vietnam, being called "children of the enemy" and were told, "Go to America." Upon arriving in the United States under the Amerasian Homecoming Act, however, they experienced disillusionment and emotional pain when they were told, "Go back to Vietnam" and encountered social denial and marginalization in the United States, despite federal recognition of their existence. For them, as for Said, "home" exists neither "here" nor "there." The affective dimension of "home" reframes it not as an imagined place, the land that never was, but as concretely and emotionally real to the exile, whether Palestinian American intellectual or Vietnamese Afro-Amerasian.

A broadening of the conceptualization of "home" is pointedly posed by Lesser (2003, 1): "Does a person have multiple homes or just one?" For refugees, undocumented workers, globalized corporate executives, and transnational professionals alike (Ong 1999; Kwong 1997; Anderson 2003) new contextual articulations of the notion of multiple homeplaces have emerged. Lesser's *Searching for Home Abroad* (2003), following the Japanese migration to Brazil and then back to Japan in recent decades and drawing on several research findings, emphasizes that the processes of "homemaking and homebreaking" are constant. For them, the search for home, linked to the notions of diaspora, citizenship, nationalism, and globalization, carries complicated and unresolved nuances.

We argue that displaced persons are not simply "objects" but often conscious "subjects" who take on an active role in carving out their new lives, making their own decisions along the way as they face new situations and cope with new contingencies. There is also a "vital double move between marking and recording the absence and lost and inscribing presence" (Bammer 1994, xiv). This leads to new, significant questions: When does this consciousness of being active subjects instead of being objects come about or come to be expressed? Can consciousness take place in the very first, immigrant generation, or does it need time and an American-born generation, better situated and more knowledgeable about the political system, to activate that consciousness? The history of Asians in the Americas tells us that time and generation are not as critical as independent factors as are the history of the immigration and the sociopolitical climate at that particular moment. Political and social activism of the 1960s did give Chinese Americans, Japanese Americans, and Filipino Americans viable impetus and opportunity to make their voices heard and to carry out their ideological ideals, be it community social service projects (Lyman 1973) or the strike for the establishment of Ethnic Studies at San Francisco State University (Umemoto 1989).

Most of these Asian American activists were of the American-born generation. But during this decade of political activism, as in the case of a new Asian American group, the Iu-Mien (MacDonald 1998), ethnic group activism and ethnic consciousness could and did also take place within the first refugee generation. For the Iu-Mien, transnational contact had served to facilitate their assertion of Iu-Mien cultural rights. It became a political mechanism for linking Iu-Mien refugees in America with Iu-Mien in Thailand and in the People's Republic of China. This contact became a subversive site where the Iu-Mien asserted their rights as scholars of their own language and culture. It thus became the site for their resistance to imposed intellectual displacement. Cultural transnational linkage, the crossing and blurring of the boundaries of nation- states, the contested rights to their own interpretive voices and self-representations, and a resistance to neocolonialism in academia are all parts of the dynamics of the Iu-Mien construction of their transnational identity. In the absence of physical colonization, ideological domination and intellectual displacement of this group of refugees nevertheless did take place in the new homeplace. As the Iu-Mien consciously plotted out the route defining where their group as a whole wanted to go, the question "Who has the right to speak?" became a critical issue for scholars and natives alike. It is at this "place of oppression and resistance" (Bammer 1994, xvii) that Iu-Mien identity continues to be constructed. Abelmann's chapter in this volume addressing "Who can teach what?" brings the issue home to the academy. Abelmann raises the issues of interdisciplinary borderland and the closed academic system of some disciplines that penalize scholars who trespass the borders. At issue then is not simply "Who can speak?" but also whose voice is the speaking voice in a particular representation. What is the underlying ideological agenda behind each articulation? What is the hidden dynamic operating in the speaking encounter between genders, between the dominant and the disfranchised, between the academics and the natives, and between academics themselves?

Conclusion

The attacks on the World Trade Center and the ensuing wars of empire reveal the sharpening contradictions of class and race on a global scale. While the establishment of an official multiculturalism serves "to contain and to neutralize [Ethnic Studies] as an emergent discipline" (San Juan Jr., this volume), in a war of civilizations multiculturalism is (again) regarded by some as the greatest threat to the nation itself (Stoddard 1920, 1927; Huntington 1996, 2004). Regardless of new orientations, from multiculturalism, postmodernism, and postcolonialism to globalization, academic institutions have become conduits of transnational business schemes and global political economies (Miyoshi 1998). "What is the way out?" E. San Juan Jr. asks in his chapter. He sees critiques of racism, class formation, and community participation, as well as the studies of cultural productions, cultural practices, and group relations understood as a function of global capitalist relations as viable strategies for reinvigorating Asian American Studies.

In his chapter "On Defiance and Taking Positions," Said (2000, 501) attributes the limitations of critical awareness among scholars to the "tendency to exclusivist, professionalized, and above all an uncritical acceptance of the principal doctrines of one's field." Said considers such limitations "a great danger within the academe for the professional, for the teacher, for the scholar." As a new theoretical paradigm, displacement bridges and opens up wider terrains of intellectual inquiry across disciplines. Analytical frameworks built on multiplicity of perspectives (LeVine 1981), multiplicity of voices, and multiple narratives (Duara 1995) hold promise for opening up analysis. The chapters in this volume also serve to remind us that the racial formations and ethnic identities of Asians in the Americas have historically been configured at the intersection of the local and global. They lead us through the Asian experience in the Americas across space and time and provide us a conceptual map with which we can engage the changing economic, cultural, and political landscapes. Immigration, displacement, and recreating a new homeplace are the cause, the beginning, the transition, as well as the contested route to the future.

NOTES

1. Immanuel Walllerstein (1974) marks the advent of a modern world system to the fifteenth century, although André Gunder Frank (1998) has argued that a Sinocentric world system preexisted this Eurocentric economy. Globalization has become one of those convenient rubrics that promise a revelation of the panoply of economic, political, and cultural transformations in late-twentieth-century capitalism. It is not surprising, therefore, that there are almost as many definitions as there are writers who deploy the term, and it is not our intention to put our dog into that fight (see, for example, Jameson and Miyoshi 1998; Featherstone 1990; Giddens 2000; Schmidt and Hersh 2000). For the purposes of this volume, following the lead of David Harvey (1989), we take globalization to be an aspect of the late-twentieth-century capitalist transition from Fordism to flexible accumulation in the United States and other core industrial states ("old" Western Europe, Japan, South Korea, Taiwan, and now parts of China and India) and its commanding dominance over states with more traditional modes of production. Although marked by increased velocity of exchange (through global and regional political and economic arrangements, investment and the transfer of money, and transportation and communications technology), globalization is radically uneven in its development both between the core and the periphery and within those sectors of the world capitalist system. Globalization has changed the nature and composition of the global working class: it has proletarianized millions of women and complicated traditional modes of labor organization. Over the past three decades, globalization thus understood has sharpened class contradictions within states and has heightened the sense of national identity among peoples within states and struggles for power between nation-states.

REFERENCES

Abelmann, Nancy, and John Lie. 1995. *Blue dreams: Korean Americans and the Los Angeles riots.* Cambridge: Harvard University Press.

Aguilar-San Juan, Karin, ed. 1994. *The state of Asian America: Activism and resistance in the 1990s.* Boston: South End Press.

Anderson, Wanni Wibulswasdi. 2003. *Lives, places, and memories.* Bangkok: Saam Charoen Press.

————. Forthcoming. *Iñupiaq narratives: Eskimo legends and stories of northwest Alaska*. Fairbanks: University of Alaska Press.

Bammer, Angelika, ed. 1994. *Displacements: Cultural identities in question*. Bloomington: Indiana University Press.

Barth, Gunther Paul. 1964. *Bitter strength: A history of the Chinese in the United States, 1850–1870*. Cambridge: Harvard University Press.

Basch, Linda G., Nina Glick Schiller, and Cristina Szanton Blanc. 1994. *Nations unbound: Transnational projects, postcolonial predicaments, and deterritorialized nation-states*. Langhorne, Pa.: Gordon and Breach.

Basso, Keith H. 1996. "Wisdom sits in places: Notes on a Western Apache landscape." In *Senses of place*, edited by S. Feld and K. Basso, 53–90. Santa Fe: School of American Research Press.

Beechert, Edward D. 1985. *Working in Hawaii: A labor history*. Honolulu: University of Hawaii Press.

Blaut, John M. 1993. *The colonizer's model of the world: Geographical diffusionism and Eurocentric history*. New York: Guilford Press.

Bulosan, Carlos. 1943. *America is in the heart*. Seattle: University of Washington Press.

Cadaval, Olivia. 1991. "Making a place home: The Latino festival." In *Creative ethnicity: Symbols and strategies of contemporary ethnic life*, edited by S. Stern and J. A. Cicada, 204–222. Logan: Utah State University Press.

Castles, Stephan. 1998. "New Migrations in the Asia-Pacific region: A force for social and political change." *International Social Science Journal* 50(156), June.

Chan, Sucheng. 1986. *This bittersweet soil: The Chinese in California agriculture, 1860–1910*. Berkeley: University of California Press.

————. 1991. *Asian Americans: An interpretive history*. Boston: Twayne.

Chan, Sucheng, and K. Scott Wong, eds. 1998. *Claiming America: Constructing Chinese American identities during the exclusion era*. Philadelphia: Temple University Press.

Chen, Ta. 1940. *Emigrant communities in South China: A study of overseas migration and its influence on standards of living and social change*. English version edited by Bruno Lasker. New York: Secretariat, Institute of Pacific Relations.

Chen, Yong. 2000. *Chinese San Francisco, 1850–1943: A trans-Pacific community*. Stanford: Stanford University Press.

Cheng, Lucie, and Edna Bonacich, eds. 1984. *Labor immigration under capitalism: Asian workers in the United States before World War II*. Berkeley: University of California Press.

Chin, Frank, Paul Jeffrey, Lawson Fusuo Inada, and Shawn Hsu Wangeds, eds. 1975. *Aiiieeeee! An anthology of Asian-American writers*. Garden City, N.Y.: Anchor.

Choy, Catherine Ceniza. 2003. *Empire of care: Nursing and immigration in Filipino American history*. Durham: Duke University Press.

Chuh, Kandice, and Karen Shimakawa. 2001. *Orientations: Mapping studies in the Asian diaspora*. Durham: Duke University Press.

Cohen, Robin. 1997. *Global diaspora: An introduction*. Seattle: University of Washington Press.

Dirlik, Arif. 1999. "Asians on the Rim: Transnational capital and local community in the making of contemporary Asian America." In *Across the Pacific: Asian Americans and globalization*, edited by E. Hu-DeHart, 29–60. Philadelphia: Temple University Press.

Duara, Prasenjit. 1995. *Rescuing history from the nation: Questioning narratives of modern China*. Chicago: University of Chicago Press.

Espina, Marina. 1988. *Filipinos in Louisiana*. New Orleans: A. F. Laborde and Sons.

Espiritu, Yen Le. 1992. *Asian American panethnicity: Bridging institutions and identities*. Philadelphia: Temple University Press.

Featherstone, Mike. 1990. *Global culture: Nationalism, globalization, and modernity: A theory, culture and society*. Special issue. London: Sage.

Frank, André Gunder. 1998. *ReOrient: Global economy in the Asian age*. Berkeley: University of California Press.

Friday, Chris. 1994. *Organizing Asian American labor: The Pacific coast canned-salmon industry, 1870–1942*. Philadelphia: Temple University Press.

Fujita-Rony, Dorothy B. 2003. *American workers, colonial power: Philippine Seattle and the transpacific West, 1919–1941*. Berkeley: University of California Press.

Gee, Emma, June Okida Kuramoto, Dean S. Toji, and Glen Iwasaki. 1976. *Counterpoint: Perspectives on Asian America*. Los Angeles: Asian American Studies Center, University of California.

Giddens, Anthony. 2000. *Runaway world: How globalization is reshaping our lives*. New York: Routledge.

Glick Schiller, Nina, Linda Basch, and Cristina Blanc-Szanton, eds. 1992. *Towards a transnational perspective on migration: Race, class, ethnicity, and nationalism reconsidered*. New York: New York Academy of Sciences.

Hagedorn, Jessica, ed. 1993. *Charlie Chan is dead: An anthology of contemporary Asian American fiction*. New York: Penguin.

Harvey, David. 1989. *The condition of postmodernity: An enquiry into the origins of cultural change*. Oxford: B. Blackwell.

Heidegger, Martin. 1993. "Building dwelling thinking." In *Martin Heidegger: Basic writings*, edited by D. Krell, 319–339. New York: Harper and Row.

Hing, Bill Ong. 1993. *Making and remaking Asian America through immigration policy, 1850–1990*. Stanford: Stanford University Press.

Hirabayashi, Lane Ryo, Akemi Kikumura-Yano, and James A. Hirabayashi. 2002. *New worlds, new lives: Globalization and people of Japanese descent in the Americas and from Latin America in Japan*. Stanford: Stanford University Press.

Hsu, Madeline Yuan-yin. 2000. *Dreaming of gold, dreaming of home: Transnationalism and migration between the United States and South China, 1882–1943*. Stanford: Stanford University Press.

Hu-DeHart, Evelyn. 1999. *Across the Pacific: Asian Americans and globalization*. Philadelphia: Temple University Press.

Huntington, Samuel P. 1996. *The clash of civilizations and the remaking of world order*. New York: Simon and Schuster.

———. 2004. *Who are we? The challenges to America's identity*. New York: Simon and Schuster.

Ichioka, Yuji. 1988. *The Issei: The world of the first generation Japanese immigrants, 1885–1924*. New York: Free Press.

Jameson, Fredric, and Masao Miyoshi, eds. 1998. *The cultures of globalization*. Durham: Duke University Press.

Jensen, Joan M. 1988. *Passage from India: Asian Indian immigrants in North America*. New Haven: Yale University Press.

Khandelwal, Madhulika S. 2002. *Becoming American, being Indian: An immigrant community in New York City*. Ithaca: Cornell University Press.

Kim Hyung-chan. 1994. *A legal history of Asian Americans, 1790–1990*. Westport, Conn.: Greenwood Press.

Kingston, Maxine Hong. 1976. *Woman warrior: A childhood amongst ghosts.* New York: Knopf.

Kondo, Dorinne. 1996. "The narrative production of 'home' community, and political identity of Asian American theatre." In *Displacement, diaspora, and geographies of identity,* edited by S. Lavie and T. Swedenburg, 97–117. Durham: Duke University Press.

Kwong, Peter. 1997. *Forbidden workers: Illegal Chinese immigrants and American labor.* New York: New Press.

Lavie, Smadar, and Ted Swedenburg. 1996. *Displacement, diaspora, and geographies of identity.* Durham: Duke University Press.

Le, Mai-Khan. 2004. "Cultural assimilation of Vietnamese Americans." Unpublished paper.

Lee, Robert G. 1996. "The hidden world of Asian immigrant radicalism." In *The immigrant Left in the United States,* edited by P. Buhle and D. Georgakas, 256–288. Albany: State University of New York Press.

Leonard, Karen. 1999. "Finding one's own place: Asian landscapes re-visioned in rural California." In *Culture, power, place: Explorations in critical anthropology,* edited by A. Gupta and J. Ferguson, 118–136. Durham: Duke University Press.

Lesser, Jeffrey. 1999. *Negotiating national identity: Immigrants, minorities, and the struggle for ethnicity in Brazil.* Durham: Duke University Press.

———, ed. 2003. *Searching for home abroad: Japanese Brazilians and transnationalism.* Durham: Duke University Press.

LeVine, Robert A. 1981. "Knowledge and fallibility in anthropological field research." In *Social inquiry and the social sciences,* edited by M. B. Brewer and B. E. Collins, 172–193. San Francisco: Jossey-Bass.

Light, Ivan, and Edna Bonacich. 1982. *Immigrant entrepreneurs: Koreans in Los Angeles, 1965–1980.* Berkeley: University of California Press.

Linger, David T. 2003. "Do Japanese Brazilians exist?" In *Searching for home abroad: Japanese Brazilians and transnationalism,* edited by J. Lesser, 201–214. Durham: Duke University Press.

Liu, John. 1976. "Towards an understanding of the internal colonial model." In *Counterpoint, perspectives on Asian American,* edited by E. Gee, J. O. Kuramoto, D. S. Toji, and G. Iwasaki, 160–168. Los Angeles: Asian American Studies Center, University of California.

Look Lai, Walton. 1993. *Indentured labor, Caribbean sugar: Chinese and Indian migrants to the British West Indies, 1838–1918.* Baltimore: Johns Hopkins University Press.

Louie, Miriam Ching Yoon. 2001. *Sweatshop warriors: Immigrant women workers take on the global factory.* Cambridge, Mass.: South End Press.

Lowe, Lisa. 1996. *Immigrant acts: On Asian American cultural politics.* Durham: Duke University Press.

Lowe, Pardee. 1943. *Father and glorious descendant.* Boston: Little, Brown.

Lyman, Standford. 1973. "Red Guard on Grant Avenue: The rise of youthful rebellion in Chinatown." In *Asian Americans: Psychological perspectives,* edited by S. Sue and N. N. Wagner, 20–44. Palo Alto: Science and Behavior Books.

Ma, L. Eve Armentrout. 1990. *Revolutionaries, monarchists, and Chinatowns: Chinese politics in the Americas and the 1911 Revolution.* Honolulu: University of Hawaii Press.

MacDonald, Jeffrey. 1998. "We are the experts: Iu-Mien (Yao) refugees assert their rights as scholars of their own culture." In *Power, ethics, and human rights,* edited by R. M. Krulfeld and J. L. MacDonald, 97–122. Lanham, Md.: Rowman and Littlefield.

Maira, Sunaina, and Rajni Srikanth, eds. 1996. *Contours of the heart: South Asians map North America.* New York: Asian American Writers Workshop.

McClain, Charles. 1994. *In search of equality: The Chinese struggle against discrimination in nineteenth-century America.* Berkeley: University of California Press.

McKeown, Adam. 2001. *Chinese migrant networks and cultural change: Peru, Chicago, Hawaii 1900–1936.* Chicago: University of Chicago Press.

Miyoshi, Masao. 1998. "'Globalization,' culture, and the university." In *The cultures of globalization,* edited by F. Jameson and M. Miyoshi, 247–272. Durham: Duke University Press.

Okada, John. 1957. *No-no boy.* Tokyo and Rutland, Vt.: Charles Tuttle.

Okihiro, Gary Y. 1995. *Privileging positions: The sites of Asian American Studies.* Pullman: Washington State University Press.

——. 2001. *Common ground: Reimaging American history.* Princeton: Princeton University Press.

Omatsu, Glenn. 1994. "The 'four prisons' and the movements of liberation: Asian American activism from the 1960s to the 1990s." In *The state of Asian America: Activism and resistance in the 1990s,* edited by K. Aguilar-San Juan, 19–70. Boston: South End Press, 19–70.

Ong, Aihwa. 1999. *Flexible citizenship: The cultural logics of transnationality.* Durham: Duke University Press.

——. 2003. *Buddha is hiding: Refugees, citizenship, the new America.* Berkeley: University of California Press.

Ong, Paul, Edna Bonacich, and Lucie Cheng, eds. 1994. *The new Asian immigration in Los Angeles and global restructuring.* Philadelphia: Temple University Press.

Palumbo-Liu, David. 1999. *Asian/American: Historical crossings of a racial frontier.* Stanford: Stanford University Press.

Portes, Alejandro. 2000. "Globalization from below, the rise of transnational communities." In *The ends of globalization: Bringing society back,* edited by D. Kalb, M. van de Land, and R. Staring, 253–272. Lanham, Md.: Rowman and Littlefield.

Railey, A., Carroll L. Riley, J. Charles Kelley, Campbell W. Pennington, and Robert L. Lands. 1971. *Man across the sea.* Austin: University of Texas Press.

Rangaswamy, Padma. 2000. *Namast America: Indian immigrants in an American metropolis.* University Park: Pennsylvania State University Press.

Rouse, Roger. 1996. "Mexican migration and the social space of postmodernism." In *Between two worlds: Mexican immigrants in the United States,* edited by D. G. Gutirrez, 8–23. Wilmington, Del.: Scholarly Resources.

Said, Edward W. 1993. *Culture and imperialism.* New York: Knopf.

——. 2000. Reflections on exile and other essays. Cambridge: Harvard University Press.

Salyer, Lucy. 1995. *Laws harsh as tigers: Chinese immigrants and the shaping of modern immigration Law.* Chapel Hill: University of North Carolina Press.

San Juan Jr., Epifanio. 1972. *Carlos Bulosan and the imagination of the class struggle.* Manila: University of the Philippines Press.

Schmidt, Johannes Dragsbaek, and Jacques Hersh, eds. 2000. *Globalization and social change.* London: Routledge.

Shukla, Sandhya. 2003. *India abroad: Diasporic cultures of postwar America and England.* Princeton: Princeton University Press.

Siu, Paul C. P. 1987. *The Chinese laundryman: A study of social isolation*, edited by J. Kuo Wei Tchen. New York: New York University Press.

Spivak, Gayatri Chakravorty. 1987. "Subaltern studies: Deconstructing historiography." In *In other worlds: Essays in cultural politics*, edited by G. Spivak, 215–219. New York: Methuen.

Stoddard, Lothrop. 1920. *The rising tide of color against white world-supremacy.* New York: C. Scribner's Sons.

——. 1927. *Re-forging America: The story of our nationhood.* New York: C. Scribner's Sons.

Tachiki, Amy, Eddy Wong, and Franklin Odo, eds. 1971. *Roots: An Asian American reader.* Los Angeles: Continental Graphics.

Takaki, Ronald. 1983. *Pau hana: Plantation life and labor in Hawaii, 1835–1920.* Honolulu: University of Hawaii Press.

——. 1993. *A different mirror: A multicultural history of America.* Boston: Little, Brown.

Tenhula, John. 1991. *Voices from Southeast Asia: The refugee experience in the United States.* New York: Holmes and Meier.

Umemoto Karen. 1989. "On strike! San Francisco State College strike, 1968–1969: The role of Asian American students." *Amerasia Journal* 15(1): 3–41.

United Nations High Commissioner for Refugees. 1995. "Indo-Chinese refugees, asylum seekers and screened-out in Thailand, as of August 1995." Bangkok.

Vô, Linda Trin. 2003. "Vietnamese American trajectories: Dimensions of diaspora." *Amerasia Journal* 29(1): ix–xviii.

Wallerstein, Immanuel. 1974. *The modern world system: Capitalist agriculture and the origins of the European world economy in the 16th century.* New York: Academic Press.

Weglyn, Michi. 1976. *Years of infamy: The untold story of America's concentration camps.* New York: William Morrow.

Wei, William. 1993. *The Asian American movement.* Philadelphia: Temple University Press.

Wilson, Rob. 2000. *Reimagining the American Pacific: From South Pacific to Bamboo Ridge and beyond.* Durham: Duke University Press.

Wilson, Rob, and Arif Dirlik, eds. 1995. *Asia/Pacific as space of cultural production.* Durham: Duke University Press.

Wilson, Rob, and Wimal Dissanayake, eds. 1996. *Global/local: Cultural production and the transnational imaginary.* Durham: Duke University Press.

Wong, Sauling. 2000. "Denationalization reconsidered: Asian American cultural criticism at a theoretical crossroads." In *Postcolonial theory and the United States: Race, ethnicity, and literature*, edited by A. Singh and P. Schmidt, 122–150. Jackson: University Press of Mississippi.

Yu, Renqiu. 1992. *To save China, to save ourselves: The Chinese hand laundry alliance of New York.* Philadelphia: Temple University Press.

Yuh, Ji-Yeon. 2002. *Beyond the shadow of Camptown: Korean military brides in America.* New York: New York University Press.

Zhao, Xiaojian. 2002. *Remaking Chinese America: Immigration, family, and community, 1940–1965.* New Brunswick: Rutgers University Press.

2

==

Diaspora, Transnationalism, and Asian American Studies: Positions and Debates

CHRISTOPHER LEE

It should come as no surprise that the borders of Asian America are not synonymous with the borders of the United States of America. Sucheta Mazumdar's often-quoted declaration that "the very genesis of Asian American Studies was international" (Mazumdar 1991, 40) underscores the ever-present, but always shifting, awareness of the transnational dimensions of the field, an awareness that exists in tension with its domestic preoccupations.[1] Mazumdar argues that the U.S.-centric focus of Asian American Studies can be traced back to the work of the Chicago school of sociologists led by Robert Park, whose paradigms of immigrant assimilation continue to influence ethnic studies by locating it in a domestic research and political agenda. Mazumdar goes on to offer an alternative, transnational genealogy of the field in an attempt to bring into conversation with other disciplines such as Asian Studies.

As part of her call for disciplinary realignment, Mazumdar identifies Overseas Chinese Studies as a precursor to Asian American Studies. Encompassing a wide range of topics from literature to business networks to family structures, this field has generally been concerned with understanding overseas communities as extensions, however remote, of a larger construct of "China." Thus questions such as the persistence of Chinese nationalism and the maintenance of social structures originating in China have been privileged themes. This research is practiced in many sites around the world, including Southeast Asia, Australia, Latin America, Europe, and China itself. Commenting on recent trends toward transnational awareness, Edgar Wickberg (2002, 1) has noted, "in the past, Chinese outside China were studied within national units, or else subnational units . . . as localized minorities, interesting for their cultural and social organization and expression. In the last decade, in line with globalization as a research construct, there has been a growing number of studies of Chinese as transnationals."[2] Although Asian American Studies has maintained a somewhat

23

distant relationship with Overseas Chinese Studies, with the latter often understood as less amendable to a domestic agenda of empowerment, growing interest in transnationalism on both sides has opened up spaces for scholarship that
can bridge and move beyond their respective disciplines.

The reframing of issues such as labor, migration, race, and gender in relation to global formations has made Asian American Studies necessarily aware
of, if not always in solidarity with, the international dimensions of its politics
and projects. From a historical perspective, transnationalism has always been
around in the field, but recent trends in ethnic studies and related disciplines
have made these issues particularly urgent. The location of the first Association
for Asian American Studies conference of the new millennium in Canada
(Toronto, March 2001) and its correspondingly appropriate theme—"Boundaries of Asian American Studies"—is just one more sign of transnationalism's
recent prominence, which parallels the growing interest in globalization across
disciplines in the humanities and social sciences (see, for example, Rowe 2000).
The recent explosion of scholarship on these topics within Asian American
Studies suggests that it would be useful to identify a renewed turn to the
transnational at this moment. This chapter does not seek to address whether
Asian America is or is not transnational; instead, the present discussion focuses
on how Asian America Studies has come to conceive its object of study as
transnational.[3] The task of this chapter is to describe some of the critical
debates that have arisen and probe into their theoretical contexts. Although
the dramatic increase in publishing in this area makes it impossible to provide
an exhaustive survey, this chapter seeks to review some recent scholarship in
relation to the issues addressed in this volume.

A key term that has emerged in the current discussion is "diaspora." Diaspora studies offer new models for researching and understanding community
and identity in an era of globalization, and the study of Asian diasporas has
become prominent in a number of projects dealing with the transnational character of Asian America. In addition, the term itself facilitates a wide range of
comparisons between different communities that have experienced displacement and dispersal. Rather early in the debate, Khachig Tölölyan argued that
diasporas are "exemplary formations of the transnational moment" (1991, 5).
Writing these words in the first issue of the leading journal *Diaspora*, he fore-
grounds a conception of diaspora that is embedded and contained in specific
historical contexts.

Etymologically, the word has long been used in Judaic studies to describe
the scattering of Jewish communities since the Babylonian captivity of biblical
times. The specific history of the term has been acknowledged in several recent
attempts to apply it to the study of non-Jewish communities. William Safran
(1991) offers a comparative account of various diasporic groups in relation to
the Jewish prototype, whereas James Clifford (1997) extends the discussion by

comparing the Jewish diaspora to Paul Gilroy's notion of the Black Atlantic (see Gilroy 1993). Writing at a more general level, Robin Cohen (1997) offers a schematic breakdown of various diasporas based on a set of broad and permeable categories, including victim, labor, trade, imperial, and cultural diasporas. His work attempts to set definitional boundaries in order to determine what formations qualify as "diasporas" and emphasizes the retention and transformation of ethnic ties within dispersed populations, again taking the Jewish example as the prototype.

As Ien Ang (2001, 25) writes, "diasporas are transnational, spatially and temporally sprawling sociocultural formations of people, creating imagined communities whose blurred and fluctuating boundaries are sustained by real and/or symbolic ties to some original 'homeland.'" Far from establishing a consensus as to what exactly constitutes a diaspora, the examples above give a sense of the range of phenomena that may potentially be included in diasporic studies. Indeed, a brief overview of the contents of *Diaspora* reveals the wide range of formations, methodologies, and debates that have accompanied the rise of diasporic studies and, as Evelyn Hu-DeHart points out in her chapter in this volume, the journal has, to date, identified more than fifty diasporas. Recently, Jana Evans Braziel and Anita Mannur (2003) have argued that the term "diaspora" should be used to name the affections, subjectivities, and identities formed in relation to real and imagined homelands. Braziel and Mannur suggest that directing critical attention to the human experiences of transnationalism can enable us to reconsider the domination of the nation-state in light of the comtemporary emergence of sites of resistance.

If nationalism has been a central feature of modernity around the world, recent reconsiderations of the nation-state, in which studies of transnationalism and diaspora figure prominently, can be understood as part of the larger critique of modernity itself.[4] The rise of radical politics in the 1960s, combined with currents in poststructuralist theory, has opened new intellectual formations such as ethnic studies and cultural studies. Stuart Hall's often-cited essay "Cultural Identity and Diaspora" (1990), which focuses on Caribbean cinema and black diasporic identity, invokes Jacques Derrida's notion of *différance* to describe processes of deferral that make the positing and recovery of stable ethnic origins impossible. Hall's anti-essentialist valorization of hybridity has deeply influenced recent scholarship in postcolonial and ethnic studies. In black cultural studies, for example, Paul Gilroy's frequently cited and debated notion of the "Black Atlantic" has made the term "diaspora" especially relevant in current research (see Gilroy 1993).[5] Like Hall, Gilroy's project can be understood as a critique of fixedness and an embrace of indeterminacy as political strategy. Ien Ang (2001) extends this argument to Asia-Pacific contexts and shows how hybridities can be mobilized in order to negotiate identity politics in embattled minority communities such as the Peranakan Chinese in Indonesia.

Arjun Appardurai (1990) has argued that the "imagination" has become central to the new global economy, and although he explores the disjunctures of globalization in a number of realms, his main focus remains on culture (for example, he examines the importation of American pop music into Filipino popular culture). This cultural turn is also evident in *Transnational Asia Pacific: Gender, Culture and the Public Sphere*, edited by Shirley Geok-lin Lim, Larry E. Smith, and Wimal Dissanayake (1999). The essays in this volume set out to map the cultural terrains of the Asia Pacific through the consideration of phenomena ranging from popular music to festivals to visual media. In "Rethinking *Diaspora(s)*: Stateless Power in the Transnational Moment" (1996), Tölölyan addresses recent attempts to displace the nation-state and cautions that diasporas can also be complicit in the function of states. Although he affirms the centrality of diaspora discourse in the arts, literature, and criticism, he also suggests, "the richness and complexity of this work on diasporic identity has entailed—though it need not have—a reduction of or an inattention to the complexity of the past and present of diasporic social formations" (28).

If many studies of diaspora have been concerned with culture, this trend has, in turn, elicited sharp critical responses. Here, I want to mention the work of scholars coming from a Marxist tradition that has tracked manifestations of transnationalism from the zenith of imperialism to recent forms of globalization. Against what they consider to be an excessive interest in discursive forms and identity politics, these critics have insisted on returning to the analysis of class in order to understand comtemporary transnationalism as a consequence of global capitalism.[6] Although this position differs methodologically from the diaspora studies discussed above, the two camps share an interest in deconstructing totalities for progressive political projects. The tools for such projects, of course, range widely from the critique of linguistic referentiality drawn from poststructuralist theory to materialist approaches that historicize social formations. Squarely in the latter camp, Arif Dirlik (1996) has argued that scholars need to pay attention to the local as a site for specific forms of resistance directed against the effects of global capital. Dirlik understands the local as a limit to totalizing concepts, which include homogenizing notions such as global proletariat and even hybridity itself. The intersections between economic and cultural resistance are mapped in Dirlik's edited volume *Asia/Pacific as Space of Cultural Production* (coedited with Rob Wilson, 1995). Focusing on marginalized (counter)cultures such as indigenous groups and immigrants, the volume argues for a sustained commitment to the local in opposition to the global. Dirlik and Wilson criticize those who privilege hybridity for turning philosophical debates over signification into descriptive accounts of material conditions. From a theoretically different standpoint, Pheng Cheah (1998a) offers a related critique of the "cultural turn" and argues that the concept of diaspora reifies ethnicity into an ahistorical construct.

In *Asian/American: Historical Crossings of a Racial Frontier,* David Palumbo-Liu clarifies the distinction between globalization, which he understands to refer primarily to economic phenomena, and diaspora, which he uses to describe the psychic realm of desires, interiorities, and identifications (1999, 355–356). His larger project locates Asian/American (written with a slash in order to emphasize the transnational linkages between the two parts) within the larger context of American modernity in order to show how it emerges at different historical moments in the cultural frontier between Asia and America. He starts with racialized discourses of American imperialism during the 1930s and concludes by tracking the recent rise of Asia-Pacific discourse through diverse phenomena such as neo-Confucianism and cyberspace. Throughout his study, Palumbo-Liu emphasizes the transnational aspects of racialization in order to draw links between culture, foreign policy, imperialism, and global economics. The need to engage constantly changing economic and political conditions is a constant challenge to scholars; in her introduction to an edited volume on Asian Americans and globalization, Evelyn Hu-DeHart (1999) notes how the 1997 Asian economic crisis interrupted the premises of her book and required her to rethink the position of Asian Americans after the collapse of the so-called "Asian economic miracle" as the collection was going to press.

Several recent anthropological studies have focused on the lived experience of transnationalism. Aiwha Ong's (1999) study of "flexible citizenship" focuses on institutions such as the family in highly mobile transnational Chinese communities located on both sides of the Pacific. Ong documents material practices of transnationalism and considers them in relation to processes of subject formation. She takes U.S.-based diaspora studies to task for narrowly defining the diasporic subject either as oppressed subaltern or elite cosmopolitan intellectual (12–14). Finding the discussion of identity in contemporary cultural studies overly abstract and "self-indulgent" (242), Ong advocates a return to anthropological research methods in order to produce an ethnography of transnationalism in the service of what she calls a new utopian intellectual practice (also see Ong and Nonini 1997). In Martin Manalansan's edited volume *Cultural Compass: Ethnographic Explorations of Asian America* (2000), contributors reflect on the role of the "native" researcher. The collection seeks to delineate methodological, ethical, and professional issues confronted by Asian American anthropologists who are intimately involved in the communities they study. In a related volume, Linda Basch, Nina Glick Schiller, and Cristina Szanton Blanc (1994) describe various experiences in which ethnographic research has led to personal involvement. Through in-depth accounts of Pilipino and Haitian-American communities, the authors focus on transnational labor formations while chronicling the development of their personal commitments to the communities they study.

Another influential topic in the development of transnational/diaspora studies is cosmopolitanism. In his introduction to the edited collection *Cosmopolitics*, Bruce Robbins locates cosmopolitanism "as an area within and beyond the nation (and yet falling short of 'humanity')" (1998, 12). He argues that the study of cosmopolitanism can untangle common misunderstandings about the relationship between capital and the nation-state. Robbins suggests that a universalist account of transnationalism is still beneficial for progressive politics, provided that the notion of the "cosmopolitan" can be expanded beyond its usual associations with elitism and privilege. In the same volume, coeditor Pheng Cheah (1998b) offers a philosophical genealogy of transnationalism, starting with a comparison between conceptions of the nation-state in the philosophical works of Immanuel Kant and Karl Marx. Whereas Kant privileges cosmopolitanism over nationalism in his vision of "perpetual peace," Marx associates the state with the encroaching power of capitalism. Cheah argues that nationalism has been an important tool for anticolonial liberation movements of the twentieth century. In the current transnational moment, "cosmopolitics" aim to balance the role of nonstate entities such as NGOs with the need to maintain forms of popular nationalism, especially in the Third World. (Cheah's more recent work [2003] continues to articulate the importance of nationalism to anticolonial struggle and provides a useful counterpoint to the tendency in postcolonial criticism to dismiss the nation-state altogether.) As a whole, *Cosmopolitics* seeks to combine theoretical exploration with materialist analysis by bringing essays by authors such as Richard Rorty and Kwame Antony Appiah in dialogue with empirical studies by Aiwha Ong and Louisa Schein, among others.

If nearly all economies of the Asia Pacific participate in the global economic system, the hegemony of that system has in turn led to attempts to theorize and articulate a distinctly Asian version of globalization. Of particular importance here are the arguments that try to place transnational capitalism within the values and traditions of "Confucian" societies in East Asia. Tu Weiming's work, especially his edited collection *The Living Tree* (1994), has elicited a range of responses in academic circles. His study of Confucian humanism defines Chinese identity by placing it within a broader "cultural China" that simultaneously decenters China as a geopolitical formation while reinforcing the centrality of Chineseness as such. Scholars such as Tu have argued against the hegemony of Western narratives of development by positing an Asian "countermodernity." In a related vein, discussions of "Asian values" has included writings from political leaders who have been associated with the development of neo-authoritarian politics (see, for example, Ishihara 1991 and Mahathir and Ishihara 1995).

According to critics, these works continue to uphold the centrality of global capitalist systems as the grounds on which to bring East and West into relation. For example, Ong (1999) links the "new Asian values" to the development and consolidation of capitalistic practices. Cheah (2001) argues that Tu's alignment of neo-Confucianism with capitalism reproduces stereotypes of Chinese as businessmen, an assumption that has fueled recent anti-Chinese movements in Southeast Asia. Palumbo-Liu (1999) reads the popularity of "Cultural China" as a form of ethnocentrism that ignores historical factors and reduces ethnic identity to abstract "values" that are themselves products of contemporary political conditions. He points out how the discourse surrounding "Asian values" is often manipulated by Western capitalists and authoritarian Asian leaders, with dangerous sociopolitical consequences for those with less access to power.

Reflecting on debates over diaspora and transnationalism, feminist scholars have repeatedly noted the exclusion of gender issues. The contributors to Inderpal Grewal and Caren Kaplan's edited anthology *Scattered Hegemonies: Postmodernity and Transnational Feminist Practices* (1994) mobilize a transnational perspective in order to reevaluate long-standing theoretical stances within Western feminism. The editors suggest that their project constitutes an intervention in several respects. First, the essays contest theories of postmodernity and postmodernism by raising previously ignored questions regarding sexual and cultural difference. Second, the study of transnationalism is expanded through studies of the local in relation to forms of gender oppression. Finally, transnational feminist scholarship aims to disrupt generalizing categories such as diaspora through comparative analyses of gender.

In situating their more recent collection *Between Woman and Nation: Nationalisms, Transnational Feminisms, and the State* (1999), editors Caren Kaplan, Norma Alarcón, and Minoo Moallem survey current theoretical debates on the nature of postmodernity and argue that they continue to exclude feminist concerns. Negotiating gender, ethnicity, and nationalism, the editors outline a project that tracks emerging forms of female subjectivity: "Women are both of and not of the nation. Between woman and nation is, perhaps, the space or zone where we can deconstruct these monoliths and render them more historically nuanced and accountable to politics" (Kaplan, Alarcón, and Moallem 1999, 12). In their essay "Transnational Feminist Cultural Studies: Beyond the Marxism/Post-structuralism/Feminism Divides," Kaplan and Grewal (1999) outline a research program that critically integrates different theoretical positions in order to recuperate often erased figures of women; the work of postcolonial subaltern studies is clearly influential here, and the work of Gayatri Chakravorty Spivak is cited as a model of transnational feminist scholarship.[7]

The premise that the nation is fundamentally structured on gender differences offers a starting point for critics who interrogate the heterosexual basis and bias of the nation. From the perspective of queer theory, the nation not only depends on the containment of femininity but also on notions of kinship and bloodline that are exclusively heterosexual. In an Asian American context, Gayatri Gopinath (1997) examines texts that locate queer desires in Asian "homelands" and questions Western-based notions of same-sex desire while placing them in a transnational frame: "The notion of a queer South Asian diaspora can be seen as conceptual apparatus that poses a critique of modernity and its various narratives of progress and development" (1997, 273). Similarly, David Eng (2001) argues that queer theory can help rethink hetero-normative assumptions stemming from the cultural nationalism of the 1960s. Eng argues that queer theory can respond to the waning of racial politics in the 1980s by energizing new political alliances based on emergent social issues such as AIDS and queer activism. These themes are also addressed by several contributors to the anthology *Q&A: Queer in Asian America* (Eng & Hom 1998). Examining topics such as Korean American identity (Lee 1998), global cultural capital (Chiang 1998), and South Asian cultural nationalism (Puar 1998), writers explore the intersection of queer, national, and racial identities in order to shed light on new cultural and social spaces previously foreclosed by the nation.

As the discussion above has shown, transnationalism and diaspora have been explored from a multiplicity of disciplines and theoretical positions. In the remainder of this chapter, I want to focus on the implications of the transnational turn on Asian American Studies, where the task of rethinking disciplinary locations in relation to transnational/diasporic processes is both urgent and promising. Recent scholarship on transnationalism and diaspora has shown, again, the instability of the term "Asian American." Not only is the salience of Asian American as a social formation in question, but the conceptual separation of Asia from America has also been challenged. A recurring theme in the study of diasporas and globalization is the oscillation between abstract theoretical frameworks and particular cases and contexts. The questioning of totalizing concepts such as "Asianness," the nation, class, or gender is often undertaken in order to recuperate the specificity of various contexts. In this sense, diaspora can be either totalizing or illuminating.

As Ien Ang (2001) writes, "the fantasmic vision of a new world *order* consisting of hundreds of self-contained, self-identical nations . . . strikes me as a rather disturbing duplication of the divide-and-rule politics deployed by the colonial powers to ascertain control and mastery over the subjected. It is against these visions that the idea of diaspora can play a critical cultural role" (34, emphasis in the original). With regard to pedagogy, R. Radhakrishnan (1996) advocates invoking diaspora as a strategy to decenter Eurocentric discourses previously considered universal. In a related discussion, Rey Chow (1993) articulates the ambivalences and contradictions of diasporic studies. She describes her use of "diaspora" as an intervention against essentialist discourses that are manifested in forms such as Orientalist epistemology or chauvinistic nationalism in the field of Asian Studies. At the same time, she exposes positions of privilege inhabited by the diasporic intellectual and argues for a vigilant stance against the idealization of the Third World from the Western metropole.[8]

The injunction to particularize offers a challenge to the study of diasporas and displacement: Does the transnational turn offer new tools to understand communities and localities or does it merely entrench a new hegemonic theory of cultural and social formations? Elaborating on these concerns, Sau-ling C. Wong's widely discussed essay "Denationalization Reconsidered" (1995) sounds a note of caution in response to the rise of diasporic studies. For Wong, "denationalization" threatens to undermine Asian American Studies' engagement with urgent domestic political issues and its overall project of "claiming America." Recently, Wong has republished the essay (2000) with a new introduction that takes stock of reactions since its original publication in a special issue of *Amerasia Journal* on "Thinking Theory in the Asian American Studies." In addition, her introduction offers a useful survey of scholarship on transnationalism and diaspora in Asian American Studies.[9]

Although most of the contributors to this volume would not share Wong's specific stand against "denationalization," the essays collected here respond to a similar set of concerns. By approaching questions of diaspora and transnationalism from a variety of sites, perspectives, and disciplines, the authors attempt to model types of scholarship that critically examine existing paradigms. For example, Scott Lucious's essay intervenes in the gap between African and Asian American Studies by mapping the Black Pacific as a site where the persistence of racism and colorism raises new questions about Asian complicity with continuing forms of discrimination. Louis-Jacques Dorais's analysis of Vietnamese Canadian communities through the category of "trans-migrants" repositions our understanding of race and ethnicity in relation to government-sponsored forms of multiculturalism, which in turn revises our understanding of how diasporas operate. As Evelyn Hu-DeHart demonstrates, a Spanish/Chinese contract for plantation laborers in Cuba reveals how local experiences can and need to be understood in relation to transnational labor systems that forge connections not only between Chinese diasporas but also to the Atlantic slave trade.

If the transnational is manifested in the local, then localities themselves cannot be understood apart from their position in transnational frames. Moving between the local and the global produces a challenge for scholars trying to find new vocabularies to bring various localities into relation with one another. A related challenge stems from the need to translate our work across disciplinary boundaries.[10] If, as the essays by Nancy Abelmann and E. San Juan Jr. point out, the establishment of ethnic studies has not overcome a long legacy of racism in the academy, the critique of that institution requires that scholars continue speaking in ways that transcend their disciplinary boundaries and local contexts.

Between the bind of the universal and the particular, the given and the new, a pedagogy of diaspora offers an intervention in the contemporary U.S. academy. The insertion of diaspora into Asian American Studies curricula offers ways to disrupt U.S.-centric nationalism while simultaneously providing strategies to rethink the foundations of the field. Radhakrishnan (1996) has suggested that objects of study that are both personal and intellectual are redefined and contested in the pedagogical interchange between student and teacher. Transnationalism and diaspora, as contested as these terms are, describe something that is, in many senses, already out there. Individuals, families, and communities around the world are located and locate themselves between national boundaries. Situated in institutions that are increasingly global sites of curricula, migration, and financing, our students are themselves more transnational than ever across race and class lines.

Asian American Studies, with its mission of making learning relevant to the experiences of its constituencies, cannot not engage transnational issues. As the more empirically oriented chapters in this collection show, the impetus for introducing transnationalism as a category does not stem merely from academic debates. Rather, to exclude these issues is to fail to adequately describe and understand the communities being studied. The challenge, then, is to link the various uses of diaspora within our work to an ongoing ethical commitment to inclusive scholarship. In this way, the divide between "idealist" diaspora studies and "materialist" critique can be effectively bridged. The task of researching and teaching the Asian diasporas lies in balancing various poles— theory-experience, global-local, universal-particular—in order to produce new intellectual projects responsible to histories and experiences.

NOTES

I thank Robert Lee and Wanni Anderson for offering the opportunity to write this chapter. I gratefully acknowledge the fellowship support of the Social Sciences and Humanities Research Council of Canada.

1. Despite the frequent characterization, by those inside and outside the field, of Asian American Studies as overly domestic in its research focus, questions of transnationalism have been debated extensively within the field for some time now. Russell Leong (2001) has chronicled how the *Amerasia Journal*, under his editorship, began to devote extensive space to these debates, starting in the late 1980s. Sau-ling C. Wong's critique of "denationalization" (1995) was written in response to the trend toward diasporic studies in the early 1990s. A special issue of *positions: east asia cultures critique*, "New Formations, New Questions: Asian American Studies" (1997) included a number of influential essays that linked Asian American cultures and communities to global capitalism and considered possibilities of resistance under such circumstances. For a recent discussion of transnationalism as a trend, see Okamura (2003).

2. I thank Edgar Wickberg for providing an advance copy of this essay in which he

discusses two recent works of Madeline Hsu's *Dreaming of gold, dreaming of home* (2000), and Wing-chun Ng's *The Chinese in Vancouver 1945–80: The pursuit of identity and power* (1999). Recent studies in this field include Chen (2000), Djao (2003), Louie (2004), McKeown (2001), and Wang (1998, 2000), and edited collections such as Benton and Pieke (1998) and Dirlik (2001). Lynn Pan, whose *Sons of the Yellow Emperor: A history of the Chinese diaspora* (1990) marked the beginning of the recent upsurge in interest in this topic, has recently edited a reference work for the field, *The encyclopedia of the Chinese overseas* (Pan 1998).

3. This chapter was originally conceived as a companion piece for this volume. My aim was to provide some background to the theoretical debates that the other contributors have responded to in order to situate their essays within a larger conversation in Asian American Studies. Much has been published in the topic of Asian diasporas since this chapter was first drafted. For example, *Amerasia* has recently produced special issues on Vietnamese (29:1) and Korean (29:3) Americans, both of which consider these groups in a diasporic context. *Amerasia* has also published a special issue on "Asians in the Americas" (28:2), which includes research on Asian communities in Central and South America. The impact of the September 11, 2001, attacks and the ensuing "War against Terror" has also been instrumental in keeping the topics of transnationalism and diaspora on the agenda. See the special double issue of *Amerasia* "After Words: Who Speaks on War, Justice, and Peace?" (27:3/28:1). In 2003, the journal *Interventions* featured a special issue on "Global Diasporas" (5:1). Other journals that have prominently featured transnational topics include *positions: east asia cultures critique*, *Public Culture*, *boundary 2*, and *Social Text*, just to name a few examples.

4. Much of this critique has been carried out in recent years in relation to debates over the nature of postmodernity. Harvey (1990) provides a comprehensive survey of the issues raised in these discussions. Two useful collections of primary theoretical documents in this regard are Waugh (1992) and Docherty (1993), both of which offer a selection of essays by important critics such as Jürgen Habermas, Jean-Francois Lyotard, Jean Baudrillard, and Fredric Jameson.

5. Edwards (2001) offers a useful genealogy of the term "diaspora" in the study of African and African-descended peoples. For a critique of Gilroy's project, see Neil Lazarus (1999, 51–67), where he faults *The black Atlantic* for sidelining the relevance of nation-states and ignoring the relevance of capitalist world systems. Thus for Lazarus, slavery (Gilroy's privileged term of analysis) cannot be understood apart from global labor systems that continue to the present in other forms.

6. See Harvey (1990) for an extended analysis of post-Fordist capitalism. Two important examples of Asian American scholarship that follow this track are Lisa Lowe's *Immigrant acts* (1996), which goes from the materialist analysis of Asian American history to the consideration of Asian American cultural politics, and *The new Asian immigration in Los Angeles and global restructuring*, edited by Paul Ong, Edna Bonacich, and Lucie Cheng (1994), which examines contemporary social formations in Los Angeles Asian communities from a social science perspective.

7. Another important collection that includes a selection of literary and visual arts in addition to critical essays is *Talking visions: Multicultural feminism in a transnational age* (Shohat 1998).

8. See particularly the introduction and the chapter entitled "Against the lures of diaspora: Minority discourse, chinese women, and intellectual hegemony" in Chow (1993)
   for a discussion of the perils and potential of "diaspora" in current academic discourse.

9. In Asian American literary studies, the essays in *An interethnic companion to
   Asian American literature* (Cheung 1997) restage the debate between diasporic
   studies (see Shirley Geok-lin Lim's essay) and domestically based studies (see
   Sau-ling Cynthia Wong's essay). Cheung's introduction attempts to mediate
   between the two positions.

10. For a useful discussion on the need to cross the disciplinary boundaries between
    Asian and Asian American Studies, see the introduction to Kandice Chuh and
    Karen Shimakawa, eds., *Orientations: Mapping studies in the Asian diaspora*
    (2001). There, the editors suggest that a rapprochement between the two fields is
    necessary in order to come to terms with how Asia and America are intercon-
    nected entities, especially in the post-Cold War period. Although the coming
    together of the two fields is undoubtedly a trend that will continue to gain
    momentum, suspicion toward area studies still runs deep in ethnic studies; for a
    discussion of these factors, see Okamura (2003).

REFERENCES

Ang, Ien. 2001. *On not speaking Chinese: Living between Asia and the West.* London:
    Routledge.

Appadurai, Arjun. 1990. "Disjuncture and difference in the global cultural economy."
    Public Culture 2(2):1–24.

Basch, Linda G., Nina Glick Schiller, and Cristina Szanton Blanc. 1994. *Nations unbound:
    Transnational projects, postcolonial predicaments, and deterritorialized nation-
    states.* Langhorne, Pa.: Gordon and Breach.

Benton, Gregor, and Frank N. Pieke, eds. 1998. *The Chinese in Europe.* New York: St.
    Martin's.

Braziel, Jana Evans, and Anita Mannur, eds. 2003. *Theorizing diaspora: A reader.* Malden,
    Mass.: Blackwell.

Cheah, Pheng. 1998a. "Given culture: Rethinking cosmopolitical freedom in transna-
    tionalism." In *Cosmopolitics: Thinking and feeling beyond the nation,* edited by
    B. Robbins and P. Cheah, 290–328. Minneapolis: University of Minnesota Press.

———. 1998b. "Introduction part II: The cosmopolitical—today." In *Cosmopolitics:
    Thinking and feeling beyond the nation,* edited by B. Robbins and P. Cheah,
    20–44. Minneapolis: University of Minnesota Press.

———. 2001. "Chinese cosmopolitanism in two senses and postcolonial national mem-
    ory." In *Cosmopolitan geographies: New locations in literature and culture,* edited
    by V. Dharwadker, 133–170. London: Routledge.

———. 2003. *Spectral nationality: Passages of freedom from Kant to postcolonial liter-
    atures of liberation.* New York: Columbia University Press.

Chen, Yong. 2000. *Chinese San Francisco, 1850–1943: A trans-Pacific community.*
    Stanford: Stanford University Press.

Cheung, King-Kok, ed. 1997. *An interethnic companion to Asian American literature.* New York: Cambridge University Press.

Chiang, Mark. 1998. "Coming out in the global system: Postmodern patriarchies and transnational sexualities in *The wedding banquet.*" In *Q&A: Queer in Asian America,* edited by D. Eng and A. Hom, 374–396. Philadelphia: Temple University Press.

Chow, Rey. 1993. *Writing diaspora: Tactics of intervention in contemporary cultural studies.* Bloomington: Indiana University Press.

Chuh, Kandice, and Karen Shimakawa, eds. 2001. *Orientations: Mapping studies in the Asian diaspora.* Durham: Duke University Press.

Clifford, James. 1997. *Routes: Travel and translation in the late twentieth century.* Cambridge: Harvard University Press.

Cohen, Robin. 1997. *Global diasporas: An introduction.* Seattle: University of Washington Press.

Dirlik, Arif. 1996. "The global in the local." In *Global/local: Cultural production and the transnational imaginary,* edited by R. Wilson and W. Dissanayake, 21–45. Durham: Duke University Press.

———, ed. 2001. *Chinese on the American frontier.* Lanham, Md.: Rowman and Littlefield.

Djao, Wei. 2003. *Being Chinese: Voices from the diaspora.* Tucson: University of Arizona Press.

Docherty, Thomas, ed. 1993. *Postmodernism: A reader.* New York: Columbia University Press.

Edwards, Brent Hayes. 2001. "The uses of diaspora." *Social Text* 19(1): 45–73.

Eng, David L. 2001. *Racial castration: Managing masculinity in Asian America.* Durham: Duke University Press.

Eng, David L., and Alice Y. Hom, eds. 1998. *Q & A: Queer in Asian America.* Philadelphia: Temple University Press.

Gilroy, Paul. 1993. *The black Atlantic: Modernity and double consciousness.* Cambridge: Harvard University Press.

Gopinath, Gayatri. 1997. "Nostalgia, desire, diaspora: South Asian sexualities in motion." *positions: east asia cultures critique* 5(2): 467–489.

Grewal, Inderpal, and Caren Kaplan, eds. 1994. *Scattered hegemonies: Postmodernity and transnational feminist practices.* Minneapolis: University of Minnesota Press.

Hall, Stuart. 1990. "Cultural identity and diaspora." In *Identity: Community, culture, difference,* edited by J. Rutherford, 222–237. London: Lawrence and Wishart.

Harvey, David. 1990. *The condition of postmodernity: An enquiry into the origins of cultural change.* Cambridge, Mass.: Blackwell.

Hsu, Madeline Yuan-yin. 2000. *Dreaming of gold, dreaming of home: Transnationalism and migration between the United States and South China, 1882–1943.* Stanford: Stanford University Press.

Hu-DeHart, Evelyn, ed. 1999. *Across the Pacific: Asian Americans and globalization.* Philadelphia: Temple University Press.

Hune, Shirley, et al., eds. 1991. *Asian Americans: Comparative and global perspectives.* Pullman: Washington State University Press.

Ishihara, Shintaro. 1991. *The Japan that can say no.* Translated by Frank Baldwin. New York: Simon and Schuster.

Kaplan, Caren, Norma Alarcón, and Minoo Moallem, eds. 1999. *Between woman and nation: Nationalisms, transnational feminisms, and the state.* Durham: Duke University Press.

Kaplan, Caren, and Inderpal Grewal. 1999. "Transnational feminist cultural studies: Beyond the Marxism/poststructuralism/feminism divides." In *Between woman and nation: Nationalisms, transnational feminisms, and the state*, edited by C. Kaplan, N. Alarcón, and M. Moallem, 349–364. Durham: Duke University Press.

Lazarus, Neil. 1999. *Nationalism and cultural practice in the postcolonial world.* New York: Cambridge University Press.

Lee, JeeYeun. 1998. "Towards a queer Korean-American diasporic history." In *Q&A: Queer in Asian America*, edited by D. Eng and A. Hom, 185–212. Philadelphia: Temple University Press.

Leong, Russell. 2001. "Creating performative communities: Through text, time, and space." In *Orientations: Mapping studies in the Asian diaspora*, edited by K. Chuh and K. Shimakawa, 57–75. Durham: Duke University Press.

Lim, Shirley, Larry E. Smith, and Wimal Dissanayake, eds. 1999. *Transnational Asia Pacific: Gender, culture, and the public sphere.* Urbana: University of Illinois Press.

Louie, Andrea. 2004. *Chineseness across borders: Renegotiating Chinese identities in China and the United States.* Durham: Duke University Press.

Lowe, Lisa. 1996. *Immigrant acts: On Asian American cultural politics.* Durham: Duke University Press.

Mahathir bin Mohamad, and Shintaro Ishihara. 1995. *The voice of Asia: Two leaders discuss the coming century.* New York: Kodansha International.

Manalansan, Martin F., ed. 2000. *Cultural compass: Ethnographic explorations of Asian America.* Philadelphia: Temple University Press.

Mazumdar, Sucheta. 1991. "Asian American studies and Asian studies: Rethinking roots." In *Asian Americans: Comparative and global perspectives*, edited by S. Hune et al., 29–44. Pullman: Washington State University Press.

McKeown, Adam. 2001. *Chinese migrant networks and cultural change: Peru, Chicago, Hawaii, 1900–1936.* Chicago: University of Chicago Press.

Ng, Wing Chung. 1999. *The Chinese in Vancouver, 1945–80: The pursuit of identity and power.* Vancouver: University of British Columbia Press.

Okamura, Jonathan Y. 2003. "Asian American studies in the age of transnationalism: Diaspora, race, community." *Amerasia* 29(2): 171–193.

Ong, Aihwa. 1999. *Flexible citizenship: The cultural logics of transnationality.* Durham: Duke University Press.

Ong, Aihwa, and Donald M. Nonini, eds. 1997. *Ungrounded empires: The cultural politics of modern Chinese transnationalism.* New York: Routledge.

Ong, Paul M., Edna Bonacich, and Lucie Cheng, eds. 1994. *The new Asian immigration in Los Angeles and global restructuring.* Philadelphia: Temple University Press.

Palumbo-Liu, David. 1999. *Asian/American: Historical crossings of a racial frontier.* Stanford: Stanford University Press.

Pan, Lynn. 1990. *Sons of the yellow emperor: A history of the Chinese diaspora.* Boston: Little Brown.

———, ed. 1998. *The encyclopedia of the Chinese overseas.* Singapore: Landmark Books.

Puar, Jasbir K. 1998. "Transnational sexualities: South Asian (trans)nation(alism)s and queer diasporas." In *Q&A: Queer in Asian America*, edited by D. Eng and A. Hom, 405–424. Philadelphia: Temple University Press.

Radhakrishnan, R. 1996. *Diasporic mediations: Between home and location.* Minneapolis: University of Minnesota Press.

Robbins, Bruce. 1998. "Introduction Part I: Actually existing cosmopolitanisms." In *Cosmopolitics: Thinking and feeling beyond the nation*, edited by B. Robbins and P. Cheah, 1–19. Minneapolis: University of Minnesota Press.

Robbins, Bruce, and Pheng Cheah, eds. 1998. *Cosmopolitics: Thinking and feeling beyond the nation.* Minneapolis: University of Minnesota Press.

Rowe, John Carlos, ed. 2000. *Post-nationalist American studies.* Berkeley: University of California Press.

Safran, William. 1991. "Diasporas in modern societies: Myths of homeland and return." *Diaspora* 1(1): 3–7.

Shohat, Ella, ed. 1998. *Talking visions: Multicultural feminism in transnational age.* Cambridge: MIT Press.

Tölölyan, Khachig. 1991. "The nation state and its others: In lieu of a preface." *Diaspora* 1(1): 1–2.

———. 1996. "Rethinking *diaspora(s)*: Stateless power in the transnational moment." *Disapora* 5(1): 3–36.

Tu Wei-ming. 1994. *The living tree: The changing meaning of being Chinese today.* Stanford: Stanford University Press.

Wang, Gungwu. 1998. *The Nanhai trade: The early history of Chinese trade in the South China Sea.* Singapore: Times Academic Press.

———. 2000. *The Chinese overseas: From earthbound China to the quest for autonomy.* Cambridge: Harvard University Press.

Waugh, Patricia, ed. 1992. *Postmodernism: A reader.* London: E. Arnold.

Wickberg, Edgar. 2002. "Overseas Chinese: The state of the field." *Chinese America: History and Perspectives*, 1–8.

Wilson, Rob, and Arif Dirlik, eds. 1995. *Asia/Pacific as space of cultural production.* Durham: Duke University Press.

Wong, Sau-ling C. 1995. "Denationalization reconsidered: Asian American cultural criticism at a theoretical crossroads." *Amerasia* 21(1 and 2): 1–27.

——. 2000. "Denationalization reconsidered: Asian American cultural criticism at a theoretical crossroads." In *Postcolonial theory and the United States: Race, ethnicity, and literature*, edited by A. Singh and P. Schmidt, 122–150. Jackson: University Press of Mississippi.

PART TWO

Displacements and Diasporas: Historical and Cultural Studies Perspectives

3

==============================

Diasporas, Displacements, and the Construction of Transnational Identities

K. SCOTT WONG

In the midst the First World War, the American social critic Randolph S. Bourne (1886–1918) published an essay that went against the grain of the widespread calls for active Americanization and national conformity through the suppression of the articulation of ethnic identities. In the face of that international crisis, Bourne resisted the notion that immigrants were required to cast their lot into the American "melting pot" and to leave behind their cultures of origin. Instead, Bourne sought to broaden Americans' understanding of their relationship to the rest of the world, advocating that notions of "citizenship" were not necessarily bound by the nation-state but could also be conceived of in a larger, international perspective. In what may be one of the first articulations of what is now commonly called "transnationalism" and "multiculturalism," Bourne wrote, "America is coming to be, not a nationality but a trans-nationality, a weaving back and forth, with the other lands, of many threads of all sizes and colors" (Bourne 1916, 96). His passionate call for a cosmopolitan and pluralistic understanding of American society and the nation's role in the world came at a time when many Americans questioned the desirability of both immigration and America's increasing involvement in global issues. For a while, the Great War brought the United States out of its isolationism and into the broader community of nations, but the aftermath of this engagement would also eventually contribute to the near-closing of the "Golden Door" to immigrants in 1924. As broad the vision was that Bourne offered in 1916, however, his primary concerns were with how Americans should incorporate immigrants from Europe into the American social landscape and how the United States should respond to a changing European polity.

By the time of his writing "Trans-National America," the United States had already had a long relationship with Asia. Although rarely acknowledged in the literature of the history of American foreign relations, one can argue that Asia has had an influence on the shaping of American culture since before the Colonial period. After all, it was Asia that Christopher Columbus and many of those who followed were seeking, not the land mass they encountered that eventually became known as the New World. This developing relationship with Asia would be fundamental in shaping the labor and trade economy of the colonies and the young republic, and the neighboring colonies of other European nations. The European, and later, American, penetration into Asia and Asian markets contributed to the diasporic movement of people and capital throughout the Pacific and Atlantic cultural spheres. For example, the Spanish colonization of the Philippine Islands in 1521 began a movement bringing Asians to the Americas possibly as early as 1565. In that year the Spanish galleon San Pablo left Cebu for Acapulco, initiating a trade route that would last for nearly three hundred years. From there, Filipinos would migrate from Mexico and settle in Louisiana as early as 1763 (Cordova 1983, 9). As the recent scholarship of John Kuo Wei Tchen (1999), Yong Chen (2000), Madeline Hsu (2000), and Adam McKeown (2001) has demonstrated, Chinese immigrants in New York, San Francisco, Chicago, and Honolulu had established transnational links with China and the Americas by the mid-nineteenth century, expanding long-standing trade and residential patterns. Throughout the nineteenth and twentieth centuries, Asians occupied important transnational positions in the Pacific and Atlantic regions, while people from various parts of the Americas would play important roles in reshaping a number of Asian countries and cultures.

Of great significance was the American presence in the Pacific region. Although American ships had long plied the Pacific trade routes, the gradual usurpation of power in Hawaii from the 1840s through the overthrow of the Hawaiian monarchy in 1893 by American sugarcane plantation owners, with the support of political and military powers, marked the beginning of American imperialism in that area that set the conditions for America's emergence as a world power (formal annexation would take place in 1898).[1] Hawaii was "caught in the crosscurrents of global mercantile trade involving Europe, the United States, and China and at the center of the burgeoning Pacific whale fishery," and it would be these competing economic, legal, and ideological forces that would eventually lead to American domination of Hawaii, including the use of the American legal system to transform the socioeconomic, political, and religious cultures of the islands. As Sally Engle Merry points out, "It was Massachusetts prototypes that formed the basis of Hawaiian criminal law, for example, because these law books happened to be in Honolulu. But it was global trade networks that brought the ships that carried the books from New England to Hawai'i" (2000, 4–6). Thus the movement of goods, capital, people, and ideologies must be taken into account simultaneously in order for the impact of transnationalism to be fully appreciated.

Whereas the Hawaiian Islands were transformed and brought into the American cultural sphere by incorporating them into the global market through the establishment of a plantation economy, coupled with missionary endeavors and military strength, the Philippine Islands came under American control through direct military aggression. In the wake of the American victory over Spain, the American government chose not to support the Filipino struggle for independence but sought instead to seize the islands and bring them under American control. To do so, however, required that the United States wage war against the Philippines, resulting in hundreds of thousands of Filipino deaths between the years 1899 to 1903.[2] Once established in both Hawaii and the Philippines, the United States dominated the Pacific trade routes and was responsible for the import and export of Asian laborers to and from their island holdings. This process of establishing and maintaining an empire in the Pacific continued the exportation of American cultural, legal, and economic ideals and ideologies to various parts of the Pacific and Asia. In turn, Asians would follow these same routes to the Americas and back, while people from the Americas would continue to maintain an influencing presence in colonial and postcolonial Asia.

While Bourne was calling for a broader incorporation of European immigrants into the American polity, another group of aspiring immigrants were being denied entry into the country. Beginning in 1875, there began a gradual but steady restriction on the immigration of Chinese, culminating in the Chinese Exclusion Act of 1882, which denied the entry of Chinese laborers for ten years. Roger Daniels points out that the Chinese Exclusion Act, the first to deny the entry of any people based on their race and class, would be the "hinge on which all American immigration policy turned. . . . [It] ended the era of free and unrestricted access to the United States" (1997, 17). This legislation would be strengthened and extended a number of times, only to be repealed in 1943 when the United States and China were allies during the Second World War. The exclusion of the Chinese set the precedent for the eventual prohibition of nearly all Asian immigration, with Japanese and Korean laborers excluded in 1907, South Asians in 1917, and Filipinos in 1934. The Immigration Act of 1924, with its prohibition of immigrants "ineligible to citizenship," would effectively shut the gates to nearly all Asian immigrants until 1965.[3]

Despite exclusionary ideologies and legislation, Asians did manage to emigrate to the Americas, and they established productive and meaningful lives there, raising families and contributing to the building and growth of the Americas and the Caribbean. The process, however, was fraught with displacement and ruptures in cultural continuity. Three of the four essays included in this section speak to the complex interactions between Asians and the residents of Latin America and the Caribbean, whereas the fourth piece looks in the other direction, to the children fathered by African American soldiers while serving in the war in Vietnam. In all of these cases, there are intertwined issues of diaspora, displacement, and the construction of transnational identities.

In her study of Chinese laborers and shopkeepers in Latin America and the Caribbean, Evelyn Hu-DeHart points to the importance of approaching Asian settlement in these areas through the lens of transnational diasporic studies. She explains that a sizable Asian population has been present in Latin America and the Caribbean throughout the twentieth century, and reminds us that the largest Japanese population outside of Japan resides in Brazil, not the United States. Hu-DeHart also provides a brief overview of how other fields have been slow to acknowledge the importance of comparative diasporic studies in terms of studying Asians outside of Asia. Chinese scholars examining the Chinese diaspora have tended to view this movement as one of migration and resettlement, but with a focus on their retention of "Chineseness" and their status as "overseas Chinese." At the same time, until recently most scholars in Asian American Studies have been concerned mainly with the immigration of Chinese, usually from southeastern China, to the western United States and Hawaii, often with a focus on the development of the anti-Chinese movement and the subsequent exclusion of Chinese labor immigrants. There was generally little interest in the movement of Chinese to other parts of the Americas and the Caribbean. Hence, for Hu-DeHart, working within a paradigm of transnational diasporas has allowed her to "overcome the limitations posed by Overseas Chinese Studies on the one hand, and cultural nationalistic Asian American Studies on the other, in that diaspora decenters China in Overseas Chinese Studies and decenters U.S.-Asians in Asian American Studies. Consequently, 'China' is enlarged to be wherever Chinese people and their descendants are to be found, and 'America' is not confined to just the United States. Multiplicities of Chineseness interact with multiplicities of Americanness, producing new and unique kinds of *mestizaje* or hybridity." By examining the presence of Chinese laborers (*huagong*) and merchants (*huashang*) in northern Mexico as agents of transnationalism, Hu-DeHart's chapter traces the development of the Chinese as both indentured laborers in Cuba and Peru, working within a contract labor system that constituted a "transitional form of labor from slave to free (wage) labor," and as the petite bourgeoisie in a "border state within a neocolonial context controlled by U.S. investments and markets." Thus by studying the Chinese diaspora in a comparative framework, Hu-DeHart is able to offer a more complete view of the role Chinese played in the development of the New World, revealing the complex relationships between emigrating peoples and their various hosts.[4]

Walton Look Lai tackles the subject of Chinese indentured labor in the West Indies in greater detail. He describes how Chinese laborers, and later, small entrepreneurs, were among those who came to the West Indies during a period of multisource and multiracial importation, during the mid-to-late nineteenth century, forming the "third largest regional grouping of Chinese arrivals to the Western Hemisphere" of the period. He argues that "as an indenture experiment, it was relatively mild, and that there was a surprising level of voluntary and even family migration, even within the framework of indentureship." He attributes this to the difference between British and Spanish methods of recruiting labor, as well as the tempering affect of Christian missionaries in the recruitment process. Focusing on the impressions others had of the Chinese migrants, Look Lai points out that they entered evolving multicultural societies and were perceived differently by the various parties already there. The newly arrived Chinese and their descendents interacted with a ruling elite of British colonial officials, white Creole planters, and former slave masters, and a laboring class made up of blacks and South Asian migrants. Each group saw the Chinese according to their own experiences of interaction and their sociopolitical and economic needs. They were perceived as industrious or lazy and inclined toward various vices, as a possible buffer between whites and blacks, as possible links to an expanding trade with Asia, as competitors for jobs, and as both perpetually foreign and desiring of assimilation. Thus Chinese West Indian migrations (or any other Chinese migration, for that matter) cannot be explained simply by the local dynamics of nationalist political economy but have to be situated within the expanding globalization dynamics of the industrial age. And by doing so, issues of labor recruitment, migration, slavery, and the rise of global capitalism come to the fore in bold relief.

Moving southeast from the West Indies, Jeffrey Lesser's work explores the construction of a Brazilian identity among Japanese immigrants and their descendants, as well as how Brazilian society and that country's national identity is defined through the presence of the Japanese. Lesser begins his essay with three "foundational fictions" in which it is suggested that "Japanese immigrants and their descendants are more 'original' or 'authentic' Brazilians than members of the European-descended Brazilian elite itself." These fictions revolve around the notion that Brazilians and Japanese are historically linked through manners, customs, linguistics, and perhaps an ancient ancestry. However, as Lesser points out, these myths of commonality do not always translate into ethnic inclusion, as third-generation Brazilians of Japanese descent are always "Japanese," rather than Japanese-Brazilian; in Brazil citizenship does not erase the condition of foreignness. This, however, does not negate their status of well-respected members of the Brazilian polity. From 1908 to 1941, some 190,000 Japanese entered Brazil and currently, more than a million Brazilians claim Japanese descent, while 200,000 of them work in Japan. Nikkei (anyone of Japanese ancestry) in Brazil have found political, economic, and social acceptance, as their "non-whiteness and non-blackness" has challenged elite ideas of national identity, as successful people in Brazil are often put in the "white" category regardless of their skin color. Nikkei thus identified with "whiteness" in order to claim a secure position in Brazilian society, despite their inherent foreignness. In fact, there were some who believed that "Japanese are the best possible Brazilians: honest, hard-working, and well-connected." As Lesser demonstrates throughout his work, the Japanese diaspora has played a role in shaping how Japanese, Brazilians, and Japanese Brazilians negotiate their identities in an era of transnationality, in which salient components of national identity—ethnicity, class, gender, and color—are questioned and reformulated by various segments of the nation-state.[5]

Bernard Scott Lucious brings this group of essays full circle, bringing the West back to Asia. Lucious seeks to broaden the critical inquiry of the "lived-experience of blackness" to include not only the "Black Atlantic," but to enlarge the study of blackness by tracing "its roots in and routes through Asian diaspo-ras" as well. He approaches this project by offering the testimonies of "mixed-heritage children born of both African American and Asian parentages . . . [allowing for an] emergent Afro-Amerasian discourse [that] indexes a spatio-temporal site beyond the Atlantic that is not exclusively African-American nor Asian-American, African diasporic nor Asian diasporic, but is all of these at once; it points to an emergent site of critical inquiry which [he has] named the 'Black Pacific.'" Lucious maps the development of the Black Pacific by present-ing it as the "cultural space at the interstices of three diasporas . . . the experi-ences of African-American men (of the Black Atlantic) who served and continue to serve in the United States military throughout the Asia-Pacific; the experi-ences of Asian women who have had affairs with American military men, or who have become either 'military brides' or 'Asian-American immigrants' as a result of the American empire's presence in the Asia-Pacific; and the experi-ences of the Afro-Amerasian children born unto African-American men and Asian women throughout the Asia-Pacific, since as early as the Spanish-American War in the Philippines. The Black Pacific, therefore, is a site of critical inquiry that is not only interracial . . . but it is also interdiasporic." The oral histories of the Afro-Amerasian children in Vietnam are insightful, at times heartbreaking. They speak of being displaced, physically and psychically, in their homeland because of their parentage. Their blackness separates them from other Viet-namese, as well as other Amerasians, as those of black parentage face a more severe discrimination than those of white fathers, a condition that Lucious labels intra-race racism, or "colorism." Thus race, ethnicity, color, and nation-ality all play vital roles in the construction of the multiracial identities of Viet-namese Afro-Amerasians. Furthermore, by tracing the presence and interaction of blacks and Asians through this region, Lucious broadens our scope of intel-lectual inquiry by emphasizing that "blackness (African Americanness) is a con-stitutive dimension of Asian and Asian American Studies, and yellowness (Asianness) of African American Studies."

These four essays all point to the idea the "concept of identity and concepts of race, ethnicity, gender, class, nationality, and the nation are interlocking and have become increasingly complex in a world ever more characterized by transnational and global exchanges" (Khu 2001, 225). As Bharati Mukherjee has so eloquently written,

> There are national airlines flying the world that do not appear in any directory. There are charters who've lost their way and now just fly, improvising crews and destinations. They serve no food, no beverages. Their crews often look abused. There is a shadow world of aircraft permanently aloft that share air lanes and radio frequencies with Pan Am and British Air and Air-India, portaging people who coexist with tourists and businessmen. But we are refugees and mercenaries and guest workers; you see us sleeping in airport lounges, you watch us unwrapping the last of our native foods, unrolling our prayer rugs, reading our holy books, taking out for the hundredth time an aerogramme promising a job or space to sleep, a newspaper in our language, a photo of happier times, a passport, a visa, a *laissez-passer.*
>
> We are outcasts and deportees, strange pilgrims visiting outlandish shrines, landing at the end of tarmacs, ferried in old army trucks where we are roughly handled and taken to roped-off corners of waiting rooms where surly, barely wakened customs guards await their bribes. We are dressed in shreds of national costumes, out of season, the wilted plumage of intercontinental vagabondage. We ask only one thing: to be allowed to land; to pass through, to continue. We sneak a look at the big departure board, the one the tourists use. Our cities are there too, our destinations are so close! But not yet, not so directly. We must sneak in, land by night in little-used strips. For us, back behind the rope in the corner of the waiting room, there is only a slate and someone who remembers to write in chalk, *Delayed*, or *To be Announced*, or *Out of Service*. We take another of our precious dollars or Swiss francs and give it to a trustworthy-looking boy and say, "Bring me tea, an orange, bread."
>
> What country? What continent? We pass through wars, through plagues. I am hungry for news, but the discarded papers are in characters or languages I cannot read. The zigzag route is the straightest. (1989, 90–91)

Refugees, businessmen, diplomats, family members seeking each other, undocumented workers, and as we now know, terrorists, all travel the routes created by transnational diasporas, now made more complex, yet perhaps easier to negotiate due to the globalization of technology and capital. But the ease by which people, capital, and ideas move across spatial and cultural boundaries because of globalization has also increased the global reach of the exploitation of labor, often along gendered and racialized lines. Lisa Lowe (1996) offers a powerful discussion of transnational labor and capital, focusing on the exploitation of Asian and Latina women in what she calls the "racialized feminization of labor" in the global restructuring of capitalism. She states,

> The focus on women's work within the global economy as a material site in which several axes of domination intersect provides for the means of linking Asian immigrant and Asian American women with other immigrant and racialized women. Asian immigrant and Asian American women are not simply the most recent formation within the genealogy of Asian American racialization; they, along with women working in the "third world," are the "new" workforce within the global reorganization of capitalism. In this sense, the active affiliations of Asian immigrant and Asian American women are informed by, yet go beyond, Asian American cultural identity as it emerged within the confines of the U.S. nation. They are linked to an emergent political formation, organizing across race, class, and national boundaries, that includes other racialized and immigrant groups as well as women working in, and immigrating from, the neocolonized world. (1996, 158)

She points out that from roughly 1850 to World War II, Asian immigration "was the site for the eruptions and resolutions of the contradictions between the national economy and the political state, and, from World War II onward, the locus of the contradictions between the nation-state and the global economy. Hence, Asian immigrant women's work must be understood within the history of U.S. immigration policies and the attempts to incorporate immigrants into the developing economy, on the one hand, and within the global expansion of U.S. capitalism through colonialism and global restructuring, on the other" (1996, 159).

In the postwar era, the globalization of capitalism has shifted manufacturing operations to Asia and Latin America as American domestic operations are "downsized" or as a former student of mine called it, "right-sized." And here again, it is imperative to look beyond the borders of the United States and examine the notion of the so-called Pacific Rim and how Asians and Asian Americans are configured in that discussion. As the flow of labor and capital has supposedly moved to the Pacific in the late-twentieth century, there has developed a discourse of the Pacific Rim that has framed the region as a "modern economic miracle" that came into being during the 1970s and 1980s. As I wrote earlier in this essay, however, this so-called Pacific Rim began earlier with the development of trade between Europe, the Americas, and Asia in the 1700s, and it steadily developed with the Gold Rush, the completion of the Transcontinental Railroad, and the American conquest of Hawaii and the Philippines. Furthermore, the common picture of the Pacific Rim has been one of robust economies generating jobs for the masses on both sides of the Pacific Ocean. Framing the picture as such, however, serves to mask the impact of the penetration of the region by the area's two dominant economies, the United States and Japan. And once the image of the "miracle" is in place, one "forgets" the history of the region, the history of American imperialism and conquest, the history of Japanese wartime atrocities, the dropping of two atomic bombs, and the Korean War, the war in Vietnam, the horrors of the Khmer Rouge, and the American program to stymie the economic development of Vietnam. The "miracle" image also serves to help us forget "the factory buses circulating through the outlying neighborhoods of a Malaysian market town, picking up throngs of young Malay and Indian women who are employed in the foreign-and-state-owned electronics and textile factories of the industrial estates and free trade zones of the Penang area; the Chinese men, women, and children in Malaysia engaged frenetically in the piecework of home labor—sewing, shoemaking, packaging, and the like—to produce commodities for the international market; or the Chinese men and women who aspire to work as illegal laborers in Japan, Taiwan, or the United States" (Nonini 1993, 162). In other words, the *Golden Venture* sails the seas of the Pacific Rim fueled by the profits to be made in the transnational economy. Let us not forget that the power of the global capital that runs the sewing machines in the sweatshops of Los Angeles and New York also runs them in Hong Kong, Taipei, Manila, Shenzhen, and Seoul.

As the globalization of capital, labor, and the movement of migrants increases, the cultural identity of those in transit and those who settle in distant lands become more fluid and decentered. Transnational identities are not necessarily fixed to a place, but perhaps to a strategy of ensuring the accumulation of needed social, economic, cultural, educational, and political capital. Stuart Hall reminds us that that cultural identity "is a matter of 'becoming' as well as of 'being.' It belongs to the future as much as to the past. It is not something which already exists, transcending place, time, history and culture. Cultural identities come from somewhere, have histories. But, like everything that is historical, they undergo constant transformation. Far from being eternally fixed in some essentialized past, they are subject to the continuous 'play' of history, culture and power" (Hall 1990, 225). The cultural anthropologist Roger Rouse frames it in this way:

> We live in a confusing world, a world of crisscrossed economies, intersecting systems of meaning, and fragmented societies. Suddenly, the comforting modern imagery of nation-states and national languages, of coherent communities and consistent subjectivities, of dominant

centers and distant margins no longer seem adequate. Certainly, in my
own discipline of anthropology, there is a growing sense that our conventional means of representing both the worlds of those we study and
the worlds that we ourselves inhabit have been strained beyond their
limits by the changes that are taking place around. (1991, 8)

Although Rouse was writing about the fluidity of the U.S.-Mexican border, his
observations are applicable to other regions as well. With the use of various
technologies, such as e-mail, the Internet, video, modern air travel, and the
global reach of modern business, the Pacific and Atlantic oceans are as porous
and elastic as the borders between many contiguous nation-states. There has
been an increase in transnational families in the postwar era, where children
and their mothers may live in the United States most of the time while the
father spends much of his time in Korea, Taiwan, Saudi Arabia, London, Bonn,
or Peru—but all are involved in the maintenance of family dynamics and decisions. Transnational technology has created not only the global village and
"hyper-extended families" but global or transnational individuals as well, with
shifting allegiances and transformative identities.

As Randolph Bourne exhorted us in 1916 to accept the "weaving back and
forth, with the other lands, of threads of all sizes and colors," he also foresaw
the dangers of not being willing to do so. He continued,

Any movement which attempts to thwart this weaving, or to dye the fabric any one color, or disentangle the threads of the strands, is false to this
cosmopolitan vision. . . . No Americanization will fulfill this vision which
does not recognize the uniqueness of this transnationalism of ours. The
Anglo-Saxon attempt to fuse will only create enmity and distrust. The
crusade against "hyphenates" will only inflame the partial patriotism of
transnationals, and cause them to assert their European traditions in
strident and unwholesome ways. But the attempt to weave a wholly novel
international nation out of our chaotic America will liberate and harmonize the creative power of all these peoples and give them the new spiritual
citizenship, as so many individuals have already been given, of a world.
(1916, 96).

The world is obviously far more complex and interrelated than it was when
Bourne wrote these words, and American society has moved beyond the sim-
plistic calls for Anglo-conformity and the incorporation of European immigrants, but the urgency of his message rings as loud and as true.

The events of September 11, 2001, and their aftermath weighed heavily on
me as I wrote this introductory piece to the following four essays. I often wondered how those events and the subsequent "war on terrorism" would be

understood by those interested in immigration, globalization, transnational-ism, and the evolution of the concept of the nation-state. Perhaps these sad and devastating developments can be seen as one result of the meeting of various overlapping diasporas, that of global capitalism, religious and political radical-ism, and centuries of the interaction of competing, complementary, and often mutually misunderstood sets of beliefs, desires, ideologies, and practices. Per-haps, too, these events will also lead people, both here and abroad, to recognize the networks of interdependence that have come with modernity, and that the complexities of the transnational movement of people, capital, labor, and ideas demand all of us to view these factors as interactive forces in the shaping of world politics and the diasporic identities of those touched by these move-ments and their long-lasting and far-reaching effects.

NOTES

1. The body of work on the American annexation of Hawaii and the subsequent development of the plantation economy is too large to cite here in its entirety. Some major and recent works include Coffman (1998), Kame'eleihiwa (1992), Merry (2000), Whitehead (1999).

2. For studies on the American war in the Philippines, see Hoganson (1998), Karnow (1989), Linn (2000), Miller (1982), and Musicant (1998).

3. The literature on the exclusion of Chinese is far too extensive to cite here. Some recent and important works are Chan (1991), Lee (2003), McClain (1994), Salyer (1995), and Wong and Chan (1998). The Immigration Act of 1924, aside from assigning each country an annual immigration quota, specified that those "inel-igible to citizenship" were barred from immigrating. At this point, citizenship was only conferred on those considered "white" or of African descent, leaving Asians largely ineligible for naturalization. See Haney-Lopez (1996), Jacobson (1998), and Ngai (1999). For the impact of the Immigration Act of 1965 on Asian immigration, see Hing (1993) and Reimers (1992).

4. For an outstanding study of Chinese immigrants in the border region of Sonora, Mexico and the United States, see Delgado (2000).

5. For his full treatment of this subject, see Lesser (1999).

REFERENCES

Bourne, Randolph S. 1916. "Trans-national America." *Atlantic Monthly* 118: 96.

Chan, Sucheng. 1991. *Entry denied: Exclusion and the Chinese community in America, 1882–1943*. Philadelphia: Temple University Press.

Chen, Yong. 2000. *Chinese San Francisco, 1850–1943: A trans-Pacific community*. Stanford: Stanford University Press.

Coffman, Tom. 1998. *Nation within: The story of America's annexation of the nation of Hawai'i*. Kane'ohe, Hawai'i: Tom Coffman/EPICenter.

Cordova, Fred. 1983. *Filipinos: Forgotten Asian Americans, a pictorial essay, 1763–circa 1963.* Dubuque, Iowa: Kendal/Hunt.

Daniels, Roger. 1997. *Not like us: Immigrants and minorities in America, 1890–1924.* Chicago: Ivan R. Dee.

Delgado, Grace. 2000. "In the age of exclusion: Race, region and Chinese identity in the making of the Arizona-Sonora borderlands, 1963–1943." Ph.D. dissertation, University of California, Los Angeles.

Hall, Stuart. 1990. "Cultural Identity and Diaspora". In *Identity: Community, culture, difference*, edited by J. Rutherford, 222–237. London: Lawrence and Wishart.

Haney-Lopez, Ian. 1996. *White by law: The legal constructions of race.* New York: New York University Press.

Hing, Bill Ong. 1993. *Making and remaking Asian America through immigration policy, 1850–1990.* Stanford: Stanford University Press.

Hoganson, Kristin L. 1998. *Fighting for American manhood: How gender politics provoked the Spanish-American and Philippine-American wars.* New Haven: Yale University Press.

Hsu, Madeline Yuan-yin. 2000. *Dreaming of gold, dreaming of home: Trans-nationalism and migration between the United States and South China, 1882–1943.* Stanford: Stanford University Press.

Jacobson, Matthew Frye. 1998. *Whiteness of a different color: European immi- grants and the alchemy of race.* Cambridge: Harvard University Press.

Kame'eleihiwa, Lilikala. 1992. *Native land and foreign desires.* Honolulu: Bishop Museum Press.

Karnow, Stanley. 1989. *In our image: America's empire in the Philippines.* New York: Random House.

Khu, Josephine M. T. 2001. *Cultural curiosity: Thirteen stories about the search for Chinese roots.* Berkeley: University of California Press.

Lee, Erika. 2003. Forthcoming. *At America's gates: Chinese immigration during the exclusion era, 1882–1943.* Chapel Hill: University of North Carolina Press.

Lesser, Jeffrey. 1999. *Negotiating national identity: Immigrants, minorities, and the struggle for ethnicity in Brazil.* Durham: Duke University Press.

Linn, Brian McAllister. 2000. *The Philippine war, 1899–1902.* Lawrence: University Press of Kansas.

Lowe, Lisa. 1996. *Immigrant acts: On Asian American cultural politics.* Durham: Duke University Press.

McClain, Charles J. 1994. *In search of equality: The Chinese struggle against discrimination in nineteenth-century America.* Berkeley: University of California Press.

McKeown, Adam. 2001. *Chinese migrant networks and cultural change: Peru, Chicago, Hawaii, 1900–1936.* Chicago: University of Chicago Press.

Merry, Sally Engle. 2000. *Colonizing Hawai'i: The cultural power of law.* Princeton: Princeton University Press.

Miller, Stuart Creighton. 1982. *"Benevolent assimilation": The American conquest of the Philippines, 1899–1903.* New Haven: Yale University Press.

Mukherjee, Bharati. 1989. *Jasmine.* New York: Grove Weidenfeld.

Musicant, Ivan. 1998. *Empire by default: The Spanish-American war and the dawn of the American century.* New York: H. Holt.

Ngai, Mai. 1999. "The architecture of race in American immigration law: A reexamination of the Immigration Act of 1924." *Journal of American History* 86(1): 67–92.

Nonini, Donald M. 1993. "On the outs on the rim: An ethnographic grounding of the 'Asia-Pacific' imaginary." In *What is in a rim? Critical perspectives on the Pacific region idea,* edited by A. Dirlik, 161–182. Boulder: Westview.

Reimers, David M. 1992. *Still the golden door: The Third World comes to America.* New York: Columbia University Press.

Rouse, Roger. 1991. "Mexican migration and the social space of postmodernism." *Diaspora* 1(1): 8–23.

Salyer, Lucy E. 1995. *Law harsh as tigers: Chinese immigrants and the shaping of modern immigration law.* Chapel Hill: University of North Carolina Press.

Tchen, John Kuo Wei. 1999. *New York before Chinatown: Orientalism and the shaping of American culture, 1776–1882.* Baltimore: Johns Hopkins University Press.

Whitehead, John S. 1999. "Western progressives, old south planters, or colonial oppressors: The enigma of Hawai'i's 'Big Five.'" *Western Historical Quarterly* 20: 295–326.

Wong, Kevin Scott, and Sucheng Chan. 1998. *Claiming America: Constructing Chinese American identities during the exclusion era.* Philadelphia: Temple University Press.

4

Images of the Chinese in West Indian History

WALTON LOOK LAI

The Chinese who entered the British West Indies in the middle and late nineteenth century formed a marginal but distinct part of the global dispersal of southern Chinese characteristic of the period. Next to those in the United States, on the one hand, and in Cuba and Peru, on the other, they formed the third largest regional grouping of Chinese arrivals to the Western Hemisphere in mid-century. About 15,000 arrived in British Guiana, with just under 3,000 going to Trinidad and Jamaica, to work as indentured laborers in the sugar industry. In the last decade of the century, these immigrants were augmented by free, voluntary small-trader and family elements, many of whom were simultaneously migrating to old and new Latin American destinations during a period of Chinese exclusion from the United States (after 1882). About 7,000 found their way into the region between the 1890s and 1940s, with most of the new arrivals going to Jamaica and Trinidad, unlike the first period, when most went to British Guiana.

Although the pattern of their entry into these new societies represented a microcosmic version of the story of the Chinese diaspora in the nineteenth century, there were a number of distinctive traits attaching to this regional experience that bear noting. As an indenture experiment, it was relatively mild, and there was a surprisingly high level of voluntary and even family migration, even within the framework of indentureship. This was largely due to the difference between the British and Spanish methods of recruiting laborers in China. The watchdog activities of abolitionist lobbies in Britain, which led to the distinctive indenture system in British India, undoubtedly played a role in British efforts to recruit Chinese labor for similar destinations within the British Empire generally. The prominent role played by Christian missionary elements in the China recruitment process also contributed to the relative mildness of the labor experiment.

The kinds of societies to which the Chinese migrants had to adjust were also more similar to the islands of the western Indian Ocean (Mauritius, Reunion) than to their hemispheric counterparts. This would include not just the sugar-plantation environment (with its prior history of slavery) but also the specific nature of the new society's multiculturalism. The society was made up mainly of white minority elites, black or colored ex-slaves, immigrants from South Asia, within the political and economic framework of European colonialism. Other similarities would include the relative marginality of the Chinese contribution to the post-slavery economic revival, due to the small numbers of Chinese laborers and their swift ascent out of the plantation environment to visible middleman minority status on the basis of mercantile activity, a trend augmented by the large numbers of the later voluntary migrants.

The Chinese were never central to the consciousness of the evolving colonial society. Never more than 1 percent of the population, they existed on the periphery of economic life and colonial consciousness for most of the early period. Hence, collective societal impressions of their presence in the West Indies would always tend to be circumscribed. Nevertheless, a study of some of these societal impressions as they evolved over time may help us to gain some insight into the special conditions of marginality inherent in their experience in the West Indies, as well as into the kind of multicultural environment being nurtured in a unique corner of the British Empire.

Who observed the Chinese in the nineteenth and twentieth centuries, and who took the time to record their observations, in whatever form? More important, how have these images altered over time, as the Chinese themselves evolved from agricultural workers to small- and large-scale traders, and as the larger society itself progressed from a state of colonial dependency to national self-determination? We have the twofold task of first distinguishing between the different social players, all of whom had their own special ways of seeing, then distinguishing between different phases in the evolution of the society, in order to see how each phase often generated both changed perceptions and new observers.

During the nineteenth-century indenture period, different elements of the ruling colonial elite assessed the Chinese as a potential and actual settler group in the society. The ruling elite was essentially made up of British colonial officials, based in the East or West Indies, and also included the white Creole planters, former slave masters, who employed the newcomers. Next to these were traveling or resident British or European writers or missionaries who took the time to record their observations on the Chinese and other peoples in the society. Besides the ruling elite, there were the views coming from fellow laborers in the society, mainly the blacks but also other immigrants entering the society at the same time, such as the Indians. Of course there was the occasional view coming from the Chinese themselves.

Second, as the Chinese progressed after the 1880s into the lower middle class, and eventually, to some extent into the upper middle class, and as the society found itself caught up after World War I in an anticolonial nationalist struggle to remove the British, new nationalist voices emerged on the scene. They came from the ranks of labor, but often also from the ranks of the increasingly vocal educated black middle classes.[1] The emerging nationalist elite would bring its own special ways of seeing the possibilities and pitfalls of the multicultural West Indies. There is also a third phase, the postcolonial phase, which sees the withdrawal of the British and the coming to power of the new black nationalist political elite in what is still a very racially stratified and unequal society. The Chinese meanwhile have been evolving still further into higher and more complex levels of economic and social influence, and generating totally new images about their place in the larger society. This corresponds with the environment of the late 1960s and after.

Colonial Elites

Colonial officials included both those who operated in China and those who functioned in the West Indies. Together they were concerned with putting into effect a colonial emigration policy, and were asked to present their views on the prospects as well as the actual experiment of the 1860s. Consular personnel and immigration officers gave a view of the Chinese as an enterprising, hardworking element who would add to the strength of postemancipation West Indian society. The earliest images are from reports of Eastern official experts on Chinese emigration to Southeast Asia, giving their views on the prospects for a West Indies-bound migration. The Chinese are generally described as an industrious, sober, and orderly people. Here are some judgments from those contemplating the first 1806 emigration to Trinidad: "The great ambition of a Chinese is to obtain a piece of ground no matter how barren, his labour and ingenuity soon making it wear the face of plenty. The indefatigable industry and habits of frugality of the Chinese, with their being the most fitted for the cultivation of the soil, seems to point out that of all people in the world they are the best calculated to transform the woody wastes and drowned parts of Trinidad into rich, fertile and productive land."[2]

Not all of this interest in Chinese labor was exclusively economic. Some saw the Chinese as a potential buffer class between the whites and the blacks, and voiced such sentiments directly, with an eye to the Haitian revolution then very much in progress to the northern Caribbean:

The events which have recently happened at St Domingo necessarily awakes all those apprehensions which the establishment of a Negro government in that island gave rise to some years ago, and render it indispensable that every practicable measure of precaution should be adopted to guard the British possessions in the West Indies as well against any future indisposition of a power so constituted as against the danger of a spirit of insurrection being excited amongst the Negroes in our colonies.

It is conceived that no measure would so effectually tend to provide a security against this danger, as that of introducing a free race of cultivators into our islands, who, from habits and feelings would be kept distinct from the Negroes, and who from interest would be inseparably attached to the European proprietors.[3]

Another motivation that expressed itself in 1806 was the desire to see Trinidad become a trade link between the East and South American trade, and Chinese settlement on the island was seen as a step in this direction: "There cannot be a doubt but that the [British East] India Company might, by a well regulated intercourse of trade from India and China, to Trinidad, render that island a depot for this commerce. That we might thereby be enabled to supply the Continent of South America with the manufactures and productions of India and China, instead of leaving that source of wealth in the hands of the Americans."[4]

In any event, the 1806 experiment was a failure; most of the 192 Chinese who arrived on the solitary vessel, the *Fortitude*, decided to return to China after a few years. It was not until the 1850s that British interest was again revived, this time in an atmosphere of worldwide Chinese migration, since this was the decade when Cantonese were emigrating in large numbers to Latin America, North America, and Australia. Similar kinds of judgments about the potential of the Chinese as settlers for the West Indies were expressed by these colonial officials: "The climate [in Guangdong], at least at this time of the year, is very similar to that of the West Indies, and I think they would enjoy health and strength in their new location. The extensive cultivation of rice and sugar in the lowlands of the two provinces Canton and Fukien would seem to qualify them for a residence in Trinidad and Demerara [British Guiana], and I believe they will be found hardy and industrious."[5]

Some of the comments were addressed to the differences between a West Indian emigration scheme and the Cuban version:

The experience of this season [1853] has fully confirmed my former views as to the disadvantage, if not danger, of leaving the emigration from China in private hands, without sufficient responsibility, and paid by bounty or by a commission on each emigrant shipped. The system will lead to abuses, and bring discredit on the country. It must be conducted by a paid officer, responsible to Government, and to a certain extent under the orders and supervision of the local Government. The headquarters of the emigration office should be at Hong Kong, but the agent should have authority to procure emigrants at other places, and to send vessels there, if necessary. There will be a good deal of expense in organising an office, and proper establishment, at the commencement, but everything must be done to inspire confidence among the Chinese, so that they may come from the country to seek for emigration of their own accord, and not at the instigation of brokers, who may probably deceive them by means which our ignorance of the mainland, and our very imperfect knowledge of their habits and language, render it impossible to discover until it be too late to apply the necessary remedy. . . .

In order to disabuse the public mind of the strong feeling that now prevails adverse to all emigration, I have had . . . notices and instructions printed. . . . (T)heir tenor will show the anxiety of Government that this new emigration should be openly and fairly conducted, and in a manner likely to be conducive to the general benefit of all parties interested in its welfare.[6]

At the close of the 1854 season, the emigration officer concluded as follows:

our acts and intentions were as different to those of the Chinese crimps as day to night. . . . Instead of collecting people by force or fraud, I . . . employed the press to sow the good seed over the length and breadth of Quantung, and to make known to those who were in poverty that the British Government offered them a new home where comparative affluence was the reward of honest labour.

Instead of the Swatow dens of filth and iniquity where the sustenance barely sufficed to support life, and where husbands and children torn from their families were caged till their purchasers called for compulsory removal to the ships, I offered the best and amplest food at houses to and from which there was *free* ingress and egress, where every information was available from maps, pamphlets and notices, and from whence the labourers were at perfect liberty to return to their old homes, or to seek the new one offered to them. Instead of forcing the emigrants to indent themselves to worse even than slavery by renunciation of the advantages of free British citizens, the current wages of the colonies, house and garden rent free, correspondence free of cost with relatives left behind, and the punctual payment at Hong Kong or Canton monthly from the day of embarkation, of such portion of the wages to be earned as the emigrants desired to appropriate in China.

Lastly, instead of placing my ships where oppression could be practised with impunity, I selected Hong Kong and Canton for their anchorage, and facilitated their inspection, by the Chinese authorities and people as much as possible.[7]

There was some discussion about whether the Chinese could adjust easily to the different societal and racial environment of the West Indies. Two different kinds of judgments were expressed. One official thought that "In all the islands and countries where the Chinese have hitherto settled as emigrants, they have found branches of the Malay family and races cognate to their own; this would not be the case in the West Indies, and I have very great doubts whether they would form connexions of a permanent character with the Negro women, so as to become contented and resident colonists. If this difficulty can be got over, I have no doubt as to the successful result of Chinese emigration on the future destinies of the West Indian colonies."[8] Another thought the opposite: "I have no doubt that the Chinese will readily amalgamate with the females they find in the country they are going to. They have no feelings of caste to restrain them in this direction, as the Hindoo coolies have. The natives of India in the Straits never intermarry with the Malays, whereas in three or four generations the Malay-Chinese females have become so numerous as to afford a sufficient supply for the Chinese population."[9]

Comments on the Chinese performance as laborers after their arrival in the West Indies varied widely among the elites, whether colonial officials or Creole planters. The migrants were a diverse group of people, and the different shipments brought all kinds of people to the islands. Many were displaced peasants (often families) seeking alternative work outside of China; many were from the unstable sectors of the urban population. A number of them were political refugees from the Taiping Rebellion. It is noticeable that there were hardly any of the entrapped debtor elements common to the Cuban and Peruvian migrations, although cases of recruitment based on false promises and false information often came to light. Official comments on the new Chinese arrivals ranged from widespread praise and enthusiasm to outright condemnation and disgust. The first arrivals of 1853 generated much enthusiasm about their future prospects as sugar workers in Trinidad and British Guiana:

> The Chinese on this estate are some of my best labourers; for strength and endurance they are equal to the Africans. Last month I had an average of 90 of these fine labourers at work every day, performing the following work, viz: cutting canes, forking cane fields, supplying canes, hauling cane trash off the fields recently cut, working on the copper wall as boilermen, working in the distillery, loading cane punts, carrying megass, etc. Without our Chinese boys I do not know how we would manage for megass carriers, as there is not a single creole working with them.[10]

An official report concluded that

> The employers found them somewhat expensive at first, and difficult to manage, but augured well of their future industry. During the first few months, however, various misunderstandings took place on the subject of work and wages, and these, for want of competent interpreters, took long to settle, and in some cases were only settled by removing the people.
>
> But this was exceptional; the majority of employers, though for some time they complained of the Chinese being difficult to manage, gradually came to look upon them as a valuable class of labourers, and those who had succeeded with them from the first preferred them to all others. . . .
>
> Many of them hold situations of high trust and responsibility upon estates, and the numbers who are independent, and conversant with the French and English languages, would inspire their newly-arrived countrymen with hope, and dissipate that lowness of spirits, which, in their own case, coupled with abuse of opium, left so many unresisting victims to the climatic remittent fever. . . .
>
> [O]f 665 Chinese now remaining from the original allotments, 310 had remained on the estates to which they were originally attached, while 255 had purchased their remaining periods of industrial residence, and about 100 were unattached, from reasons given in the Annual Report for 1857.
>
> The Canton coast is a sugar-growing country, and its inhabitants have been officially reported, on the best authority, by Sir Frederic Rogers, in his letter of 7 January 1853, to be strong, thrifty, intelligent and industrious, and of all Chinamen the best adapted for labour in the West Indies. The wages near Canton are $2 per month with rice, and the people would certainly be content to emigrate for $5 and rice, or $7 without allowances.[11]

At the end of the 1860s, after the arrival of most of the immigrants, another official report in 1871 compared the Chinese with their fellow workers as follows:

> The Chinese labourer possesses greater intelligence than either the Indian or the Negro, and is much quicker at learning to manage machinery than either of them. He is also very careful and neat in his work in the field or buildings; is much more independent than the Coolie, and not so easily led away by discontented persons; rarely making a frivolous complaint. . . . Possessing a keen sense of justice where his own rights are concerned, he is very capable of strong resentment at anything that appears to him unjust.

The Chinese, as far as we are aware, have never combined with the Indians in disturbances on estates; but, on the other hand, have occasionally taken the side of the employer in opposing them.

They have not the same objection to living with females of a different race from themselves that the Indians have. This may be owing in some degree to the small proportion of women who have emigrated from China, but the principal reason for it is that the Chinese have not the difficulty of *caste* to get over that the Indian has, and are more cosmopolitan in their habits.[12]

Many of the complaints centered on the immigrants' rebelliousness and tendency to run away (in Belize they even ran away and lived among the native Indians), propensity to evade work, engage in praedial larceny, or sponge off their fellow workers (whether of their own race or others). There were also complaints about excessive gambling and opium addiction: "Opium smoking is carried on by some to great excess, and it is not uncommon to see many of them quite emaciated, and almost unfit for work, from excessive use of this drug. It appears, unhappily, that opium smoking is not altogether confined to the Chinese; a few Indians have picked up this habit from them."[13] They often fought among themselves, on board the ships as well as on the plantations, if they came from different regions or ethnic groups, such as Fukienese and Cantonese, or Hakka and Punti. One voyage in 1853 to British Guiana threatened to break out into a mutiny, and the passengers were later described as "quite savage, many of them never having seen a European before coming to Amoy to go away, and having as little idea of right and wrong as the wandering savages of the wildernesses of America. They are fierce, cunning, ill-natured, revengeful, and hypocritical; and we have far more to do to keep anything like order among them than if they were so many monkeys."[14]

Preconceived planter prejudices abounded. One group who landed in Antigua in 1882 were described on the first day as "the most miserable looking batch of humans that could ever be seen." One week later the same planter-journalist wrote that "they are not such a miserable batch as we had mentioned, but the majority are fine looking strong men." However, he was still of the view that their introduction was a waste of money.[15]

While the planters and officials were passing judgments on their worth as laborers, many missionaries and independent critics of the indenture system commented on the exploitation of both the Chinese and the Indians. Chief Justice Beaumont, a severe critic of the indenture system, spoke out against the violence of the system, and gave several accounts of individual Chinese who suffered under it, including "The use of personal violence towards them on the part of their superiors." He continued:

No doubt, to some extent, the immigrants suffer in this way in common with the Negro and other Coloured labourers, and indeed as to mere acts of contumely they, perhaps, do not suffer to the same extent as these; but as to more serious and systematic outrages of this nature they are far more exposed to them, are practically far less protected against them, and in fact suffer far more from them. The most common forms which they take are forcible intrusions into and extrusions from their houses, imprisonment without warrant upon the estates or at the adjoining station-houses, and assaults by managers, overseers, drivers and other persons in authority. . . .

The details of the case [of Low-a-Si] are too shocking and harrowing to bear unnecessary repetition. . . . It appears by the [coroner's inquisition] proceedings that this poor Chinaman was, for no other reason than that he protested that he was too sick to work, brutally beaten and kicked to death by some of the staff of overseers and drivers of a "first-class estate," in the face of the whole staff of the estate's buildings, a multitude of hands at work there, including many of his own countrymen. This barbarous murder was effected by a series of assaults thus publicly committed, and which were continued during a space of more than an hour, the actors coming and going, and the poor wretch piteously wailing, bleeding, vomiting, and yet feebly attempting the work which he pleaded in vain with his dying breath that he was too sick to do. (1871, section 3, paragraphs 3–5)

The *Royal Gazette* in British Guiana was equally graphic with individual case studies of migrants under pressure.

Cho-a-King was flogged for stealing plantains at Canal No. 1. He pleaded guilty but was so severely beaten. On the Chinaman being examined he was found to be covered with bruises from neck to foot, and was so stiff from the punishment he had received, that he could hardly walk. Considering the severe beating the man had already received the Magistrate felt justified in discharging him. (March 2, 1866)

It has been reported that two nights ago a Chinaman who was stealing plantains at the Sisters' Estate near Plantation Wales was shot dead. Occurrences of this kind are rare nowadays compared to what they were a couple of years ago, and this we ascribe to the wholesome dread which most people entertain for the cat-o'-nine tails. (April 16, 1867)

Many immigrants complained of having been deceived by recruiters about the nature of the work they were expected to perform in the new environment. The *Royal Gazette* wrote: "We fear that, in the anxiety to procure a sufficient number of emigrants from China, the emissaries of our Agent have misled the people and that numbers of tradesmen and others have been induced to leave the country under the impression that they would be allowed to follow their own occupations, or else that the prospect of remuneration has been represented in colours far too flattering" (July 13, 1860).

One missionary in Trinidad told the gruesome tale of a Chinese tailor who had been tricked into indenturing himself with a promise that he could practice his profession in the new environment, and who was brutally forced to work on the sugar plantations after arrival, whereupon he shot himself in the head before his startled superiors. "The evening of the third day after work he put on his best clothes and in the presence of the people of the estate before they had the time to stop him he blew his brains out. This act made the one who told me about it say that the English government is essentially false. Its politics are crooked" (Massé 1988; journal entry for February 6, 1882).

Post-Indenture Adjustment

Many of the missionaries commented on the Chinese after the period of indenture was over, in the 1870s and 1880s. Sometimes the comments were about their peculiar cultural appearance or habits, sometimes about their swift acquisition of wealth, often about their assimilation into the society via Christianity or intermarriage. Commentaries about their vices such as gambling or opium usage continued.

The *Royal Gazette* carried descriptions of their celebration of the Chinese New Year in British Guiana in 1880:

> The Chinese inhabitants of the city have been celebrating their New Year last week, after the fashion of their countrymen at home. For a succession of nights they marched through the principal streets in procession, dressed in costume, bearing aloft immense bright coloured paper lanterns of various clever devices, but mostly fish-shaped, and beating gongs and tom-toms. They were followed by a large crowd of the unwashed, who we have no doubt would gladly have had some horseplay at the expense of the celestials, if a number of policemen, wisely furnished by the Brick dam authorities, had not accompanied the procession to maintain order. In the Charlestown district of the city, where the Chinese most do congregate, the New Year festivities were held with much feasting, fuddling and gambling, but though the people were very hilarious and very noisy there was no single instance of conduct requiring the interference of the police. (February 24, 1880)

In Trinidad in the 1890s, the Reverend Cothonay (1893) was saying:

If there is under the sun a clever and industrious people . . . who enrich themselves where others go bankrupt, that people are the Chinese. We have in Trinidad a good number of Chinese, and I assure you that their character, dress and customs contribute not a little to the stamp of originality of our population. All come here penniless, naturally, since these bands of emigrants are the rabble of Canton and other villages in the Chinese Empire. Today, some are extremely rich merchants, and the others at least comfortable in their roles as small shopkeepers or big traders. In the heart of the smallest village, if you find a shop, be sure it is owned by a Chinese. The creoles, and especially the blacks, are almost incapable of withstanding the competition. . . . There are no Chinese labourers here at all. Their preference is for trade. (1893, 143)

On race relations, commentaries appear to be contradictory, with some observers noting the levels of intermarriage with the locals, others noting the exact opposite, and still others noting the high level of unmarried bachelors among the Chinese immigrants. The Reverend Cothonay felt that Chinese and coolies intermingled willingly enough, creoles and coolies never. A good number of children were the offspring of Chinese and coolies; even after several generations one could recognise the descendants by their almond-shaped eyes (1893, 143). The Reverend Bronkhurst wrote:

between the Black creoles and Chinese there has existed a strong, bitter prejudicial feeling towards each other, and so far as I have been able to ascertain there is no likelihood of a Chinaman ever marrying a Black woman, or a Black man ever marrying a Chinese woman. A similar feeling exists among the East Indian coolies also towards the Black race. Of course I do not refer to the isolated cases of such marriages which have taken place in the Colony, nor do I refer to the illicit intercourse between the Chinese, East Indian immigrants, and Black women: but I speak of the immigrants as a whole. (1883, 124)

Still other observers wrote: "They freely marry creole women, and are careful in selecting those who are handsome" (Hart 1865, 100). "As Chinese women are scarce, the Chinaman has always a coloured woman as a concubine, and they generally manage to get the best looking girls in the place" (Kirke 1898, 160). The *Royal Gazette* in British Guiana commented on the "bachelor" nature of the Chinese immigrants: "In respect to immigration generally, the disproportion between the sexes is very great, particularly as regards the Chinese, and . . . neither Chinese nor Coolies, except in very rare instances, ever mate with the other races in the Colony. As a necessary consequence the surplus males die out without progeny" (January 26, 1864).

Chinese women, of whom we catch passing glimpses during the period of their arrival in the 1860s, were viewed in a sometimes flattering but often demeaning light. Individual vessels in Trinidad sometimes brought hardworking, loyal families, but some brought individuals who established unstable male-female relations that generated desertion or domestic violence. The *Royal Gazette* told the tale of many women who were involved in domestic disputes with their husbands, and subsequently committed or tried to commit suicide or murder in the process. Many had undergone the foot-binding process before embarkation to the West Indies: "little eyes, plump rosy lips, black hair, regular features, void however of beauty—their feet are unnaturally small, or rather truncated; they appear as if the fore-part of the foot had been accidentally cut off, leaving the remainder of the usual size, and bandaged like the stump of an amputated limb. Their dress is somewhat like that of the men" (Hart 1865, 100).

By the 1880s, however, the social mobility evident among the Chinese had transformed their womenfolk as well. The Reverend Kingsley, who visited Trinidad in the 1880s, noted with some curiosity the Westernized Chinese females among his congregation:

> [At] the end of the sermon—I became aware, just in front of me, of a row of smartest Paris bonnets, net-lace shawls, brocades and satins, fit for duchesses; and as the center of each blaze of finery . . . the unmistakable visage of a Chinese woman. Whether they understood one word; what they thought of it all; whether they were there for any purpose save to see and be seen, were questions to which I tried in vain, after service, to get an answer. All that could be told was, that the richer Chinese take delight in thus bedizening their wives on high days and holidays; not with tawdry cheap finery, but with things really expensive, and worth what they cost, especially the silks and brocades; and then in sending them, whether for fashion or for loyalty's sake, to an English church. (1871, 106)

Comments on the Chinese passion for gambling and opium smoking continued. A Catholic missionary stated in the 1880s:

> Every day in Trinidad there are Chinese who ruin themselves by gambling and others to the contrary who recover their wealth. I was asking one day of a small Chinese girl the state of her father, she replied: "Formerly my father had several shops. He gambled and he has lost them. Now he is still gambling, sometimes he wins, other times he loses. When he has lost everything, his friends lend him a few dollars and he reimburses them when he wins." There is the life not only of this Chinaman but of many. They are nearly all merchants. Selling their merchandise at exorbitant prices they get rich quickly. But as the proverb

says: "a good thing badly acquired profits the same." They ruin themselves as easily. The passion for gambling is so strong with them that even those who are communicants succumb sometimes to the temptation. (Abbe Masse, March 22, 1881)

The *Royal Gazette* commented in 1884 on "the dens of infamy in the Charlestown district carried on by the Chinese [which] are increasing in number and promise, before long to furnish material wherewith to mark a dark page in the colony's history. The poor, the starving, and the obscene are always amongst the visitors to these dens of iniquity—both women and men carry the few pence which they can either beg for, borrow, or steal, to be swallowed up by John Chinaman, and the visitors have to depart sadder, but by no means wiser, people" (November 15, 1884).

By the turn of the century, the upward mobility of the Chinese in West Indian society was very marked. The community of the 1910s and 1920s was by then a mixture of older, highly mobile Westernized traders and professionals, and the new immigrants, comprising small-scale and itinerant mercantile elements. One of the most interesting commentaries comes from the pen of a visiting Chinese journalist, who wrote for the *China Weekly Review* in 1929:

With each succeeding generation, the picture of the land of Confucius grew more blurred, and finally disappeared altogether. First, celestial manners gave way to local customs, then Chinese speech was dropped, and, in many instances, Westernised surnames were substituted for the high-sounding Chinese titles. Chinese by blood, they were as English as Britishers. They knew as much of China as Indians. They had never heard of Li Po. The great arts of the Sung dynasty was unknown to them. Chinese music grated on their ears. Chinese speech was anathema. They were Britishers under yellow skins.

Unlike their fellow countrymen in America who are mostly engaged in the chopsuey and laundry business, the Chinese in the West Indies are engaged in shopkeeping and planting. There are practically no Chinese labourers. Every Chinese aspires to own a shop or a plantation. The stigma that China is a nation of shopkeepers is almost true, if applied to the West Indies, for under the freedom of British rule, the retail trade, especially in the towns and villages of the West Indies, are predominantly a Chinese monopoly. Black, white, mulatto trade with their yellow brother without any trace of racial awareness.

The new generation of Chinese in the West Indies, however, is more ambitious than their forefathers. Brought up in Western schools, they seek freedom from their hemmed-in lives and aspire to callings superior to those of shopkeeping and planting. That this ambition has been largely realised today is found in the fact that the Chinese in the

West Indies have found a footing in the professions and higher commerce. . . .

When China made its attempt to cut itself off from the old monarchical form of government in 1910, a latent patriotism in the hearts of West Indian Chinese came to the surface. They were in sympathy with the movement, and contributed their financial bit to its support.

The period following the Chinese Revolution saw the birth of a number of Chinese clubs in the West Indies. Some were social; others political; and the majority a blend of the two. Speakers on China were popular, and an October Tenth anniversary was made the occasion of great celebration. . . .

While the belief is general that the overseas Chinese usually hoard their money to return to China, it is not true of those in the West Indies. Here the Chinese are contented. As British subjects, they have opportunities to embark in any adventure, enterprise, or project as any other citizen. What savings are made are usually invested in West Indian property. Then, too, the young Chinese are not acquainted with Chinese customs or language, and were they to return to China, they would be as foreign as Americans.[16]

Many people in the host society, however, continued to see the Chinese as an essentially alien and mysterious element. A white Creole writer in Trinidad in the 1920s described them as follows:

As an economic class in Trinidad they are the most powerful section of what can be called here the middle class. They range from clerks, grocers, merchants down to not too large scale financiers. They possess a free masonry of their own which is very powerful. In fact so powerful that with a few exceptions they do not bother to watch their interests in the political field. Like the class of which they form so representative a part they seem to be entirely devoid of public spirit and to be arrogantly individualistic.

As a race, physically they have remained comparatively Chinese, mixing to a very small extent with the other races of the island. But culturally they have lost almost all connection with the country of their origin. In no other part of the world has this happened so finally and so completely. In San Francisco, in New York and even in London the Chinese inhabitants have their native festivals and follow the ways of their people also. Here in Trinidad they ape the religion and manners of the white merchants whom they are emulating in the unscrupulous acquisition of commercial wealth. It is to be wondered if they are aware that those whom they imitate are backed by powerful home governments in their ventures and that while they might tolerate another

racial group playing second fiddle in their commercial games they
would certainly and seriously resent any threat to their commercial
superiority.

In art the loss of their traditional background shows painfully. They
who belong to the race that has the finest most delicate art values of
all mankind make pretty-pretty water colour sketches and horrible
concoctions of modern European painting that are not worthy of a
pupil of a correspondence art course. The houses they build are quite
the worst among the worst in the Western world. Their only artistic
contribution to Trinidad seems to have been in the exquisite features
and limbs of their women. (Boissiére 1945, 26)

The View from Below

Turning now to the view from below, we have to recognize several distinct
stages in the relationship between the Chinese and the majority black society.
First would be the relationship between the early indentured Chinese and their
fellow laborers (1850s–1870s), then the larger societal attitudes toward the Chinese as they steadily evolved from being a part of the rural proletariat to
belonging to the small and eventually large merchant class (1880s–1900s). Even
later, when these voices became more imbued with the sentiment of anticolonialism and nationalism after the First World War, a further question would be
to what extent perceptions of the Chinese were influenced by these larger
forces.

As far as the first period is concerned, the West Indies has produced nothing like the autobiography of the Cuban runaway slave Esteban Montejo, who
recorded some very acute observations on the Chinese coolies in Cuba during
the mid- and late nineteenth century. What views we have from the blacks we
derive from the colonial documents relating to incidents involving both groups,
and often three groups of people. These accounts tend to be scant in nature.
There are newspaper criticisms from the independent black press in 1850 con-
demning the whole idea of Chinese immigration, reminding the readers that
the 1806 experiment had been a signal failure, and that in Mauritius in the
1840s it had not proved successful either (Look Lai 1993, 167).

There are not many work-related commentaries from the black community
during the indenture period. Most of these came from the white officials. There
are several accounts of clashes between the Chinese immigrants and black
workers in British Guiana in the 1860s. In one early clash with black villagers
arising out of language and communication difficulties, six Chinese were sent
to jail, and the black villagers later promised the authorities that they would try
to live on good terms with the Chinese, whom they claimed to consider more
"respectable" than the Indian coolies.[17] There are accounts of rebellious Chi-

nese laborers killing black drivers or foremen in plantation-related disputes, as well as accounts of harsh treatment by the latter group toward immigrant laborers. There are also accounts of clashes between Chinese and Indian workers, as well as Chinese siding with one side or the other in Indian-black clashes (Sue-a-Quan 1999, chapter 6).

There are also many accounts of both groups participating in each others' recreational pastimes. Blacks are supposed to have learned gambling games from the Chinese, and even Indians are supposed to have picked up opium smoking from them, while Chinese often participated in the celebration of a few Indian religious processions: "This year the Coolies called in the aid of the Chinese to build their gaudy temples, and these ingenious fellows gave the Coolies better temples than they have ever had before. As on former occasions the black people followed the procession in thousands, and seemed to look on the [Tadja] festival as one designated as much for their spiritual benefit as for that of the Coolies."[18] Once the Chinese left the plantations in the 1870s and 1880s, however, and became small peasant gardeners and rural shopkeepers, new images began to appear. Altogether, there are three distinct phases in the society's evolution (and consequent attitudes to all other groups): the late nineteenth century, the nationalist emergence (early twentieth century), and the postcolonial period (post-1960s).

In all phases, one constant has been an element of amused and bemused tolerance of a foreign entity with distinctive physical and cultural traits. This was shared not only by the white elite but also by the larger society at all levels. Sometimes this judgment would be tinged with affection, often by malice, almost always with serious ignorance about who the Chinese were as a group. This aspect has remained to this day, and expresses itself in daily life at all levels, often by the educated as well as the uneducated. Ironically, it is often expressed by creolized Chinese themselves in a self-conscious, self-deprecating fashion.

The main preoccupation, however, has been with the economic emergence of the Chinese. There were those who praised their economic advancement as a model to emulate, and there were those who expressed concern that they were becoming a kind of economic threat. They are seen as vigorous competitors with black retailers in Jamaica, and with Portuguese and Indians in Trinidad and British Guiana.

A letter in the *San Fernando Gazette* as early as the 1880s declared: "The Chinese do not raise agricultural products, they are not laborers; but reap the benefits of others' labor, and become prosperous, while the poor people, proprietors and others are gradually getting ruined. The Chinese are to be compared to horse leeches, or to a parasite which settles on a plant not vigorous to throw it off, and which it saps of its strength. They resort to all manners of devices to cheat the people even in the buying, selling, weighing and gambling."[19] Emerging into

the ranks of the foreign middleman minority, a figure familiar to many Third
World societies, the Chinese found the response of the larger society to be
ambivalent. Influencing the societal perceptions was the extent to which the
Chinese were viewed as a group apart, or as a group with an inclusive attitude
toward black society. Evidence of racial intermarriage was usually seen as a
good sign. Even though in Trinidad and British Guiana there is evidence that no
more than 20 percent of the original indentureds entered into interracial liaisons,
most of them conforming in fact to the stereotype of the bachelor immigrant;
nevertheless the perception in the society was one of readiness by many to
intermarry into the larger society. At that level, then as well as later, a comparison was always being made with the more racially exclusivist Indian community (Look Lai 1993, chapter 7). The presence of a large Indian community, on
whom the blacks always vented most of their racial antipathies, tended to generate a more ambivalent attitude toward the Chinese in Trinidad and British
Guiana over time, despite the anxieties mentioned above. David Lowenthal has
mentioned that in this multicultural atmosphere, the Chinese often appeared
in the role of conciliators and arbiters between the two groups, rather than as
stark middlemen exploiters (1972, 207).

This situation did not exist in Jamaica, which experienced very little Indian
immigration; this fact probably helps to explain the widespread phobia that
developed toward the Chinese in the early twentieth century. During this
period there was a very noticeable increase in the Chinese voluntary migration
to Jamaica, an island that had not experienced a large Chinese indenture phase.
From 481 in 1891, the community leapt to 2,111 in 1911 and to 3,696 in 1921. A vigorous correspondence in the Jamaican press took place in 1912 and 1913 protest-
ing the "Chinese invasion." In 1918, a year of worker unrest generally in Jamaica
(and the rest of the West Indies), this hostility erupted into a major anti-Chinese
riot in the parish of St Catherine (Look Lai 1998a). A community meeting resolution best expressed Jamaican popular attitudes:

RESOLUTION PASSED BY THE PAROCHIAL BOARD OF ST. ANN AT ITS
MEETING ON THURSDAY 4TH OCTOBER 1917

Resolved

That in the opinion of this Board the time has come (in the absence of
Trade Unions etc. in this island) when it is the duty of this government
to protect the native shopkeepers as well as the community against
the overincreasing number of Chinese shopkeepers throughout the
island for the following reasons:

(1) They are not desired in any enlightened and progressive country.

(2) Their custom and manner of living along with the skilful manipu-
lation of their goods make it impossible for the natives to compete.

(3) Directly or indirectly they are the cause of many bankruptcies, vagrants, paupers; and a very large percentage of our best citizens who have left the island for foreign parts have lost their business or jobs on this account.

(4) Present war conditions demand that something be done to protect the fathers, mothers and relatives of the men who have gone to fight, while the Chinese are left to become rich and enjoy all safety and privileges; not even a special tax levied on these aliens to compensate the men fighting for them.

That the other Parochial Boards of the island be asked to cooperate with a view of putting the matter strongly before the government.[20]

Similar cries over the new immigration came from British Guiana. The *Daily Chronicle* editorialized in 1923:

today we would direct the attention of our readers to . . . the steady influx of Chinese immigrants to the colony for some while past. Perhaps, at the outset we should say we have no fundamental objection to Chinese colonists. Those already with us have made exemplary citizens. They are the most law abiding section of the community, without exception; frugal and painstaking in all their undertakings, they provide a worthy example to other colonists; while they have identified themselves with every form of colonial endeavour. But, nevertheless, we suspect that this section of the community, no less than any other, is as anxious as ourselves in their desire to ward off the evil we would today indicate.

Steamer after steamer arriving in the colony brings its quota of Chinese immigrants, small in number it is true, but they come just the same, and were we assured that all these immigrants were of a desirable class we would have nothing to say about the matter; but are they? Jamaica has had rather bitter experiences lately, and it behoves this colony to take steps before it finds itself in that into which Jamaica was plunged. Communities, no less than persons, must benefit from the lessons of their neighbours. In Jamaica the stream commenced in quite the same way as we now see it in British Guiana. First there was a trickle, then it grew to a brook, and persons raised their eyebrows in gentle protests; whereupon a benign government stepped in, and introduced an ordinance drafted, we believe, by no less a person than the Hon. Hector Josephs.

At this sign of government appreciation of the danger ahead, public apprehensions were allayed. Unfortunately, however, the ordinance became a dead letter, gradually the brook became a wider stream, and eventually developed into a flood. When the good people of Jamaica awoke in the tossing deep they realised that their armour and defences, duly provided, had been sadly neglected, and the island was in the grip of an economic situation brought about by the large influx of a most undesirable type of immigrant. Immigrants who were neither agriculturists nor colonists in any sense, but just parasites: gamblers, thieves and cutthroats were everywhere. Some embarked upon trade to the great sorrow of those who gave them credit; others just gambled, and devoted their wits to the exploitation of the unwary, while the growing effect upon the morale of the community was being gradually undermined in another direction altogether, since these men, of an extraordinarily low type themselves, consorted with such women as they could find, possibly equally depraved as their husbands, and produced a type of half caste which is even a greater menace than their fathers.

These are dangers we would warn the community against today. The colony needs agriculturists, not petty traders and laundrymen. However, we do not think it is particularly the province of the government to keep out traders and laundrymen, provided that in admitting men of that type we do not admit undesirables of the class we have indicated! Already the city is flooded with Chinese laundries, and the homely old washerwoman is being gradually driven out of business. . . .

[It] would possibly be an advantage if the local government would explore the policy pursued by the United States of America in its latest immigration policy, that only a given percentage of the population of any one race already resident may be admitted as residents in any one year; always, of course, in so far as this colony is concerned, excluding immigrants brought in as agriculturists under any well thought out and approved scheme with due protection for those already in our midst, even of that class.[21]

In 1924, the Jamaica Chinese Benevolent Society reported to the Chinese ambassador in London of the murders of six immigrants by Jamaicans, and the atmosphere of fear and violence in which they lived (Look Lai 1993, 342 n. 56). Anti-Chinese riots occurred again in Jamaica in 1938, again a year of general labor unrest throughout the British West Indies, and twice after Independence: in 1965, and during the 1970s. These occurrences of anti-Chinese activism by the larger populace in Jamaica can be compared to similar outbreaks against the Chinese in Mexico in the 1920s and 1930s, although the end result was not official support for mass expulsion, as happened in Mexico.

Nationalist anticolonial sentiment during the early and mid-twentieth century definitely influenced perceptions of the Chinese, whenever social observers bothered to comment on their presence (which, it has to be stressed, they did not always). There were those who were baffled by Chinese "inscrutability," unsure of where they stood and whose side they were on in the developing anticolonial struggle against the British dispensation. There were those whose positions were influenced by nationalist idealism about the multiracial and multicultural potentialities of West Indian society, and who yearned to see a new kind of society emerge in the region that would be an example to the rest of the world. There were those of more leftist persuasion, from Marcus Garvey in the 1920s to Walter Rodney in the 1960s, who sought to locate the Chinese in West Indian society in ideological-universalistic terms, seeing them essentially as a conservative and antinationalistic petite bourgeoisie.

The new West Indian novelists, whenever they did mention the Chinese at all, either saw them as valuable additions to the multicultural mosaic of the Caribbean, like George Lamming in *Of Age and Innocence* or Wilson Harris in *The Whole Armour*, or saw them as part of a complex and problematic multiculturalism with more problems than solutions, like Edgar Mittelholtzer's *Morning at the Office*. Lamming's *Of Age and Innocence* is a fictional account of a nationalist leader and movement in a fictional Caribbean island, San Cristobal. In a visionary outburst, his main character declares: "Here Africa and India shake hands with China, and Europe wrinkles like a brow begging every face to promise love. The past is all suspicion, now is an argument that will not end, and tomorrow . . . is like the air in your hand. I know San Cristobal. It is mine, me, divided in a harmony that still pursues all its separate parts. No new country, but an old old land inhabiting new forms of men who can never resurrect their roots and do not know their nature" (1958, 58).

More often than not, the Chinese are presented as peripheral figures in stereotypical roles, as inscrutable or clever or linguistically deficient rural shopkeepers, preoccupied with money and profit. Such characters appear in the novels of Samuel Selvon, Michael Anthony, V. S. Naipaul, and even in the short stories of the Chinese Trinidadian Willie Chen.[22]

Even Calypsonians in Trinidad often voiced similar ambivalent sentiments about the Chinese in an age of anticolonialism.

> Smiley, a calypsonian who often sings on racial themes (What is wrong with the Negro man; The Chinese) identified the Chinese negatively as a small exploitative commercial group.
> "Them Chinese don't lend, they don't give, they don't spend. . . . According to Mr Guy, they sucking the country dry" (Rohlehr 1990, 510)

Leftist activist Walter Rodney also picked up the refrain in Jamaica, giving it a special ideological twist.

The Chinese are a former labouring group who have now become bastions of white West Indian social structure. The Chinese of the PRC
have long broken with and are fighting against white imperialism, but
our Chinese have nothing to do with that movement. They are to be
identified with Chiang-Kai- Shek and not Mao-Tse-Tung. They are to
be put in the same bracket as the lackeys of capitalism and imperialism who are to be found in Hong Kong and Taiwan. Whatever the circumstances in which the Chinese came to the West Indies, they soon
became (as a group) members of the exploiting class. They will have
either to relinquish or be deprived of that function before they can be
re-integrated into a West Indian society where the black man walks in
dignity. (Rodney 1970, 28–29)

He is careful to make the same criticism of the mulatto class: "The same applies
to the mulattoes . . . characterised by ambiguity and ambivalence . . . the vast
majority have fallen to the bribes of white imperialism, often outdoing the
whites in their hatred and oppression of blacks. Garvey wrote of the Jamaican
mulattoes: 'I was openly hated and persecuted by some of these coloured men
of the island who did not want to be classified as Negroes but as white'" (Rodney 1970, 29).

One of the consequences of the society's ambivalence toward the Chinese
middlemen in an age of anticolonialism has been the sporadic outburst of ani-
mosity toward them (and other middlemen minorities) during the intense stages
of the anticolonial struggle (Jamaica in the 1960s and 1970s, Trinidad and Guyana—
formerly British Guiana—in the 1970s), and the nervous migration of a sizeable
segment of this community away from the region to metropolitan destinations
such as Canada, the United States, or Europe in the last thirty years (Look Lai
1998b, 252–253). This despite the fact that in all of the regional nationalist movements, there were often several Chinese figures who were themselves prominent and influential supporters of the new nationalism.

Ironically, the age of globalization (post-1980s) has witnessed a new and
renewed interest in the Chinese community by the mature postcolonial nationalist leadership. This is a situation which is still evolving, and it lacks clear direction. But the signs are that after many decades in which the community was
seen as a fringe minority incidental (or hostile) to nationalist aspirations, a new
appreciation of its potential to assist in the development efforts of the society
is being forged. The impetus for these changed and changing perceptions comes
primarily from external factors, principally the changed parameters of the new
global economic order: first, the post-Cold War shift in global geopolitics and
ideologies, and second, the global ascendancy of Asia (especially China), which
has had a beneficial impact on Caribbean public attitudes toward the Asian

minorities in their midst. Increasingly, local-born Chinese professionals are finding themselves thrust into positions of major decision making in the region, in keeping with their acquisition of professional skills and (perceived) international outreach capabilities. This signals a new departure in societal attitudes, a transition from relative marginality and peripheral status to one of growing centrality and significance to the nation-building effort. It may be a regional microversion of the kind of evolution that has already taken place in other societies, or it may prove to be just a current ethnic fad in transition. Whatever it ultimately proves itself to be, it is clear that the century-long passage from foreign sugar worker to peripheral minority petite bourgeoisie to prized multicultural citizen represents a new stage of self-identification in the transition from sojourner to settler in these young and still growing societies of the Caribbean region.

NOTES

1. The rise of West Indian creative literature, for example, was a direct product of this era of nationalist sentiment, reflective of the voice of the new nationalism, rather than the voice of the established colonial elite.

2. Colonial Office Correspondence, C.O.295, Vol. 2, July 16, 1802, excerpts from Captain William Layman's "Hints for the Cultivation of Trinidad."

3. Colonial Office Correspondence, C.O.295, Vol. 17, February 18, 1803, Secret Memorandum from the Colonial Office to the Chairman of the Court of Directors of the East Indian Company.

4. Ibid.

5. British Parliamentary Papers (hereafter P.P.) 1852–53, LXVIII (986), Dispatches respecting Chinese immigrants introduced into British Guiana and Trinidad, 80; White to Barkly, July 19, 1851.

6. P.P.1852–53, LXVIII (986): Duke of Newcastle to Lt Governor Walker, June 29, 1853, Enclosure to Dispatch No. 16, Sub-Enclosure No. 1.

7. Twentieth General Report of the Colonial Land and Emigration Commissioners, Appendix No.45. P.P., Emigration Series (Irish University Press), Vol. 14.

8. P.P. 1852–3, LXVIII (986), Dispatches respecting Chinese immigrants introduced into British Guiana and Trinidad, p. 73: White to Barkly, June 21, 1851.

9. P.P. 1854–5, XXXIX (O.7) Dispatches respecting Chinese immigrants introduced into British Guiana and Trinidad, p. 7: Winchester to Bow-ring, July 22, 1854.

10. P.P.1852–53, LXVIII (986): Acting Governor Walker to Duke of Newcastle, Dispatch No. 16, July 8, 1853, Enclosure No. 3.

11. Nineteenth General Report of the Colonial Land and Emigration Commissioners (1859), Appendix No. 42: P.P., Emigration Series (Irish University Press), vol. 14.

12. P.P., 1871, XX (C.393): Report of the Commissioners appointed to enquire into the treatment of immigrants in British Guiana.

13. Ibid.

14. P.P. 1852–53, LXVIII (986): Governor Barkly to Duke of Newcastle, Dispatch No. 11, March 12, 1853, Enclosure No. 2.

15. *Antigua Times*, February 1 and 8, 1882.

16. Arthur Young, *China Weekly Review*, May 11, 1929.

17. Thirteenth General Report of the Colonial Land and Emigration Commissioners (1853), Appendix No. 50: Great Britain, Parliamentary Papers, Emigration Series (Irish University Press), vol. 12.

18. *Royal Gazette*, March 11, 1873.

19. *San Fernando Gazette*, October, 12 1889. See also Look Lai (1993), 207.

20. British Foreign Office , F.O. 228/3466. Overseas Chinese, 1917–1927. No. 6A. Chinese in Jamaica. US Consuls to take charge of interests of: L. Probyn to Rt Honourable Walter H. Long, M.P., Secretary of State for the Colonies, September 30, 1918, enclosure.

21. *The Daily Chronicle*, Sunday April 1, 1923, editorial.

22. See, for example, the short stories by Samuel Selvon, "The calypsonian," "Holiday in five rivers," "Down the main" (Salkey 1960; Selvon 1957); by Michael Anthony, "Many things," "Drunkard of the river," "Village shop" (all in Anthony 1973); by Willi Chen in *King of the carnival and other stories* (1988); and Naipaul's *House for Mr. Biswas* (1961) and *Miguel Street* (1959). The conservative V. S. Naipaul went furthest in his novel *Guerillas* (1975), essentially a commentary on the mass movements of the 1960s and 1970s. Here his main character was portrayed as a person of mixed Chinese blood, a frightening pathological product of the radical movement. This portrayal is unusual, since political commentaries usually tended to see the Chinese as conservative rather than as radicals.

REFERENCES

Anthony, Michael. 1973. *Cricket in the road.* London: Andre Deutsch.

Beaumont, Joseph. 1871. *The new slavery: An account of the Indian and Chinese immigrants in British Guiana.* London: W. Ridgway.

Boissiére, Jean de. 1945. *Trinidad: Land of the rising inflexion.* Trinidad: n.p.

Bronkhurst, Rev. H.V.P. 1883. *The colony of British Guyana and its labouring population.* London: T. Woolmer.

Chen, Willi. 1988. *King of the carnival and other stories.* London: Harisib.

Cothonay, Marie Bertrand. 1893. Trinidad: Journal d'un missionaire dominicain des Antilles anglaises. Paris: V. Retaux et fils.

Hart, Daniel. 1865. *Historical and statistical view of the island of Trinidad with chronological table of events from 1782.* London: Judd and Glass.

Kingsley, Charles. 1871. *At Last: A Christmas in the West Indies.* London: Macmillan.

Kirke, Henry. 1898. *Twenty-five years in British Guiana, 1872–1897.* London: S. Low, Marston.

Lamming, George. 1958. *Of age and innocence.* London: M. Joseph.

Look Lai, Walton. 1993. *Indentured labor, Caribbean sugar: Chinese and Indian migrants to the British West Indies, 1838–1918.* Baltimore: Johns Hopkins University Press.

———. 1998a. *The Chinese in the West Indies, 1806–1995.* Kingston, Jamaica: University of the West Indies Press.

———. 1998b. "The Chinese in the Caribbean." In *The encyclopedia of the Chinese overseas*, edited by L. Pann. Singapore: Archipelago Press.

Lowenthal, David. 1972. *West Indian Societies.* London: Oxford University Press.

Massé, Abbé Armand. 1988. *The diaries of Abbé Armand Massé, 1878–1883.* Translated by M. L. de Verteuil. Port of Spain, Trinidad: n.p.

Naipaul, V. S. 1959. *Miguel Street.* New York: Vanguard.

———. 1961. *House for Mr. Biswas.* New York: Knopf.

———. 1975. *Guerillas.* New York: Vintage Books.

Rodney, Walter. 1970. *The groundings with my brothers.* London: Bogle-L'Ouverture Publications.

Rohlehr, Gordon. 1990. *Calypso and society in pre-independence Trinidad.* Port of Spain, Trinidad: G. Rohlehr.

Salkey, Andrew, ed. 1960. *West Indian stories.* London: Faber and Faber.

Selvon, Samuel. 1957. *Ways of sunlight.* London: MacGiven and Kee.

Sue-a-Quan, Trev. 1999. *Cane reapers: Chinese indentured immigrants in Guyana.* Vancouver: Riftswood.

5

==

On Coolies and Shopkeepers

The Chinese as *Huagong* (Laborers) and *Huashang* (Merchants) in Latin America/Caribbean

EVELYN Hu-DeHART

For almost twenty-five years I have been studying the history of migration and settlement of the Chinese in a part of the world not commonly associated with Chinese diaspora studies, or, as the study of Chinese migration and resettlement is known outside the United States. Overseas Chinese Studies (*huaqiao shi*). Although the Chinese in the United States and even in Canada have constituted a central focus of the field, the rest of the Americas—that is, Latin America and the Caribbean—have been largely ignored until very recently. Similarly, for the most part, the field of Latin American/Caribbean Studies has also historically slighted the study of Chinese immigrants and communities; this is true even for those who focus on social history, immigration history, the study of "foreigners" (*extranjeros*), and it is true for U.S.-based and Latin America/Caribbean-based scholars.[1] Until recently, the same kind of inattention was true of studies of the Japanese in this region, as well as of another significant immigrant group from Asia, the East Indians or South Asians. Two of the leading scholars who have taken monumental steps to remedy this situation are included in this volume: Walton Look Lai of Trinidad and Jeffrey Lesser of the United States.

The election of Alberto Fujimori to the presidency of Peru fifteen years ago has made it no longer feasible to deny the existence of Asians in Latin America and the Caribbean. Now, if we care to look, we will find that the largest community of Japanese-descended people outside Japan reside in Brazil, not Los Angeles; that besides Fujimori, other descendents of Asian immigrants have assumed presidencies in the region, such as Cheddi Jagan of Guyana. (If we include descendants of Middle Eastern immigrants—variously known as Arabs, Turks, Lebanese, Syrians, Palestinians—who are historically included among "Asians" in Latin America, the list grows long, and would include former Prime

Minister Edward Seaga of Jamaica, President Saul Menem of Argentina, and the recently deposed President Mahoud of Ecuador. Lebanese-Mexican industrialist/financier Carlos Slim Helú is widely acknowledged as Mexico's wealthiest citizen today.)

The belated attention paid to Asians in Latin America and the Caribbean is surprising for another reason: when examining censuses of many countries in the region from the late nineteenth century through the entire span of the twentieth century, distinctive Asian ethnic/nationality groups are often noted. A good example is Mexico, whose eleven national censuses taken state by state between 1895 and 1990 delineate and differentiate among Chinese, Japanese, Indian (or Hindustani), Korean, Filipino, even Laotian/Cambodian/Vietnamese (noted as early as 1920 and 1930), as well as Lebanese and Syrian, Palestinian, Turk, Iranian, and "other Asians."[2]

Another source of impetus for the study of Asians in the Americas is Asian American Studies, a branch of ethnic studies, that is, the study of racial formation and race relations. Not long after its inception, some people in Black Studies (now African American Studies) began to break away from a cultural nationalistic approach to embrace the concept of the *black diaspora,* thus following the pattern established by the Atlantic slave trade that distributed African slaves throughout the Western Hemisphere. In other words, the shared history of slavery compelled scholars to adopt (borrowing from the Jewish diaspora) a new paradigm that was transnational and comparative, decentered from Africa yet connected through blackness or race.

When I first encountered Asian American studies in the mid-1970s and tested its receptivity to the study of Asians in Latin America and the Caribbean, I found the field still largely U.S.-centric (just as Overseas Chinese Studies remains Chinacentric). When early on I began to use the concept and term of "diaspora" to force open interest of the Chinese in the Americas to include Latin America and the Caribbean, I found little resonance among Asian Americanists at the time, but no overt resistance, either. The term was simply not used at the time in Asian American Studies, having not yet entered the consciousness of those working in the field, who still preferred the immigration model to examine successive waves of Chinese migration from one location (the homeland, primarily south China), to the United States (primarily California and the American West, and Hawaii). The idea of "diaspora" resonated even less—hardly at all, in fact—with Asia-based overseas Chinese scholars, for there is no word in Chinese to capture the term or its essence. (Ling-chi Wang's translation of "diaspora" as *luo-di-shen-gen*—"putting down roots where landed"—is better than "overseas Chinese," but does not do the job.)

Suddenly and rapidly, it seems, within the past ten years the idea of "diaspora" has taken off. Now, every nationality and ethnic group some of whose members have left home and relocated in more than one place has a diaspora, even as many of us still stumble over its proper pronunciation (is it di-aspora with a long *i* or a short *i*, or diaspo-ra, with emphasis on the *o*?) A few years ago, I encountered in the *New York Times Magazine* (March 12, 2000) a reference to a "vast Tibetan diaspora." The excellent journal *Diaspora*, in its tenth year of publication, has now identified at least fifty diasporas throughout history and around the globe, not having met a diaspora it does not want to acknowledge. The proliferation of diasporas has made it difficult to theorize diaspora. It is not the primary purpose of this paper to theorize diaspora, but those of us who use it need to provide at least a rationale for its deployment.

For me, working with the model of diaspora allows me to overcome the limitations posed by Overseas Chinese Studies, on the one hand, and cultural nationalistic Asian American Studies, on the other, in that diaspora decenters China in Overseas Chinese Studies and decenters U.S.-Asians in Asian American Studies. Consequently, "China" is enlarged to be wherever Chinese people and their descendants are to be found, and "America" is not confined to just the United States. Multiplicities of Chineseness interact with multiplicities of Americanness, producing new and unique kinds of *mestizaje* or hybridity. Moreover, by taking a hemispheric and global approach to the study of Chinese outside China, analysis of the Chinese diaspora is by definition and necessity comparative, thereby bringing to light many otherwise hidden facets of their experiences.

In the case of the Americas, although a few diasporic Chinese returned to the homeland, the vast majority did not, and others remigrated to other points in the hemisphere. For example, among the first Chinese in New York City were remigrants from Havana, following a well-established and well-traveled path across the Caribbean waters from Havana to New York. Chinese coolies on Cuban plantations were sent to Mississippi plantations to fill an acute labor shortage in the 1860s (see Cohen 1984). Despite the Chinese Exclusion Act, Chinese on both sides of the U.S.-Mexican border interacted freely and frequently, while big Chinese merchant houses in San Francisco and Los Angeles opened and stocked branch stores in Mexico, Cuba, and Peru. Chinese labor contractors in California introduced Chinese workers to open up vast tracts of virgin land in Baja California for large-scale cotton cultivation in the Mexicali Valley.

Chinese *huaqiao* (immigrants) in the diaspora shared common experiences, whether as *huagong*, workers, or as *huashang*, merchants. Throughout the Americas, they entered already multiracial societies that were nevertheless dominated by European ethnicities and a white power structure. The exact nature of their work and social relationships in the workplace, and the exact nature of their businesses and business opportunities varied across time and space.

Sharp contrasts in economic development and degree of globalization affected Chinese integration into society and their social relationships with others. By the time Chinese were recruited to work in the U.S. West in the mid-nineteenth century, the United States had become a powerful, autonomous, and expansionist capitalist society practically free of political and economic domination by England, its former colonial master. Their need for cheap wage labor prompted railroad and agricultural entrepreneurs in the American West to recruit mostly male Chinese workers, while the country simultaneously beckoned unprecedented numbers of diverse European immigrants who came with families to homestead the expanding frontier carved out of territorial incorporation of Indian and Mexican land. European immigrants, constructed as "white," were promised land, freedom, and citizenship, but the Chinese were denied these same rights, while being forced to join already racialized blacks, Indians, and Mexicans as inferior, nonwhite minority groups. Although undoubtedly miscegenation occurred in this multiracial environment, U.S. laws strictly prohibited interracial marriages in order to keep the races apart and pure, the better to maintain racial hierarchies and privileges. (Enacted by the states, the last of these antimiscegenation laws were not abolished until the late l960s.)

By contrast, the Chinese experience in Latin America and the (Spanish) Caribbean has to be framed within the context of first Spanish colonialism, followed by U.S. imperialism or neocolonialism in the hemisphere. Unlike all European colonies in Asia and British and French colonies in the Caribbean, Spain's American colonies became settler societies built by massive numbers of European immigrants as colonists with access to land. Europeans mixed with native populations to produce hybrid peoples and cultures. Thus, Chinese were brought into colonial Cuba as contract laborers in the mid-nineteenth century to work alongside black slaves on white-owned and -operated sugar plantations. There they occupied an in-between space between black and white, slave and free. Similarly, Chinese men from the same region of south China and during the same period of time were also recruited to work on coastal Peruvian plantations shortly after its independence from Spain. With black slavery abolished, coastal plantations revived by foreign capital introduced Chinese contract laborers as the sole labor force until they were replaced by indigenous Peruvian workers from the highland. This chapter will, first, examine the Chinese contract laborer on nineteenth-century Cuban and Peruvian plantations as the earliest system of *huagong* in the Americas, predating Chinese labor in the American West, which took on a different form.

When Chinese were induced to migrate to Mexico beginning in the late nineteenth century, they concentrated along the long northern border with the United States, which was receiving a massive infusion of U.S. capital investment in mines, railroads, and commercial agriculture; this migration coincided with the enactment of Chinese exclusion in the United States. In this situation, the Chinese were desired not so much to provide cheap labor—there were plenty of Mexicans for that—as to build a commercial infrastructure to provide commodities and services for a local population that was making a partial transition from a peasant (subsistence) economy to a dependent capitalist economy of wage labor and export markets. In their proliferation as shopkeepers, street hawkers, food vendors, itinerant traders or peddlers; fruit and vegetable (truck) farmers or market gardeners; tailors and cobblers; owners of boardinghouses, canteens and restaurants, and hand laundries; and as small manufacturers, they dominated small retail trade in the local economy, becoming in effect the regional petite bourgeoisie. This chapter will also examine in detail the formation of the Chinese as the local petite bourgeoisie in a northern Mexican border state within a neocolonial context controlled by U.S. investment and markets. Both time and place-specific studies were conducted and apprehended against a comparative background presented by the Chinese diaspora.

Huagong: Contract Laborers in Cuba and Peru

When Chinese workers, largely male, were introduced to California and the American West in the mid-nineteenth century to work in mines, railroad construction, and agriculture, slavery as a form of labor in the American south was being seriously challenged and on its way out. It was thus neither politically nor economically feasible to extend slavery to the newly acquired Western states, despite their enormous demand for cheap labor. Chinese labor came to the rescue, until European immigrants led by the Irish pushed them out of jobs, and their immigration was eventually banned outright. When Hawaii was annexed to the United States and plantations flourished there, Asian labor—Chinese, Japanese, and others—again came to the rescue. Nowhere on U.S. territory, wherever Chinese and other Asian labor was introduced, however, was it seriously suggested that they constituted a new form of slavery or an extension of slavery, regardless of the actual conditions of their work.

Those were precisely the questions asked, however, when Chinese contract workers, or coolies, were introduced to Cuban and Peruvian plantations in the mid-nineteenth century. Between 1847 and 1874, some 225,000 Chinese male workers embarked for Latin America: 91,412 arrived in Peru, and 124,813 in Cuba (Table 5.1). They came with bilingual Spanish-Chinese eight-year contracts. In the case of Cuba, still a Spanish colony, they worked alongside African slaves whose numbers they replenished in the waning days of the Atlantic slave trade; in the case of Peru, which abolished slavery shortly after it became independent in 1821, they became the sole labor force. The questions immediately asked at the time by observers in Cuba and Peru, as later by scholars, were: Did Chinese contract laborers constitute an extension or prolongation of slavery in Cuba, and did it constitute a new form, a revival or recreation of slavery in Peru? Obviously, Chinese proximity to slavery—spatially in Cuba and temporally in

TABLE 5.1

Coolie Imports to Cuba and Peru (1847–1874) Correlated with Slave Imports (Cuba Only) and Sugar Production

	Peru		Cuba		
Year	Coolies	Sugar (metric tons)	Slaves	Coolies	Sugar (metric tons)
	(1)	(2)	(3)	(4)	(5)
1847					
1848	4,754			571	
1853			12,500	4,307	391,247
1854			11,400	1,711	397,713
1855	2,355		6,408	2,985	462,968
1856	4,220		7,304	4,968	416,141
1857	405		10,436	8,547	436,030
1858	300		19,992	13,385	426,274
1859	321		30,473	7,204	469,263
1860	1,092	618	24,895	6,193	428,769
1861	2,116	885	23,964	6,973	533,800
1862	1,691	1,257	11,254	344	454,758
1863	1,620	1,615	7,507	952	445,693
1864	6,562	2,864	6,807	2,153	525,372
1865	5,943	1,463	145	6,400	547,364
1866	6,725	5,111	1,443	12,391	535,641
1867	3,360	3,431		14,263	585,814
1868	4,307	9,352		7,368	720,250
1869	2,861	12,479		5,660	718,745
1870	7,544	13,175		1,227	702,974
1871	11,812	13,141		1,448	609,660
1872	13,026	14,022		8,160	772,068
1873	6,571	21,696		5,093	742,843
1874	3,827	31,940		2,490	768,672
1875		56,102			750,062
1876					626,082
1877					516,268
Total	91,412			124,813	

Sources: Cols. 1 and 2: Rodríguez Pastor (1988, 27, 296); Col. 3: Rebecca Scott (1985); Col. 4: Scott (1985, 10); Col. 5: Pérez de la Riva (1966).

Peru—made these questions inevitable and necessary. Elsewhere I explored these questions in depth and concluded that Chinese coolies were not slaves, although they did suffer slavelike conditions at work (Hu-DeHart 1992). This was in large part because the Europeans who recruited them in China and transported them across the Pacific, and those who bought up their contracts on the other end and consigned them to hard labor on their plantations, treated them as they did slaves, a system with which they were thoroughly familiar. Relatively short-lived at only twenty-five years, the Chinese contract labor system did constitute a transitional form of labor from slave to free (wage) labor.

One thing was certain in both cases: Chinese workers were indispensable to the viability and vitality of the plantation sugar economies, no less in Cuba where their labor enabled sugar production to continue its upward curve when the last shipment of slaves in 1866 ended that source of workers. Concurrent with the cessation of the African slave trade, the largest shipments of Chinese coolies arrived in 1866 (12,391) and 1867 (14,263); over 50 percent of the total number to Cuba arrived after 1865 (64,500) (see Table 5.1).

The use of indentured labor, based on formal contracts, seemed to have been a common practice throughout the Chinese diaspora in the nineteenth century, wherever European plantations thrived. It is known generally as the coolie system in Asia and in the Americas; the Dutch used it on their Southeast Asian plantations, the British employed both Chinese and East Indian coolies on their West Indian (Caribbean) estates after slavery; and of course, the Spaniards in Cuba and the newly independent Peruvians also adopted this system of labor. (Despite widespread use of the term "coolie" to refer to Chinese laborers, no formal indentured labor system involving Chinese existed in the United States.) My own work has examined Chinese indentured labor on the Cuban and Peruvian plantations of the mid to late nineteenth century (Hu-DeHart 1992).

The contracts were issued in both Chinese and Spanish and in duplicate, one to the coolie to be kept on his person for the duration of his bondage, the other to the contracting agency, which transferred it to the master when he purchased the contract. Printed in clear type in both versions, usually on a fine blue paper, it included the name of the onsite agent as well as the contracting agency in Havana or Lima, sometimes the name of the coolie ship, and was signed by the Spanish consul in China and the local authorities (local Portuguese authorities when the trade was transferred from the uneasy Chinese government in south China to the more amenable Portuguese colonial regime in Macao).

In the Spanish-language contracts, Cubans and Peruvians rarely referred to the Chinese as coolies or workers, but rather euphemistically as *colonos asiáticos*. On the other hand, and in an apparent inconsistency, those who bought their contracts were referred to as *patrón* or *patrono,* and in Peru, sometimes as *amo,* which is a paternalistic term for "master." The contracts had the heading *Libre Emigración China para la Isla de Cuba* (or *para el Perú*)—Free Chinese Immigration to Cuba (or Peru)—which explains the references in the document to *colono* and not worker. In the Chinese-language version, the entirely different heading refers to a "Labor Employment Contract" (*Gu-kong-he-tong*), making no allusion to immigration or colonization, but only to work. Consistent with this construction, those who contracted with the Chinese were known as "employers." Since the Chinese-language contract was supposedly read by local authorities to the recruited workers, presumably the Chinese knew they were going somewhere to work and not to settle permanently. In fact, to ensure this understanding, very few women were sent to Cuba or Peru.

Throughout the years of the trade, some of the basic terms of the contract remained constant: the eight years of servitude almost never varied, nor wages of one peso a week, or four a month. In addition to salary, coolies were paid in food and clothing, usually some specific amount of rice, meat or fish, yams or vegetables, as well as two changes of clothing, one jacket, and one blanket a year. Housing was also provided. The contract specified three days off during New Year, and usually Sundays as well, although this was rarely honored even when stipulated. Furthermore, the contract provided for medical attention, although it also stipulated under what condition the *patrono* could withhold pay until recovery. In other words, no work, no pay. In practice, it meant that missed days of work, even when the worker was legitimately ill, were tacked onto the original eight-year term, thus lengthening the service term. The coolie was also advanced eight to fourteen pesos at time of departure for passage and a new change of clothes, which constituted a debt to the *patrono* to be repaid by deductions from his salary at the rate of one peso a month.

In Cuba, the initial contracts were reinforced by the first coolie regulations issued on April 10, 1849, entitled "Government Regulations for the Handling and Treatment of Asian and Indian Colonists" (Pérez de la Riva 1978, 117). In issuing these rules, Governor-General Conde de Alcoy bluntly stated the need for rules that assured coolie "subordination and discipline" as well as rules to "protect their rights." Whereas nowhere in the contract was corporal or other forms of punishment specified, the 1849 regulations clearly spelled out the conditions—insubordination and running away—under which corporal and other severe punishment could be meted out, including floggings (*cuerazos*), leg chains or shackles (*grillete*), and confinement in stocks (*cepo*). These familiar-sounding punishments were borrowed wholesale from long-standing practices in slavery.

The regulations also contained two articles that implied a differentiation between Chinese coolies and black slaves. One stipulated that whenever there were ten coolies on any one estate, the planter must assign a white overseer to supervise and care for them, and help them with their work. Another stipulated that only the white overseer could mete out corporal punishment to coolies, and never in the presence of slaves. A new set of regulations was issued in 1854, along with slight modifications to the contract itself. Corporal punishment of coolies was abolished, although there is no shortage of evidence to demonstrate that such punishments continued.

The new contract contains a clear statement stipulating that, upon completion of the eight-year term, "I will be free to work as I wish without being forced to extend this contract, not even under the pretext of debt, obligations, or promises that I might have made." The new regulations also attributed a clear legal personality to the coolie, recognizing him basically as a free man, thus free to marry, reproduce, and assume parental rights over his children. He had a right to preserve his marital relationship and familial obligations—married coolies with children could not be forcibly separated, for example. He could acquire and dispose of private property, bring charges against others, including his master, in court, and had recourse to colonial authorities in the event of abuse, which, if severe enough, could even result in the recision of his contract.

The regulations carefully spelled out the coolie's right to freedom and under what conditions. Upon reaching twenty-five years of age, or upon completing six of the eight-year term of service, the *colono* had the right to have the rest of his contract voided by providing a fair indemnization to the *patrono*. Other ways to gain his freedom would be to compensate the owner for the cost of his upkeep and maintenance (food, clothing, job training, tools), or compensate him for the cost of finding his replacement. One exclusionary clause was built in: none of the means to freedom could be exercised during the cane harvest (*zafra*), or when other urgent tasks needed to be performed.

In Peru, aside from various versions of the contract, there were fewer comprehensive regulations governing the coolie system. Peru did not come under equally intense world (especially British) scrutiny as did Cuba, which, because of its continuing practice of slavery at a time when the British were bent on terminating it, could not escape having considerable attention trained on the coolie system as well. Consequently, the Cubans had to respond constantly to international pressures to moderate the excesses of the coolie system; hence the series of regulations. In the mid-1850s, Spain and Peru also transferred their coolie trade operations from under the glaring eyes of the British and Chinese authorities in the treaty ports of South China to the relaxed gaze of the Portuguese colonial authorities in Macao.

Other than a few three-year contracts during the early years, the Peruvian contracts were for eight years, with other terms also very similar to those in the Cuban contracts. By 1868, in response to international outcry, the government had outlawed sending coolies to the guano pits with their utterly deplorable conditions, a prohibition explicitly stated on the contracts but ignored up to that point. The contracts also contained statements that the coolie agreed to work in Peru "of my own free will," and that, after the eight years, no pretext could be used, not even debts, to prolong servitude. The freed coolie would then be "free to work as I wish." Unlike the Cuban contracts, the Peruvian ones made no reference to wage differentials between different kinds of workers on the coastal plantations, because the Chinese were the bulk, sometimes the exclusive, labor force, whereas Cuban plantations had a mixed labor force of slave, contracted, and free.

In other respects, the contracts and the regulations made clear that during the eight-year term of servitude, the coolies were their masters' properties, constituting moreover a fixed capital investment in his enterprise. In the Peruvian account books, when a coolie died before his contract expired, the estate manager noted the premature death as a "loss" (*pérdida*) (Rodríguez Pastor 1988, 35–36). Despite various recourses legally available to the coolie to complain against abuses, excesses, and violations of the contract, other stipulations made it clear that the daily life and work of the coolies were pretty much left to the discretion of those who held their contracts. Various clauses also made clear that the contract—and by extension the rights and needs of the *patrono*—took precedence over rights and needs of the *colono*. One common article in the contracts stated that the *colono*, upon signing his contract, "renounces the exercise of all civil rights which are not compatible with the compliance of contract obligations." He had very little freedom of mobility, being specifically prohibited from leaving his place of work without the written permission of the *patrono*, or risk being arrested as a runaway (*cimarrón*). To exercise many of his personal legal rights, such as marriage and owning property, he needed to obtain prior approval of his master. Although he could in theory buy out his contract (*coartación*) and hence gain his freedom, the terms were so stringent that it was practically impossible. The selling and buying of contracts, as well as the renting out of contracts, in practice differed little from the practices of buying, selling and renting out slaves. The laws, in effect, particularly on the plantations, were flagrantly disregarded, the contract a mere piece of paper. In other words, on a day-to-day basis, life on the plantations for the Chinese contract laborers were not materially different from that of slaves. In less guarded moments, plantation owners referred to their contracted Chinese workers as *brazos*, or cheap, unskilled labor, almost never as the *colonos* or settlers noted on the contracts. They were "convenient" and "indispensable" substitutes for slaves.

The nature, terms, and conditions of coolie contracts took a sharp new turn in Cuba with the issuance of the 1860 "Regulations for the Introduction of Chinese Workers to the Island of Cuba" (see Pastrana 1983). The new law required coolies who had completed their original eight year term to recontract with the same or another master, or leave Cuba at their own expense within two months of contract termination. In other words, it rendered moot all talk about freedom explicitly delineated in the contract itself and earlier regulations. With so few workers able to save enough for the return fare, most stayed and recontracted. Such compulsory and successive recontracting perpetuated servitude indefinitely, to the point that the legal distinction between indenture and slavery became truly blurred.

There is no doubt that the Cubans compelled recontracting in order to keep as many as possible of this semi-captive, alien labor force on the plantations, knowing full well that few could afford to purchase a passage home. Although recontracting was coercive and abusive, the terms of the new contracts varied considerably from the original eight-year contract and from each other. A batch of early recontracts from 1868 reveals that their terms were short, generally six months or one year. The pay varied greatly, from a low of four pesos, two reales a month for one year, to thirteen pesos per month for one year. Others were paid eight and one-half pesos, twelve pesos, twelve and three-fourths pesos. Some were given food, clothing, and medical attention in addition to cash. Two workers who recontracted with the same master were offered quite different wages of eight and one-half pesos and twelve pesos. Unfortunately, no other information was provided in these agreements to help explain the wide differential in wages during the same year, and even on the same estate. These recontracts then suggest that the planters were not able to dictate uniform terms, and that, more important, the coolies appeared to wield some leverage in negotiating the terms of employment. If this were true, then some degree of labor market forces seemed to have been at work.

The other side of the recontracting requirement was its extremely coercive and abusive nature. Among Chinese workers still under some kind of contract when the coolie trade ended in 1874, many testified to a visiting Chinese commission that they were forced into successive recontracting. Cuban authorities and planters were determined to keep the Chinese in the labor market by denying them the *cédula*, or certificate of completion of contract service, which would have permitted them freedom of movement, residency, and occupation if they stayed in Cuba. When freed from the plantation, they almost always preferred to move to the towns and cities to own or work in a small business. Between contracts, those unable to meet exorbitant demands by local authorities of up to 140 pesos to issue the all-important *cédula* (by law the document was supposed to be issued free of charge), would be sent to the municipal *depósitos* or holding cells. There they waited to be recontracted, or were put to work on public works projects at no pay whatsoever. In this sense, the *depósitos* functioned as a labor reserve for the planters or anyone else in need of temporary help at low cost.

But regardless of how they were treated at work, the Chinese were keenly aware that they were free men under contract, very distinct from the slaves who were chattel for life. The Cuban archives contain numerous protests and complaints filed by coolies against *patronos* and local authorities who they felt had violated the contracts of some regulations—for example, those forbidding corporal punishment. Of the 1,179 depositions taken from coolies by the visiting Chinese commission in 1874, most demonstrated a keen awareness of their position and expressed deep frustration that, while legally free and protected from abuses, they were in fact not properly treated, either by the *patronos* or by the authorities charged with protecting them (Cuba Commission Report 1993).

Huashang: Petite Bourgeoisie in Mexico

This is a story of how an immigrant group in Mexico entrenched itself in a regional economy in Mexico, then found itself racialized and expelled from the country, its businesses confiscated and redistributed to native Mexicans. It can be argued that the Chinese became a kind of "pariah capitalist" in northern Mexico, not unlike Chinese and Jews in different times and different parts of the world.

That Chinese became successful and ubiquitous shopkeepers and merchants is not uncommon in the diaspora; what stands out here is the degree to which the Chinese came to control local small businesses, to the extent that they became in effect the region's petite bourgeoisie, holding a virtual monopoly over local retail trade. We will trace here the historical process by which Chinese immigrants to the northwestern state of Sonora (bordering Arizona) during Porfirian Mexico (1875–1911) and through the active years of the Mexican Revolution (1910–1920) entrenched themselves in the local economy. Statistical data uncovered in Mexican municipal, state, and federal archives on population (total numbers and geographical distribution within the state), occupations and types of businesses, and capital investment and size of businesses, will demonstrate just how widely and deeply the Chinese had penetrated the state's economic structure.

Toward the end of the regime of dictator Porfirio Díaz, in 1910, the Chinese population in Sonora had reached 4,486, in a total state population of 265,383, making them the largest foreign colony in Sonora, exceeding North Americans (3,164) and many more than Spaniards (259) and Germans (183). In 1910, there were 13,203 Chinese in all Mexico; only 82 were women (Table 5.2). The Chinese community in Sonora reached a high point in 1919 of 6,078, indicating heavy Chinese immigration to Mexico during the most turbulent revolutionary years of 1910–1917. This number dropped precipitously during the following decade, until the community numbered 3,571 in 1930, at the beginning of the Great Depression and on the eve of its expulsion from Sonora (Table 5.3). The Chinese community in Sonora and all Mexico was consistently predominately male. Even as late as 1930, the census noted only 119 women within Sonora's Chinese population of 3,167.

TABLE 5.2
Chinese Population in Mexico, 1900–1930

State	1900	Women[a]	1910	Women	1921	Women	1927[b]	1930	Women
Aguascaliente	102		21		14		31	47	18
Baja California Norte	188		532		2,806	14	5,889	2,982	
Baja California Sur			319		175	3		139	3
Campeche	5		70		61	1	108	113	38
Coahuila	197	5	759	14	52	16	707	765	153
Colima	5		80	2	32	1	43	38	14
Chiapas	16		478	1	645	30	1,261	1,095	238
Chihuahua	328	2	1,325	9	533	16	1,037	1,127	229
México, D.F.			1,482	5	607	18	1,062	886	141
Durango	147	1	242	2	46		197	229	33
Guanajuato	11		102		21	3	37	37	12
Guerrero	3		27		3		7	10	3
Hidalgo			38		50	1	98	70	18
Jalisco	20		70	1	53	1	192	151	48
México	15		58	1	25		78		24
Michoacán	4		26		5		8	12	1
Morelos	5		18		3		9	3	
Nayarít					152		164	170	27
Nuevo León	90		221		89	2	216	165	4
Oaxaca	81		262		158	6	254	158	50
Puebla	11		31		17	1	22	44	12
Querétaro	1		5		1		1	2	
Quintana Roo	3		5		2		10		4
San Luís Potosi	32		109		105	2	288	271	18
Sinaloa	233	1	667	4	1,040	4	2,019	2,123	438
Sonora	850	9	4,486	37	3,639	66	3,758	3,571	412
Tabasco	236	1	48	4	67		64	23	
Tamaulipas	38		213	2	2,005	21	2,916	2,117	242
Tepic	29		173						
Tláxcala									
Veracruz	116		434	1	847	10	1,908	1,238	162
Yucatán	153		875		773	5	1,726	972	153
Zacatecas	19		41		19		113	142	25
Total	2,718	18	13,203	80	14,498	185	24,218	17,865	2,522

Sources: Mexican censuses for 1900, 1910, 1921, and 1930 in Salazar Anaya (1996).

For 1927, see "Extranjeros residentes Estados Unidos. For 1927, see "Extranjeros residentes Estados Unidos de México. Resumen del censo practicado por la Secretaría de Gobernación en 1927, y extrajeros, distribucción por estados, 14 marzo 1928," Archivo Histórico del Gobierno del Estado de Sonora, vol. 1930.

[a]These women were counted within the total; they were erratically counted and not completely reliable; in later years, Mexican women married to Chinese men could have been included in this count.

[b]Women were not noted separately by state in the 1927 census, but a total figure of 1,772 was given.

TABLE 5.3

Chinese Population in Sonora

Year	Population	Total state population
1887	100	–
1890	229–270	221,682
1900	850	–
1904	2,414	–
1910	4,486	265,383
1919	6,078	–
1925	3,435	–
1927	3,758	–
1930	3,571	–

Sources (in chronological order): Consul A. Willard to U.S. State Dept., Guaymas, December 31, 1887, U.S. National Archives, General Records of the Department of State, Record Group 59, M284, Roll 4, #851; Willard to State, May 8, 1890, RG59/M284/Roll 5/#983; Corral 1891, v. 1, pp. 586–602; Censo Mexicano 1900; "Comisión oficial encargada del estudio de la inmigración asiática en México, 18 nov. 1903," informes presentados por los prefectos en 1904, Archivo Histórico del Gobierno del Estado de Sonora (AHGES), vol. 1900; Censo Mexicano 1910; "Gobierno del Estado de Sonora, censo de los residentes chinos, presentado por los presidentes municipales, 1919," AHGES, vol. 3345; "Estado de Sonora, Sección de Estadística, Año de 1925, Censo chino," AHGES, vol. 3741; "Extranjeros residentes en los Estados Unidos Mexicanos. Resumen del censo practicado por la Secretaría de Gobernación en 1927; y distribución de extranjeros en el Estado de Sonora, 14 marzo 1928," AHGES, vol. 50, 1930; Censo Mexicano 1930.

The distribution of the Chinese within Sonora was also significant. When they first arrived in the late nineteenth century, they congregated in Guaymas, the port of entry, and in the capital city of Hermosillo. Then they moved to other growing towns, such as Magdalena, south of Hermosillo on the newly con-structed rail line, and to the company town of Cananea in the northeast corner of the state, close to the U.S. border.

Table 5.4 indicates that by 1904, Chinese could be found in each of the

TABLE 5.4

Distribution of the Chinese Population in Sonora in 1904

District	Population
Alamos	57
Altar	10
Arizpe	1,106
Guaymas	427
Hermosillo	409
Magdalena	350
Moctezuma	39
Sahuaripa	5
Ures	11

Source: "Comisión oficial encargada del estado de la inmigración asiática en México, 18 nov. 1903; informes presentados por los prefectos de distrito en 1904," Archivo Histórico del Gobierno del Estado de Sonora, vol. 1900.

eight districts of the state. They continued to be prominent in Guaymas, Hermosillo, and Magdalena, but by far the largest number had gone to Arizpe district, where Cananea and smaller mining camps as well as border towns were located. Cananea had 800 of Arizpe's 1,106 Chinese. Conversely, the districts of Altar, Sahuaripa, and Ures, with no significant mines, commercial agriculture or railroads, had few Chinese.

Occupationally, contrary to expectations as well as against unfounded common charges leveled against the Chinese, they tended to shun low-paying menial laboring jobs. There were in the nineteenth century a small number of contract laborers—200 at most—for the mines, but not much is known about them. A number of Chinese could always be found working as cooks, domestics, and chauffeurs, especially for American families in the mining towns. Another small number hired themselves out as day laborers (jornaleros). By far the greatest number of Chinese started their own small businesses, or worked as partners and employees of other Chinese in business.

Among the first Chinese to arrive in Mexico were a few with capital. As early as 1876, the Chinese shoe factory Tung, Chung, Lung was established in

Guaymas, followed by Siu Fo Chong in 1890 in Guaymas, and several others in Hermosillo and Magdalena. Some of these shoe factories also branched out into manufacturing rough or coarse clothing. All of them hired exclusively Chinese workers. By 1902, Tung, Chung, Lung alone was producing annually 80,000 pairs of shoes, worth 130,000 pesos (see Hu-DeHart 1980). In Governor Ramón Corral's 1890 count of 229 Chinese, who were second in numbers among foreign residents only to the 337 North Americans, noted that over half (161) were shoemakers, tailors, and ironers employed in Chinese shoe and clothing factories. Other Chinese occupations included day laborer, truck farmer, cook, baker, one *minero* (miner), one *cirujano* (surgeon—Chinese doctor?), and twenty *comerciantes*, merchants or shopkeepers (Corral 1891, 502).[3]

Throughout the 1870s and 1880s, large commerce on the West Coast of Mexico was limited to the big towns, such as Guaymas, and was almost exclusively in the hands of Germans, Spaniards, and Englishmen. The United States had a very small share of Mexico's import-export trade, due largely to the absence of American representatives promoting such a relationship. Whereas most Americans were involved with the mining economy, almost all the Europeans were merchants, industrialists, or manufacturers.

By 1890, Chinese with a little capital began to establish *abarrotes*, or small grocery stores, starting in Guaymas, then spreading quickly to other towns. Their capital worth of 600 to 800 pesos each was much more modest than the 5,000 and 8,000 pesos of Tung, Chung, Lung and Siu Fo Chong, the shoe factories. During this decade, in mining towns such as Minas Prietas and La Colorado, Chinese were already noted as itinerant traders or peddlers (*ambulantes*). Since foreign mining companies generally opened company stores (*tienda de raya*) to supply essential food and goods to their Mexican workers, Chinese peddlers either attempted to compete with them by selling at lower prices, or supplemented company stores that were stocked with different products. A third type of small Chinese business appearing at this time were canteens and restaurants, many in mining camps or railroad towns. These were mostly third-class establishments cooking for male workers in the absence of their own womenfolk.[4] By this time, it had become obvious to U.S. consuls in Guaymas and Mazatlán (Sinaloa state, south of Sonora) that, aside from working for their compatriots, the Chinese shied away from laboring jobs, because the wages were so low that "even a Chinaman could not exist thereon." Nor were they eager to accept domestic employment, as the wages they sought were higher than those Mexicans asked.[5]

By the end of the nineteenth century, two levels of Chinese commercial activity had emerged: at the top was a handful of well-capitalized shoe and clothing factories, located in cities such as Guaymas, Hermosillo, and Magdalena. In addition to producing shoes and clothing for working people in and near these towns, they actively distributed their products to the interior. An

1897 advertisement by Siu Fo Chong in a Guaymas paper announced: "Special Attention to Orders from the Interior of the State." These large Chinese firms expanded from manufacturing shoes and clothing into wholesale and retail trade of a range of food and consumer items: fresh and canned goods, cereals and flour, dry goods, imported luxury products and general merchandise of every kind. Printed on its letterhead just below the Fon Qui company name was this notice: "Shoe Factory; Wholesale and Retail; Groceries; National and Foreign Goods."[6] Both firms established their own branch stores, starting with nearby railroad and mining towns such as Imuris and Santa Ana, moving eastward to Cananea and southward to Hermosillo and Guaymas, and, in the twentieth century, into the commercial agricultural zones of the Yaqui and Mayo river valleys.

So small they were initially imperceptible to the state's large business directories, Chinese-owned small businesses spread into every municipality in the state: groceries, general stores, canteens, restaurants, truck farms, itinerant traders, hand laundries, shoe repairs, tailors. They even expanded into two remote sierra communities that had never had any retail outlets. Local newspapers, however, did not miss the picture. By the end of the century, local papers such as Guaymas's *El Tráfico* frequently decried the growing Chinese commercial presence in Mexican communities. Its shrill and virulent voice specifically noted that the Chinese were at the point of monopolizing the small business sector of the local economy, much to the detriment, it claimed, of humble Mexicans trying unsuccessfully to compete with them.[7]

During the Mexican Revolution, while much of Mexican life was severely disrupted, Chinese merchants and shopkeepers actually prospered. Despite numerous incidents of violence against their persons and properties—from 1910 to 1916 an estimated one hundred Chinese were killed by revolutionaries of various factions in Sonora—the ability to survive and thrive in the midst of such turmoil would further solidify the Chinese position in the local economy, but also deepen Mexican resentment. The revolution also seriously disrupted European mercantile ties with old German and Spanish firms in Sonora, in some cases forcing their withdrawal from the state and from the country, leaving a vacuum for the Chinese to fill. Juan Lung Tain and Fon Qui became increasingly aggressive, importing primarily from the United States via the recently completed railroads. Thus, the Chinese not only prospered but also helped strengthen U.S.-Mexico commercial ties, a relationship that had been notably weak before the revolution. U.S. consuls repeatedly expressed their pleasure at this fortuitous turn of events, at times arguing for the necessity of the U.S. government to protect Chinese merchants when they came under revolutionary attack, in order to protect American business contacts and credits in Mexico (Bell 1923, 32–34).

Chinese businesses were further boosted by the need of all revolutionary armies marching up and down, in and out and through Sonora, to be fed and provisioned. To a large extent, Chinese stores supplied their needs—not always voluntarily, to be sure, and not always adequately compensated, if at all. Frequently, revolutionary soldiers simply sacked and stripped Chinese stores of their merchandize. At other times, more responsible generals and captains appropriated food and goods but left behind with the Chinese proprietor a promissory note for payment later.

From these promissory notes we gain a glimpse into the well-stocked shelves of the Chinese merchants such as Juan Lung Tain: corn, flour, coffee, beans, wheat, salt, sugar, canned goods (lard, salmon, sardine), sacks of sago (a meal-like food) and peppers, cinnamon, tea, pastas, iron works, white stationery paper, household goods, jute, khaki, wool and sacks, soap, cowhide, alcohol, lanterns, coffee makers, iron cooking pots and pans, horseshoes, hobnails, shirts and pants of different materials, men's wool suits, various types of cloths and clothing materials (wool, linen, silk, percale, Indiana, satin, pique, taffeta), woolen blankets, socks of various materials, women's silk stockings, corsets, laceworks, embroidered works, lace trimmings, taffeta ribbons, metal flower pots, sombreros, American shoes and spats, Mexican shoes, women's shoes, children's shoes, silk shawls, silk handkerchiefs, silk blouses, silk and cotton vests, underpants, multiple brands of perfume and power, pewter tankards, Turkish opium, shoe polish, tweed and yellow khaki, teakettles, padlocks, spoons, thread, knives, various brands of cigar, bathtubs, crystal glasses, dish sets, spurs, bridles, carts, mules, mares, machine grease, tobacco, leather bags, plows, furniture.

Chinese businesses fortunes were also contingent on the fortunes of American investors. As long as American mines continued to operate in spite of revolutionary wars, the Chinese had clients, so closely did they follow the trail of American investment. Besides opening their own businesses to serve workers employed by Americans, the Chinese established more direct relationship and dealings with the American companies. Some operated company mess halls; others bought supplies from company stores for resale later in smaller quantities. One American mine owner actually sold his *tienda de raya* (company store) to a Chinese, who then operated it as his own business. Another American mine owner paid his Mexican workers in tokens redeemable at the local Chinese store.[8]

Tables 5.5 and 5.6, based on 1913 information, illustrate the progress Chinese had made during the last decade of the Porfirian regime and first years of the revolution. Although more Chinese had joined the ranks of the large bourgeoisie, their numbers and total capital were still modest in comparison to the total Mexican-owned and other foreign-owned capital: There were only 15 Chinese large businesses compared to 238 owned by Mexicans and other foreigners, and 731,830 pesos in capital compared to 18 million. The average Chinese

TABLE 5.5

Profile of the Chinese Business Community, 1913

Town	General merchandise	Grocery/ fruitstand	Combi- nation	Notions/ fabrics	Restaurant	Hotel	Laundry	Clothing factory	Shoe factory	Others
Alamos	3									
Bácum	3									
Cananea			24	1		1	4	1		
Carbo		4								
Cócorit	7									
Cumpas	2	2						1		
Cumuripa	1			1						
Fronteras			7							
Guaymas	11				39	1	4		1	
Hermosillo		65				1	1			2ª
Imuris	4	1								
Llano	3				1					
Nacozari	1									
Magdalena			9			1				
Minas Prietas			4				3			
Nácori			3				4			
Pilares	3									
Navojoa	4									
Nogales			21							
Ortíz	4									
Pótam	5									
Realito	2									
San Miguel	1									
Santa Ana			6							
Santa Cruz	3									
Tórin			8						1	
Total	57	72	82	2	40	4	16	2	2	2

Source: International Chinese Business Directory, 1913.
ªListed as pharmacy, silk.

TABLE 5.6

Businesses with Capital over 20,000 Pesos, 1913

| District | Mexicans, Europeans, and U.S. citizens | | Chinese | |
	Number	Capital	Number	Capital
Hermosillo	79	6,418,193.20	5	127,200.00
Guaymas	50	3,812,466.20	6	225,000.00
Alamos	45	2,280,540.80	1	25,000.00
Magdalena	22	1,386,435.40	2	256,224.00
Altar	3	71,446.00	0	
Arizpe	22	3,339,088.10	1	26,560.00
Ures	238	18,000,875.00	17	792,707.45

Source: "Lista de los causantes sujetos a la contribución directa ordinaria que tienen capitales de $20 000 en adelante (1913)," Archivo Histórico del Gobierno del Estado de Sonora, vol. 2968.

Note: Sahuaripa district is not included in this list, which probably means it had no business capitalized above 20,000.00 pesos.

business was capitalized at 48,788.67 pesos, compared to an average of 75,630.62 for other businesses. Furthermore, the range within the 15 Chinese businesses is much narrower than the range within the rest of the large business community: with three exceptions (Fon Qui, Juan Lung Tain, and On Chong), the Chinese firms had less than 50,000 in capital. By contrast, 98 non-Chinese firms were capitalized above 50,000.

Table 5.5 lists 279 small to medium Chinese businesses spread among twenty-six municipalities or towns (*municipios*). Most of them were general merchandize or grocery stores, 40 were restaurants, 16 laundries, 4 hotels, 2 dry goods stores, 2 clothing factories, 1 shoe factory, and 2 drugstores (herbalists?). The actual number of Chinese businesses was probably more than the 279 included in this list found in the *International Chinese Business Directory*. For example, the U.S. consul in Cananea noted in 1915 that there were 60 Chinese businesses in that town, although there were just 31 included in the 1913 directory.[9]

As soon as the fighting began to wind down in 1915 and 1916, the Chinese were ready to expand again. From 1917 to 1920, Chinese entrepreneurs formed some ninety-four "mercantile societies," that is, companies or business partnerships. Some of these, such as Juan Lung Tain, were old firms under reorganization;

TABLE 5.7

**Chinese Merchantile Societies
(Partnerships), 1917–1920**

Capital (pesos)	Number
Less than 1,000	20
1,000–5,000	59
6,000–19,000	8
20,000–50,000	4
More than 50,000	3[a]

Source: "Sociedades civiles y mercantiles en Sonora, 1912, 1917, 1918, 1919, 1920," taken from the Registro Público de la Propiedad (property registry) of each district. Archivo Histórica del Gubierno del Estado de Sonora, vol. 3432.

[a]The three largest were: Fon Qui, with 80,000 pesos; Juan Lung Tain with 67,000 pesos; and the Canton Commercial Co. of Cananea, with 50,000 pesos (the only one involved in mining).

most others were new enterprises. Table 5.7 breaks down these companies by amount of capitalization. Again, it can be seen that the vast majority of these firms were small to medium in size, capitalized at 5,000 pesos or less, while non-Chinese firms (Mexican, European, North American and other foreign) were commonly capitalized at 25,000, 50,000, up to hundreds of thousands of pesos, and even up to one and two billion, represented by the Crown Graphite Company and the Arizona Mexico Land Company.

In 1917–1920, Mexico finally began to unify under one revolutionary leadership, the northerners led by Sonoran generals Alvaro Obregón and Plutarco Elías Calles. By then, the Chinese had attained an undeniable position of strength in the local economy, a fact acknowledged by the Chinese themselves, as well as by the North Americans and the Mexicans. This growth occurred in spite of the first organized anti-Chinese campaign in the state from 1916 to 1919, spearheaded by a Magdalena schoolteacher who was himself a small businessman, José María Arana.[10] In January 1920, Martín Wong, president of the Guaymas chapter of the Chinese Fraternal Union, claimed that "Chinese business has recently increased a hundred percent." U.S. Consul Bartley Yost added that "the trade in groceries, dry goods, and general merchandise in Sonora is largely controlled by the Chinese." This development actually pleased North Americans because of the close commercial ties they had established with Chinese merchants in Sonora over the course of the revolutionary decade.[11] For this reason, U.S. consuls in Mexico consistently protected the Chinese from harassment and persecution, even to the point of granting them temporary asylum on the U.S. side of the border at a time when Chinese persons could not legally be admitted into that country (see Cumberland 1960).

In 1919, the state government and the federal Labor Department conducted independent surveys of the Chinese population and their business activities in Sonora. These surveys yielded similar results and the most complete and detailed reports on the Chinese to date.[12] The governor's report, based on information submitted by municipal authorities, found 4,667 Chinese residing in fifty-eight municipalities. Only four very small and remote places in Sahuaripa and Ures districts indicated no Chinese presence at all. The total would have been higher, but for some reason Cananea, a principal center of Chinese residence and business, did not submit a report. The Labor Department's report was based on information supplied by the Chinese Fraternal Union. It counted 4,477 Chinese, distributed among all nine districts (Table 5.4).

The Chinese community in 1919 was composed overwhelmingly of young to middle-aged men, that is, men of working age. Among them, 62 percent were between the ages of twenty-six and forty, increasing to 84 percent for those between twenty-one and forty-five, and to an astounding 92 percent if the upper age limit were extended to fifty. Only 331 individuals, or 5.4 percent, were younger than twenty, and only 170, or 2.8 percent, older than fifty-one.

In terms of years of residence, the Labor report indicated that, as of 1919, 41 percent of the Chinese had been in Mexico for ten to twenty years, and another 38.7 percent had lived there for five to ten years. Thus the vast majority, almost 80 percent, had at least five years experience in the country. It also meant that most had arrived in Mexico between the years 1899 and 1914, with another 1,459 persons, or 24 percent, landing during the tumultuous revolutionary years of 1912 to 1915.

Both the governor and the Labor report noted that the Chinese were predominantly *comerciantes*—merchants or shopkeepers. The Labor report provided a clear occupational breakdown by district, as summarized in Table 5.8. Fully 70 percent—4,258 of them—were *comerciantes*, with day laborers (*jornaleros*) a distant second at 12.8 percent. Farmers (*agricultores*, truck farmers or market gardeners) and miners (*mineros*) constituted 3.4 percent and 3.2 percent, respectively. There were eight "industrialists" (*industriales*), which probably designated the owners of shoe or clothing manufacturing facilities. Slightly under 1 percent and slightly over 1 percent were cooks (*cocineros*) and laundrymen (*lavanderos*), numbers so insignificant they should put to rest any

TABLE 5.8
Chinese Occupations in Sonora in 1919

District		Store owner or peddler	Truck (garden) farmer	Miner	Cook	Laundry-man	Shoe-maker (repair)	Craftsman (jeweler, carpenter)	Tailor	Butcher, tanner	Baker	Day laborer	Minors	Vagabond
Moctezuma	521	1	25	75	5	6	8	1	2	4	5	75		35
Guaymas	1,156		50		5	15	8		2	1	9	65		35
Sahuaripa	46		2		1	1					1	6		
Altar	146		15	1	4	2	1		1		3	15		5
Alamos	492	2	15		5	6	5		2		2	100		35
Ures	51		3		1	1				1	1	8		5
Arizpe	758		20	120	15	18	15	1	8	6	10	287	100	70
Magdalena	516	2	53		15	12	8		4		7	147		35
Hermosillo	579	3	24		7	8	24	1	4	3	1	75		35
Total	4,258	8	207	196	58	69	69	3	23	15	39	778	100	255

Source: Departamento de Trabajo. Sección de Conciliación. "Informe que rinde el Jefe de la Sección sobre la situación de las colonias asiáticas en la Costa Occidental de la República, 1919." E. Flores, comisario. Archivo General de la Nación/Trabajo, México, D.F.

lingering notion that Chinese anywhere in the American diaspora were predisposed to these occupations or businesses. The rest of the Chinese in this survey were artisans and craftsmen of various kinds: tailors, shoemakers, jewelers, carpenters, bakers, tanners, constituting another 2 percent. Finally, there were 100 children and 255 vagrants, men without fixed occupations.

Not only did merchants dominate the total picture but in every district they led the way. This category included fixed shops as well as ambulatory traders, hotels, and restaurants. In addition, industrialists, truck farmers, and many of the artisans and craftsmen should also be considered small businesses, as many of them owned their own establishments, or worked for Chinese who did.

The diligent Labor Department commissioner also gathered extremely useful information on the amount of Chinese and non-Chinese commercial capital invested in Sonora, information summarized in Table 5.9. The non-Chinese category can be broken down in this way:

1. 755,000 pesos were accounted for by the company stores (*tiendas de raya*) of the large, primarily North American-owned mining towns, such as Green Copper in Cananea, Moctezuma, El Tigre, and Minas Lampazos.
2. 1,808,000 pesos belonged to businesses owned by North Americans, Germans, French, Arabs, Japanese, and other non-Chinese foreigners.
3. That left only 978,000 pesos belonging to Mexicans.

As for the Chinese, they controlled over 2 million pesos in commercial investment, equal to the approximately 2 million controlled by other foreigners. But there were numerically almost twice as many Chinese businesses as all other combined, for a lower amount of capital per business. This meant that the average Chinese business capital, 2,644 pesos, was considerably smaller than the non-Chinese, at 6,482 pesos. Table 5.10, which breaks down the 827 Chinese businesses by amount of capital invested, highlights their predominantly petit bourgeois nature.

In terms of industrial strength, the Chinese were much weaker than other industrialists in the state, Mexican and otherwise. Chinese owned only a small number of so-called industries, which were properly speaking small and medium craft and artisan shops manufacturing products for local consumption by the working class, such as common shoes and ready-made clothing, sweets, *masa* or cornmeal for tortillas, pastas, and small leather and metal goods. In fact, like the numerous and ubiquitous outlets, restaurants, and hand laundries, these Chinese businesses were also petit bourgeois in nature. Completely eluding Chinese hands were major industries, such as flour mills (which were primarily controlled by large Sonoran *hacendados*—large landowners), utilities, railroad, cattle ranches and, of course, mines, these latter mostly controlled by North Americans.[13]

TABLE 5.9

Commercial Establishments and Capital in Sonora in 1919

		Chinese			Mexicans and others	
District	No.	Capital (pesos)	Average per estab-lishment	No.	Capital (pesos)	Average per estab-lishment
Moctezuma	81	220,520.00	2,722.47	28	522,270.00	18,652.50
Guaymas	248	854,110.00	2,443.99	54	936,805.00	17,348.24
Sahuaripa	6	27,000.00	4,500.00	29	40,550.00	1,398.28
Altar	30	61,404.00	2,046.80	42	73,810.00	1,759.38
Alamos	102	185,100.00	1,814.71	44	104,400.00	2,372.73
Ures	25	48,900.00	1,956.00	28	45,400.00	1,621.43
Arizpe	110	196,320.00	1,748.73	67	546,555.00	8,157.54
Magdalena	107	320,621.00	2,996.46	54	168,400.00	3,118,52
Hermosillo	827	272,960.00	2,313.22	88	375,350.00	4,265.34
Total	1,536	2,186,935.00	2,644.42	434	2,813,540.00	6,482.41

Source: Departamento de Trabajo. Sección de Conciliación. "Informe que rinde el Jefe de la Sección sobre la situación de las colonias asiáticas en la Costa Occidental de la República, 1919." E. Flores, comisario. Archivo General de la Nación/Trabajo, México, D.F.

Economic reports in the early to mid-1920s further confirmed the consolidation of Chinese commercial power in Sonora. An American named Harold Arnold conducted a business survey between 1921 and 1924.[14] He examined every one of the state's seventy-four municipalities, and counted 572 Chinese businesses compared to 316 Mexican-owned ones, followed very far behind by 31 North American, 11 French, 5 Spanish, 6 German, 5 "other European," 12 Arab, and 13 Japanese-owned. There were 13 communities, mostly in the districts of Altar, Ures, and Sahuaripa, that had no Chinese businesses. Not surprisingly, these were the state's least developed districts, where the economy was still based on traditional peasant or subsistence agriculture, with little mining, railroad, or commercial agricultural activities whatsoever.

More significantly, in nine towns, all businesses were Chinese owned. A few of these were small, sparsely populated communities located in the above-named, slow-developing districts. Five, however, were growing towns in the rapidly developing southern part of the state, specifically in the Yaqui and Mayo river valleys of Guaymas and Alamos districts, where commercial agriculture

TABLE 5.10

Chinese Commercial Establishments in 1919

Capital (pesos)	Number
1,500–5,000	740
5,000–10,000	76
More than 10,000	11

Source: Departamento de Trabajo. Sección de Conciliación. "Informe que rinde el Jefe de la Sección sobre
la situación de las colonias asiáticas en la Costa
Occidental de la República, 1919." E. Flores, comisario.
Archivo General de la Nación/Trabajo, México, D.F.

underlay the newest and most dynamic sector of the economy, and where U.S.
investment capital predominated. Just as in the northern part of the state
where, earlier, Chinese followed in the wake of mining and railroad development, so in the south they trailed closely behind colonization and commercial
agricultural growth. In other words, wherever the local economy was making a
transition from subsistence to market, Chinese shopkeepers were there, and
usually there first.

In 1925, in the midst of a vigorous renewed anti-Chinese campaign in Sonora,
which urgently called for the expulsion of the Chinese from the state, the state
government conducted another census of the Chinese population and compiled statistics on Chinese versus Mexican commercial and industrial capital.
Table 5.11 summarizes the findings of this report, as well as an earlier one conducted by the state treasury in 1922.

In 1925, Chinese preeminence in local commerce remained intact. Despite
rising anti-Chinese persecution, they managed to hold on to their position.
According to Table 5.11, 1,570 of the 3,435 Chinese were *comerciantes*, which
included owners and "partners" (*socios*), the term Chinese business owners
preferred to use for their Chinese employees. Add to this the 465 *agricultores*,
most of whom were small businessmen who leased land from Mexicans and
North Americans to plant vegetables and fruits, which they then carted and
sold in local produce markets; the 93 *industriales* and 13 *profesionales*, and
even the 98 shoemakers, 37 tailors, and 73 laundrymen, most of whom also
probably owned their own businesses, some 70 percent of the Chinese population were involved in providing goods and services of a wide variety.

TABLE 5.11

The Chinese Commercial Bourgeoisie, 1925

Town	No. of individuals	Women	Occupation										Capital (pesos)	
			Shop-keeper	Poultry farmer	Employee	Shoe-maker	Tailor	Cook	Factory owner	Profess-ional	Day laborer	Laundry-man	Chinese capital invested	Mexican capital invested
Aconchi	5	1	2										2,000	500
Agua Prieta	107	7	75	4	3		2	8	2		1	2	21,950	3,200
Altar	15		5	5				1					19,600	50,405
Alamos	8		6	1					1				3,900	23,450
Arizpe	29	2	15	6				2	1	1	1		16,500	28,550
Arivechi	2													1,000
Atil	2		2										3,000	1,200
Bacadeh	2										2			
Bacanora	10		5	2							3			500
Bacerac	2		2										3,250	
Bacoachi	31		5	19							1		11,915	4,000
Bácum	65		49	2	1				5		3			7,500
Banámichi	5	3	4	1									12,183	15,100
Batuc	3		3											2,500

Baviácora	13	11	2									10,010	3,040
Bavispe	6	5								1		2,200	3,300
Caborca	18	4	9				5					5,000	12,450
Cananea	410	204	22	16	17	11	21	7		56	23	172,323	42,200
Cócorit	169	72	13	24			5	11		22	1	124,610	1,200
Cucurpe	4	1								3			15,740
Cumpas	58	18	9		2				1	1		33,330	
Etchojoa	76	27	3	14				1		6		45,450	
El Tigre	92	17	15	1	1	2	3	1		31		27,040	14,400
Fronteras	172	24	15					1		31		26,240	
Granados	3	2	2				1						
Guaymas	363	193	39	16	3	4	24	19	1	2	7	256,840	880,670
Hermosillo	404	258	34		45	4		15	1		19	211,785	729,665
Huachinera	2	2										3,658	250
Huásabas	6	3	1							1		2,000	1,300
Huatabampo	84	49	16	17				1		1		68,950	
Huépac	7	5		1						1		6,700	3,725
Imuris	68	7	53	6						1		8,500	1,200
La Colorado	36	16	2	6			1	1		6		20,900	1,000
Magdalena	106	52	38	2		1	4	1		2		174,070	76,240
Mazatán													
Moctezuma	30	13	7	1				1	1	2		14,840	13,240

(continued)

TABLE 5.11 **The Chinese Commercial Bourgeoisie, 1925** (continued)

Town	No. of Individuals	Women	Occupation										Capital (pesos)	
			Shop-keeper	Poultry farmer	Employee	Shoe-maker	Tailor	Cook	Factory owner	Profess-ional	Day laborer	Laundry-man	Chinese capital invested	Mexican capital invested
Movas	2		2											
Muletas	1										1			
Nacori Ch,	3		1											
Nacozari	148	7	43	21	13	11				2	3		48,593	
Navojoa	165	24	53	1	50	17						1	126,340	89,100
Nogales	263	23	136		33		7	12	18	2	18	17	152,670	254,655
Nuri														3,050
Opodepe	9		6	1	1				1					
Oputo	8		4								4		8,340	6,700
Oquitoa	5		1	2				1					3,000	1,000
Pilares	64		39				6	6	2		11		20,750	11,000
Pitiquito	10		9	1										37,598
Quiriego	16		10	2	3						1		2,700	1,200
Rayón	7		6	1									10,310	6,700
Rosario	9	3	3											500
Sahuaripa	17		6	6				1	1	1	2		8,300	22,550
San Ignacio	21		2	13							5			

San Felipe														3,000
San Javier	1													3,000
San M. Horc.	28		23	3				2			1		10,800	182,900
San Pedro	2		2										5,000	
Santa Ana	85	6	29	18	20	1		1	4			1	23,505	29,200
Santa Cruz	27		3						1		24		5,000	3,000
Sáric	15		6	7	1				1				6,700	2,000
Soyopa														4,500
Suaqui														5,300
Tepache	7		5	1									2,020	350
Trincheras	2		2	2									1,080	1,050
Tubutama	11	1	2	4						1			3,200	
Tacupeto	1		1										2,500	800
Ures	24		20	4					4				30,834	65,450
Villa Seris	70		6	64									7,300	20,500
V. Pesqueira	1			1										1,200
Yécora	2		2											
Total	3,435	174	1,570	465	230	98	37	98	93	13	247	73	1,784,436	1,697,803

Source: For population and occupation: "Estado de Sonora. Sección de Estadística. Año de 1925. Censo chino." Archivo Histórico del Gobierno del Estado de Sonara (AHGES), vol. 3741. For capital: "Noticias estadísticas comparativas de los giros comerciales e industriales con especificación de su capital invertido de nacionales y chinos establecidos en el Estado de Sonora," June 2, 1925. AHGES, vol. 3758.

TABLE 5.12

**Chinese and Mexican Commercial/
Industrial Capital Compared, 1925**

Capital (pesos)	Chinese	Mexican
Up to 4,900	471	1
5,000–10,000	41	27
11,000–99,000	4	28
Over 100,000	1	5

Source: "Noticia estadística comparativa de los giros comerciales e industriales con especificación de su capital invertido, de Nacionales y Chinos establecidos en el Estado de Sonora," June 2, 1925. Archivo Histórico del Gobierno del Estado de Sonora, vol. 3758.

Table 5.12 summarizes the detailed survey of Chinese and Mexican businesses capitalized above 1,000 pesos. Like Table 5.10, this survey also clearly illustrates the solid, petit bourgeois nature of the Chinese commercial community, and how completely the Chinese dominated this class. Of the 517 Chinese establishments in 1925, the vast majority, 471 of them, had less than 5,000 pesos in capital, and most of these were worth only 1,200 to 2,500 pesos. Of Mexican-owned business, only one fit into this category, while the vast majority, 55 out of 61, fell into the larger two categories of 5,000 to 10,000 pesos and 11,000 to 99,000 pesos. Finally, only one Chinese firm, the venerable old Juan Lung Tain capitalized at 195,000 pesos, was included in the largest category of firms with over 100,000 pesos; five Mexican firms were included in this category.

The 417 Chinese businesses were spread over 65 of the state's municipalities; by contrast, the 61 Mexican-owned businesses were represented in just fourteen towns. As in 1919, a handful of small, economically traditional communities in Ures, Altar, and Sahuaripa districts had no Chinese presence; but these towns had no retail outlets of any kind. On the other hand, some remote communities, such as Atil, Tubutama, and San Pedro de la Cuevas, had only Chinese-owned stores. By contrast, the commerce of mining towns, such as Nacozari de García near Cananea, was exclusively in Chinese hands, as was true of rapidly growing agricultural towns in the southern part of the state, such as Cócorit in the Yaqui Valley, with 42 Chinese businesses (most capitalized under 3,000 pesos), Etchojoa and Huatabampo in the Mayos Valley, with 20 and 26

Chinese merchants, respectively. So by sheer numbers and widespread geographic distribution, Chinese businesses distinguished themselves from all other businesses combined. For the moment, their commercial dominance could not be denied, nor was it seriously challenged by any group of competitors.

Table 5.12 also provides convincing demonstration that the Chinese represented, and indeed, dominated, the petit bourgeois sector of the state's economy. The first two categories, representing businesses with capital up to 10,900 pesos, constituted the most numerous group, and they were overwhelmingly Chinese. In sharp contrast, the second two categories, representing capital from 11,000 to over 100,000 pesos, the numbers were extremely few—only thirty-eight—and mostly Mexican. Four of the five Chinese businesses included in these categories were located at the lower end of the scale, capitalized under 99,000 pesos, and as low as a mere 11,000 pesos.

Constituting a virtual monopoly that formed over the course of the past half century, Chinese predominance in local retail trade did not escape the attention of state and international observers. Indeed, this development probably explains the number of successive and detailed surveys and reports conducted by various state agencies as well as private individuals and groups (including the Chinese themselves) to document this increasingly obvious phenomenon.

Conclusion

As noted in the introduction, the purpose of this chapter is not to theorize the Chinese diaspora, although unquestionably that needs to be done, especially as a body of literature is fast building up. I do suggest that the term "diaspora" inspires and compels one to think comparatively and to work within a comparative framework. My purpose here is to share some of my own research on the Chinese diaspora in the Americas, emphasizing the relatively neglected region of Latin America and the Caribbean. Specifically, my plan is to illustrate two fruitful areas of research on the Chinese in this vast region: Chinese as contract laborers on colonial and neocolonial plantations, focusing on the nature of these contracts, and Chinese as a petite bourgeoisie in a neocolonial environment, focusing on their historical formation. The idea of a formal and state-organized indentured system of *huagong,* and the idea of a *huashang* so predominant that Chinese merchants actually constituted the local petite bourgeoisie (going far beyond being simply actively involved in local commerce and trade), would probably elude our attention if we did not study the Chinese diaspora in Latin America and the Caribbean. Although Chinese indentured labor did occur in other European colonies in Asia and the British Caribbean, we need to examine the variations in this system of labor, and why, for example, formal indenture was not practiced in the United States, when a large, cheap, and captive labor force was needed and deployed for mining and railroad construction at about the same time in the nineteenth century. Although Chinese shopkeepers were known everywhere in the diaspora, did Chinese merchants anywhere in the world dominate local retail trade so extensively and conclusively as they did in Sonora at the beginning of the twentieth century? This is what I mean by asserting that diaspora studies are necessarily comparative, historically contingent, and locally or regionally contextualized.

NOTES

By permission of editors Anderson and Lee of this volume, an earlier version of this work was published in *Amerasia Journal* 28:2 (2002): 64–90.

1. See, for example, the issue of the scholarly journal *Historias* (October 1994–March 1995), published by one of Mexico's preeminent historical research institutes, the Dirección de Estudios Históricos of the Instituto Nacional de Antropología e Historia. The issue was dedicated to the study of the "immigrant experiences" and to "foreigners" in Mexico, and included essays on the English, French, Spanish, Jewish, Lebanese, Central American, and Caribbeans, but none on the Chinese.

2. See the census tables compiled in Salazar Anaya (1996).

3. Of the eleven Chinese noted as artisans in Guaymas in 1911, ten were shoemakers, the eleventh a cigarmaker. "Censo de comerciantes, industriales y artesanos en el municipio de Guaymas, 1881," Biblioteca y Museo de Sonora, Archivo Histórico, Hermosillo, Sonora, México (hereafter BMS), vol. 496.

4. "Lista nominal de los vecinos principales de cada población," 1892. Reports by district, but missing Hermosillo, BMS, vol. 647; "Oficina de Fiel Contraste. Noticia de las averiguaciones de pesas y medidas (Office of Weight and Measure Control) Minas Prietas and La Colorado, 1896, BMS, vol. 791.

5. Consul Louis Kaiser to Department of State, December 31, 1890, U.S. National Archives, General Records of the Department of State, Record Group (RG) 59, M284, Roll 1022.

6. See Fon Qui's letter to secretary of the State Government, regarding a consignment to him from Jesús Contreras, Mexican *hacendado* (large landowner), of 30 loads of flour for retail sale *en comisión*. Magdalena, April 5, 1900, Archivo Histórico del Gobierno e Estado de Sonora, Hermosillo, Sonora, México (hereafter AHGES), vol. 1556.

7. *El Tráfico*, Guaymas, 1899–1901. Hemeroteca Nacional, México, D.F. The newspaper's denunciations of Chinese encroachments in local commerce used extremely strong, crude, and quite racist language. One editorial, for example, described the Chinese with such colorful phrases as "loathsome, despicable and dangerous," as "a terrible plague," and "an abominable race" (April 5, 1899).

8. Samuel Wong and Manuel Lee, President and English Secretary (interpreter) of the Chinese colony of Nacozari, to State Government, regarding harassment by local authorities, June 5, 1916, and reply of local authorities to State Government on Chinese charges, June 19, 1916, AHGES vol. 3975, pt. 2; various reports from the police commissioner of Lampazos, October 1918, AHGES, vol. 3377; Jim Joe, Chinese businessman of Cananea, bought from Alfonso Charlot, owner of the Triunfo mine, his company store; various documents in 1900 and 1910, in AHGES, vol. 2556.

9. U.S. Consul A. Adee to Department of State, Cananea, July 24, 1915, "Records of the Department of State relating to the Chinese question in Mexico, 1910–1929," Univer-

sity of Arizona Microfilm, documents copies from the U.S. National Archives, General Records of the Department of State, Record Group 59 (hereafter NA Chinese).

10. For more on the anti-Chinese campaigns, see Hu-DeHart (1980).

11. U.S. Consul Bartley Yost to Department of State, Guaymas, January 21, 1920, in NA Chinese; see also Bell (1923).

12. Actually, Governor Calles gathered his information on orders from the Secretary of Gobernación (Internal Affairs) of the federal government. The Department of Labor sent its own commissioner, E. Flores, to the northwestern states of Colima, Nayarit, Sinaloa, and Sonora. He was greatly aided by the Chinese communities themselves, through associations such as the Chinese Fraternal Union. For the State Department report, see AHGES, vol. 3345. Full citation of the Department of Labor report: Departamento de Trabajo. Sección de Conciliación, "Informe que rinde el Jefe de la Sección sobre la situación de las colonias asiáticas en la Costa Occidental de la República," 1919 (E. Flores, comisario), Archivo General de la Nación (México, D.F.), Trabajo.

13. "Confederación de Cámaras Industriales de los Estados Unidos Mexicanos," report on Sonora submitted by State Government, March 17, 1920, AHGES, vol. 3385.

14. Harold Arnold, "Sonora: The golden state of the west coast of Mexico," (mimeograph), AHGES, vol. 3683. The manuscript contains no date, but its content indicates 1921, and it was filed in the 1924 volume in the state archives.

REFERENCES

Bell, P. L. 1923. *Mexican west coast and lower California: A commercial and industrial survey*. Washington, D.C.: Government Printing Office.

Cohen, Lucy M. 1984. *Chinese in the post-civil war south: A people without a history*. Baton Rouge: Louisiana State University Press.

Corral, Ramón. 1891. *Memoria de la administración pública del estado de Sonora*. Guaymas.

Cuba Commission Report. 1993. *The Cuba Commission Report: A hidden history of the Chinese in Cuba: The original English-language text of 1876*. Baltimore: Johns Hopkins University Press.

Cumberland, Charles. 1960. "The Sonora Chinese and the Mexican Revolution." *Hispanic American Historical Review* 40(2)(May): 191–211.

Hu-DeHart, Evelyn. 1980. "Immigrants to a developing society. The Chinese in northern Mexico, 1875–1932." *Journal of Arizona History* 21 (Autumn): 49–85.

———. 1992. "Chinese coolie labor in Cuba and Peru in the nineteenth century: Free labor or neoslavery?" *Journal of Overseas Chinese Studies* 2(2)(April): 149–181.

Pastrana, Juan Jiménez. 1983. *Los chinos en la historia de Cuba, 1847–1930*. Havana: Ed. Ciencias Sociales.

Pérez de la Riva, Juan. 1966. "Demografía de los culies chinos en Cuba (1853–74)." *Revista de la Biblioteca Nacional José Martí* 57(4)(October–December): 57–86.

———. 1978. *El Barracón. Esclavitud y capitalismo en Cuba*. Barcelona: Ed. Crítica.

Rodríguez Pastor, Humberto. 1988. *Hijos del celeste imperio en el Perú (1850–1900). Migración, agricultura, mentalidad y explotación*. Lima: Instituto de Apoyo Agrario.

Salazar Anaya, Delia. 1996. *Población extranjera en México (1895–1990). Un recuento con base en los censos generales de población*. México: Instituto Nacional de Antropología e Historia.

Scott, Rebecca. 1985. *Slave emancipation in Cuba*. Princeton: Princeton University Press.

6

==================================

From Japanese to Nikkei and Back

Integration Strategies of Japanese Immigrants and Their Descendants in Brazil

JEFFREY LESSER

Foundational Fictions

1. In the early 1920s, Hachiro Fukuhara, a wealthy businessperson from Japan, decided to set up a farming colony in the Amazon that would be populated by Japanese immigrants. He returned from an exploratory trip to area north of Blem do Pára, at the mouth of the river, claiming that Brazil was "founded by Asiatics" since "the natives who live along the River Amazon look exactly like the Japanese. There is also a close resemblance between them in manners and customs . . . [and] a certain Chinese secretary in the German Embassy at Rio [has] made a careful study [of language] and concluded that these Indians descended from Mongols." Fukuhara even stated that he knew of a Buddhist ceremony performed in the Himalayas where a woman holds a tree as she is bearing a child and her husband walks around her, exclaiming happily "I saw the same thing in the Amazon."[1]

2. Rokuro Koyama came to Brazil in 1908 on the first ship bringing Japanese immigrants. He was one of the interpreters on the ship, since he spoke some Spanish. He settled in Bauru, a small city in the interior of the state of São Paulo, and was known as the "father of Nikkei journalism" after establishing the *Seishu Shinpo* (*São Paulo Weekly*) in 1921. Koyama became fascinated with Brazil's indigenous population after having a vision of a naked Indian, who "looked like a Japanese," crouching naked on a huge rock alongside a railroad line. This fascination led to a study of the Tupi language and he asked in the introduction to his Tupi-Japanese-Portuguese dictionary: "Did we Japanese and Tupi-Guarani originally come from and share the same Polynesian seed? Do we meet again now, after four thousand years? Was the language of the Tupi-Guarani natives the same as that of the very ancient Japanese?" (Koyama 1951, 1).

3. A large float representing the *Kasato-Maru*, the ship that brought the first Japanese immigrants to Brazil, is preceded by a smaller one topped by a fifteen-foot-high bottle of Sakura soy sauce with giant plastic sushi and sashimi revolving around it. On top is the *sushiman*, a Caucasian painted to "look" Japanese. The dancers are dressed as carnivalized samurais and geishas. Together they sing their samba:

BURAJIRU, MEU JAPÃO BRASILEIRO
MY BRAZILIAN JAPAN

Geishas with patterned kimonos, taught to serve and seduce with love. . . . Monks, warriors, samurai, the Buddha is the religious image and in judo my Brazil is champion. . . . From the country of soccer to the empire of the Rising Sun, I mix sake with samba to make our people happy. I mix sake with samba to make our carnival happy.[2]

Background Meanings

These three foundational fictions all have something in common. Each suggests that Japanese immigrants and their descendants are more "original" or "authentic" Brazilians than members of the European-descended Brazilian elite itself. The reasons are not hard to fathom. Brazil is a country where the social insecurity of the elite is paramount, and thus hyphenated identities simply do not exist. Indeed, for at least the past one hundred years Brazilians have placed successful people in the "white" category, regardless of their skin color. This reflects the widely accepted upper- and middle-class notion that Brazilians whose ancestry is mixed and includes some African heritage are problematic elements in the building of the nation. Japanese-Brazilians, on the other hand, are neither white nor black, and the messages about them have been mixed. On the one hand, we might see integration if we looked at the advertisement for the very popular 1980s soap opera "The Immigrants" that went: "Portuguese, Japanese, Spanish, Italians, Arabs—Don't Miss the Most Brazilian Soap Opera on Television."[3] Yet a different impression emerges when we examine the language that Brazilians use to describe ethnicity: a third-generation Brazilian of Japanese descent remains "Japanese," and not Japanese-Brazilian—put differently, being a Brazilian citizen has never ended the condition of foreignness.

How were Nikkei ethnic identities and perceptions constructed in Brazil during the twenties, thirties, and forties, and how did these function as a kind of mirror in which national identity confronted itself? The temporal boundaries marked a period of enormous demographic change, massive economic growth, and authoritarian rule, and they were also years when what it meant in a public sense to be a "Brazilian" was widely contested. By examining strategies used by Nikkei, I will show how markedly Brazilian national identity was redefined prior to World War II. Nikkei provide a fascinating case study of ethnic negotiation. Between 1908 and 1941, about 190,000 Japanese entered Brazil, and today, more than one million Brazilians claim Japanese descent. Some 200,000 of these self-defined Nikkei currently work in Japan. Nikkei have found wide success in the political, economic, and social spheres; and it was exactly the "non-whiteness and non-blackness" of the group that most challenged elite notions of Brazilian identity (Levy 1974).[4] By examining public Nikkei ethnicity as expressed in the language of the majority (in newspapers and books, on the political stage, and in the academy), I want to suggest that the definitions of virtually all of the components of national identity—ethnicity, class, color, gender, and even the very boundaries of the Brazilian state—were successfully negotiated by certain groups.

There are two main actors in this story. On one side are members of the majority elite, composed of politicians, intellectuals, journalists, and business-people. Almost all were well educated, generally in the same few schools of law and medicine, where they learned about eugenics and other forms of scientific racism. Although this shared learning created a common methodology for understanding the role of immigrants and their descendants in Brazilian society, it did not create a common viewpoint. Instead, the elite was sharply divided between those who saw the "whitening" of Brazil as a goal that would be achieved through the physical transformation of the skin color of the masses and others who saw "whiteness" as related to economic growth and domestic production. For the former, only Europeans could be white and Africans and Asians simply had to be banned from entering; the latter position is best summed up by a federal deputy who declared in 1935, "the Japanese colonists . . . are even whiter than the Portuguese [ones]."[5]

On the other side of the story was an immigrant and minority elite, also composed of politicians, intellectuals, journalists, and businesspeople. They too were well educated, and their goal was to establish a place for their particular group. Like those in the majority, they were markedly divided, and from this three very flexible strategies emerged during the first half of the twentieth century. Prominent among these responses was an apparent auto-decultura-tion, where minorities insisted on their own whiteness, placing themselves neatly into a pantheon of traditionally desirable groups. More measured gestures gravitated toward a bicultural compromise where "whiteness" was not a necessary component of Brazilianness. Instead, these minority elites promoted the idea that Brazil would improve by becoming more "Japanese," formulations that partake of the basic impulse to construct a national hierarchy by identifiable ethnic characteristics. Productivity, class status, and nationalism thus became markers of identity, allowing ethnicity to be maintained even as its importance was dismissed. The final, and most extreme, strategy was an apparent radical ultranationalism, as different groups attempted to recreate an imagined ethnic future. These three strategies all emerged in the early years of the twentieth century and were used by Nikkei and other groups over the next fifty years.

Ethnicity as Strategy

Almost 200,000 Japanese settled in Brazil between 1908 and 1941, helping to create an explosion in Brazilian-Japanese commercial relations. Many exports were produced in immigrant colonies, and just fifteen years after the arrival of the first Japanese settlers rice went from being an import to being one of Brazil's top exports. Yet elite interest in Japanese immigrants and their descendants was not only about production; many desperately wanted to mirror Japanese international status, its powerful military, and its imagined homogenous society, and saw a "Japanized" society as part of the answer.

These impressions of Japan placed Nikkei in a strong position to negotiate their place in Brazil. For example, when Nikkei suggested that Japan's particularly nationalistic culture meant that they were superpatriotic Brazilians, the idea resonated widely among the elite. Thus when Cassio Kenro Shimomoto and José Yamashiro, students at São Paulo's prestigious São Francisco Law School, volunteered for the São Paulo state forces during the unsuccessful 1932 Revolution, they were hailed for their decision, especially after Shimomoto declared to a reporter that he was "before anything . . . a Brazilian."[6] Yamashiro's moment of fame came when São Paulo's largest newspaper published a letter from his farmer father that complimented José "as a Brazilian and Paulista, for obeying the natural impulse to pick up arms to defend his State."[7] The use of the word "natural" is critical here; I think that it really means biological, and that it suggests that nationalistic Brazilians—better Brazilians—would be created through Japanese immigration. Put differently, members of the Japanese "race" had a genetic propensity toward loyalty, and that mystery gene, in the children of immigrants, would make them superpatriotic. Who was a better Brazilian than one whose loyalty to the state was natural?[8]

Nikkei did more than assert their genetic patriotism. They also heavily invested in the promotion of their own whiteness. These notions came to the broader Brazilian public via newspapers, books, and magazines that regularly published photographs of "Brazilian"-looking children who were, at least ostensibly, of Japanese and Euro–Brazilian parentage.[9] The photos were uniform: Japanese men married to white Brazilian women who had produced white children. Each gave the message that Japanese immigrants were an elite, only interested in, and able to attract, those of high racial status. Japanese immigrants were whitening Brazil even as they made it more productive. As Bruno Lobo, a professor at the Rio de Janeiro Medical School, noted in a book published by the Brazilian government, "it is not an exaggeration to say that more than 94,000 Nipo-Brazilian children have already been born, children of resident Japanese immigrants, almost 100,000 little future Brazilians" (Lobo 1935, 144).

Whereas whiteness and genetic patriotism seem obvious ways in which a group might assert its place within the Brazilian nation, the use of ultranationalism targeted toward other countries might not. Yet a number of seemingly non-Brazilian nationalist movements became critical to the negotiations over national identity in the first part of the last century. Japanese nationalism, a phenomenon that was strong since the early part of the century among immigrants and Nikkei, showed its most public face after Brazil ended its flirtation with fascism and joined the Allies in 1942. An official "Brazilianization" campaign banned foreign-language schools and newspapers and led to intense anti-Japanese propaganda. Bela Lugosi's *Yellow Peril* played to large crowds in São Paulo, Zero scares were common, and anti-Japanese lyrics found their way into popular songs.[10]

Some immigrants and Nikkei responded to these challenges by keeping as low a profile as possible; but others responded to the racist policies and discourse by forming secret societies that insisted that Japan won the war. What makes these groups particularly interesting is their size—they claimed over 150,000 members—and that their influence exploded *after* World War II ended. How, in 1946 and 1947 and 1948, could 150,000 literate people living in Brazil believe that Japan had won the war? The technical reasons are that the idea of Japan's defeat had little resonance among immigrants, since the Japanese-language media was banned and few in rural areas had access to Brazilian newspapers or newsreels (Kumusaka and Saito 1970, 169). This meant that secret newspapers found a willing audience among the many immigrants educated to believe in Japan's superiority and invincibility.

One did not have to "believe" that Japan had won the war, of course, to support the societies in their demand for a space for Japanese-Brazilian ethnicity. Indeed, secret societies were a counterattack on the way national identity was defined. The most powerful was the Shindo Renmei (Way of the Subjects of the Emperor's League), which emerged in late 1945. The society's initial goals were to maintain a permanent Japanized space in Brazil through the preservation of language, culture, and religion among Nikkei and the reestablishment of Japanese schools.[11] What the Shindo Renmei did *not* promote was a return to Japan. Home was Brazil, and by the end of 1945 the group had 50,000 members who believed, or claimed to believe, that Japan had won the war.[12] News of Japan's defeat was dismissed as nothing more than U.S. propaganda, and just a week after Emperor Hirohito broadcast his surrender message, the Shindo Renmei released its own statement:

Emperor Hirohito has been forced to abdicate in favor of a Regent. . . .
The Imperial combined fleet has been given the order for immediate
action, and in a furious battle in Okinawan waters the Japanese Navy
and Air Force destroyed about four hundred Allied warships, thus
deciding the course of the war. The Japanese employed for the first
time their secret weapon, the "High Frequency Bomb." Only one of the
bombs killed more than one hundred thousand American soldiers on
Okinawa. [This led to the] "unconditional surrender of the Allies (and)
the landing of Japanese expeditionary forces in the United States."[13]

The "news" spread quickly, and by mid-1946 the Shindo Renmei claimed 130,000
members, and its propaganda included altered photos of President Truman
bowing to Emperor Hirohito and "press" reports of Japanese troops landing in
San Francisco and marching toward New York.[14] When a group of prominent
Nikkei circulated the actual surrender documents they were accused of being
traitors, and the community quickly divided into two camps: the *kachigumi*
(victorist) and *makegumi* (defeatist), who called themselves *esclarecidos* in
Portuguese (clear-headed or enlightened) (Handa 1987, 651–655).

What brought the Shindo Renmei to the attention of the wider public was
a series of killings by young people recruited to assassinate community members who publicly insisted that Japan had lost the war. The press sensation grew
still more when captured Shindo Renmei members insisted that "Japan did not
lose the war. As long as there is one Japanese on earth, even if he is the last,
Japan will never surrender" (Handa 1987, 673). Not all Nikkei agreed with these
tactics, and Brazil's government, itself in a moment of transition after Vargas
was forced to leave office in 1945, was equally concerned about its inability to
control the hostilities. Thus, in mid-1946, four hundred Shindo Renmei leaders
were arrested, and Brazilian diplomats had the new Japanese government prepare documents outlining the Allied victory. The papers, however, were immediately dismissed as false.[15]

The Brazilian government had a number of options in dealing with the situation. They could have ignored it as an internal "Japanese problem," since
political killings were, and are, far from atypical in Brazil. They could have sent
out the army, made mass arrests, and imposed martial law in communities with
large Japanese and Nikkei populations. Yet this is not what happened. Rather,
in July 1946, one of Brazil's most powerful politicians, José Carlos de Macedo
Soares, invited police, military officials, diplomats, and Shindo Renmei members, including those in jail, to a friendly meeting at the governor's palace.
Imagine the scene: one of the two or three most important politicos in Brazil
taking four hundred people out of jail, putting them in the same room with
other leaders of a secret of society that claimed 130,000 members, and calling

them "the most important part of the Brazilian population." Those in the audience understood the rules of the game, and Sachiko Omasa laid out the deal: "We Japanese do not believe . . . in Japan's defeat. If Your Excellency want [*sic*] to end the disputes and terrorist acts, begin by spreading word of Japan's victory and order that all false propaganda about defeat be stopped."[16]

At this point Macedo Soares could have dismissed the Shindo Renmei as a bunch of kooks, but he did nothing of the sort. Instead he prohibited newspapers from publishing news of Japan's defeat and ordered the term "unconditional surrender" taken out of all official communications. The killings stopped, and large-scale Nikkei efforts to raise funds for Japanese victims of the war helped to marginalize the extreme "victorist" groups. The last gasp came in early 1950, when the Japanese Olympic swimming champions arrived in Brazil. An exhibition match at a major soccer arena was a sellout and included the presence of the governor of São Paulo. But during an interview the swimmers expressed shock when presented with the idea that Japan had *won* the war. As a result the remaining Shindo Renmei activists began a poster campaign claiming the swimmers were Koreans masquerading as Japanese.[17] The suggestion was ludicrous, and public support for the secret societies ended, in large part because a space, albeit a contested one, for Nikkei had emerged in postwar Brazil.

Conclusions?

This chapter, although not intended as a critique of the "diasporic" or "displacement" approach that many scholars of ethnicity or immigration take, does not fit comfortably into those models. Indeed, I have tried here to show that "Brazilian" part of the implicit hyphen in the word "Nikkei" is much stronger than the "Japanese" part that was, among those born in Brazil, imagined in the Andersonian sense (Anderson 1983). When discussing ethnicity in Brazil's public sphere, members of the Nikkei elite *were* Brazilians, using widely accepted national discourses to widen spaces for ethnicity within national identity. The subject of this article cracked open and reassembled the discourses on Brazilian identity through strategic negotiations of race, ethnicity, and nation.

The question remains, however, whether Brazilian national identity includes Nikkei. Certainly the narrow national paradigm of a "white" or "European" Brazil was expanded during the first half of the twentieth century, as the notion that ethnicity and Brazilian citizenship could coexist became increasingly accepted. Yet all this took place within a context of open prejudice. In a new research project that focuses on post-World War II Brazil, I am examining how ethnicity was transformed during the age of industrialization, hyperinflation, and military dictatorship. My preliminary work suggests that in many ways success and discrimination go hand in hand. In the last fifteen years, for example, some quarter of a million Nikkei have settled in Japan, and many speak of discrimination at home and a search for identity as motivations for migration. At the same time, assertion of whiteness by minority groups carries a racism of its own, and it appears that a strong feature of the postwar minority struggle against discrimination was an aggressive mimicking of the racism of the majority.

Are the situations that I have focused on in this article more than symbolic? For me, the answer is a resounding yes. In the postwar period, to marry a Brazilian of Japanese descent became a positive action, regardless of the class status of the individuals involved. The Brazilian state promotes itself by using images of certain ethnic groups, and a major bank has advertised itself for the last twenty-five years with a close-up of a Nikkei and the caption "We need more Brazilians like this Japanese." A powerful federal politician, whose leftist politics and Okinawan parents insure his lack of Nikkei support, recently discussed his successful campaign strategy with me. "I need to remind voters," he told me, that "Japanese are the best possible Brazilians: honest, hard-working, and well-connected." This is just the most recent formulation of the great Brazilian paradox—that policies constructed to remake Brazil as "white" in fact created a multicultural society. Today the Nikkei and Syrian-Lebanese communities are broadly successful in the economic, political, military, and artistic arenas. Both groups seem more part of the Brazilian nation than do, for example, Afro-Brazilians or Polish-Brazilians.[18]

Examining the different strategies used by Nikkei to negotiate their Brazilianness reminds me of Griel Marcus's comment that history is the result "of moments that seem to leave nothing behind, nothing but the spectral connections of people long separated by place and time, but somehow speaking the same language" (Marcus 1989, 4). The connections here are indeed spectral: Were Japanese white? If Amazonian Indians had descended biologically from Japanese ancestors, were new immigrants from Asia more Brazilian than most members of the European-descended elite? In the end, Brazil emerged as a nation that is multicultural but hyphenless.

NOTES

This article is an abridged and modified version of Lesser (1999), chapters 4 and 5.

1. Hachiro Fukuhara, "Brazil founded by Asiatics?" in the *Japan Times and Mail*, June 26, 1927. The Kanegafuchi Cotton-Spinning Company was known for its innovative use of dormitories and health services as a means of maintaining female labor; "Nipponese gets 2,500,000 acres as a basis for a vast colony." *Japan Times and Mail*, May 11, 1930.

2. Sociedade Educativa e Recreativa Escola de Samba, Unidos do Cabuçu, Rio de Janiero Carnival, 1994.

3. Advertisement for the Bandeirantes Television Network tele-novela "Os Imigrantes" (1981) in *Jornal do Imigrante* 4(422) (September 1981): 2.

4. "Discriminação por Nacionalidade dos Imigrantes Entrando no Brasil no Período 1884–1939." *Revista de Imigracão e Colonização* 1(3)(July 1940): 617–638.

5. Speech of Acylino de Leão, September 18, 1935. Republica dos Estados Unidos do Brasil, *Annaes da Camara dos Deputados: Sessões de 16 a 24 de Setembro de 1935*, vol. 17 (Rio de Janeiro: Off. Graphica d' "A Noite," 1935), 432.

6. *Brasil e Japão* (1934), 238–240.

7. *O estado de São Paulo*, September 19, 1932. Yamashiro (1996), 111–117.

8. *Nippak Shinbun* (São Paulo), July 1932.

9. *Folha da Manhã* (São Paulo), July 5, 1934; Lobo (1926), 159; Calvino Filho (1934), 17, 33, 97, 112; *Cruzamento da ethnia japoneza* (1934).

10. *Diário da Noite* (São Paulo), September 30, 1942.

11. Hekisui Yoshii, "Gokuchû kaiko-roku" [Memories from prison], manuscript, 1948. Cited in translation by Susumu Miyao and José Yamashiro, "A comunidade nipônica no período da guerra" in Comissão de Elaboração da História dos 80 Anos da Imigração Japonesa no Brasil (1992), 262. Translation of Shindo Renmei documents can be found in "Perigosa atividade nipônica em São Paulo" *Arquivos da Polícia Civil de São Paulo* 8:2 (1944): 567–571. Willems and Saito (1947), 143. Two excellent studies of the Shindo Renmei and similar movements are Maeyama (1970), and Miyao and Yamashiro, cited above, 265–360.

12. See translation of Shindo Renmei objectives and statutes in report of João André Dias Paredes to Major Antonio Pereira Lira (State Police Chief, Paraná), April 30, 1949. Secretaria de Estado de Segurança Pública, Departamento da Polícia Civil, Divisão de Segurança e Informações. No. 1971—Sociedade Terrorista Japonesa. Arquivo Público Paraná, Curitiba. Botelho de Miranda (1948), 11. Tigner (1954), 42.

13. Article by José Yamashiro in *Paulista Shinbun* (São Paulo), April 29, 1947. Translated and reprinted in Tigner (1954), 44.

14. *O estado de S. Paulo*, March 26, 1946; *Correio da manhã*, April 6, 1946; *A Noite* (Rio de Janeiro), April 13, 1946. Neves (1960), 97, 124.

15. "As atividades das sociedades secretas japonesas e ação repressiva da polícia de São Paulo, publicadas pela impressa." *Arquivos da Polícia Civil de São Paulo* 12(2)(1946): 523–530.

16. Information on the meeting from: *A Gazeta* (São Paulo), July 20, 1946; *Jornal de São Paulo*, July 20, 1946; Miyao and Yamashiro, "A Comunidade Enfrenta um Caos sem Precedentes," 300–305.

17. *Folha da Noite* (São Paulo), March 21, 1950. Handa (1987), 746–752.

18. *Folha de São Paulo*, October 19, 1995. Fausto, Truzzi, Grün, and Sakurai (1995). *Vida e Sangue de Polacko*, documentary film directed by Silvio Back (Curitiba, Paraná), in Coleção Silvio Back, Museu de Imagen e Som, São Paulo, C 309/93. Ianni (1972), 169–198.

REFERENCES

Anderson, Benedict. 1983. *Imagined Communities: Reflections on the Origin and Spread of Nationalism*. London: Verso.

Botelho de Miranda, Mário. 1948. *Shindo Renmei: Terrorismo e Extorsão*. São Paulo: Edição Saraiva.

Brasil e Japão: Duas civilizações que se Completam. 1934. São Paulo: Empreza Graphica da "Revista dos Tribunaes."

Calvino Filho, ed. 1934. *Factos e opinões sobre a immigração japoneza*. Rio de Janeiro: n.p.

Comissão de Elaboração da História dos 80 Anos da Imigração Japonesa no Brasil. 1992. *Uma epopéia moderna: 80 anos da imigração japonesa no Brasil.* São Paulo: Editora Hucitec.

Cruzamento da ethnia japoneza: Hypothese de que o japonez não se cruza com outra ethnia. 1934. São Paulo: Centro Nipponico de Cultura.

Fausto, Boris, Oswaldo Truzzi, Roberto Grün, and Célia Sakurai. 1995. "Imigração e política em São Paulo." São Paulo: Editora Sumaré/FAPESP.

Handa, Tomoo. 1987. *O imigrante japonês: História de sua vida no brasil.* São Paulo: T. A. Queiroz: Centro de Estudos Nipo-Brasilieros.

Ianni, Octavio. 1972. *Raças e classes socias no Brasil.* Rio de Janeiro: Editora Civilização Brasileira.

Koyama, Rokuro. 1951. *Tupi tango shu* [The Tupi lexicon]. São Paulo: Teikoku Shoin.

Kumusaka, Y., and H. Saito. 1970. "Kachigumi: A collective delusion among the Japanese and their descendants in Brazil." *Canadian Psychiatric Association Journal* 15(2): 167–175.

Lesser, Jeffrey. 1999. *Negotiating national identity: Immigrants, minorities and the struggle for ethnicity in Brazil.* Durham: Duke University Press.

Levy, Maria Stella Ferreira. 1974. "O Papel da migração internacional na evolução da população brasileira (1872 a 1972)." *Revista de Saúde Pública*, supplement 8: 49–90.

Lobo, Bruno. 1926. *Japonezes no Japão-no Brasil.* Rio de Janeiro: Imprensa Nacional.

———. 1935. *Esquecendo os antepassados: Combatendo os estrangeiros.* São Paulo: Editorial Alba Ltda.

Maeyama, Takashi. 1970. "Ethnicity, secret societies and associations: The Japanese in Brazil." *Comparative Studies in Society and History* 15 (April): 589–610.

Marcus, Greil. 1989. *Lipstick Traces: A Secret History of the Twentieth Century.* Cambridge: Harvard University Press.

Neves, Herculano. 1960. *O processo da "Shindo-Renmei" e demais associações secretas japonesas.* São Paulo: n.p.

Republica dos Estados Unidos do Brasil. 1935. *Annaes da Camara dos Deputados: Sessões de 16 a 24 de Setembro de 1935.* Vol. 17. Rio de Janeiro: Off. Graphica d' "A Noite."

Tigner, James L. 1954. "The Okinawans in Latin America." *Scientific Investigations in the Ryuku Island (SIRI)* Report 7. Washington, D.C.: Pacific Science Board—National Research Council, Department of Army.

Willems, Emilio, and Hiroshi Saito. 1947. "Shindo Renmei: Um problema de Aculturação." *Sociologia* 9: 133–152.

Yamashiro, Jos. 1996. *Trajetória de duas vidas: Uma história de imigração e integração.* São Paulo: Aliana Cultural Brasil-Japão/Centro de Estudos Nipo-Brasileiros.

7

===

In the Black Pacific

Testimonies of Vietnamese Afro-Amerasian Displacements

BERNARD SCOTT LUCIOUS

American critical inquiries of the lived-experience of blackness continue to explore the inherent heterogeneity of African diasporas, yet such inquiries focus almost exclusively within a specific spatio-temporal site.[1] This transnational and transcultural site, which is more commonly known today as the "Black Atlantic," is a symptomatic formation of the transculturation of many African diasporic cultures, linked primarily by the history of the Atlantic slave trade: it overlaps and connects black cultures in the Caribbean, Europe, Africa, and the Americas.[2] Beyond the Black Atlantic, however, another counterhegemonic discourse emerges and calls attention to the need for American literary and cultural studies to map the lived-experience of blackness in terms of its roots in and routes through Asian diasporas. Informed by the lived-experience of blackness of Afro-Amerasians—the mixed-heritage children born of both African American and Asian parentages—the emergent Afro-Amerasian discourse indexes a spatio-temporal site beyond the Atlantic that is not exclusively African-American nor Asian-American, African diasporic nor Asian diasporic, but is all of these at once; it points to an emergent site of critical inquiry which I've named the "Black Pacific."

"Black Pacific" is introduced in this essay as a neologism, which discursively names an emergent site of critical inquiry and cultural space at the interstices of three diasporas. The first diaspora is informed by the experiences of African-American men (of the Black Atlantic) who served and continue to serve in the United States military throughout the Asia-Pacific.[3] Ever since Commodore Matthew Calbraith Perry led the first United States naval expedition to Asia (1852–1855), blacks have participated in the American empire's military operations and ventures in the Asia-Pacific. In his personal journal, Perry noted that when he reached Edo (Tokyo) Bay in 1853, two black guards escorted him;

together, they proceeded to march into the city to meet the emperor (see Perry and Pineau 1968). Since the Perry expedition, black men have continued to serve in the American military in the Asia-Pacific, throughout the wars there: the Spanish American War, World War II, and the Korean and Vietnam wars.

The second diaspora is informed by the experiences of Asian women who have had affairs with American military men, or who have become either "military brides" or "Asian-American immigrants" as a result of the American empire's presence in the Asia-Pacific. In *The Politics of Life: Four Plays by Asian American Women*, Velina Hasu Houston (1993) explains that Asian women faced the difficult challenge of loving their American men, whether black or white, while attempting to remain loyal to their people; because the American empire's presence was challenged by the Asian people, interracial affairs were complicated by not only the taboo of interracial sexuality but also the expectation of national allegiance among Asians. Consequently, Asian women who had interracial relationships with African-American men were often accused of being traitors of their race and nation.

The third diaspora is informed by the experiences of the Afro-Amerasian children born to African-American men and Asian women throughout the Asia-Pacific, since as early as the Spanish-American war in the Philippines (see Shade 1980, 23).[4] The Black Pacific, therefore, is a site of critical inquiry that is not only interracial (shaped by the interracial relationships between African-Americans and Asians, and the Afro-Amerasian offspring of such relationships), but it is also interdiasporic.[5]

What I am calling here "Black Pacific" is an example of what James Clifford (1997) recognizes as a translational term. "[U]sed for comparison in a strategic and contingent way," the translational term is a comparative concept that signifies cross-cultural exchanges, linkages, or identities that emerge as two or more cultures converge; such terms, as identified by Clifford, include "diaspora," "borderland," "immigration," "migrancy," "tourism," "pilgrimage," "exile," and "travel" (11). "Black Pacific," like these translational terms, is shaped by what Clifford describes as "cultural processes that complicate, cross, and cross-up national boundaries" (39). The (inter)diasporic, (trans)cultural processes, which transgress national boundaries within the Black Pacific, call attention to the need to rethink, conjoin, and therefore translate other translational terms such as "Black Atlantic," "Asia-Pacific," and "American Pacific."[6] As a translational term, "Black Pacific" denotes the convergence of African and Asian diasporic spaces. Furthermore, it connotes that blackness (African Americanness) is a constitutive dimension of Asian and Asian American Studies, and yellowness (Asianness) of African American Studies. Although my usage of "Black Pacific" as a translational term begins by defining it with respect to black existence in the Asia-Pacific since the emergence of the American empire, I redefine it more broadly to embrace not only the histories of Afro-Amerasians and African Americans but also the histories of indigenous blacks throughout the Asia-Pacific.[7]

Thinking about the lived-experience of blackness in the Black Pacific, particularly the ways in which it has been marked by the displacement of black bodies, this discussion focuses on the testimonies of Vietnamese Afro-Amerasians, which are, I believe, among the most revealing texts informing the Afro-Amerasian discourse; these testimonies appear in *Children of the Enemy: Oral Histories of Vietnamese Amerasians and Their Mothers*, published by Stephen DeBonis in 1995. In *Children of the Enemy*, the term "Amerasian" is used to identify all Amerasians—those born of both European-American and African-American heritages, collectively. Although I also use the term "Amerasian" to denote the collective—Amerasians of all heritages—I employ the prefixes Euro- and Afro- to differentiate between white/Euro-Amerasians (those of European American heritage) and black/Afro-Amerasians (those of African American heritage). Although *Children of the Enemy* includes both Euro-Amerasians and Afro-Amerasians, my discussion is limited to the testimonies of Afro-Amerasians, not only because they provide a unique opportunity for exploring and mapping an unexplored terrain (throughout the Black Pacific, particularly black existence in Vietnam), but especially because Afro-Amerasian testimonies give voice to experiences specific to the black body. For example, the testimony of a man named Vu explains, "In Vietnam, people always look at me strange because I am different. Even if I am reading a book or a newspaper, I catch people looking at me because I am a black boy. The Vietnamese look down more on the black Amerasian than the white. I don't know why, but I know it is so" (120). In another example, a woman named Pha adds to Vu's testimony about the Vietnamese Afro-Amerasian struggle with antiblack racism in Vietnam: "I didn't go to school [in Vietnam], I was embarrassed of my skin. I started to go in Long Anh, but the students always insulted me, called me 'black girl.' People always talked bad about me because I was black. . . . My family didn't love me, they didn't love my mother. They looked down [upon] us. Before [the fall of Saigon to the Vietcong in] '75, it was not so bad, but after '75, the family didn't want to keep me at home. They were scared of the VC, they wanted to send me away where nobody could see me" (105–106). These testimonies reveal that Vietnamese Afro-Amerasians experienced the heaviest load of discrimination in Vietnam (see DeBonis 1995, 14).

Focusing on the testimonies of Vietnamese Afro-Amerasians in *Children of the Enemy*, this chapter attempts to understand and map the lived-experience of blackness in Vietnam, and the ways in which it has been burdened and conditioned by the displacement of Vietnamese Afro-Amerasian bodies (black bodies) throughout the Black Pacific (in Vietnam and throughout the Asia-Pacific).

It begins by defining the Vietnamese Afro-Amerasian testimony as a "black testimony" and explores the conditions of its emergence within the Asian diaspora. Second, it delineates a cultural-historical contextualization of intrarace racism—or "colorism"—in Vietnam, drawing attention to the testimonies' revelation of Vietnamese discrimination toward (the "blackness" of) Afro-Amerasians. Finally, it traces the pervasiveness of colorism in Vietnamese culture throughout several contact zones—cultural spaces where Vietnamese Afro-Amerasians are confronted by colorism. This essay argues that the multiplicity of Vietnamese Afro-Amerasian displacements is rooted in the pervasiveness of colorism in Vietnam and is routed through several contact zones. By examining the testimonies as discursive markers of the roots and routes of Vietnamese Afro-Amerasian displacements, it argues that the testimonies collectively index the constellation of contact zones, and mark the interdiasporic site of critical inquiry that I am calling here the Black Pacific. The central underlying claim is that Vietnamese Afro-Amerasian testimonies tell the story of black resilience in the Black Pacific: how the displaced black body, in any given contact zone, has agency and the capacity to (re)define itself; specifically, how it has endured, resisted, subverted, or simply survived the colorism in Vietnam. These testimonies bear witness to the survival strategies used to withstand the challenges of the lived-experience of blackness in cultures of the Asian diaspora, and more specifically, the Vietnamese diaspora.[8]

Black Testimony

"Black testimony," which bears witness to one's personal struggle against antiblack racism, has traditionally been understood as a distinctive literature of the African diaspora.[9] That distinction, however, is challenged by Vietnamese Afro-Amerasian testimonies, which reveal that black testimonies must also be recognized as a distinctive literature of the Asian diaspora. The emergent testimonies of Vietnamese Afro-Amerasians are first-person accounts that provide provocative glimpses of the lived-experience of blackness within postwar Vietnam, and in a much broader context, throughout postcolonial, postimperial, and postwar Asia.

Revealing the complexities of the lived-experience of blackness in Asia, Vietnamese Afro-Amerasian testimonies occasion several questions. Two implicit questions are: What is a black testimony and what are the conditions of its emergence within the Asian diaspora, particularly, within a postwar, Vietnamese, diasporic culture? Raising the question of the meaning of "black testimony" at the outset, this discussion invokes multiple definitions. For Natasha Tarpley, the black testimony is a critical practice in which one tells a story about one's survival and endurance of antiblack racism; she adds that it is a story that opens a discursive space for learning about, accepting, affirming, and loving one's blackness. In *Testimony*, Tarpley explains that her understanding of "testimony" was derived

> from the verb to testify: to bear witness, to bring forth, to claim and pro-claim oneself as an intrinsic part of the world. The act of testifying or giv-ing testimony has deep roots in African American history, reaching back to slavery (and before), to the places our ancestors created—behind somebody's wood cabin doubling as a makeshift church or meeting house, or in a nearby clearing—where they opened themselves out to one another, showed their scars, spoke of their day-to-day life, their hopes and dreams, prayed to their God, and tried to remember everything they had lost. Testifying, although it has strong religious connotations, has also performed the important secular function of providing means by which the slave could make herself visible, in a society which had ren-dered her invisible; by which he could explore the sound of his voice when he had been rendered silent . . . testimony is not only a way to com-mune with one's Creator, but is also a way to define and redefine one's humanity; to ground oneself in community; to revel in the touch of hands and bodies familiar with the testifier's pain or joy. . . . And it is these simple gestures—touching and being touched, raising up one's voice—that helped to fill in the frame of the [black] body. (1995, 2–3)

While Tarpley recognizes both religious and secular connotations, she shows that the black testimony has evolved as a secular, discursive activity through which one bears witness to an audience or community sympathetic to black lived-experiences. Her recognition of the black testimony's nonreligious func-tion is supported by Geneva Smitherman (1977), who explains that "testifyin" is a concept that "came out of the black church"; however, in the secular world, it is a "concept referring to a ritualized form of black communication in which the speaker gives verbal witness to the efficacy, truth, and power, or some experi-ence in which all blacks have shared" (58). Tarpley's "black testimony" is understood as the act, or process, of telling a story by which one defines, rede-fines, proclaims and affirms one's black body. It enables the black body to become visible, to be heard, to commune, and to legitimize its existence.

For Henry Louis Gates, the black testimony is the critical practice of inscribing one's individual "race history" in language, and thereby adding to a "collective history of 'the race'" (1991, 4). He explains, "If the individual black self could not exist before the law, it could, and would be forged in language as a testimony at once to the supposed integrity of the black self and against the social and political evils that delimited individual and group equality for all African-Americans" (4). Gates's "black testimony" is a counterhegemonic activ-ity, not only because it goes against the grain of the law and of other social and political evils, but also because it goes against the grain of major literary genres, "while fiction would seem to be the major genre practiced by black writers today, the impulse to testify, to chart the peculiar contours of the individual protagonist on the road to becoming, clearly undergirds even the fictional tradition of black letters, as the predominance of the first person form attests" (4).

Building on these definitions, the Vietnamese Afro-Amerasian testimony can be understood as a critical practice that bears witness to one's struggle against antiblack racism in Vietnamese cultures. It is a first-person representation of the lived-experience of blackness in language, and is a counterhegemonic activity by which Vietnam's black bodies subvert the dominant discursive practices that pose a nihilistic threat and render its invisibility in culture. Vietnamese Afro-Amerasian testimonies, however, represent a critical departure from the tradition of black testimonies imagined above: they testify about the displacement of black bodies in the Black Pacific, beyond black communities and cultures traditionally linked to the African diaspora, throughout cultures of the Asian diaspora. This critical departure, which shifts the framework of black critical inquiry beyond the African diaspora and into the Asian, raises the question (the second implicit one mentioned above): What are the conditions of the emergence of Vietnamese Afro-Amerasian testimonies—black testimonies—in a postwar, Vietnamese, diasporic culture?

The emergence of Vietnamese Afro-Amerasian testimonies has been conditioned, primarily, by the Congressional passing of the Amerasian Homecoming Act in 1987. Twelve years after the fall of Saigon and the U.S. military's withdrawal from Vietnam, this act permitted Vietnamese Amerasians to enter the U.S. as immigrants, "while at the same time granting them refugee benefits such as pre-entry, English-as-a-Second-Language training in the Philippine Refugee Processing Center [PRPC] and resettlement assistance in the United States" (DeBonis 1995, 3). Between 1982 and 1988, the Orderly Departure Program brought approximately 11,500 Vietnamese Amerasians and their relatives out of Vietnam; with the passing of the Amerasian Homecoming Act, that number jumped to 67,028 in 1991. Displaced, transnationally, from their Vietnamese homeland, and en route to the United States, black and white Amerasians spent some time in the Philippines at the PRPC where Stephen DeBonis, one of the Americans working at the site, interviewed them. Reflecting upon his interviews with Amerasians, DeBonis explains:

My own interest lies not in numbers of departures and cases processed, but in the stories behind them. From 1982 to 1992, I worked in the Philippine Refugee Processing Center in Bataan [Philippines] as a supervisor in a State Department-funded educational program. This program was mandated to prepare U.S.-bound refugees for life in America. Three hundred and seventeen thousand Khmer, Lao, Hmong,

Vietnamese and Amerasians passed through the center from its inception in 1980 to December 1991, to take five-month courses in English-as-a-Second-Language (ESL), Cultural Orientation, and Work Orientation, prior to resettlement in the United States. Amerasians and accompanying family members began trickling into the PRPC in 1985. (1995, 3)

Between 1991 and 1992, DeBonis conducted over one hundred interviews; some of the interviews were translated and included in *Children of the Enemy*.

Discursively, a process of multiple dimensions has conditioned the emergence of Vietnamese Afro-Amerasian testimonies. These testimonies stem from not only the Amerasians' willingness to testify in an interview; more complexly, they stem from a process compounded further by practices other than the testimony, yet specific to the interview: transcription (from oral to written), translation (from Vietnamese to English), compilation (by Stephen DeBonis, in book form), publication (as a new text of American literature), and appropriation (in this chapter, and throughout my critical inquiry of Afro-Amerasians in the Black Pacific). This discursive multiplicity (or discursive process of multiple dimensions) provides a framework for thinking about the issue of agency: who, in fact, is speaking through the Vietnamese Afro-Amerasian testimonies? Although Vietnamese Afro-Amerasian agency is formulated as the Vietnamese Afro-Amerasians are testifying, telling their own stories of black resiliency in the Black Pacific, it subsequently takes the form of (and is framed by) the discursive multiplicity. Therefore, Vietnamese Afro-Amerasian agency is multidiscursive—it stems from the testimonies of Vietnamese Afro-Amerasians, yet it is mutually implicated in the discursive practices and agencies of others (such as the Vietnamese-to-English translation of the interview translator, the editorial inclusion or exclusion of DeBonis's compilation, or the mapping of the Black Pacific throughout my own critical inquiry).

Within the Vietnamese Afro-Amerasian testimonies, the discursive multiplicity signifies a mixture not only of agencies but also and especially of languages and cultures; each testimony can also be understood in terms of its "accent"—mixture of multiple languages (English and Vietnamese) and cultures (African-America and Vietnam). The inherent Vietnamese Afro-Amerasian accent of (these black testimonies) points to Mikhail Bakhtin's linguistic model of hybridity (see Young 1995, 20). Invoking Bakhtin, I am suggesting that these black testimonies challenge us (American audiences, communities sympathetic to the struggles of black lived-experiences) to hear and to reflect critically upon the (bicultural) accent of (Vietnamese Afro-Amerasian) critical practices and cultural productions in the Asian diaspora. Each Vietnamese Afro-Amerasian testimony should be heard/read as "a mixture of two social languages within the limits of a single utterance . . . an utterance that belongs to a single speaker, but that actually contains mixed within it two utterances, two speech manners, two styles, two 'languages', two belief systems" (cited in Young 1995, 20). The complexity of the Vietnamese Afro-Amerasian accent, for example, is echoed in the poignant testimony of a woman named Mai Linh:

> You can call me Mai Linh. I'm from Cam Ranh. My card says I'm twenty-two, but I'm really twenty-five. . . . In Cam Ranh [my mother] lived together with one "soul brother," black. That man be my father. . . . He was in the army, airborne, the Thirty-third. That's all my mother told me. Before, my mother had pictures, had a paper that say she stay with him. . . .
>
> When the VC [Vietcong] were coming, she heard that they would look for the white baby, the black baby, the American baby. They want to know who is the woman that stay with the Americans. So my mother be scared, she burn all the pictures, all papers. Because VC say he hate Americans, he don't like no girl who worked for the Americans, got baby American. He say if he sees black American or white American, he gonna kill them. . . .
>
> [O]ut of many American black and white [Vietnamese Amerasian] children, tens and thousands, only have ten who go to study. The Vietnamese talk bad, they beat American children, they slap them. They say, "You a black girl, you a white man, how come you don't go to America? How come you live here?" Make anybody feel bad, that's why we don't want to study. . . . I don't want to go [to school] because they call me "black," they make me feel bad inside. (DeBonis 1995, 110–111)

As this testimony suggests, multiple domains of difference (for example, American/Vietnamese and racial purity/racial impurity) have conditioned the Vietnamese Afro-Amerasian accent. Mai Linh's testimony explains that both black and white Amerasians experienced Vietnamese racism in these domains of difference: they were despised, targeted, and threatened by the Vietcong; taunted, slapped, and beaten by other Vietnamese people; and ultimately, prompted to leave their mothers' Vietnamese homeland and flee to their fathers' American homeland.

The Vietnamese racism against which Mai Linh testifies is informed by the popular stereotype that black and white Vietnamese Amerasians are the illegitimate children born to the American enemy and Vietnamese bar girls or prostitutes. In another passage in DeBonis's book, Mai Linh recalls a direct confrontation with this stereotype of illegitimacy: "one Vietnamese girl, she talks bad to me and my friend Hue. She say, 'I don't like black girl, I don't like white girl, because their father American, because their mother be bad, be a whore.' So I slap her" (110). Because postwar Vietnam looked down upon black and white Amerasian bodies as signifiers of illegitimacy, it was not uncommon for Amerasians to testify about the legitimacy of their parents' unions, and to affirm the legitimacy of interracial affairs and interracial identities in Vietnam. Mai Linh, for example, testifies that she was neither the product of simply a casual encounter nor of prostitution, but instead, she was a legitimate Amerasian; also, that her mother lived together with the African-American man ("soul brother") who was her father, and that her mother "had pictures, had a paper that say she stay with him." Delegitimization is just one example of the many forms of racism that posed everyday challenges to Amerasians in postwar Vietnam; however, other forms existed and posed different challenges. Mai Linh's experience with delegitimization is mentioned here in order to suggest that the Vietnamese Afro-Amerasian testimony is a practice of legitimization, which "affirm[s] the legitimacy of interracial affairs and interracial identities in Vietnam."

Although both black and white Amerasians experienced delegitimization and encountered many forms of Vietnamese racism, the Amerasians of African-American descent encountered antiblack racism that was believed to have caused greater suffering and heavier burdens. One Vietnamese woman, the mother of both a black and white Amerasian, contends that anti-black racism posed a heavier burden, and observes that black bodies were more often at risk of displacement than white bodies: "Vietnamese say, 'You go back to America, you dirty American, go back to America. You lose the war already, go back.' They say like that many times to my daughter, 'cause she is black. My son is white, not so many problems" (5). This mother's contention that the burdens of antiblack racism were greater than antiwhite racism is supported by Huong's testimony. She contends, "All my life people had been mean to me there [in Vietnam] because of my color. My skin is black, and my hair is curly, not like the Vietnamese, and they didn't like that" (5).

Black and white Amerasians whom DeBonis interviewed at the PRPC experienced (trans)national displacement—they were uprooted and forced beyond Vietnam's national border, traveled through the Philippines, and then eventually migrated into the United States; their immediate family members accompanied many of them, and collectively, they represented one dimension of the Vietnamese diaspora. "Displacement," in the context of mass migrations from postwar Vietnam, across national borders, throughout cultures of the Vietnamese diaspora, signifies a *transgression* of a national border. Although this diaspora can be understood as a symptomatic formation of a *national displacement*, the testimonies of Vietnamese Afro-Amerasians also suggest that it is especially a symptomatic formation of *racial displacement*; the displacement of black (Vietnamese Afro-Amerasian) bodies, inside and outside of Vietnam, shows that Asian displacements are not just simply national but they are also racial.

Underscoring the multiplicity of Vietnamese Afro-Amerasian displacements (national, racial, and others), I use the plural form, "displacements," which

Angelika Bammer (1994) defines as "[t]he separation of people from their native culture through either physical dislocation (as refugees, immigrants, migrants, exiles, or expatriates) or the colonizing imposition of a foreign culture" (xi). For Bammer, "displacements" denotes not only the movement(s) of people across national borders, but also within: "people who are not expelled [transnationally] from but displaced within their native [national] culture" due to "internal and external processes" such as colonialism, imperialism, or racism. "Obviously," she writes, "not all of the 23 million who lived under French imperial rule in Indochina, say, or the 340 million British subjects from the Indian subcontinent can be said to have been displaced [transnationally] by colonial rule" (xi). However, they did experience various forms of displacement within their national cultures:

> the expropriation of land that often left indigenous peoples with merely a small, and mostly poorer, portion of their land; the pass laws that controlled and regulated their physical movement; the economic shifts that forced them into new centers of imperial employment thus creating new patterns of migratory labor; the presence of a foreign ruling power that disappropriated local cultures—effected massive displacements of indigenous peoples in ways that cannot be added up in numbers and did not end with official decolonization. (xi–xii)

Here, Bammer refers to the expropriation of land, control and regulation of the body's physical movement, and forced economic migration, in order to underscore the multiplicity of displacements, both transnational and intranational.

My use of the plural form—"displacements"—in the title and throughout this chapter, builds on Bammer's definition and calls attention to the inherent multiplicity and variations of Vietnamese Afro-Amerasian experiences: displacements stem from movements that may be either voluntary or involuntary, transnational or national; more broadly speaking, they stem from shifts from a range of familiar places/spaces (such as a home, neighborhood, community, or nation) into unfamiliar ones. To understand the profoundness of Vietnamese Afro-Amerasian displacements, one must first consider its roots in colorism.

Colorism

The term "colorism," as defined by Alice Walker (1983, 290), refers to the "prejudicial or preferential treatment of same-race people based solely on their color." It refers to the hostility that exists among individuals within the same racial group when skin color differences are perceived: usually, a contrast is made between people who appear to be either lighter-skinned/darker-skinned or racially pure/racially mixed. Sometimes referred to as "intraracial color discrimination," "skin color bias," and also "color complex," colorism has been described as "a psychological fixation about [skin] color and [phenotypic] features that leads Blacks [or any other individuals within the same racial group] to discriminate against each other" (Russell, Wilson, and Hall 1992, 1–2). In 1903, W.E.B. Du Bois's "Of the Dawn of Freedom" observes that "The problem of the twentieth century is the problem of the color-line—the relation of the darker to lighter races of men in Asia and Africa, in America and the island sea. It was a phase of this problem that caused the Civil War" (Du Bois 1995, 54). Alice Walker's "If the Present Looks Like the Past, What Does the Future Look Like?" (in Walker 1983) extends the scope of Du Bois's observation of the color-line problem by stating: "the problem of the twenty-first century will still be the problem of the color-line, not only 'the relation of the darker to the lighter races of men [sic] in Asia and Africa, in America and the island sea,' but [also] the relations between the darker and the lighter people of the same races, and of the women who represent both dark and light within each race. It is our 'familial' relations with each other in America that we need to scrutinize. And it is the whole family, rather than the dark or the light, that must be affirmed" (310–311). Walker's critique of Du Bois's observation of racism—"the problem of the color-line"—is that "it omits what is happening within the family, 'the race,' at home [in African-America]; a family also capable of *civil* war." Racism exists between dark-skinned and light-skinned people belonging to different racial groups, as Du Bois observed; but, according to Walker, it also exists between those belonging to the same racial group—especially within the black American racial group or the African-American racial "family." Although Walker's observation calls attention to colorism among African-Americans in the United States (the problem of the color-line at "home" in African-America), it omits what is happening to Afro-Amerasians displaced throughout Asia, away from "home" beyond the United States.

The testimonies of Vietnamese Afro-Amerasians like Mai Linh's extend the scope of Walker's observation of colorism by shifting the focus away from "home"—from African-America—to Asia. More specifically, Vietnamese Afro-Amerasians call attention to the need to reconsider the question of colorism, transnationally, racially, and culturally, by observing the lived-experience of blackness in Vietnam. This reconsideration calls for two epistemological shifts from the dominant discourse of blackness.

The first shift is from a nationalist to a transnationalist framework. Paul Gilroy (1993) has argued that black critical inquiries, especially in African-America, must get beyond "national and nationalistic perspectives" and also "far beyond the well-policed borders of black particularity" (6–7). Accordingly, Vietnamese Afro-Amerasian testimonies challenge black critical inquiries to think about black lived-experiences transnationally—particularly Afro-Amerasian experiences with colorism, outside of the United States, in the Asia-Pacific.

The second shift from the dominant discourse of blackness demands a move from a black and white (black-white) to a black and yellow (black-yellow) racial dialectic.[10] It has been argued by bell hooks (1994) that "the black body has always received attention within the framework of white supremacy. . . . Against this cultural backdrop, every moment for black liberation in this society . . . has had to formulate a counter-hegemonic discourse of the body to effectively resist white supremacy" (127). Against the cultural backdrop of a black-white America, Vietnamese Afro-Amerasians draw attention to *yellow supremacy* (a presumption of the purity of yellowness) in Vietnam; their encounters with colorism shift the focus of the discourse of blackness to a black-yellow racial dialectic. Colorism, therefore, is not simply a black-white color-line problem of the African diaspora; it is also a black-yellow color-line problem of the Asian diaspora.

Even though Walker notes that it is "based solely on . . . color," any inquiry of Vietnamese Afro-Amerasian experiences must first recognize that colorism is a more complex problem at the black-yellow color-line because of the multiple forms of discrimination. For Vietnamese Afro-Amerasians, colorism is compounded by discrimination toward black skin, mixed blood, and foreignness.

The first form of discrimination is toward the black skin. In Vietnam, Afro-Amerasians experienced the most discrimination because their black skin was perceived as relatively darker than the skin color of other Vietnamese people (especially white/Euro-Amerasians). The claim that black skin carries a stronger stigma than white skin in Vietnam was made in a formal study of Vietnamese Amerasian mental health, issued in 1989 as "Vietnamese Amerasians: Practical Implications of Current Research" (Felsman et al. 1989). This psychological study administered "questionnaires to determine the level of mental health symptomatology in a group of 259 Amerasians awaiting U.S. placement at the PRPC, Bataan, Philippines." (This PRPC is the same site where DeBonis conducted his interviews for *Children of the Enemy;* see McKelvey, Mao, and Webb 1992, 912). "Overall," in the study by Felsman et al., "Vietnamese Amerasians were found to have a high level of mental health symptomatology differentiating them significantly from [other] Vietnamese unaccompanied minors . . . [having black skin, or being 'Afro-American' were among the] risk factors in Vietnamese Amerasians . . . found . . . to be 'significantly associated with psychological distress'" (Felsman et al. 1989).

Vietnamese Afro-Amerasians experienced more discrimination because black skin made them physically conspicuous in Vietnam's largely homogeneous society. Several reasons may account for Vietnam's discrimination toward black skin. In "From Dust to Gold: The Vietnamese Amerasian Experience," Kieu-Linh Caroline Valverde (1992) explains that the "Vietnamese, much like other Asian groups, look down on dark skin, which they equate with the lower peasant class or *ethnic* minorities" (147). Also, DeBonis suggests that Vietnam's "negative attitudes may have been initially shaped by their experience with the 'black French,' the North African troops of France's colonial army. . . . [T]hese troops acquired a terrible reputation for pillage, cruelty, and especially rape. Whatever the reason, the brunt borne to those [Amerasians] fathered by blacks seems to have been heavier" (5).

The second form of discrimination is toward "mixed blood." According to Pearl S. Buck (1966), the first American woman to receive both the Pulitzer Prize and Nobel Prize, Amerasians have encountered discrimination toward their mixed blood because they are caught between two conflicting ideas of citizenship: *jus sanguis*—the rule of descent by blood—which bases citizenship on the nationality of the father at the time of birth, and *jus solis*—the right of the soil—which bases citizenship on the territory where the child is born, regardless of the parents' nationality. With the Vietnamese favoring *jus sanguis* and the Americans insisting on *jus solis*, Amerasians fall into a double bind, whereby they inherit nothing from either side of their mixed lineage—neither a nation nor a recognized identity (see Bass 1996, 39–40). Valverde (1992) notes that Amerasians endured ostracism from Vietnam's physically homogeneous society because they were of mixed blood and labeled as worthless half-breeds (144). Furthermore, Valverde explains that "The Vietnamese subjected Amerasians to racial abuse on a daily basis in the form of name-calling"; among the names were *con lai* (half-breed or mixed-blood) and also *my lai* (American mix) (see DeBonis 1995, 146).

Despite the usage of several pejorative terms for "mixed blood," the naming of Amerasians has not always been an exclusively negative practice. In fact, the term "Amerasian" was coined by Pearl S. Buck (1966) as a positive term, to call attention to the displacement of countless mixed-blood children, born of both American and Asian bloodlines, throughout Asia. Buck visited Asia in the 1960s and became conscious of the plight of Amerasians, whom she first recognized as "half-American children" but then later renamed:

> I went to Japan to work on a film and one day, indeed the first morning after my arrival, I saw a child with Japanese features, but his eyes were blue and his hair brown. "What child is this?" I asked my Japanese friend and guide. With diffidence he answered me, ending with the sentence that fell on my heart. "We believe there are some two hundred thousand of them. It is impossible to know the number. Usually their births are not registered anywhere. Their mothers are ashamed of them." "And their fathers?" I asked. "They are gone," he replied simply. "They are Americans." I was silent, but thereafter wherever I was I searched for this child, on the streets, in orphanages, in village and town. . . . That same autumn I went to Korea at the invitation of the Korean people, and there the child was again, wandering on the streets, lost and alone, segregated in poverty-stricken orphanages, swarming around American camps. . . .

When I came home again I knew something must be done for these half-American children, who are our blood relatives through our sons and brothers. (43–44)

After her visits to postwar Japan and Korea, Buck introduced "Amerasian" as a critical new term in America's English language, hoping to raise the American cultural consciousness about the displaced, mixed-blood children of America's black and white "sons and brothers."

The term *Amerasian* names a genealogy that can be traced back as far as 1898 at the time of the Spanish American War in the Pacific Archipelago, today known as the Philippines (see Shade 1980). During this war, the Philippines witnessed not only the demise of Spanish colonialism but also the rise of American imperialism; Spanish colonialism in the Philippines was replaced by American imperialism, and American soldiers replaced Spanish soldiers. At this time, the first generation of Amerasians was born. In addition to the *mestizo* offspring of Spanish-Filipino unions, the Amerasian offspring of American-Filipino unions were born throughout the American-occupied islands. According to a U.S. military census report, "some 18,000 American-Mestizoes were living in and about Manila in 1920" (cited in Shade 1980, 23). Since then, Amerasians or "American-Mestizoes" have been born in the Philippines to American citizens, servicemen, and businessmen of both European-American and African-American heritages. In the early 1980s, it was estimated that [at least] two million Amerasians have been born since U.S. troops first landed in Asia during the Spanish-American War (Shade 1980, 21). Throughout postwar Asia, particularly where U.S. troops have been present, Amerasians have been born in such countries as Korea, Laos, Cambodia, Taiwan, Japan, Thailand, and Vietnam.

"Amerasian" may be the synthesis of two terms "American" and "Asian," but culturally "Amerasian" signifies the mixed blood(lines) of multiple domains of difference: Occident/Orient, America/Asia, First World/Third World, white/yellow, and black/yellow. The term "Amerasian," which Buck used interchangeably to denote the "half-American" children's mixture of "race" and "nation," is another example of Clifford's "translational term." It is a term that implies that "American" identities and cultures are somehow intertwined with the "Asian," and that the "local" and the "global" are mutually implicated in one another.

Implicit in Buck's "mixed blood" neologism is the notion of "global analytic dimension" that Donald Pease (1993) discusses in the introduction to *Cultures of United States Imperialism*, a collection of essays that critique the part imperialism has played in the history of U.S. culture. Pease argues: "the introduction of a global analytic dimension to otherwise local struggle enables the subjects positioned there to understand the production of racial, gendered, regional and class subjectivities as mutually implicated and to recognize, as a corollary, that a group who successfully overcame cultural oppression in the first world may have depended, for their surplus cultural resources, on . . . the so-called Third World" (24). The idea of the global analytic dimension, which enables us to understand that a group in the "First World" may somehow be mutually implicated in the "Third World," calls attention to cultures that are transnational; they are mutually implicated in other cultures that exist across their borders. The term "Amerasian" challenges the American empire to recognize that its imperialist bloodline flows across America's "borders" transnationally and globally. Buck's neologism is therefore a translational term, in the sense that it translates both "American" and "Asian" bloodlines, and names or introduces a more positive or critical consciousness of the mixed blood.

The third form of discrimination is toward foreign blood. DeBonis explains that "In relatively homogeneous Vietnam, foreign blood carries a strong stigma. Outsiders in the land of their birth, fatherless children in a culture where identity flows from the father, Amerasians were generally relegated to the fringe of society. These offspring of Americans were considered fair game for abuse" (5). The Amerasians' foreign blood, whether black or white, was subjected to discrimination because it represented the bloodline of antinationalist opposition to Vietnam during and after the Vietnamese-American War. In postwar Vietnam, the Amerasian children of Vietnam's war enemy experienced discrimination because they appeared as constant reminders of the war that threatened the Vietnamese nation.

Also, the Amerasians' foreign blood appears as an antinationalist threat in Vietnam because it represents the legacy of American imperialism. In the Vietnamese schools, lessons were taught that warned against the "American imperialists." According to DeBonis, "History classes decrying America's role in the destruction of Vietnam were intensely embarrassing for the Amerasians because they emphasized their status as children of the enemy, often turning their classmates against them" (6). In addition to the school lessons, a postwar "anti-American campaign" was launched in Vietnam, therefore encouraging the discrimination toward the Amerasians' American, foreign blood (see Valverde 1992, 146).

The discrimination toward the Amerasians' foreign blood is linked to American imperialism but is compounded further by French colonialism. Throughout French colonial Vietnam, many Eurasian (half-French, half-Vietnamese) children were born; and like the Amerasians, Eurasians were recognized as problems due to foreign occupation in Vietnam. In *Vietnamerica: The War Comes Home*, Thomas Bass (1996) writes:

> By 1900, Eurasians formed a recognizable subclass of petty criminals and prostitutes in Saigon, and soon a spate of articles was appearing in the French Press about Indochina's "Eurasian problem." . . . [A] 1929 report on Eurasians contends that the "half-breeds" tend to be the "malcon-

tents and rabble-rousers who give the most trouble to the local authorities . . . they are all the more dangerous for having a foot in each camp
and possessing natural qualities of intelligence and flexibility that he can
be tempted to put to bad use. (84–85)

Eurasians and Amerasians were both "problems" in Vietnam because they both
possessed "foreign" blood that appeared antinationalist—the bloodlines of both
colonialism and imperialism. There was one fundamental difference between
the two perceived problems, however: France immediately took care of their
Eurasians upon withdrawing from Vietnam, whereas America neglected the
Amerasians for nearly a decade after the war. In 1954, the French withdrew from
Vietnam after being defeated at the battle of Dien Bien Phu; for some, this withdrawal marked the end of the French colonialist era in Vietnam and throughout Indo-China. That same year, the French government brought twenty-five
thousand Franco-Asian (half-French, half-Asian) children to France, guaranteed them citizenship, and also provided for those who stayed behind in Vietnam with their mothers. In 1975, the Americans withdrew from Vietnam as the
South Vietnamese government fell to the North; upon their withdrawal, the
Americans left behind not only MIAs and POWs, but also between thirty thousand and eighty thousand Amerasian children. In Vietnam, Amerasians existed
as "foreigners"; they were denied both Vietnamese and American citizenship
because many were born illegitimately, outside of marriages. In 1988, the
Amerasian Homecoming Act went into effect, just a year after it was signed; as
a result, many Amerasians left their Vietnamese homelands hoping to escape
discrimination and poverty and to find their American fathers. Displaced out of
Vietnam, Vietnamese Afro-Amerasians encountered colorism and its inherent
complexities along the black-yellow color-line.

Contact Zones

Compounded by black skin, mixed blood, and foreign blood, the problem of
colorism that confronts Afro-Amerasians in Vietnam is so pervasive that it
reveals itself through the multiplicity of the black body's displacements: it can
be traced throughout several contact zones, within and beyond Vietnam. The
concept of the contact zone, as I am using it here, has multiple resonances.
Mary Louise Pratt (1992) coined the term "contact zone" to invoke the "social
spaces where disparate cultures meet, clash, and grapple with each other, often
in highly asymmetrical relations of domination and subordination—like colonialism, slavery, or their aftermaths" (4). Introducing this concept in her study
of European expansion and travel writing, she suggests that the location of
these in-between cultural spaces appears at the "frontiers of nations and
empires" (4). Pratt's usage underscores the *international* dimension of contact

zones. James Clifford (1997), on the other hand, extends Pratt's concept of the
contact zone by shifting the focus from the periphery (the "frontiers") back to
the center (the "nations"), and from foreign to domestic spaces; he calls attention to the location of contact zones within the nations and empires (204). Clifford's usage underscores the *national* dimension of contact zones. For Tchen (in
Desai, Machida, and Tchen 1994), the contact zone can be located not only in
between collective bodies (nations or other social groups) but also within individual bodies; he argues, for example, that the Asian body becomes a "zone of
contact" when it appears under the American Orientalist gaze, in front of racist
stares. Tchen's usage underscores the *corporeal* dimension of contact zones.
Building on Pratt, Clifford, and Tchen, I am suggesting that Vietnamese Afro-
Amerasian contact zones appear as "zones of contact" of international,
national, and corporeal dimensions.

Vietnamese Afro-Amerasian contact zones are cultural spaces where the
black body comes in contact with colorism and its many discursive practices
(such as name-calling, abandonment, or displacement). The racialized cultural
space of displacements is what Frantz Fanon describes as "a zone of nonbeing,
an extraordinarily sterile and arid region, an utterly naked declivity where an
authentic upheaval can be born" (1967, 8). In the antiblack zone of nonbeing,
the black body is displaced by racism or more specifically, in the case of Vietnamese Afro-Amerasians in Vietnam, colorism.

Displaced, in an antiblack world, the black body emerges in the zones of
nonbeing or contact zones because of two oppositional processes: the masking
and the unmasking of the black body. The first process, the masking of the
black body, is a hegemonic process in which black bodies, notably the bodies of
black-skinned people of African descent, are masked or racialized as "black";
and then ultimately dehumanized as "nonbeing." Here, racism territorializes
the black body, confining it to Fanon's "zone of nonbeing." The second process,
the unmasking of the black body, is a counterhegemonic process in which black
bodies seek liberation from racism, and transcendence out of the shadowy
domain. Here, antiracism reterritorializes the black body, shifting it beyond the
confines of a "zone of nonbeing" into an emergent, counterhegemonic zone—a
zone of transcendence. Ultimately, therein, a revolutionary and "authentic
upheaval" is born. Racism displaces the black body into a zone or space of
racism; but conversely, it is the revolutionary upheaval of antiracism that calls
upon the black body to challenge the displacement by exploring new zones of
being—or new zones of transcendence. A contact zone, therefore, is a site of
critical inquiry shaped by both the hegemonic process of racialization and the
counterhegemonic process of re-racialization; it is the location where the black
body is masked or territorialized by racism and unmasked or reterritorialized by
antiracism.

Throughout the dominant discourse on the lived-experience of blackness (the discourse on blackness), the black body's contact zone has been recognized primarily in terms of its location at a black-white color line. Fanon observes that "not only must the black man be black, he must also be black in relation to the white man . . . the Negro has been given two frames of reference within which he has had to place himself . . . there are two camps: the white and the black . . . [the] white man is sealed in his whiteness. The black man in his blackness" (11). Fanon contends that a color line (or racial dialectic) exists, which separates and seals the white from black. Fanon's observation suggests that black bodies and white bodies coexist unequally within the contact zone—each one on different sides of the black-white color line: in the contact zone, the black body is displaced at the margins of an antiblack world, and the white body is privileged at the center. The Fanonian observation of the black body's zones is one that looks, almost exclusively, at its location along the black-white color line. However, the testimonies of Vietnamese Afro-Amerasians shift the focus of black critical inquiries to the black-yellow color line. Calling attention to the black body's location at the black-yellow color line, Vietnamese Afro-Amerasian testimonies can be understood as reformulations of Fanon's observation of zones of nonbeing; they point to contact zones that may be signified linguistically by the racial-spatial metaphor "black skin, yellow masks."[11]

The testimonies reveal that the contact zones specific to Vietnamese Afro-Amerasian displacements are located in three primary contexts: corporeal, national, and international. In the corporeal context, the contact zone emerges as the Vietnamese Afro-Amerasians' physical body itself; the displacements herein bring about a physical dislocation and violate the black body. In the national context, the contact zones appear within Vietnam's national border, at the margins of society; the displacements herein push the black body aside, into the periphery of the Vietnamese Afro-Amerasians' homeland. In the international context, the contact zones extend across the Vietnamese national border, into other countries; the displacements herein move the black body from the Vietnamese Afro-Amerasians' native culture into a foreign culture.

In addition to the three primary contexts—corporeal, national, and international—the location of the contact zones are marked further by two critical dimensions intrinsic to Vietnamese Afro-Amerasian displacements: trajectory and transgression. In the first dimension, the *trajectory* signifies the path of the Vietnamese Afro-Amerasians' displacement between two domains: familiar and unfamiliar. It locates the movement of the displacement throughout the contact zone, from one site to another, beginning with the original, familiar domain. In the second dimension, the *transgression* differentiates between the various forms of border crossings; transgressions, for example, may be either national or racial; they may also be characterized as physical, social, cultural, or even discursive, depending on how and where they move the black body across perceived borders.

What follows is a mapping of seven of the most formative contact zones indexed by Vietnamese Afro-Amerasian testimonies. Each one quoted below (in this section) appears in *Children of the Enemy*. Collectively, the testimonies (or mappings) of the contact zones underscore the pervasiveness of colorism and its various manifestations in the multiplicity of Vietnamese Afro-Amerasian displacements. Individually, each of these black testimonies bears witness to the many contexts and dimensions of the black body's displacements—delineating between various trajectories and transgressions. Collectively, they bear witness to black resilience: the Vietnamese Afro-Amerasians' endurance and survival of the circumstances of colorism.

Corporeal

In the first contact zone, which appears within the corporeal context, colorism permeates individual Vietnamese Afro-Amerasians bodies; herein, discrimination literally pierces and enters the flesh itself.

The first contact zone of the black body's displacement is located at the Vietnamese Afro-Amerasian body itself. The displaced black body's trajectory in this corporeal contact zone can be traced from one layer (the outer layer) of the black skin to the other (the inner layer), throughout the physical body; it originates on the surface of the Vietnamese Afro-Amerasians' black skin and then continues its path downward, piercing the flesh, under the black skin. In his description of scars visible on one Vietnamese Afro-Amerasian man's body, DeBonis wrote: "Raised, pendant-shaped burn marks define the length of his right arm in neat, grisly rows of three. These were self-inflicted with a lit cigarette in Chi Hoa prison during a period of dejection. His right forearm has been slashed into a mass of scar tissue. Running down the right calf is a tattooed message in Vietnamese roughly translatable as, 'If your lover betrays you, be true to yourself.' On the inside of the left calf, 'Life is unjust, hatred everlasting'" (1995, 122). In this description, the Vietnamese Afro-Amerasian body appears as a contact zone in which discrimination is literally inscribed upon the flesh itself.

The implosion of the black skin, along the trajectory between its outer and inner layers, causes both voluntary and involuntary displacements. The voluntary type of displacement in the corporeal context is recognized by DeBonis as an "almost ritual scarification" practiced by many Vietnamese Amerasians (122). This ritual involves using not only cigarettes but also razors to inflict wounds upon one's body. In his testimony, one man named Hung accounts for his scars: "You ask me about my scars. All my life people despised me, they called me a 'bastard,' a 'nigger.' I didn't care about myself. I wanted to die. So I took a razor and slashed myself all over. People see my scars and they think, 'Oh, he's a tough guy, he a troublemaker.' They judge me. But it's not like that, I just wanted to die. I tried to kill myself four times. All my life has been sad. I never had a father's love, only a mother's, and that was not enough for me" (99). For Hung and many others, ritual scarification was often practiced during times of extreme depression and imprisonment. This practice, however, was not exclusive to men. This is evidenced in Mai Linh's testimony: "Before, in Vietnam, I stay in my house, I be all by myself. I feel bad, angry, I do anything. I drink whiskey and take a razor and cut myself on the arms. That's how I got these scars. You think I'm crazy, but I'm not crazy. I do it to forget, but sometimes I can't forget" (122). The testimonies of Hung and Mai Linh indicate that the self-inflicted burns and slash marks signify externalizations of despair, sorrow, anger, and shame—the (physical, corporeal) consequences of colorism. The Vietnamese Afro-Amerasian body externalizes inner turmoil not only because it seeks to forget it but also because it chooses to symbolize and testify about the extremities of colorism. Although ritual scarification is a voluntary, albeit violent, act practiced by both black men and women in Vietnam, it is deeply rooted in Vietnamese colorism and caused by discrimination toward the Vietnamese Afro-Amerasians' black skin, mixed blood, and foreign blood.

The involuntary type of displacement in the corporeal context takes the form of the sexual molestation of Amerasian youth. This is illustrated in the account of one young woman named Thuy who was homeless in Saigon and slept on Le Lai Street. There, on that street, the owner of a local restaurant took her in—offered her a job, food, a place to stay, and also promised to protect her if she ever encountered trouble on the streets. One night, after working there for about a year, Thuy was approached by the owner during her sleep, and was told that if she didn't allow him to sleep with her, she would find herself back on the streets again. In her testimony, Thuy recalls:

> He was around thirty, I was only about seventeen. . . . When I was three months pregnant, his wife confronted me and put me out. So I was seventeen and pregnant, no home. I just wandered around, finding work as a dishwasher in little food stalls, sleeping on the street. When the time came to have my baby, I couldn't get to the hospital. I gave birth on the street, right on the sidewalk. Some strangers, some passersby helped me. After the birth, I kneeled on the street with my baby in my pants, the cord still attached. I was too weak to hold the baby. I tried to get a taxi to take me to the hospital, but none would stop. Finally, after two hours, one did, and I got to the hospital. (86)

Thuy's testimony shows that the Vietnamese Afro-Amerasian body is not only a racialized contact zone, but also a gendered one. Exploited because of her gender—coerced into having sexual intercourse with the married, thirty-year-old restaurant owner—seventeen-year-old Thuy experienced involuntary displacement of her black female body. Despite the exploitation, she chose to survive:

wandering about homeless while pregnant, working odd jobs, giving birth on the streets, and waiting for a taxi, hour after hour, to go to the hospital for the sake of her own well-being and that of her newborn.

Whether voluntarily or involuntarily displaced, the Vietnamese Afro-Amerasians' black skin becomes wounded and violated, due to burning, slashing, or penetration. The voluntary and involuntary displacements of the black body, under the black skin, in the corporeal contact zone, signify the transgression of a racial border: the displaced black body crosses a racial border—during the ritual scarification and the sexual molestation—because it is black and devalued in Vietnam.

National

In the second, third, fourth, and fifth contact zones, which appear within the national context, Vietnamese Afro-Amerasians encounter socioeconomic displacements and are pushed aside to the margins of Vietnamese society.

The second contact zone of the black body's displacement is located at the "homeplace." The path of the displaced black body's trajectory in this national contact zone originates inside the Vietnamese homeplace and then continues beyond the family nucleus, sometimes outside (of the dwelling place of the Vietnamese Afro-Amerasians, their family members, and their ancestors). Typically, displacement within the homeplace stems from a family's internalization of colorism and social shame; often, however, it stems from fear of punishment by the Vietcong. One Vietnamese Afro-Amerasian woman named Pha explains: "Before '75, it was not so bad, but after '75, the family didn't want to keep me at home. They were scared of the VC, they wanted to send me away where nobody could see me. Around 1977 the government told mothers of Amerasians to come to a meeting. Some they let go, some they sent to jail. My mother was afraid at this time, and she was arguing with my grandmother, so we left for Ho Chi Minh City" (106).

The homeplace is a contact zone in which the Vietnamese family displaces the Vietnamese Afro-Amerasians away from their home. This alienation by family members usually takes the form of either abandonment or abuse. In the case of abandonment, the children are given away at birth. One woman named Hahn recalls: "When I was four, my father returned to America, and my mother went away. She just left me with the baby-sitter and didn't come back, and that baby-sitter became like my stepmother. My mother didn't tell the baby-sitter that she was leaving. She just abandoned me there" (46). In the case of abuse, a stepfamily or foster family often mistreats the Afro-Amerasian children. In her testimony, Thuy relates her experience of abandonment, which parallels Hahn's, but she also describes her experience of abuse:

> When I was still young, maybe seven or eight years old, my mother gave
> me away to the baby-sitter. That lady became like my stepmother. . . . My

stepmother had three children, and she made me take care of them. I received little affection from the family. My stepfather didn't abuse me, but my stepmother tormented me. She hated me because I was black. She thought I was dumb. She called me stupid, and she beat me. One time she hung me upside down. When I was about as old as this girl [Thuy points to an eight-year-old-child], she made me strip to the skin and stand outside in the hot sun. Sometimes I would hide under the bed and wait until she left before I came out to eat. (82)

Whether through abandonment or abuse, the displacement of the black body away from the homeplace, in the national contact zone, signifies the transgression of an ancestral-familial border: the presence of the black family member in the Vietnamese household brings about a disruption within the homeplace, consequently leading to the disavowal of the black body away from the sacred grounds of the Vietnamese ancestors and family. Abandoned, abused, and homeless, the Vietnamese Afro-Amerasians nonetheless exhibited resilience. For example, many like Thuy often returned home, despite being shunned by their families:

I began to think, even though I had been mistreated when I was a girl in Phan Thiet, wasn't it my homeland? So I got on a bus and went back there, back to my home province. . . . The neighbors told me that my stepmother had died of hemorrhagic fever. I was sad despite the way she had treated me. Some neighbors told me that my real mother was living in a small village, not too far [away]. . . . When I found my mother's house, we recognized each other and cried, overcome with emotion. . . . We got along well for the first month, but after that my mother and her husband started arguing. He didn't want me to live in their house. . . . Finally my mother and I had an argument. She told me, "You are stubborn because of your mixed blood." I became angry. I told her, "If I were white and beautiful, you would never have left me." My mother didn't say anything, she just cried. Soon after that I left my mother's house. I just slipped out without telling anyone. I did not want to disrupt the harmony of her house or disrupt her marriage. (84–85)

Like Thuy, some returned home while others simply continued to believe in and to practice ancestor worship; for many Vietnamese Afro-Amerasians, revering the ancestors remained important, despite their family's alienation.

The third contact zone of the black body's displacement is Saigon's street culture—the streets of Saigon. The path of the displaced black body's trajectory in this national contact zone originates from the Vietnamese Afro-Amerasians' individual, personal, and private space, and then continues its path onto the streets of Saigon, into a collective, impersonal, public space. Homeless Vietnamese Afro-Amerasians resort to living on the streets, often as adolescents or teenagers desperately seeking ways to earn money. In her testimony, Thuy explains:

> I went over to the Ba Chieu market and begged for scraps. I slept at the market with some other beggars. After about a week, I went over to Quach Thi Trang Park and began shining shoes. I worked with a group of Amerasians—two boys and two girls, all black like me. . . . [W]e slept in the bus station, or if it was not raining, we sometimes slept in the park. You know at that time, the black and white Amerasians stayed separately, not like now. Now they mix very freely, but then white Amerasians didn't want to make friends with me. This group taught me how to shine shoes . . . we pooled our money in the group, that's how we lived. I also worked as a dishwasher in a boardinghouse and as a newspaper seller. I would take a bath and wash my clothes at the public faucet. . . . Sometimes bad things would happen [in the streets], but nobody bothered me. . . . I think maybe I had a look about me, and people left me alone. (84)

For some, like Tuan Den (roughly translatable as "smart and black"), street life included gang life:

> When I was a teenager, I went out to live on the street and to earn some money. I was part of a group of kids, shining shoes and sleeping on the street. . . . Eventually, I got into street crime. We cornered people at knifepoint, at night, in dark places. We'd tell them to give up their money. . . . When we got the money, we had to give it to the gang leader. . . . Even if I was the one who did the robbery, he would let me keep just a little of the money. I didn't like that, but there was nothing I could do. I didn't feel close to the people in the gang, but I needed them to survive. The life of crime didn't bother me. I just thought of it as business. (53)

For Thuy, Tuan Den, and others, surviving "street life" means begging, shoe shining, sleeping in bus stations, in parks, and on the streets, bathing and washing clothes in public faucets, and working with a group, such as a gang. The displacement of the black body into the streets of Saigon, in the national contact zone, signifies the transgression of a social border: the body is displaced into a public (collective) domain and therefore is denied a private (individual) domain.

The fourth trajectory of the black body's displacement is the school. The path of the displaced black body's trajectory in this national contact zone originates inside the classrooms of Vietnamese children, and then continues outside the school, into and beyond the schoolyard. Confronted by colorism in the classrooms and out on the schoolyards, Vietnamese Afro-Amerasians suffered many forms of abuse, which often caused their withdrawal from school. One man's testimony explains, "I only went to school up to the second grade. The students don't like black skin, they hate it. They like to play with the fair-skinned people. They never let me forget I was black and that I had no father. They always called me names and made me feel ashamed, so I stopped going" (99). The harm of colorism at school was not limited to verbal name-calling; it was also physical. For example, Vu's testimony explains that he was forced to sit in the corners of classrooms and was beaten: "in the class, I often got something like discrimination. The classmates look at me like I am a low type of person. . . . In my last three years of high school, I did very well, but in the first year I could not, because the students forced me to sit in the corner of the class and taunted me. I was alone, I could not go against them. I did not dare to complain to the teacher, because when I finished the class they would beat me up" (116–117).

At school, not only the Vietnamese children but also the parents threatened Vietnamese Afro-Amerasians verbally and physically. For example, Mai Linh recalls an incident at her school and notes:

> a man and a woman over there, they slap me. They say, "You black, you can't sit down with my children." So that's why I didn't go to school. . . . I go home, and my mother says, "Mai Linh, you go to school?" I say, "Yes," but she looks at my schoolbook, and she sees I didn't go, and she slaps me. Then I tell her, "I never go to school no more." She says, "Why?" I say, "You crazy. I go to school, some people slap me, they slap my friend. They say they don't want no black, they don't want no white American." So I tear up that paper [*school registration*], and I never go to school no more. (110)

Confronted by antiblack discrimination and hostility at school—in the form of both verbal and physical abuse from parents and classmates, Vietnamese Afro-Amerasians felt they could not remain in school. Threatened by the consequences of colorism at school, their black bodies were displaced from the classrooms, beyond the schoolyard. The displacement of the black body away from school, in the national contact zone, signifies the transgression of an educational border: the Vietnamese Afro-Amerasian body is displaced outside of the institution of learning and, therefore, is denied access to a formal education. Withstanding the educational discrimination, they resorted to an informal education: for example, Hanh learned how to read Vietnamese from her friends (47), and Mai Linh learned how to read English from her grandmother's neighbor (112).

The fifth contact zone of the black body's displacement is the labor camp. The path of the displaced black body's trajectory in this national contact zone

originates from a space of individual freedom, or free space, and then continues into the labor camps, at the margins of society. Many Vietnamese Afro-
Amerasians and their mothers were forced by the government to live and work
in labor camps, sometimes called "New Economic Zones" or "State Farm for
Agricultural and Industrial Education and Labor." Coerced by propaganda to
"do the duty of building the defense economy," they were forced by the Vietcong to work in the camps with other marginalized people in Vietnam: street
people, vendors, the homeless, prostitutes, criminals, women who had affairs
with the American enemy, and other mixed-blood *children of the enemy.*

In their testimonies, Vietnamese Afro-Amerasians call attention to at least
four different labor camps in which they endured hardships. The first two
camps are described from the point of view of two women: Pha and Thuy. Pha
describes Dong Ban, in Tay Ninh province, and recalls, "There was nothing
there but mountains, trees, and a few huts, no market at all. For that we had to
go to the nearest town. My mother worked clearing land for rice fields. She cut
down trees and cut up the wood, and I would carry the wood out. We worked
every day, Saturday, Sunday, we didn't take holidays. And that has been my life
even until now" (106–107). Thuy describes Cay Truong 2, in Song Be province,
and recalls:

> We lived on newly cleared land on the edge of the jungle and mountains.
> We built a hutch out of palm thatch, and that's where we stayed. I cleared
> land, dug holes, planted rice and vegetables. All labor, all hard. We
> planted manioc. We didn't get paid for our work, but we sold part of the
> vegetables we grew for a little cash. I made a little stove out of three
> stones. They gave us some rice a few times a week. I had to borrow pots
> to cook in. I was voted in as leader for distribution of goods, but there
> wasn't much to distribute. Rice was lacking, we had to eat manioc. . . . It
> was too hard to live there. It was difficult to get water, food was scarce.
> (86–87)

Pha's and Thuy's testimonies show that the daily conditions of life and labor in
the camps were extremely intense and included such tasks as clearing land, digging holes, and planting vegetables; typically, laborers received no cash payment, and only small portions of food.

The next two camps are described from the point of view of men: Dung and
Hung. Dung describes Tien Lanh, a labor camp in Quang Nam Da Nang
province and recalls, "Tien Lanh means Angel, and the joke was that you had to
be an angel with wings to escape. . . . Tien is a labor camp, and most of the labor
is farm work—clearing land, planting rice. . . . If you tried to make a break, they
[the labor camp guards] would shoot you. If you work slowly or try to stop for a
while, they beat you with a rifle butt. If you try to escape, they fire in the air
three times to alert the other guards. If they catch you, they beat you really bad,

almost to death" (125). In his testimony, Hung describes Duyen Hai district and recalls that it is "on a kind of peninsula. One side is facing the ocean, and one side has a river. It's difficult to escape, but not impossible. Who do they send there? Young people they don't like, vendors, homeless people, prostitutes, criminals, people they suspect of committing a crime or anybody who opposes them. We are forced to labor there. We had to dig canals to channel the seawater into the fields. These became shallow salt ponds, where we harvest the salt. The work is very hard, a lot of digging" (100–101).

The displacement of the black body into the labor camps, in the national contact zone, signifies the transgression of an economic border: forced and condemned into labor camps, Vietnamese Afro-Amerasians appear in the excess of Vietnam's economy, in the "new economic zones." Like Pha and Thuy, Dung and Hung endured daily hardships in the labor camps; their testimonies, however, reveal an anxiety about the possibilities and impossibilities of escape (102, 124–125).

International

In the sixth and seventh contact zones, appearing within the international context, Vietnamese Afro-Amerasians enter voluntarily, hoping to escape Vietnamese discrimination.

The sixth contact zone of the black body's displacement is the Vietnamese-Cambodian borderland. The path of the displaced black body's trajectory in this international contact zone originates from within the Vietnamese Afro-Amerasians' homeland, and then continues over the national border in the southwestern part of Vietnam, across Cambodia's border. The space conjoining and overlapping Vietnam and Cambodia is what I am calling here the Vietnamese-Cambodian borderland. Borderlands, according to Gloria Anzaldúa (1987, i), "are physically present when two or more cultures edge each other, where people of different races occupy the same territory, where under, lower, middle and upper class touch, where the space between two individuals shrinks with intimacy." A borderland, therefore, appears when two worlds, separated by a border, merge together and form a third.

Dwelling in the Vietnamese-Cambodian borderland, and freely crossing the border between both countries, is a privilege that one Vietnamese Afro-Amerasian woman attributes to her ability to "pass" (racially and ethnically) as a Khmer. Thuy explains:

> Some friends of mine heard that it was easy to make money in Cambodia, so they decided to go there. I went along with them. We crossed the border at Dinh Zuong village, Dong Thap province. Because I was black, they didn't question me. They thought I was Khmer from one of the border villages. These people often cross back and forth, so I walked right

across. My Vietnamese friends had to sneak around, but I walked right through because I am black like a Khmer. We took a bus to Prey Veng city. I set up a stand near the Buddhist temple frying bananas and selling them. At night, I slept in the market. In a few months, I began to do general buying and selling. I bought from Vietnamese and sold to Vietnamese and Khmer. The Khmer like me better than the other Vietnamese because my color was more like theirs. They would say that my skin is like a Khmer, but my face is different. I went to sell at the market with Vietnamese who were born in Cambodia and spoke the language fluently, but the people used to think I was Cambodian because of my color, and I was the one they would talk to. This was different than Vietnam, where they hate my black skin. (85)

The displacement of the black body across the Vietnamese-Cambodian borderland, in the international contact zone, signifies the transgression of a racial-national border: Thuy crosses the racial border that separates the Vietnamese from the Cambodians by freely passing as a member of one of Cambodia's dark-skinned (indigenous "black") racial minority—a Khmer. Therefore, crossing the border between Vietnam and Cambodia becomes a strategic act of survival whereby one "passes" and transgresses the borders or discursive boundaries of one's "race" and "nation."

The seventh contact zone of the black body's displacement conjoins and overlaps Vietnam and America; this transnational, transpacific space is what Bass calls "Vietnamerica." In his book *Vietnamerica: The War Comes Home*, Bass focuses on Amerasian displacements and existence in Vietnamerica. Forming a new translational term, Bass's neologism invokes a trans-Pacific history: the United States presence in Vietnam and the subsequent Vietnamese immigration to the United States. "Vietnamerica" names the space of migration during and after the Vietnamese-American war. The path of the displaced black body's trajectory throughout Vietnamerica, in this international contact zone, originates from within Vietnam, and then continues its path over its national border, across the South China Sea and the Pacific Ocean, into and throughout the United States, the homeland of the Vietnamese Afro-Amerasians' fathers.

The passing of the Amerasian Homecoming Act granted black and white Amerasians (and their families) greater access to the United States, their fathers' homeland; it produced a policy that not only legitimized the Vietnamese Afro-Amerasians' mixed blood and American ancestry, but also opened the door for immigration from Vietnam. When it was passed in 1987, the act enabled black and white Amerasians, and their families, to be airlifted from Vietnam to America: "The last casualties of war were finally being evacuated," according to Bass. Furthermore, Bass contends that the act was a postwar humanitarian gesture: "Twenty thousand, thirty thousand Amerasians—no one knew the number for sure—would be transplanted across the Pacific. Teenagers at the bottom of Vietnamese society, many of them homeless and illiterate, would be flown [to America]. . . . Overnight Amerasians in Vietnam went from being bui doi, 'the dust of life,' to 'gold children' endowed with the power to fly themselves and their family members around the world" (1996, 3). Consequently, a Vietnamese market for Amerasians developed; as DeBonis (1995, 11) notes, "those who had reviled the Amerasians for their American blood were now eager to exploit them as tickets out of impoverished Vietnam to the United States."

Leaving behind their Vietnamese homeland and entering into Vietnamerica, Amerasians yearned for a better life in America. The testimonies of the Vietnamese Afro-Amerasians revealed that they yearned to seek employment and education opportunities in America, to reunite with their fathers and form new families, and especially to escape discrimination in Vietnam. Thuy's testimony points to a yearning for both employment and education, "I hope that my husband can get a job in the United States. . . . I can be a laundry woman or do ironing, something like that. What I would really like is to be a saleslady—sell watches and cassette players, something like that. I just want to support my kids. I want my children to go to school. But I am worried. We learned that in America everything is run by machine. How can I work? I never went to school" (89). Mai Linh's testimony expresses a desire for a family in America:

> Maybe when I go to America, I find a man who be good. . . . I think I better wait till I go to America, maybe find an American man. When I get to America, first thing, I want to find my father but I don't know how. If I had a picture, maybe, but I don't know. I don't know anything, even his [last] name, but my mother don't let me know. [Mai Linh is in tears] Maybe he die already. What I wanna do in America? What I do? I go to America, I have to study. Daytime I study, nighttime I get a job and I go to work. That's all, what else can I do? In America I don't want to stay with Vietnamese. I don't want no Vietnamese to be my mother, my father. If I can't find no American to be my mother or father, I stay by myself. (113–114)

Like Mai Linh's testimony, Vu's underscores a yearning to escape discrimination in Vietnam; but it also expresses deep concern about and anticipation of discrimination even in America:

> In Vietnam, people always look at me strange because I am different. Even if I am reading a book or a newspaper, I catch people looking at me because I am a black boy. The Vietnamese look down more on the black Amerasian than the white. I don't know why, but I know it is so. I have an inferiority complex. I have had it for years. It's very hard to

explain in English. For example, I am looked down upon by the people
who live around me. Little by little, day by day, it is impressed on my
memory. If I am busy, working for example, I don't think about it. But
when I am alone, it stays in my mind. I worry about discrimination in
America, from Americans. I have seen it in the TV, and I read about it
in the newspaper. I am worried about that. I have seen the white and
the black fighting together, and one or two months ago I saw in the TV
about the violence in Los Angeles. Men that live in the world must be
united together, friendly. (121)

The displacement of the black body, into Vietnamerica, in the international
contact zone, signifies the transgression of a national-imperial border: Vietnamese Afro-Amerasians leave behind their homelands, crossing both the Vietnamese border and the American border. On one hand, they are crossing the
national borders of two distinct nations, on the other hand, they are trans-
gressing a boundary imposed by American imperialism—until the American
empire passed the Amerasian Homecoming Act, Amerasians were left in the
empire's overseas' battlefield, in war-torn Vietnam, and were denied legal
access to America. Migrancy in Vietnamerica, in between Vietnam and America, is perhaps, the clearest evidence of Vietnamese Afro-Amerasian endurance
and survival: it is a testament to the newly found freedom to move from the
periphery (Vietnam) and to legally enter into the center (America).

In the Black Pacific

As these testimonies of displacements have shown, the lived-experience of
blackness of Vietnamese Afro-Amerasians is rooted in the pervasiveness of colorism in Vietnam and routed throughout the multiplicity of contact zones. The
constellation of Vietnamese Afro-Amerasian contact zones—corporeal, national,
and international—emerges as a space for rethinking "blackness" (in terms of
its roots and routes) in the Black Pacific (the interdiasporic site of critical
inquiry along the black-yellow color line, at the interstices of Afro-Amerasian,
African-American, and Asian diasporas). Through their testimonies, Vietnamese
Afro-Amerasians have illustrated that although their existential situations have
been marked primarily by the displacement of their "blackness," they continue
to endure and to survive.

Although Vietnamese Afro-Amerasians owe their black genealogies exclusively to their African-American fathers, their lived-experience of blackness,
however (particularly with colorism, contact zones, and displacements), is due
heavily to Vietnam's multilayered black history: first, the presence of the Afro-
Amerasians themselves before and after the Vietnam-American War; second,
the presence of African-American soldiers whose interracial affairs with Viet-

namese women defied Vietnam's patriarchal, national, and racial-ethnic mores (not only because black men were dating Vietnam's women, but especially because such unions produced mixed-blood children); third, the presence of the "'black French,' the North African troops of France's colonial army" who had earned a "reputation for pillage, cruelty, and especially rape" (5); and fourth, the presence of the Montagnard people, Vietnam's "aboriginal black," "darker-skinned," "Negrito" ethnic group, whose marginalized status in Vietnam precedes the Vietnamese Afro-Amerasians.[12]

Collectively, these multiple black histories in Vietnam, underscored by the Vietnamese Afro-Amerasian testimonies, present an epistemic challenge to the Black Atlantic's dominant discourse on blackness: they go against the grain of the long-standing cultural logic of "the one-drop rule" which has traditionally framed "blackness" in terms of the "Negro," "Negroid," or "black" genealogies of the African diaspora.[13] In the Black Pacific, however, critical inquiries of the lived-experience of blackness must also explore frameworks that focus on the plight of all blacks in the Asia-Pacific: Afro-Amerasians, African-Americans, Africans, and aboriginal blacks throughout Asian diasporas.

NOTES

I am grateful to Malini Schueller, Nell Painter, Colin Palmer, Noliwe Rooks, Lyndon Dominique, and Michelle Fowles for their comments and encouragement. Also, I wish to thank Wanni W. Anderson and Robert G. Lee of Brown University for the comments on this study. A fellowship at the Princeton University Program in African-American Studies enabled me to write this chapter and to do the necessary research on Afro-Amerasians in the Black Pacific.

1. I use the term "lived-experience of blackness" to call attention to the existential situation in which black people encounter antiblack *racism*, and also challenge the hegemonic representations, practices, and processes that objectify them, discursively and socially, as a ("black") race without agency or voice. For critical discussions, see Fanon (1967), and Judy (1996). Judy notes that the proper translation of the title that Fanon gave to his fifth chapter "L'experience vecue du Noire" (in *Black skin, white masks*) is not Charles Lamm Markmann's translation, "the fact of blackness"; more accurately, it should be understood as "the lived-experience of the Black." According to Judy, "Fanon struggled to get beyond the consideration of the black as an object to a consideration of the 'authentic forces' at work in human existence" (54). The implication here is that blackness should not be seen as a fixed race, but rather as part of what Judy describes as "a moment in the process of consciousness becoming in-itself and for-itself and for-others" (54). See also Gordon (1997). Gordon cautions against theories or critical inquiries that fail "to address the existential phenomenological dimension of racism"; he contends that such interrogations suffer "from a failure to address the situational dimension, what Fanon called l'experience vecue ('lived-experience'), of race" (70).

2. The term "Black Atlantic" comes from Gilroy (1993). Gilroy's usage of "Black Atlantic" names the transcultural formation that has emerged since the Atlantic slave trade, between black cultures of Africa, Europe, the Caribbean, and the Americas. Upon

reading an earlier version of my essay "In the Black Pacific: Testimonies of Vietnamese Afro-Amerasian displacements," Colin Palmer (Princeton University Professor of History and African-American Studies) noted that this appellative—Black Atlantic—excludes much of the black world; and that it is not synonymous with the African diaspora. With this in mind, "Black Atlantic" should be understood as a synecdoche; it represents a part, but not the whole of the black (cultures of the) world. My coinage and usage of "Black Pacific," as I explain later in this essay, represents another part.

3. For critical discussions on "Asia-Pacific" see, for example, Palumbo-Liu (1999) and Dirlik (1992).

4. The U.S. military census states that "some 18,000 American-Mestizoes were living in and about Manila in 1920" (Shade 1980).

5. My coinage of the term "interdiasporic" is an attempt to invoke the cultural space between (at the interstices of) multiple diasporas, which is a site of critical inquiry and cultural production that is often marginalized in studies of diasporas. With this in mind, I am suggesting that the study of the Black Pacific, and its Asian, African-American, and Afro-Amerasians diasporas, is an inherently interdiasporic one. Studies of an emergent interdiaspora can be comparative, cross-cultural, transnational, and quite often interracial.

6. See Gilroy (1993), Palumbo-Liu (1999), Dirlik (1992), and Dudden (1992). Dudden uses the term "American Pacific" to name the "geopolitical actuality" formed by United States imperialism throughout the Asia-Pacific region. According to Dudden, the American Pacific has emerged in between cultures that have acquired economic or military significance since the China trade, and throughout the major wars in the Asia-Pacific.

7. My redefinition and recontextualization of "Black Pacific," which appears in the latter part of my discussion, illustrates the distinction that Lewis Gordon makes between "black" and "Africana" philosophies. Gordon (2000) writes, "By *black philosophy* what is meant is the philosophical currents that emerged from the question of blackness. I distinguish Africana philosophy and black philosophies because the latter relate to a terrain that is broader than Africana communities. Not all black people are of African descent: indigenous Australians, whose lived-reality is that of being a black people, are an example. . . . There are black people whose cultural formations show a convergence of many cultural formations—from Africa, Europe, Asia, Australia, and the Americas" (5–6).

8. I use the term "Vietnamese diaspora" to describe the dispersion (and the cultures formed as a result) of Vietnamese people in multiple geographical and historical contexts: on the one hand, I am thinking about the migration of Vietnamese people to France, during and after French colonization; and on the other hand, I am thinking about Vietnamese migrations to "second-asylum" countries such as the United States, Canada, Australia, China, in addition to France, during and after the war with the United States.

9. See Blassingame (1977), Gates (1991), Smitherman (1977), and Tarpley (1995).

10. On the one hand, I am thinking about here the emergence of "yellow" identity and consciousness in America, which privileged the discourse and model of the Black Power movement. For a discussion of this, see Wei (1993). Wei explains, "By emphasizing racial pride and African American culture, the Black Power Movement inspired Asian Americans, especially middle-class college students, to assert themselves as people of color" (42). Consider, for example, the conference "Asian American Experi-

ence in America—Yellow Identity" held at the University of California, Berkeley, on January 11, 1969 (see Uyematsu 1971). On the other hand, I am thinking about the processes and histories of "yellowface" and "yellow peril," and also the Asian and Asian American critiques of them. See Desai, Machida, and Tchen (1994). In that collection, Tchen notes that the "process of yellowface enculturation has broad yet largely unacknowledged relevance for both Asians and Americans. Virtually any person of Asian descent—American or non-American—has been perceived by 'Occidentals' of European descent as an 'Oriental' other in some zone of contact" (13). See Lee (1999), and Lowe (1996).

11.　The location of the black body in contact zones at the black-white color-line is marked in language by the term "black skin, white masks"; this racial-spatial metaphor is the English translation of "peau noire, masques blancs," the title of Fanon's psychoanalytic study on racism, colonialism, and the lived-experience of blackness, originally published in French in 1952. "Black skin, white masks" calls attention to a discourse that recognizes the black body's location at the black-white color line—underscored primarily by the history of European colonialism and slavery, and by the displacement of black-skinned people of African descent throughout the diaspora; however, within that discourse on blackness, the black body's location at the black-yellow color line—underscored primarily by the history of black experiences within the Asian diasporas, particularly throughout Asian America—remains relatively unnoticed, unmapped, and marginalized therein.

12.　For critical discussions of Asia's "aboriginal black," "Negrito" people, see for example, Diamond (1999), and Van Sertima and Rashidi (1988).

13.　See Davis (1991).

REFERENCES

Anzaldúa, Gloria. 1987. *Borderlands: The new mestiza = la frontera*. San Francisco: Aunt Lute Books.

Bammer, Angelika, ed. 1994. *Displacements: Cultural identities in question*. Bloomington: Indiana University Press.

Bass, Thomas A. 1996. *Vietnamerica: The war comes home*. New York: Soho Press.

Blassingame, John W., ed. 1977. *Slave testimony: Two centuries of letters, speeches, interviews, and autobiographies*. Baton Rouge: Louisiana State University Press.

Buck, Pearl S. 1966. *For spacious skies: Journey in dialogue*. New York: John Day.

Clifford, James. 1997. *Routes: Travel and translation in the late twentieth century*. Cambridge: Harvard University Press.

Davis, F. James. 1991. *Who is Black?: One nation's definition*. University Park: Pennsylvania State University Press.

DeBonis, Steven., ed. 1995. *Children of the enemy: Oral histories of Vietnamese Amerasians and their mothers*. Jefferson, N.C.: McFarland.

Desai, Vishakha N., Margo Machida, and John Tchen, eds. 1994. *Asia/America: Identities in contemporary Asian American art*. New York: Asia Society Galleries.

Diamond, Jared M. 1999. *Guns, germs, and steel: The fates of human societies*. New York: W. W. Norton.

Dirlik, Arif. 1992. "The Asia-Pacific idea: Reality and representation in the invention of a regional structure." *Journal of World History* 3(1): 55–79.

Du Bois, W.E.B. 1995. *The souls of black folk*. New York: Signet Classic.

Dudden, Arthur Power. 1992. *The American Pacific: From the old China trade to the present.* New York: Oxford University Press.

Fanon, Frantz. 1967. *Black skin, white masks.* New York: Grove.

Felsman, K. J., M. C. John, F.T.L. Leong, and I. C. Felsman. 1989. "Vietnamese Amerasians: Practical implications of current research." Unpublished manuscript. Office of Refugee Resettlement, Washington, D.C.

Gates, Henry Louis, ed. 1991. *Bearing witness: Selections from African-American autobiography in the twentieth century.* New York: Pantheon.

Gilroy, Paul. 1993. *The Black Atlantic: Modernity and double consciousness.* London: Verso.

Gordon, Lewis R., ed. 1997. *Existence in Black: An anthology of Black existential philosophy.* New York: Routledge.

———. 2000. *Existentia Africana: Understanding Africana existential thought.* New York: Routledge.

hooks, bell. 1994. "Feminism inside: Toward a Black body politic." In *Black male: Representations of masculinity in contemporary American art,* edited by Thelma Golden, 127–157. New York: Whitney Museum of American Art.

Houston, Velina Hasu, ed. 1993. *The politics of life: Four plays.* Philadelphia: Temple University Press.

Judy, Ronald A. T. 1996. "Fanon's body of Black experience." In *Fanon: A critical reader,* edited by L. R. Gordon, T. D. Sharpley-Whiting, and R. T. White, 53–73. Cambridge: Blackwell.

Lee, Robert G. 1999. *Orientals: Asian Americans in popular culture.* Philadelphia: Temple University Press.

Lowe, Lisa. 1996. *Immigrant acts: On Asian American cultural politics.* Durham: Duke University Press.

McKelvey, Robert S., Alice Mao, and John A. Webb. 1992. "A risk profile predicting psychological distress in Vietnamese Amerasian youth." *Journal of the American Academy of Childhood and Adolescent Psychiatry* 31(5): 911–915.

Palumbo-Liu, David. 1999. *Asian/American: Historical crossings of a racial frontier.* Stanford: Stanford University Press.

Pease, Donald E. 1993. "New perspectives on U.S. culture and imperialism." In *Cultures of United States imperialism,* edited by A. Kaplan and D. Pease, 22–37. Durham: Duke University Press.

Perry, Matthew Calbraith, and Roger Pineau. 1968. *The Japan expedition, 1852–1854: The personal journal of Commodore Matthew C. Perry.* Washington, D.C.: Smithsonian Institution Press.

Pratt, Mary Louise. 1992. *Imperial eyes: Travel writing and transculturation.* New York: Routledge.

Russell, Kathy, Midge Wilson, and Ronald E. Hall. 1992. *The color complex: The politics of skin color among African Americans.* New York: Harcourt Brace Jovanovich.

Shade, John A. 1980. *America's forgotten children: The Amerasians.* Perkasie, Pa.: Pearl S. Buck Foundation.

Smitherman, Geneva. 1977. *Talkin and testifyin: The language of Black America.* Boston: Houghton Mifflin.

Tarpley, Natasha., ed. 1995. *Testimony: Young African-Americans on self-discovery and Black identity.* Boston: Beacon.

Uyematsu, Amy. 1971. "The emergence of yellow power in America." In *Roots: An Asian American reader,* edited by A. Tachiki et al., 9–13. Los Angeles: University of California, Asian American Studies Center.

Valverde, Kieu-Linh Caroline. 1992. "From dust to gold: The Vietnamese Amerasian experience." In *Racially mixed people in America*, edited by M.P.P. Root, 144–161. Newbury Park, Calif.: Sage.

Van Sertima, Ivan, and Runoko Rashidi, eds. 1988. *African presence in early Asia*. New Brunswick, N.J.: Transaction.

Walker, Alice. 1983. *In search of our mothers' gardens: Womanist prose*. San Diego: Harcourt Brace Jovanovich.

Wei, William. 1993. *The Asian American movement*. Philadelphia: Temple University Press.

Young, Robert. 1995. *Colonial desire: Hybridity in theory, culture, and race*. New York: Routledge.

PART THREE

===========================

Displacements and Diasporas: Anthropological Perspectives

8

==

Lived Simultaneity and Discourses of Diasporic Difference

NINA GLICK SCHILLER

It is one thing to speak of diasporas, ethnoscapes, hybridity, and transnational communities, and quite another to carefully research the life worlds, performance of culture, and social relationships of migrants and their children. Whether we begin that exploration through participant observation or ethnographic interviews, as soon as we begin to examine how migrants and their descendants live their lives, we move beyond the domain of diasporic discourse and confront the complexity of the migrant experience. Concepts of assimilation versus diasporic identities, situational or multiple identities—in fact any discussion of migration solely in terms of identities, values, norms, or cultural repertoires—cannot capture the processes of social connection that link migrants to more than one location and immerse them in various, sometimes overlapping and sometimes competing, identity projects.

To understand the lived experience of migrants, it is urgent that we understand that it is possible to become incorporated within a locality, its economy, its institutions, and its forms of cultural production and at the same time live within social networks that are intimately tied to elsewhere. These ties to elsewhere often link people to an economy, institutions, and cultural production framed by the political processes of other nation-states, even as these ties produce actors whose experience crosses multiple political borders and social boundaries (Basch, Glick Schiller, and Szanton Blanc 1994; Morowska 2001).

Wanni Anderson, Louis-Jacques Dorais, and Sunaina Maira provide us with descriptions of three different sets of locales and networks in what is sometimes glossed glibly as the "Asian diaspora." Through their work we meet Lao women college students in Rhode Island, Vietnamese from age twenty-one to retirees in Montreal and Quebec City, and Indian-American youth in the New York metropolitan area. These studies provide us with provocative glimpses into what it means to forge social relations and cultural representations within what many have called transnational social spaces or fields (Faist 1999; Glick Schiller, Basch, and Blanc-Szanton 1992; Glick Schiller 1999). And these glimpses remind us that metaphors of space are only useful if we remain keenly aware that space is not a product of nature but is socially delimited by the intersections and overlays of institutions of family, economy, school, culture, and politics. That is to say, these authors, in their own ways, remind us that to be transnational is to confront differences in power experienced within the simultaneous production and reconfiguration of gender, race, and class in specific geographic locations. Although the authors of the three studies discussed here are not presenting us with comprehensive ethnography or a survey of a representative sample, each study contains research that challenges existing approaches to diasporic and transnational studies and provides invaluable perceptions on which we can all build.

In this discussion, I will explore how a comparison of Anderson, Dorais, and Maira's descriptions of the settlement of Asian migrants revisits the conceptualization of Asian diasporic identities and moves us beyond the essentialized concept of diaspora. The term "diaspora" definitely has its uses, both conceptual and political. It gives us a way to envision migrant populations as part of broader transborder connections, histories, and cultural politics, and in dialogue with but differentiated from concepts of identity that are rooted in the building of territorially based nation-states (Gilroy 1993). The concept of diaspora, however, as Maira points out, participates in a form of cultural politics that creates unity through concepts of shared essentialized biological descent-based identities (see also Gabbacia 2000 for an ethnographically and historically grounded critique). Maira's examples are telling. The cultural politics of diaspora can keep us from seeing the kinds of overlapping and interactive racialized identifications of Indians in Britain when they embrace blackness or Indian youth in New York when they situate themselves within hip hop. Diasporic consciousness can prevent us from seeing, theorizing, and taking political action in relationship to the simultaneous setting in and transnational reaching out that marks so many migrant experiences, including those of second-generation Indians in New York, Laotians in Rhode Island, and Vietnamese in Quebec and Montreal described by these three authors.

The migrants described in these three studies are both settlers and transmigrants who live within multiple forms of transnational connection. They can best be understood by reformulating our approach to migration so that we can conceptualize simultaneity—that is, the incorporation of migrants in social fields that extend into the new land and transnationally through networks to many other localities, including the ancestral homeland. To comprehend their complex and multiple social embeddedness we must discard concepts of assimilation or a progression of increasing loss of identification with the homeland as one generation replaces another (Alba and Nee 1997; Rumbaut 1997). Transmigrant and well-incorporated immigrants are not two opposing categories. The new assimilationism, which contests transnational migration as a significant migrant experience, casts it as a first-generation phenomena, ignores it in discussions of immigrant incorporation, or poses it as an alternative immigrant strategy, misses the point (Faist 1999; Gerstle 1999).

Assimilation, whether conceptualized in the United States as Anglo-conformity or melting-pot culture, in France as republicism, or in the German idiom of "integration into the national culture," provides us with a description of an aspect of public policy of nation-states and the methodological nationalisms of social scientists. It has never been a concept that adequately describes migrant behavior, either past or present (Wimmer and Glick Schiller 2002; Joppke 1999). Milton Gordon's (1964) distinction between acculturation and assimilation provides us with a somewhat more useful approach by conceptually distinguishing between cultural performance and social structure. Migrants can continue to mark cultural differences through a set of practices while participating in the institutional life of a country. Indian women who go to work in saris provide us with an example. Obversely, migrants can take up the cultural practices of the mainstream culture but maintain a separate set of institutions. Vietnamese organizations in Montreal who participate in local politics can be said to be participating in a form of acculturation despite structural separation. Moreover, as Gans (1979) pointed out in his work on "symbolic ethnicity," migrants can maintain or revive identities, despite acculturation and assimilation. But to date discussions of assimilation, acculturation, and symbolic ethnicity have failed to addresses the transnational connections, cultural elaborations, and identifications that many migrants still maintain or construct anew, even as they settle into a new location.

Anderson's description of Lao women in Rhode Island aptly captures the simultaneity of settlement and transnational linkage. Anderson, as well as Dorais, Maira, and myriad recent studies of transnational migration, make it clear that migrants, both past and present, often acculturate and become structurally incorporated in a new land to which they have come as immigrants or refugees, yet still maintain not only homeland ties but ongoing social networks. Yet, as Anderson's perceptive ethnography makes clear, the dichotomous framework, which places homeland identifications and transnational social and cultural connections in opposition to the acculturation and assimilation of immigrants, still preoccupies her Laotian informants' own understanding of their relationship to new land and old. In fact this dichotomy becomes a poltergeist that continues to haunt Anderson, threatening to disrupt the clarity of her analysis. Anderson documents that Laotian refugees in Rhode Island, through their nostalgia for a purer and simpler past, construct and revitalize this dichotomy and live it. Anderson's respondents' narratives of the idealized contrast between homeland and new land structure their sense of self, collective identity, and settlement, and thus shape their behavior.

The tendency to compare, contrast, and dichotomize the realities of homeland and land of settlement, which proves to be central to Anderson's Lao narratives, extends far beyond the Laotian experience of migration. Globally, the nostalgia of migrants and refugees for a past life that never was mediates and shapes settlement and the maintenance or reconstitution of homeland ties (Glick Schiller and Fouron 2001a, 2001b; Fouron and Glick Schiller 2003). By invoking their shared past, migrants, their descendants, and people within the homeland bridge the chasms of time, space, generation, and dramatically different daily experience that divide them. Collectively they recall that "in the past we practiced this, we believed that, families were cohesive, men and women each knew their place, and we were happy and now life is less pure, less satisfying, more complex and fraught with tension." This is an old song, but it is also a factually wrong song, both because it simplifies the past, with its conflicts of gender, class, and power, and because it disregards the fact that the homeland culture was and continues to be a changing mosaic of influences. Global processes and transnational communication, social relations, and connections now affect all localities of the world.

Anderson documents the disparity between migrant nostalgia and the contemporary culture of the homeland as it is shaped by global forces, including the transnational flows of ideas and objects provided by the migrants themselves. Both the Lao young women in Rhode Island and those "back home" in Laos experience global forces via videos and changing patterns of consumption, and think about gender relations through this lens. When Lao young women arrive in Rhode Island—through processes of family unification, transnational marriage arrangements, or visits to relatives—they come with notions of what it means to be a Lao woman forged in transnational space. In effect, once transnational migration is firmly established, complete with the dispersal of money and material objects from abroad, all individuals who grow up within the transnational social field are part of a transnational second generation (Fouron and Glick Schiller 2001).

Transnational relationships, transnational flows of ideas and objects, and the nostalgia that filters both social connections and cultural flows do not automatically or necessarily translate into identity with a homeland or slow the processes of migrant settlement. Transnational connections to a homeland can exist without identification with that homeland, and settlement in a new land can take place, despite a strong identification with the homeland. Illustrating these contradictory processes, Anderson confirms that as they live their daily lives within transnational social fields, Lao young women in Rhode Island are drawn into debates about whether they are Lao or Laotian and whether either shared nation signifier can be transmuted into a hyphenated Laotian-American identity. Standing back from this debate, we can see that the parameters of the argument reflect an internalization by all participants of the bias against simultaneity. This bias reflects hegemonic nation-state building projects that obscure the possibility not only of multiple identities but also of multiple incorporations (Basch, Glick Schiller, and Szanton Blanc 1994).

Dorais's data on Vietnamese in Quebec City and Montreal, echoing Anderson's, also provide evidence of simultaneous incorporation and transnational connection. Dorais makes it clear that whether or not persons of Vietnamese origin in Montreal or Quebec identify as Canadians, as part of a Vietnamese-Canadian ethnic group, or as members of a Vietnamese diaspora is not an indicator of their degree of transnational connections. He notes that the word "diaspora" is in fashion and used so broadly that all immigrant and refugee populations become diasporas. The problem with such a broad definition of "diaspora" is that it begs the question of assuming ongoing identification across time, space, and generations. As did previous approaches to migration, which assumed that immigrants were uprooted and disconnected from their homeland and home ties, the current trend at redefining immigrants and refugees as a diaspora precludes investigation of just when the term "diaspora" is most usefully deployed: What kinds of connections and identification, in what circumstances, and in which generations? In response to the simplification of processes of incorporation, connection, and identification that he finds in discourses of diaspora, Dorais argues, in effect, that whether or not the presence of migrants from elsewhere, even those with transnational connections, can be taken as evidence of a diaspora is a matter of empirical investigation.

His research makes clear that this investigation must address the role of migrant-sending states and of the growth of ideologies of long-distance nationalism. Although family networks engage the Vietnamese in Quebec and Montreal with kin who participate in the politics and cultures of multiple states and location, all of these actors must come to terms with a politics generated from their homeland and about their homeland. The government of Vietnam defines persons of Vietnamese origin as nationals, whatever their legal citizenship, labeling them Viet Kieu (Vietnamese sojourners). The Vietnamese organizations studied by Dorais in Montreal contest the legitimacy of the Vietnamese government but not the claim that those abroad remain part of Vietnam. Refugee politics can fuel an ideology of continuing claims and political actions taken on behalf of the homeland and against its current regime.

Once we begin to talk about homeland politics that extend across international borders, we have entered the domain of long-distance nationalism. The concept of "long-distance nationalism," deployed without elaboration or definition by Benedict Anderson (1993, 1994) and Arjun Appadurai (1993), and employed increasingly by scholars of transnational migration, provides an analytical lens that brings into focus both the processes through which migrants of varying class and gender positions relate to their homeland and through which different sectors of the homeland population, from the poor and disempowered to the political leadership, relate to a dispersed population settled abroad (Glick Schiller 1999). Skrbiš (1999), describing the ideology and practices of Croatians in Australia; Fuglerud (1999), studying the connections of Tamils to the struggle in Sri Lanka; and Matsuoka and Sorenson (2001), describing the homeland politics of Eritreans settled in Canada, have found this term useful and have contributed to documenting the global significance of long-distance nationalism as a political ideology and a set of practices.

Georges Fouron and I (Glick Schiller and Fouron 2001a, 2001b; Fouron and Glick Schiller 2001, 2003) have defined long-distance nationalism as a set of ideas that link together people living in various geographic locations and motivate or justify their taking action in relationship to an ancestral territory and its government. Through such ideological linkages, a territory, its people, and its government become a transnational nation-state. Long-distance nationalism does not exist only in the domain of the imagination and sentiment. It leads to specific action. These actions link a dispersed population to a specific homeland and its political system. Long-distance nationalism binds together immigrants, their descendants, and people who have remained in their homeland into a single transborder citizenry. It provides the transborder nationalist narratives that constitute and are constituted by everyday forms of state formation. As in other versions of nationalism, the concept of a territorial homeland governed by a state that represents the nation remains salient, but national borders are not thought to delimit membership in the nation. Citizens residing within the territorial homeland view emigrants and their descendants as part of the nation, whatever legal citizenship the émigrés may have.

By delineating and defining long-distance nationalism, we are better able to differentiate between a political identity specifically linked to the politics of a homeland and the type of diasporic consciousness. Diasporic consciousness provides an identity for individuals and populations whose history reaches beyond the borders of a specific nation-state but who remain aloof from a state of origin or any specific nationalist project. The black diaspora as described by Paul Gilroy (1993), Jewish consciousness before Zionism and Israel, and the Asian diaspora as it is used in diasporic studies are examples. (See Tölölyan's [2001] parallel efforts to conceptualize changing Armenian ideologies of identity and dispersal, using the terms "exilic nationalism" and "diasporic nationalism.")

Are the members of Dorais's sample long-distance nationalists? Are they members of a Vietnamese diaspora? With only two exceptions, the persons in Dorais's sample are linked to Vietnamese elsewhere in Canada, in Vietnam, and in other countries through family connections. In this sense they live their lives across borders and could be considered a diaspora. Few members of his sample actively participate in overseas Vietnamese community organizations, although they apparently know such organizations. However, at least the first-generation migrants Dorais interviewed also continue to identify with Vietnam as their homeland, despite their incorporation into Canada.

At the same time, the Vietnamese interviewed by Dorais were also settlers. Moreover, the Vietnamese organizations in Montreal and their leaders were, in 1990, simultaneously—and I stress that this word is key—ethnic organizations funded to serve as brokers of newcomers in a multicultural Canada and long-distance nationalists, working to engage Vietnamese abroad in reclaiming their homeland from its current communist government. Dorais, seeking to conceptualize simultaneity of incorporation and transnational connection, suggests the concept of "double belonging."

Employing another productive approach to the study of transnational relations, Dorais also looks at the transnational economic activities of Vietnamese in Canada. He rightly warns us that focusing on transnational economic activities and discarding other aspects of transnational connection as nothing new, as Portes (1996) at one point suggested, undercuts our ability to understand the nature of migrant relationships to both settlement and maintenance of homeland ties. In fact, Dorais pushes us to probe the relationships between the flow of goods across borders and identity constructions, emphasizing the materiality of cultural processes. Goods circulated globally can become signifiers of ethnic difference—understood as the symbolic differentiation of distinct populations incorporated within and subordinated to a single nation-state—as well as persisting symbols of connection with a homeland.

Both Dorais and Maira remind us that there are many forms of cross-border networks. They cannot all be explained in the same way, or connected to a single identity politics, although the same individuals may engage in more than one form of connection across borders. Some connections contribute to nation-state building while other kinds of cross-border activities may challenge such projects. Yet items used to construct or maintain ethnic identifications as migrants settle into a new state, and nationalist identifications that link them to a homeland, may deploy the same trading networks and cultural circuits in both projects—and actors may engage in both kinds of identity projects at the same time.

Whereas Dorais tends to see persisting Vietnamese familial connections as emanating from basic values within Vietnamese culture, family as a source of transnational connection plays a prominent role in Anderson's description of Lao migrants and Maira's description of second-generation south Indians. Lest anyone build from this some generalized cultural conception of an Asian mode of transnational connection, it is important to note that comparative studies in transnational migration make it clear that the maintenance of family ties is central to the migrant experience for almost all populations (Glick Schiller

1999; Foner 2000). In fact, this may be a cultural universal in the face of the global economic and political precariousness of migrant-sending locations and the insecurity, discrimination, and loss of status that migrants experience as they resettle. Within this setting, both persons left behind and persons who have migrated see family ties as a form of social capital, sometimes the only form available to them.

Although many of the patterns such as the centrality of family ties described by all three authors resonate with descriptions of other migrating populations, the specificity of culture, time, and place do matter. Maira's observations of the New York hip-hop scene that shapes the identities of second-generation South Asian youth, when coupled with Dorais's and Anderson's descriptions of the gaps between the discourses of diaspora and the multiple incorporation strategies of their respondents, provide a useful corrective of the generalities projected by diaspora studies. Maira is particularly skillful at highlighting the significance of locality as a factor that shapes the nature of incorporation of migrants and their transnationality. The existence of organizations that claim to represent a transnational community or a diaspora, the existence of local politics that highlight ethnic identities, and the local configurations of the politics of race all shape the degree to which transborder identities are articulated and whether local modes of incorporation employ racial or ethnic signifiers.

Maira captures the fluidity of the New York context and of the "desi scene," a Manhattan youth culture created by Pakistani and Indian youth who experience themselves as South Asian young people growing up in New York and participating in the production of a hip-hop subculture that stands outside of whiteness. Moving toward a more nuanced reading of dispersal, one that examines the actual nature of border connections, Maira selects the term "transnational" for certain cross-border social relations that structure cultural production, because these relations are "mediated heavily by the structures and ideologies of nation-states and still deeply concerned with notions of 'place' and processes of 'localization.'" As she points out, "hybridity, though fashionable in cultural theory and also literally in 'ethnic chic' is not always easy to live, for social institutions and networks continue to demand loyalty to sometimes competing cultural ideals that may be difficult to manage for second generation youth."

Maira's thoughtful critique of concepts of cultural hybridity builds on her understanding of both the significance of locality and the nature of transnational connections. Her disquiet with the concept of cultural hybridity reflects her dissatisfaction with the false dichotomy between the culturally pure homeland and the impure ethnic cultures of immigrants. Discussions of hybridity, Maira argues, do not adequately describe the form of cultural production she documents. The youth in New York among whom she worked construct identities not only from transnational cultural flows such as music videos in India but also in response to the transnational social fields in which their households in New York are situated. Their cultural mix is in dialogue with their life experience of transnational relations and the racial politics and racialization processes of New York City.

Whether we speak of long-distance nationalism, double belonging, the simultaneity of incorporation and transnational connection, or transnational cultural production, however, we simplify the influences of migrant networks that extend globally into many nation-states. And the complexity of these cultural and social processes of connection brings us back to the virtues of the concept of diaspora, with all its risks of essentializing identities, minimalizing the variations shaped by history and locality, and ignoring the continuing role of nation-state building in both the homeland and the specific land of settlement. The strength of the concept of diaspora is that it does not locate subjectivity or identity politics and practices within the confines of any single state or territory. If used within the context of careful ethnography and skillful studies of transnational processes, relationships, and connections, the concept of diaspora can assist in describing moments in which Asian migrants experience and mechanisms by which they articulate their historical connections and contest inequalities of local, national, and global power. However, to be useful, formulations of diasporic identity must not obscure our understanding that migrants may enter the daily life of the locality in which they have settled, although they identify not with that locality but as a dispersed people. In point of fact, and once again, our analytical mantra must be: all identity constructions can obscure the complexity of social relations because they are statements about relationships of unequal power.

REFERENCES

Alba, Richard, and Victor Nee. 1997. "Rethinking assimilation theory for a new era of immigration." *International Migration Review* 31(Winter): 826–874.

Anderson, Benedict. 1993. "The new world disorder." *New Left Review* 193 (May/June): 2–13.

———. 1994. "Exodus." *Critical Inquiry* 20 (Winter): 314–327.

Appadurai, Arjun. 1993. "Patriotism and its futures." *Public Culture* 5(3): 411–429.

Basch, Linda, Nina Glick Schiller, and Cristina Szanton Blanc. 1992. *Towards a transnational perspective on migration: Race, class, ethnicity reconsidered.* New York: New York Academy of Sciences.

———. 1994. *Nations unbound: Transnational projects, postcolonial predicaments, and deterritorialized nation-states.* London: Gordon and Breach.

Faist, Thomas. 1999. "Transnationalization in international migration: Implications for the study of citizenship." *Transnational Communities*, Working paper series: 99–108.

Foner, Nancy. 2000. *From Ellis Island to JFK: New York's two great waves of immigration.* New Haven: Yale University Press.

Fouron, Georges, and Nina Glick Schiller. 2001. "The generation of identity: Redefining the second generation within a transnational social field." In *Migration, transnational-*

ism, and the political economy of New York City, edited by H. Cordero-Guzman, R. Grosfoguel, and R. Smith, 58–86. Philadelphia: Temple University Press.

———. 2003. "Killing me softly: Violence, globalization, and the apparent state." In *Globalization, the state, and violence*, edited by J. Friedman, 203–248. Walnut Creek: Altimira.

Fuglerud, Oivind. 1999. *Life on the outside: The Tamil diaspora and long-distance nationalism*. Ann Arbor: University of Michigan Press.

Gabbacia, Donna R. 2000. *Italy's many diasporas*. Seattle: University of Washington Press.

Gans, Herbert. 1979. "Symbolic ethnicity: The future of ethnic groups and cultures in America." *Racial and Ethnic Studies* 2(1): 1–20.

Gerstle, Garry. 1999. "Liberty, coercion and the making of Americans." In *The handbook of international migration: The American experience*, edited by C. Hirshman, P. Kasinitz, and J. DeWind, 275–293. New York: Russell Sage.

Gilroy, Paul. 1993. *The black Atlantic: Modernity and double consciousness*. Cambridge: Harvard University Press.

Glick Schiller, Nina. 1999. "Transmigrants and nation-states: Something old and something new in the U.S. immigrant experience." In *The handbook of international migration: The American experience*, edited by C. Hirshman, P. Kasinitz, and J. DeWind, 94–119. New York: Russell Sage.

Glick Schiller, Nina, Linda Basch, and Cristina Blanc-Szanton, eds. 1992. *Towards a transnational perspective on migration: Race, class, ethnicity, and nationalism reconsidered*. New York: New York Academy of Sciences.

Glick Schiller, Nina, and Georges Fouron. 2001a. *Georges woke up laughing: Long-distance nationalism and the search for home*. Durham: Duke University Press.

———. 2001b. "'I am not a problem without a solution': Poverty, transnational migration, and struggle." In *New poverty studies: The ethnography of politics, policy and impoverished people in the United States*, edited by J. Maskovsky and J. Good, 321–363. New York: New York University Press.

Gordon, Milton M. 1964. *Assimilation in American life: The role of race, religion, and national origins*. New York: Oxford University Press.

Joppke, Christian. 1999. *Immigration and the nation-state: The United States, Germany, and Great Britain*. Oxford: Oxford University Press.

Matsuoka, Atusko, and John Sorenson. 2001. *Ghosts and shadows: Construction of identity and community in an African diaspora*. Toronto: University of Toronto Press.

Morowska, E. 2001. "Disciplinary agendas, analytic strategies, and objectivity of (im)migration research: Advantages in interdisciplinary knowledge." Paper presented at Social Science Research Council Workshop conference, "Transnational migration: Comparative perspectives," Princeton University, June 30–July 1.

Portes, Alejandro. 1996. "Transnational communities: Their emergence and significance in the contemporary world system." In *Latin America in the world economy*, edited by R. P. Korzeniewicz and W. Smith, 151–168. Westport, Conn.: Greenwood Press.

Rumbaut, Ruben. 1997. "Paradoxes and (orthodoxies) of assimilation." *Sociological Perspectives* 40(3): 483–512.

Skrbiš, Zlatko. 1999. *Long-distance nationalism: Diasporas, homelands, and identities*. Brookfield, Vt.: Ashgate.

Tölölyan, Khachig. 2001. "Elites and institutions in the Armenian transnation." Paper delivered at Social Science Research Council Workshop conference, "Transnational migration: Comparative perspectives," Princeton University, June 30–July 1.

Wimmer, Andreas, and Nina Glick Schiller. 2002. "Methodological nationalism." Paper delivered at Social Science Research Council Workshop conference, "Transnational migration: Comparative perspectives," Princeton University, June 30–July 1.

9

From Refugees to Transmigrants

The Vietnamese in Canada

LOUIS-JACQUES DORAIS

According to the Canadian federal census, some 137,000 residents of Canada claimed a single or multiple Vietnamese ethnic origin in 1996. Without debating the accuracy of this figure—Canada had only 94,000 Vietnamese in 1991, and births and new arrivals could in no way have reached a total of 43,000 over the following five years—it shows that people from Vietnam now constitute a sizeable group among Canadian immigrants. Even when those Vietnamese who define themselves primarily as Chinese or Khmer from Vietnam are left out of statistics, we remain with around 100,000 ethnic Vietnamese living in Canada. Cities such as Toronto (with 41,735 Vietnamese in 1996), Montreal (25,340), Vancouver (16,870), Calgary (10,110), Edmonton (7,775), or Ottawa (6,615) have now become metropolises of sort among Canadian ethnic Vietnamese, Chinese Vietnamese, and Khmers from Vietnam.

As in the United States and elsewhere in the world, the vast majority of Vietnamese migrants came to Canada as refugees, or as relatives of refugees when more recent, family-sponsored arrivals were arranged. Their migration was directly or indirectly provoked by the fall of South Vietnam in April 1975. On January 1, 1975, only 1,500 persons of Vietnamese ancestry were living in Canada, most of whom resided in the province of Quebec. With few exceptions, they were students or recent graduates from Canadian French-speaking universities or the children of these students and graduates. Most of them were males, and a good number had married local, non-Vietnamese women (Dorais 1999). By the end of the year, though, 3,100 more Vietnamese had entered Canada, and a further 2,500 arrived in 1976.

This was nothing in comparison with the much higher numbers of Vietnamese (and, also, Cambodian and Laotian) refugees who were admitted during and just after the so-called "boat-people crisis" of the late 1970s. Between 1979 and 1982, some 59,000 individuals whose last country of residence had been Vietnam entered Canada (as against 7,100 refugees from Cambodia, and 7,500 from Laos). About 60 percent of them were ethnic Vietnamese, the remainder Chinese or Khmer Vietnamese. This high rate of admission continued through the 1980s, a period during which the Canadian government encouraged family reunification. It started slowing down after 1990, and since 1995, fewer than 5,000 Vietnamese a year have entered Canada.

Vietnamese who arrived in Canada in 1975 and afterward were identified as refugees. Newspapers, the electronic media, and public opinion, as well as government officials and resettlement personnel, commonly referred to them as "Vietnamese refugees," "Indochinese refugees," or "boat people." This seemed all natural, even if, as Indra (1987) has shown, the mere concept of "refugee" was not devoid of political connotations, since the definition of who was or was not a refugee had been constructed by politicians and policymakers. As for the vast majority of Vietnamese, they also willingly defined themselves as refugees ("Vietnamese," rather than "Indochinese"), given the fact that they had left their country (or refused to return there) in view of their nonacceptance of the current regime. In their case, too, this definition was political, because they considered their flight as a testimony to their anti-Communist opinions.

This, however, happened more than twenty years ago. Since then, most refugees from Vietnam, their children, and the relatives who joined them through family reunification have become Vietnamese Canadians or, in the case of many young persons, Canadians of Vietnamese ancestry. Even if some individuals and ethnic associations may still claim publicly that they will never cease being refugees, in Canada as elsewhere, Vietnamese have now formed complex communities of immigrants and children of immigrants, whose members are increasingly integrated within mainstream economic and social organization, but who generally preserve several aspects of their culture and ethnic identity.

The existence of these communities, which maintain numerous transregional and transnational relations with co-ethnics living elsewhere in Canada, as well as in Vietnam and other countries, entails two closely related questions: To what extent may Vietnamese Canadians be considered transmigrants, and what are the most salient features of their transnational activities? Answers to these questions will be tentative. They will be principally based on data collected in 1997–98 in Montreal and Quebec City as part of a research project on transnational identities among the Quebec Vietnamese (cf. Dorais 1998a).[1]

Transnationalism and Transmigrants

Basch, Glick Schiller, and Szanton Blanc (1994) define transnationalism as a process through which immigrants develop and maintain multiple social relations that link together their societies of origin and of resettlement. Individuals involved in this process construct social fields that go across geographical, cultural, and political boundaries. It may be added (Glick Schiller, Basch, Blanc-Szanton 1995) that the daily life of these transnational migrants, or "transmigrants," is based on multiple and constant interconnections that transcend international borders.

In their introduction to a special issue of *Ethnic and Racial Studies* on transnationalism, Portes, Guarnizo, and Landolt (1999) stress the fact that if this phenomenon is to be considered a special area of investigation, it must be defined with some precision. Nothing is gained by calling immigrants transmigrants if the activities of these so-called transmigrants are essentially the same as those of any other immigrant:

> For purposes of establishing a novel area of investigation, it is preferable
> to delimit the concept of transnationalism to occupations and activities
> that require regular and sustained social contacts over time across
> national borders for their implementation. . . . The occasional contacts,
> trips and activities across national borders of members of an expatriate
> community . . . contribute to strengthening the transnational field but,
> by themselves, these contacts are neither novel enough, nor sufficiently
> distinct, to justify a new area of investigation. (Portes, Guarnizo, and Landolt 1999, 219)

According to these authors, the term "transmigrant" should, therefore, only apply to people who actually commute across national borders on a regular basis, chiefly for professional or political reasons. Broadly speaking, the dynamics of transnational activities can be summarized in three substantive propositions: "1) The emergence of these activities is tied to the logic of capitalist expansion itself; 2) while following well-established principles of social network development, transnational communities represent a phenomenon at variance with conventional expectations of immigrant assimilation; 3) because transnational enterprise is fuelled by the dynamics of capitalism, it has greater potential as a form of individual and group resistance to dominant structures than alternative strategies" (Portes, Guarnizo, and Landolt 1999, 227–228).

In an earlier article, one of the authors of the text just quoted, Luis E. Guarnizo, had called in question the third proposition above. For him (Smith and Guarnizo 1998), transnational practices and hybrid identities may be potentially counterhegemonic, but they are by no means always resistant, because they can be used for the purposes of capital accumulation (as in the case of the contemporary overseas Chinese). Moreover, since some states encourage their subjects living abroad to maintain their allegiance to the homeland and to participate in its politics, transnationalism does not necessarily lead to the emergence of citizens of the world. It may rather reinforce traditional nationalism through a deterritorialized expansion of the nation-state.

Vietnamese as Transmigrants

The situation of most overseas Vietnamese seems to correspond to the definition of transnationalism found in Basch et al. (1994). As we shall see, they maintain multiple social relations that link together their societies of origin and of resettlement, and such relations are significant for them. They are conscious enough of their specificity as Vietnamese residing abroad to designate themselves (and be designated by homeland people) with a special name, Viet Kieu (Vietnamese sojourners).[2]

In a general way, the dynamics of their transnational activities are congruent with those summarized in Portes et al. (1999). Even if most Viet Kieu claim, often with good reason, that they are, or were, political refugees, their emigration from Vietnam also has economic connotations. One of the chief reasons given for having left their homeland is an alleged lack of educational and professional opportunities for their children, who are often barred from entering higher education and prestigious careers because of the past activities and/or class position of their parents.[3] Another is a desire to escape being sent to the New Economic Zones (Dorais, Pilon-Le, and Nguyen 1987).[4] Vietnamese thus see their resettlement in Canada, the United States, or elsewhere as a way of economic mobility, through education and technical knowledge rather than through trade and entrepreneurship.[5] Because young Viet Kieu wish increasingly to bring their knowledge acquired abroad back to Vietnam, by way of international cooperation, their acquisition of professional skills has transnational connotations (Methot 1995; Richard 2000).

In accordance with the third proposition of Portes et al., these professional and economic activities, which include money remittances sent to Vietnam from abroad, operate within family and other intraethnic social networks. It remains to be seen, though, the point to which they really constitute an alternative to mainstream capitalist structures. Those involved in the networks through which they operate are eager to participate in capitalist markets, albeit in a generally modest way, particularly since the inception in 1986 of the Vietnamese *doi moi* policy of economic opening. Be that as it may, these networks can help Viet Kieu to escape total assimilation to their host societies, as envisioned by Portes et al. in their second proposition.

The propositions of Portes et al. are of a general nature. If they define the broader framework through which transnationalism operates, they do not tell much about the microsociology of transmigration. Moreover, these authors' definition of transnationalism insists mainly on the economic aspects of this phenomenon, transmigrants being considered primarily as international entrepreneurs. Researchers interested, as is the author of the present chapter, in defining transnationalism as a way of organizing personal relations, representing cultural identity, and developing economic and political ties that cross international borders, should, perhaps, look elsewhere to find a relevant analytical model.

In her chapter in the *Handbook of International Migration*, Nina Glick Schiller (1999) offers an interesting and, in the eyes of this author, productive definition and description of what she calls transnational migration (rather than transnationalism): "Transnational migration is a pattern of migration in which persons, although they move across international borders and settle and establish social relations in a new state, maintain social connections within the polity from which they originated. In transnational migration, persons literally live their lives across international borders. That is to say, they establish transnational social fields" (Glick Schiller 1999, 96).

According to Glick Schiller, the term "transmigrant" should only apply to "people who claim and are claimed by two or more nation-states, into which they are incorporated as social actors, one of which is widely acknowledged to be their state of origin." Transmigrants are different from simple immigrants who just move across international borders to settle elsewhere, whether or not these immigrants establish transnational networks. Transnational migration implies continuing participation in the economy, politics, and social organization of one's state of origin, while, at the same time, being more or less fully involved in one's country of adoption. Contrary to what many social scientists seem to think, it is not a recent phenomenon. Even in the nineteenth century, immigrants to the United States contributed actively to the formation of nation-states in their countries of origin, while shaping "the ways in which U.S. national identity was debated and represented" (Glick Schiller 1999, 104).[6]

Transnational migration should also be distinguished from diasporas, which Glick Schiller defines as "dispersed populations who attribute their common identity, cultural beliefs and practices, language, or religion to myths of a common ancestry" (Glick Schiller 1999, 96). Unlike transmigrants, who participate in two active nation-states, members of a diaspora share in a sense of common heritage that is not necessarily linked to any contemporary state.

Overseas Vietnamese do participate in transnational networks, and these often involve contacts with Vietnam as a country, as well as with individual Vietnamese still living in the homeland (Dorais 1998b).[7] At the beginning of this section, we saw that their situation seems to correspond to the propositions of Portes et al. on the general dynamics of transnationalism. It remains to be seen, though, to what extent this situation and the activities it generates correspond to tighter definitions of transnational migration, such as the one just described.

Glick Schiller (1999, 97) asserts that research on transmigrants should investigate "the range and multiplicity of social networks that immigrants establish." Among various fields where such networks operate, three seem particularly important to the study of transnational migration: 1) economic activi-

TABLE 9.1

Survey Respondents by Gender and Age

	Male	Female	Total
Between 21 and 24 years old	4	6	10
Between 25 and 49 years old	3	5	8
50 years old and over	6	4	10
Total	13	15	28

ties, including remittances sent to the home country; 2) political discourses and organizations; and 3) personal relations across national borders. We will now examine how Canadian Viet Kieu behave in each of these fields.

A Transnational Economy?

As mentioned in the introduction, data for this paper stem principally from a research project completed in 1998 (cf. Dorais 1998a). It consisted of in-depth interviews with twenty-eight Vietnamese Canadians (seven in Quebec City and twenty-one in Montreal) on the nature and importance of their local and transnational social networks. In terms of gender and age, the sample was distributed as shown in Table 9.1.

This sample included individuals who belonged to the various waves of Vietnamese immigration to Canada: pre-1975 former students (two persons); first wave (1975–1978) refugees (four persons); second wave (1979–1982) boat people (eight persons); post-1982 family reunification cases (ten persons); and young people born in Canada (four persons). With two exceptions (a half-Cambodian and a half-Chinese), all of them were ethnic Vietnamese.

In occupational terms, the sample was not truly representative of Vietnamese Canadians in general. Ten of the informants (all of them in their twenties) were students, seven (over sixty-five years of age) were retired, and one was a housewife. Among those active on the labor market, two worked in the service sector (one was a store clerk, the other a waitress), while eight held a professional or administrative position. This is at variance with general statistics. In 1996 (according to census data), 54 percent of all Viet Kieu over fourteen years of age living in the province of Quebec were holding a job or searching for one (as against 36 percent in the sample), and 48 percent of these were working as factory operatives, laborers, or employees in the service sector (Richard 2000).

Thus it should be kept in mind that my conclusions apply above all to upper-middle-class ethnic Vietnamese Quebecers, that is, to professional—or formerly professional—college-educated people whose income generally is or used to be above average. This entails two consequences related to the economic aspects of transnational activities: first, the informants are upper middle class, they can devote financial resources to transnational activities potentially unavailable to other Viet Kieu; and second, since, among the Viet Kieu, international business is, for the most part, in the hands of people of Chinese origin or ancestry, the sample should not be expected to participate in large- or middle-scale trade networks involving Vietnam, even if such networks do exist. The sample's transnational economic relations should, therefore, comprise money remittances and other forms of cross-border aid, rather than entrepreneurial activities.

Money remittances play a major role in the contemporary economy of Vietnam. It has been estimated that in the early 1990s, between US$600 and $700 million a year were sent back to families in Vietnam by relatives living abroad (Economist Intelligence Unit 1995, 4). This amount may have decreased recently, because of some improvement in economic conditions in Vietnam, but it still exceeds half a billion dollars a year. According to the Viet Nam News Agency (the government of Vietnam's official news medium), in 1999 alone, the 21,810 overseas contract workers from Vietnam remitted US$220 million to their homeland (Vietnam News 2000a).[8] And this did not include money sent back by those Viet Kieu who reside abroad permanently.

Interview data show that Vietnamese Canadians from Montreal and Quebec City do participate in these kinds of economic activities. Sixteen out of twenty-eight informants state that they or their parents aid their relatives on a more or less regular basis. This support includes, but is not restricted to, kin living in Vietnam. As a matter of fact, aid is—or was, in the case of families settled since long—often aimed at relatives in the process of resettling abroad, whether in Canada or elsewhere. Some informants assert that the necessity of mutual help is lower now than it used to be because the economic situation in Vietnam and among Viet Kieu has greatly improved. Here are some excerpts from interviews:[9]

> We bring, I would say, financial support. Normally, this fund-raising is done here in Canada, and in the United States. We do it within the extended family, and we tell them money was gathered in California, Florida, and Canada. Aid is not only financial. For instance, from time to time, my uncle goes back to Vietnam [. . .] to bring a presence, some form of physical support. (Twenty-five-year-old male, Quebec City)

> My parents opened a restaurant and it worked very well right from the beginning. [. . .] And it often happened that uncles and aunts came

and asked them to lend them money to open a business, or things like that. It happened often, but now, it is less the case. (Twenty-two-year-old male, born in Canada, Quebec City)

Every year, once or twice, we send money to relatives in Vietnam, but amounts are quite small. People in my family are very close one to another. If I need money to pay my telephone or electricity bills, my mother will give it to me. (Twenty-nine-year-old male, Montreal)

We send financial support to our relatives in Vietnam. At first, we aided them on a regular basis, but since two or three years it is almost finished, because things have improved for them. (Seventy-eight-year-old female, Montreal)

I do not help really, but my parents do. Among brothers and sisters, they help each other for many things, and not only money. (Twenty-one-year-old female, born in Canada, Montreal)

Informants seem to include money and other remittances within the broader context of family support. One should support relatives—and be supported by them—whenever needed, whether these relatives live in Vietnam, Canada, or elsewhere.

Another aspect of transnational economic activities is the existence of a thriving cross-border Viet Kieu market dealing in ethnic food, books, and newspapers in Vietnamese, audio and video cassettes and CDs, and various other goods and services. Cities such as Montreal, Toronto, or Vancouver harbor a multiplicity of Vietnamese—or Chinese-run shops, restaurants, drugstores, business offices, and medical clinics whose customers are chiefly Vietnamese Canadians. Quebec City, with fewer than 800 Viet Kieu residents, has thirty-two Vietnamese restaurants, five Asian grocery stores, and a dozen other Vietnamese-owned businesses.

Most goods sold in these stores, restaurants, and offices originate from outside Canada. Some—cultural products and culinary specialties, for example—come from Vietnam, but others (books, newspapers, audio and video cassettes and CDs, and some food items) are produced by Viet Kieu living in the United States or, more infrequently, Australia or France. The bulk of these goods, however, including basic foods (such as rice, noodles, tea, and sauce), cloth, jewelry, and traditional Asian remedies, are imported from Thailand, Hong Kong, and China by overseas Chinese wholesalers.[10] Since most retailers in Canadian Viet Kieu commercial neighborhoods are also Chinese—from Vietnam, Laos, or Cambodia—ethnic Vietnamese do not play a very active part in transnational business, except as consumers.

This is why a majority of Vietnamese Canadians do not feel really concerned with the transnational economic networks linking Vietnam, Thailand, Hong Kong, and China with Viet Kieu—and overseas Chinese—communities around the world. Even if a few ethnic Viet Kieu conduct business in Vietnam and other countries, overseas Vietnamese generally perceive import-export and trade as a domain controlled by, and reserved to, the Chinese. For them, the transnational economy mainly consists of sending money remittances and other goods to their relatives living in Vietnam or elsewhere.[11]

Transnational Politics: Associations and Discourses

Besides cross-border economic relations, transnational migration is character-ized by political activities that incorporate transmigrants simultaneously in two nation-states: their homeland and their host country. In the case of their home state, this may entail two types of action (Glick Schiller 1999, 110–111). Some states include emigrant populations as members of their political community by recognizing them as nationals or citizens of their native (or ancestral) country.[12] Such is the case with Vietnam, which considers that all Viet Kieu and their descendants are Vietnamese nationals, whatever their actual citizenship.

Other states feel that without having to become nationals, emigrants should continue to identify with their home nation. In both cases, political dis-courses emanating from the homeland invite transmigrants to define them-selves as part of their ancestral country. According to Glick Schiller: "Within a globalized economy, transnational narratives may provide political leaders with claims to populations or resources that can bolster the position of their state within global geopolitics" (1999, 111).

Here again, Vietnam is a good case in point. For the Vietnamese govern-ment, emigration plays an important part in the development of the country. In its temporary form, that of guest workers sent abroad, it is seen as a strategy to alleviate unemployment and poverty. In a declaration made in the spring of 2000, Prime Minister Phan Van Khai stated that Vietnam "should try to send hundreds of thousands or even millions of workers and experts to work abroad in order to solve redundancy in labor and contribute to poverty alleviation" (Vietnam News 2000a, 1).

Overseas Vietnamese too—the Viet Kieu—are considered potential contrib-utors to the process of nation building. At a meeting held in Hanoi on April 30, 2000, on the occasion of the twenty-fifth anniversary of the surrender of South Vietnam to northern forces—the event that triggered massive emigration out of the country—Phan Van Khai "called upon all Vietnamese people, at home and abroad, regardless of their social status, political conviction and past history, to join hands in making Viet Nam a prosperous and happy country" (Vietnam News 2000b, 1). According to the Prime Minister, Vietnam must modernize and industrialize, and everyone should join efforts in developing the nation. Khai concluded his speech by declaring: "All Vietnamese at home and abroad, regardless of their past history, are entitled to have their niche in the country's great national unity as long as they join efforts in building a prosperous, peaceful, independent and democratic Viet Nam" (Vietnam News 2000b, 4).

Viet Kieu are, thus, part of the nation. There exists in Hanoi a State Committee for the Viet Kieu, whose task it is to encourage and support overseas Vietnamese in their efforts to help develop Vietnam. Among other activities, it publishes a weekly newspaper (with a Web version) in the Vietnamese language, *Que Huong* (Fatherland), aimed at "Vietnamese living in foreign countries" (*nguoi Viet Nam o nuoc ngoai*). The journal includes news about Vietnam and Viet Kieu, or guest worker communities abroad; pieces on Vietnamese culture and history; and official opinions on various topics.

The essence of transnational migration being participation in two nation-states, transmigrants also belong to their country of adoption. Glick Schiller (1999, 110) asserts that modern states are explicitly redefining themselves as transnational thanks to multiculturalism: "Within immigrant-receiving countries such as the United States, Canada, and Australia, a range of actors, from government officials to educational institutions, are responding to immigrant populations by proposing a concept of multiculturalism that recognizes immigrant roots but envisions them as 'transplanted' within the multicultural terrain of their new country."

In Canada, multiculturalism has been official policy since 1971. According to McLeod (1983, 243–244), Canadian multiculturalism is based on four principles:

1. Equality of status: all ethnic groups are equal to the other.
2. Emphasis on Canadian identity: ethno-cultural pluralism constitutes the very essence of Canadian identity.
3. Possibility of choice: a greater choice of lifestyles is a positive factor in shaping a society.
4. Protection of civil and human rights: no Canadian resident should be discriminated against because of his/her ethnic origin, race, culture, language, or religion.

Canada is often described as a mosaic of many different cultures—aboriginal, French, English, and immigrant—each of them equal to the others.[13] It is the task of the federal and provincial governments to ensure that these ethno-cultural groups maintain harmonious relations among themselves with respect to law and order. Emphasis is thus laid on the management of ethnic relations rather than on transnational ties between immigrants and their homelands, though official encouragement of the preservation of ancestral cultures and the establishment of ethnic communities cannot but foster some sort of linkage with the countries of origin for a good part of the migrants.

Vietnamese refugees started arriving in Canada during the mid-seventies, just after the inception of the Canadian official policy on multiculturalism. Along with other groups of immigrants, they were encouraged by the federal government to establish ethnic associations in their cities of residence, and financial support was available to help them doing so. The main objective of these associations was to act as brokers between Canadian Viet Kieu and the federal and provincial authorities, so that resettlement could be conducted— and services offered—in an orderly manner. The associations also played a political and cultural role. Their leaders considered it a duty to help Vietnamese Canadians preserve their ancestral culture, which many asserted was endangered by Communism in the homeland.[14]

Most Canadian Viet Kieu thus experienced the political aspects of transnational migration as an invitation to participate in the activities of various ethnic associations and organizations. These generally conducted a discourse that upheld the necessity of preserving Vietnamese identity abroad while becoming full members of mainstream Canadian society. In Montreal alone, the number of Vietnamese associations witnessed an exponential growth. There were two of them (both student clubs) in 1970, sixteen in 1980, and sixty-three in 1990 (Dorais 1992).[15] Some associations were affiliated with international Viet Kieu organizations, such as the Association of Vietnamese Physicians, Pharmacists and Dentists of the Free World; the Vietnamese Buddhist World Order; or the National [anti-Communist] Liberation Front.

Because the vast majority of Vietnamese Canadians consider themselves refugees—or children of refugees—from Communism, most Viet Kieu associations overtly condemn the present Vietnamese government.[16] Public meetings and celebrations routinely exhibit symbols of the anti-Communist struggle (such as the flag and national anthem of the former Republic of [South] Vietnam), and the leaders of some associations regularly denounce attacks on human rights in Vietnam, or Canadian aid to this country. They consider that genuine Vietnamese culture survives only outside Vietnam, and that the preservation of this culture abroad constitutes a political act of national affirmation in the face of Communist internationalism, which, according to them, now dominates Vietnam (Dorais 1992).

At a workshop on the arrival of Vietnamese refugees in Canada, organized by the Vietnamese Canadian Federation on April 29, 2000, the keynote speaker, Professor Ton That Thien, a distinguished Viet Kieu political scientist, explained why, in his mind, Communists had won on April 30, 1975 (Ton That Thien 2000).[17] He attributed their victory to a lack of common sense on the part of Vietnamese and foreign intellectuals, who believed that South Vietnam's National [anti-American] Liberation Front was a democratic nationalist organization, rather than Hanoi's puppet. This led to the dispersal of Vietnamese refugees all over the world. In Professor Thien's opinion, Communists "are heartless cynics and inveterate liars" (Ton That Thien 2000, 7). They therefore cannot hold any legitimacy in a culture (the Vietnamese one) where legitimacy is primordial. It is because of this illegitimacy that refugees had to flee Vietnam by hundreds of thousands. Communist cynicism and insincerity are, thus, responsible for the exile of the Viet Kieu.

Such a discourse enters into direct contradiction with the already-mentioned invitation to all Vietnamese, at home and abroad, to "join hands in making Viet Nam a prosperous and happy country" (Vietnam News 2000b, 1). In Canada, official opinions of this latter type are conveyed chiefly by the local chapters of two pro-Hanoi international organizations, the General Union of Vietnamese and the Congress of Vietnamese, which are run by a small number of predominantly pre-1975 immigrants from Vietnam. According to these associations, the Viet Kieu must preserve their culture and identity in order to help Vietnam hold out against the assaults of Western consumerism and individualism.

Vietnamese Canadians are thus exposed to two sets of political discourse and organization, one anti-Communist (which predominates) and the other pro-Hanoi.[18] This means that transnational politics forms a permanent part of their environment. It remains to be seen, however, to what extent the Viet Kieu find it important to participate in such movements. Hundreds of people may gather once a year in front of huge South Vietnamese flags to celebrate Tet, the lunar New Year, but the leaders of ethnic associations are few in number—the same individuals sit on the boards of several different organizations—and they often complain that nobody wants to take any responsibility in the community (Dorais 1992).

When asked if overseas Vietnamese may be considered a well-organized collectivity, a majority (nineteen out of twenty-eight) of my informants from Quebec City and Montreal answer negatively:

> In comparison with the Chinese, I believe that Vietnamese around the world do not form an organized collectivity. Not well organized like the Chinese. [. . .] Vietnamese are a little more relaxed, not as rigid as Chinese are. I'm under the impression that there are no networks. (Fifty-one-year-old male, Quebec City)

> I don't know. Family is the most important thing; and family solidarity; and Buddhist temples. (Seventy-two-year-old female, Montreal)

> I know that every year, Vietnamese Catholics get together in August to celebrate the Holy Virgin. And there are people from Canada, the United States, maybe Australia. [. . .] But it is not all of the world's Vietnamese that get together like that. (Twenty-four-year-old female, Quebec City)

> No, each community minds its own business. (Forty-two-year-old male, Montreal)

For most of my informants, cross-border family solidarity is more important than community organizations when it comes to the settlement of individual or collective problems among overseas Vietnamese. When asked which Viet
Kieu institutions are the most important for them, they spontaneously mention
the family, religion, and/or ancestors' worship, rather than any formal association or other type of organization:

> Family, ancestors' worship, and religion. (Seventy-year-old female, Mon-
> treal)

> Religion, family, and the ancestors. (Fifty-year-old male, Montreal)

> Maybe the family. (Twenty-four-year-old female, Montreal)

> The family, religion [ancestors' worship], and education. (Twenty-three-
> year-old male, born in Canada, Montreal)

If formal organizations play any role, it is at the local level (organizing the
yearly celebration of Tet, for instance), not the international one. This does not
mean that informants are not interested in transnational politics. On the contrary, the majority of them feel concerned with political and other developments in Vietnam, even if no respondent, irrespective of age or professional
situation, expresses a wish to move back there:

> Yes I'm really interested with what happens in Vietnam, I'm eager to see
> the country develop because, you know, this Communist mentality still
> exists. Vietnam is the country of origin of my parents; I want to know
> what happens there. (Twenty-two-year-old male, born in Canada, Que-
> bec City)

> We always read magazines that tell about Vietnam. It is important for
> those who will be left [after our generation] because I think that some
> day, they will go back there to rebuild the nation without the Commu-
> nists. (Seventy-eight-year-old female, Montreal)

> It is my country, I love her and I worry about her. (Fifty-year-old male,
> Montreal)

> It is important for me because I love the people there. I don't want them
> to suffer or live in poverty. I deeply believe that people have a right to
> live as they want; nobody chooses to die. (Forty-six-year-old female,
> Montreal)

> When something important happens, I like to be informed, but nothing
> more than that. It is important, though, to get informed, because it is the
> country of our parents. (Twenty-three-year-old male, born in Canada,
> Montreal)

These are my origins and I don't want to disavow them. . . . It is our ancestral country, our roots, then it is important [to feel concerned], to know where we are coming from. (Twenty-four-year-old male, Montreal)

Transnational politics may, thus, be said to exist among Canadian (and other) Viet Kieu. Divergent discourses, often representing contradictory interests, invite them to fight Communism or to join hands with the Vietnamese government in reconstructing the country. Ethnic associations, some of them operating across national borders, try to enroll them on one side or the other. It seems, however, that the Canadian Vietnamese, with the exception of a minority of leaders and other activists, do not consider that such discourses and organizations have an important part to play in their lives. They feel concerned with Vietnam as a nation—and this may be considered an expression of transnational politics—but, for them, family relations and ancestors' worship appear much more significant than formal organizations.[19]

Transnational Family Relationships

The central importance of the family in Vietnamese culture and society does not have to be discussed here (cf. Liljestrom and Tuong Lai 1991; Luong 1984; Nguyen Khac Vien 1994; Papin 1999). Research on the Viet Kieu (for example, Chan and Dorais 1998; Gold 1992; Kibria 1993; Knudsen 1988; L Huu Khoa 1985; Nash and Nguyen 1995) has amply shown that despite emigration, family dispersal, and changing living conditions, most Vietnamese try to preserve some unity within their families.[20] In many cases they still consider their parents and relatives as the only persons they can really trust, whatever the physical distance between them. This receives a symbolical expression in the belief that deceased ancestors are able to assist their descendants wherever they live, and that these descendants should worship them from time to time (Dorais 1989). For my Montreal and Quebec City informants, Vietnamese culture principally consists in the preeminence of family relationships, respect for the elderly, and ancestors' worship (Dorais 1998a, 33).

In contemporary Vietnam, family is sometimes seen as a replacement for social services (education, health care, access to a basic income) that the government is no longer able to provide for its citizens. Traditional family virtues are, therefore, officially praised, and the importance of money remittances sent by relatives abroad is fully recognized (Tuong Lai 1991; Papin 1999).[21] No wonder, then, if transnational family relationships are particularly important and significant to the Viet Kieu.

My research data from Montreal and Quebec City yielded up the following conclusions as to the family networks and transnational activities of informants (Dorais 1998a, 57):

1. The extended family (*dai gia dinh,* "big family") of a vast majority of informants is spread over several cities and countries, but their immediate (most often nuclear) family has generally been able to gather in one location (Montreal or Quebec City), which most informants consider their final place of settlement.

2. Regular—but not necessarily frequent—relations are maintained with outlying members of the extended family (and, of course, with one's own nuclear family) and, to a lesser extent, with close friends.

3. Such relations may take various forms: letters (including e-mail), phone calls, visits, financial support.

4. Only four informants (out of twenty-eight) do not take part in such transnational networks and activities.

Answers given by informants did not show any systematic variation according to gender, professional occupation, or year of arrival in Canada.[22] Age had a role to play, but in a limited way. Young people maintain many fewer contacts with their extended kin than their elders, but they generally belong to nuclear families where parents regularly maintain such contacts.[23] The sample may, therefore, be described as participating in a cluster of networks made up of relatives and friends spread out over the world (including Vietnam), and among which various types of contacts are maintained.

Twenty-four out of twenty-eight informants state that they have relatives and friends living in a Canadian or foreign location other than Montreal or Quebec City. More than half of the sample (fifteen of twenty-eight) can mention at least three different places where these relatives may be found:

> My older brother was a boat people. He was accepted by France. The second brother, younger than I am, studied in Japan since he was fifteen, and from Japan, he came to Canada, to Quebec City. He sponsored us, and he also sponsored a third brother. And my youngest brother was a boat people too. He was in Toronto and after a few years, they migrated from Canada to the United States, with his wife's family who live in Houston. (Fifty-one-year-old male, Quebec City)

> My closest relatives live here in Montreal, but the rest of the family, they all stayed in Vietnam. But I have a female cousin in California. (Twenty-nine-year-old male, Montreal)

> We are all here, in the province of Quebec; my wife and I, and our four children: a daughter, the eldest, and three sons. In Toronto, I have a big brother. Other siblings live in the United States, but they only got there in 1992. I have two older brothers in Paris. They went to France to get an education, and they remained there afterwards. The others are in the

United States, because they thought that down there, it is a rich country where you can do very well. (Sixty-five-year-old male, Montreal)

All my family on my mother's side are in the province of Quebec. On my father's side, they live in Vietnam. My friends are here. I also have relatives in the United States. (Twenty-three-year-old female, Montreal)

I have many relatives here, in the Montreal area. On top of that, we have a few cousins in the United States, and in Germany too. (Twenty-one-year-old female, born in Canada, Montreal)

Except for the four individuals without family outside Quebec, all informants—including those born in Canada—say that they get in touch at least twice a year with relatives and friends living in the United States, Europe, Vietnam, or elsewhere in Canada. Younger respondents often mention that their parents maintain many more contacts with outlying relatives than they do. Such contacts include phone calls, letters and parcels, travel, and, increasingly, e-mail messages:

We get in touch by phone from time to time. We must know how people live there [in the United States], what are their problems there. And they want to know the same thing concerning us. [. . .] We chat about that. I visited them twice. (Forty-seven-year-old female, Quebec City)

We phone each other occasionally, but phone calls are expensive. [. . .] We write from time to time, for Christmas, the New Year, holidays; we send postcards. [. . .] My cousin went to Prince Rupert [northern British Columbia] to visit my aunt. My mother went to Vietnam last winter and she is returning this summer. I was there three years ago. My father and brother never went back, though. We don't have time; and no money. Travel is expensive. (Twenty-four-year-old female, Quebec City)

I keep in touch by mail, by telephone, sometimes I travel. [. . .] I like traveling, but I cannot do it any more. My relatives who live abroad come and visit me from time to time. (Eighty-two-year-old male, Montreal)

Yes, I have a lot of contacts. I travel, I call, and I write too. (Sixty-five-year-old male, Montreal)

I do not contact very often my relatives and friends living in France or Vietnam; we may speak twice a year on the phone, but not more. (Forty-six-year-old female, Montreal)

My grandfather visited us once, a long time ago. My mother went back to visit her family [in Vietnam] some years ago. But I never went to

Vietnam. My parents frequently phone my uncles there, to see if they are okay. (Twenty-three-year-old male, born in Canada, Montreal)

As for my relatives outside Quebec City, we write, we phone and we e-mail each other. We travel a lot because I often participate in conferences in the United States. There is a lot to do. I travel to the United States, and to Vietnam. (Fifty-one-year-old male, Quebec City)

Despite their geographical dispersion, family members seem to be able to keep in touch quite regularly. As already mentioned, contacts are not limited to the exchange of information. They may also include financial support, which gives them an economic function. Whatever their nature, however, these contacts occur primarily within the limits of the extended family.[24] At the basic level, that of individuals and households, Viet Kieu transnational networks are thus predominantly based on kinship relations.

This is so because, for a majority of Vietnamese, family is still considered one of the most significant elements in life, even if it may now appear endangered by contacts with Western society, and if younger individuals may be ambivalent about some of its aspects.[25] Let me quote my informants one last time:

I believe that family preserves its importance here. In my own family, my grandson is married to a French Canadian girl. He is very close to our family. His father told us to speak Vietnamese to his wife, so that she can understand our language. (Seventy-eight-year-old female, Montreal)

Family is the most important thing for the Vietnamese. Everything revolves around the family; it is the basis of life. It must be important for young people too. This is what adults teach them through family education. (Fifty-year-old male, Montreal)

Yes, I think that family preserves its importance. [. . .] But some young people, teenagers for the most part, they have parents who give a lot to their kids, but who impose on them restrictions. They [kids] find it difficult. Sometimes, they want to go out, work part-time, but parents don't accept that. They want their children to study seriously. The children want to study too, but also to go out and do things. (Twenty-six-year-old female, Montreal)

The first generation still preserves the sacred character of the family. As for the second generation, they adapt very well to Quebec society. They are professionals, have a good job, a good salary, they adapt well. I mean they are more open. They adapt well to change, but for them—as is the case with me—we always try to preserve family relationships. Because it is important. (Twenty-five-year-old male, Quebec City)

Family is still very important. It may not be as important for young people, though, because we have other things to do, like going to school and finding a job. Maybe when we get older, it will become more important. It is important, but not as important as it is to our parents. (Twenty-three-year-old male, born in Canada, Montreal)

Family is of the utmost importance. For young people too. But this depends on your family and on the way you've been raised. [. . .] I visit my mother and the rest of the family every weekend. She lives in Longueuil [a suburb of Montreal]. Everybody gathers there. We phone each other very often. If I don't see my mother for three days, I freak out. And my [French Quebecer] boyfriend freaked out too when he realized that! (Twenty-three-year-old female, Montreal)

Family relationships, whether local or transnational, appear as both important and significant for Vietnamese Canadians. They structure their social networks and, as it seems, they play a major part in the day-to-day operation of Viet Kieu communities, which are based on these networks.

Conclusion

In the introduction to this chapter, two questions were asked: To what extent may Vietnamese Canadians be considered transmigrants? And what are the most salient features of their transnational activities? Answering these questions depends, of course, on how transmigrants and transnationalism (or transnational migration) are defined.

We saw, with Portes et al. (1999), that the broader framework through which transnationalism operates implies a dynamic whereby transmigration is characterized by its ties with the logic of capitalist expansion, and by the development of cross-border social networks at variance with conventional expectations of immigrant assimilation. I mentioned that at the macrosociological level, such dynamics might apply to the situation of Vietnamese Canadians— and of the Viet Kieu in general—for whom resettlement in Canada, the United States, or elsewhere entails economic mobility and social networking, even if they generally perceive themselves as refugees who fled insufferable political and economic conditions.

At a more basic, microsociological level, though, it is doubtful if Canadian and other Viet Kieu may be fully considered transmigrants. According to Portes et al. (1999, 219), this term should only apply to people who actually commute across national borders on a regular basis, chiefly for professional or political reasons. This is the case with only a handful of overseas Vietnamese. For Glick Schiller (1999), transnational migration implies continuing participation in the economy, politics, and social organization of one's state of origin and, at the same time, more or less full involvement in one's country of adoption. Here again, only a small minority of Viet Kieu entrepreneurs and politically vocal community leaders correspond to the definition.

Observation and interview data from Montreal and Quebec City show that "ordinary" Vietnamese Canadians are primarily interested in their own family. What really counts for them, besides earning a living or studying to acquire some professional competence, is the well-being of their parents, children, siblings, and other relatives. Even young people, who may be ambivalent about authoritarianism within the traditional Vietnamese family, see family cohesion with pride and often criticize North American individualism (Guilbert 1993; Chan and Dorais 1998). Canadian Viet Kieu know well about the competing political discourses (anti-Communist vs. pro-Vietnam) conveyed by their ethnic associations and media, but when asked which institutions are the most important for them, my informants spontaneously mention the family, religion, and/or ancestors' worship, rather than any formal association or other type of organization.

The social and symbolic importance of family life makes kinship relations the very basis of Viet Kieu communities. In a context where many families have been dispersed around the world, kinship-based social networks often include individuals living in different nation-states. In Canada and, most probably, in other First-World countries, these individuals genuinely wish to participate as best they can in mainstream economy and society. But, at the same time, they feel they still fully belong to their family and, in many cases, to their ancestral culture. This generates activities that are de facto transnational. These may be economic (money remittances and parcel gifts sent to Vietnam), social (letters, phone calls, and visits to outlying relatives and friends), cultural (audition of Vietnamese or Viet Kieu tapes and CDs), or mixed (purchase of ethnic food, periodicals, cassettes, and other products imported from Vietnam or elsewhere). The family-based (and culture-based) nature of these transnational activities may be said to constitute their most salient feature.

A majority of Vietnamese Canadians might, therefore, be considered—in want of a better term—as passive transmigrants.[26] Except for a small number of individuals, they do not conduct business in, or with, Vietnam, nor do they have an active part to play in the operation of local and international ethnic associations, or in the production of anti-Communist or pro-Vietnam discourses.

On the other hand, though, most of them are interested and concerned with Vietnam as a nation-state. They feel it is important to know what is going on in their homeland, politically and socially. Many people send remittances to their relatives there, a growing number of Viet Kieu visit Vietnam during their holidays, and several young Vietnamese Canadians wish to spend some time in that country, working for international development projects. More important, perhaps, the mere fact of belonging to cross-border family networks entails, for a vast number—probably a majority—of Canadian Viet Kieu regular transnational contacts at the individual or household level.

Research should be expanded in at least four directions. As I have mentioned, my sample from Montreal and Quebec City is almost exclusively composed of upper-middle-class individuals. It should be investigated whether working-class Viet Kieu share the same transnational activities and interests as their more educated and upscale compatriots. It should also be seen if family relationships are influenced by one's actual involvement in Vietnamese affairs. In other words, are political and ethnic activists more insistent than "ordinary" people in displaying the importance of the family, because it is perceived as a hallmark of Vietnamese culture? Differences in transnational involvement between ethnic and Chinese Vietnamese would constitute an equally worthwhile research topic. Finally, the transnational activities of the young Viet Kieu should become the object of longitudinal research. It is they, after all, who will decide if Vietnamese Canadians of the future shall be considered as refugees, transmigrants, or Canadians of Vietnamese ancestry.

NOTES

Thanks to a grant from Heritage Canada, the Canadian federal department in charge of culture and citizenship. The author also acknowledges support received from the organizers and discussants of the symposium "Diaspora and Displacement: Teaching and Researching the Asian Diasporas" (Brown University, April 15, 2000), where a very preliminary version of this chapter was presented

1. Research was conducted among ethnic Vietnamese; the choice of this study group was motivated by the fact that over the preceding twenty years the author had already investigated various aspects of their social organization.

2. Estimations vary greatly (between one and two million) as to the total number of Viet Kieu. One and a half million is probably a good guess.

3. Another reason may be opportunities for themselves, in the case of those individuals forbidden to hold a job after their liberation from reeducation camp, or whose business was expropriated by the government.

4. The New Economic Zones were pioneer agricultural areas set up by the Vietnamese government after 1975, in order to alleviate overpopulation in the cities. From 1978 on, several thousand urban dwellers were forced to migrate to these areas (Papin 1999, 39). This contributed much to the boat-people crisis of 1979–1980.

5. Although, as we shall see later, there exists a thriving ethnic market—partly in the hands of Vietnamese Chinese—of foods, services, and cultural products adapted to the tastes of the Viet Kieu.

6. Vertovec (1999, 448) mentions that if transnational activities have existed for long, it is "the scale of intensity and simultaneity of current long-distance, cross-border activities especially economic transactions" that make them different from earlier forms of transnationalism.

7. Some authors, including myself (cf. Chan and Dorais 1998), have called the Viet Kieu a diaspora, without really discussing the concept. The question of whether or not overseas Vietnamese should be considered a diaspora, interesting as it may be, is too complex to be treated here.

8. According to the agency, these temporary migrants lived in thirty-eight different countries, but their highest numbers were to be found in Japan, South Korea, and North Africa.

9. Excerpts from interviews conducted by Sarah Gilmore, Eric Richard, and Stephanie Tailliez, for the research project already mentioned. Translated from French by the author. All informants are born in Vietnam, except when stated otherwise.

10. Even the most commonly found brands of *nuoc mam* (fish sauce), the archetypal ethnic Vietnamese food item, are produced in Thailand by overseas Chinese (and sold in bottles labeled in four languages: Vietnamese, Chinese, Thai, and English).

11. It may be argued, of course, that as consumers they participate objectively in the global transnational market economy, thus contributing to the accumulation of capital in the hands of Chinese and other traders. But as far as their personal social life is concerned, such participation has no signification for them.

12. The difference between nationals and citizens is that the former are full-fledged members of the nation, but without the same political rights as the latter (voting and standing as candidate in an election, for instance).

13. Such a vision is not endorsed by all Canadians, of course. The aboriginal peoples, as well as most French Canadians—those from Quebec in particular—consider themselves as belonging to specific sociological nations within the Canadian nation-state. As such, many of them think they should enjoy a larger measure of political autonomy.

14. Most of these leaders were well-educated males who had lived abroad since before 1975, or had left South Vietnam with the first wave of refugees in 1975. Comparisons between Viet Kieu communities show that the absence of such a category of individuals impeded the development of Vietnamese ethnic organizations in some locations (cf. Dorais 1991, 1998b).

15. These associations could be divided into four types (Dorais 1992, 221–223): mutual-aid associations (thirty-seven of them in 1990), sociocultural organizations (nine), religious associations (eleven), and political movements (six).

16. They consider Communism responsible for the deterioration of economic conditions and, allegedly, of public morality in post-1975 Vietnam.

17. The Vietnamese Canadian Federation, established in 1980, coordinates the activities of fifteen major Vietnamese Canadian mutual-aid associations.

18. The same political dichotomy is also found in other Viet Kieu communities. For French examples, see Lê Huu Khoa (1985) and Bousquet (1991).

19. Political involvement may vary according to migration history. Boat people are said by many Viet Kieu to be more vocal in their anti-Communism than migrants who arrived legally, thanks to a program of family reunification. Opinions also vary in time. Since the economic and social opening of Vietnam in the late 1980s, most Vietnamese Canadians have deemed it politically correct to visit the country and conduct some transnational business there. It should be added, too, that if

political pluralism existed in Vietnam, more Viet Kieu might be tempted to get involved in homeland politics.

20. A way of doing that is to sponsor the immigration of one's close relatives (parents, brothers, sisters), so that the family is reunited in one location.

21. Traditional family virtues were condemned as "feudal" before the implementation of the *doi moi* (Vietnamese perestroika) policy in the late 1980s.

22. As already mentioned, however, my sample is mostly upper middle class. Working-class informants might have given slightly different answers (their more limited financial means preventing them, for instance, from traveling abroad to visit relatives).

23. Richard (2000) draws the same conclusion from a sample of sixteen second-generation Vietnamese Montrealers.

24. They may sometimes include unrelated friends, however.

25. On this ambivalence (which also applies to gender relations) in a North American Viet Kieu context, see Kibria (1993), Guilbert (1993), Thomas (1997), Chan and Dorais (1998).

26. This chiefly applies to ethnic Vietnamese. As mentioned earlier, Chinese from Vietnam are much more actively involved in transnational business and other activities.

REFERENCES

Basch, Linda G., Nina Glick Schiller, and Cristina Szanton Blanc. 1994. *Nations unbound: Transnational projects, postcolonial predicaments, and deterritorialized nation-states.* Langhorne, Pa.: Gordon and Breach.

Bousquet, Gisele L. 1991. *Behind the bamboo hedge: The impact of homeland politics in the Parisian Vietnamese community.* Ann Arbor: University of Michigan Press.

Chan, Kwok Bun, and Louis-Jacques Dorais. 1998. "Family, identity, and the Vietnamese diaspora: The Quebec experience." *Sojourn* 13(2): 285–308.

Dorais, Louis-Jacques. 1989. "Religion and refugee adaptation: The Vietnamese in Montreal." *Canadian Ethnic Studies* 21(1): 19–29.

———. 1991. "Refugee adaptation and community structure: The Indochinese in Quebec City, Canada." *International Migration Review* 25(3): 551–573.

———. 1992. "The Vietnamese associations in Montreal: Their adaptive role." In *The quality of life in Southeast Asia*, edited by B. Matthews, 221–229. Montreal: Canadian Asian Studies Association.

———. 1998a. *Identités transnationales chez les Vietnamiens du Québec.* Quebec: Université Laval, Département d'anthropologie.

———. 1998b. "Vietnamese communities in Canada, France, and Denmark." *Journal of Refugee Studies* 11(2): 107–125.

———. 1999. "Vietnamese." In *Encyclopedia of Canada's peoples*, edited by P. R. Magocsi, 1312–1324. Toronto: University of Toronto Press.

Dorais, Louis-Jacques, Lise Pilon-Le, and Huy Nguyen. 1987. *Exile in a cold land: A Vietnamese community in Canada.* New Haven: Yale University, Council on Southeast Asia Studies.

Economist Intelligence Unit. 1995. "Country report, Vietnam." London: Economist.

Glick Schiller, Nina. 1999. "Transmigrants and nation-states: Something old and something new in the U.S. immigrant experience." In The handbook of international migration: The American experience, edited by C. Hirshman, P. Kasinitz, and J. DeWind, 94–119. New York: Russell Sage Foundation.

Glick Schiller, Nina, Linda G. Basch, and Cristina Blanc-Szanton. 1995. "From immigrant to transmigrant: Theorizing transnational migration." *Anthropological Quarterly* 68(1): 48–63.

Gold, Steven J. 1992. *Refugee communities: A comparative field study.* London: Sage.

Guilbert, Lucille. 1993. "Transfert, transformation et transform culturel." In *Transferts Orient-Occident: Populations, savoirs et pouvoirs*, 67–121. Quebec: Université Laval, Groupe d'études et de recherches sur l'Asie contemporaine.

Indra, Doreen M. 1987. "Bureaucratic constraints, middlemen and community organization: Aspects of the political incorporation of Southeast Asians in Canada." In *Uprooting, loss and adaptation: The resettlement of Indochinese refugees in Canada*, edited by K. B. Chan and D. M. Indra, 147–170. Ottawa: Canadian Public Health Association.

Kibria, Nazli. 1993. *Family tightrope: The changing lives of Vietnamese Americans.* Princeton: Princeton University Press.

Knudsen, John C. 1988. *Vietnamese survivors: Processes involved in refugee coping and adaptation.* Bergen: University of Bergen.

Lê Huu Khoa. 1985. *Les Vietnamiens en France: Insertion et identité: Le processus d'immigration depuis la colonisation jusqu'à l'implantation des réfugiés.* Paris: L'Harmattan/C.I.E.M.

Liljestrom, Rita, and Tuong Lai. 1991. *Sociological studies on the Vietnamese family.* Hanoi: Social Sciences Publishing House.

Luong, Hy V. 1984. "'Brother' and 'uncle': An analysis of rules, structural contradictions, and meaning in Vietnamese kinship." *American Anthropologist* 86(2): 290–315.

McLeod, Keith A. 1983. "Multicultural education: A decade of development." In *Two nations, many cultures: Ethnic groups in Canada*, edited by J. L. Elliot, 243–259. Scarborough: Prentice-Hall Canada.

Methot, Caroline. 1995. *Du Viet Nam au Quebec: La valse des identités.* Quebec: Institut Québecois de Recherche sur la Culture.

Nash, Jesse W., and Elizabeth Trinh Nguyen. 1995. *Romance, gender, and religion in a Vietnamese-American community: Tales of God and beautiful women.* Lewiston, N.Y.: E. Mellen.

Nguyen Khac Vien. 1994. "Ancestors' Worship." *Vietnamese Studies* 3(113): 6–46.

Papin, Philippe. 1999. *Viet-nam. Parcours d'une nation.* Paris: La Documentation Française.

Portes, Alejandro, Luis E. Guarnizo, and Patricia Landolt. 1999. "The study of transnationalism: Pitfalls and promise of an emergent research field." *Ethnic and Racial Studies* 22(2): 217–237.

Richard, Eric. 2000. "Un transnationalisme familial: L'experience de jeunes Vietnamiens de Montreal." M.A. thesis. Université Laval, Montreal.

Smith, Michael P., and Luis Guarnizo. 1998. *Transnationalism from below.* New Brunswick, N.J.: Transaction.

Thomas, Mandy. 1997. "Crossing over: The relationship between overseas Vietnamese and their homeland." *Journal of Intercultural Studies* 18(2): 153–176.

Ton That Thien. 2000. "Sober thoughts on April 30: The South Vietnam Liberation Front and Hanoi, myth and reality." http://www.vietfederation.ca/30-40-00/TonThatThien.htm.

Tuong, Lai. 1991. "Introduction." In *Sociological studies on the Vietnamese family*, edited by R. Liljestrom and T. Lai, 3–11. Hanoi: Social Sciences Publishing House.

Vertovec, Steven. 1999. "Conceiving and researching transnationalism." *Ethnic and Racial Studies* 22(2): 447–462.

Vietnam News. 2000a. "Emigration as a tool to alleviate poverty." http://vietnamnews. vnagency.com.vn/2000–06/10.

———. 2000b. "A nation looks back to the future." http://vietnamnews.vnagency.com.vn/ 2000–04/30.

10

Between Necessity and Choice

Rhode Island Lao American Women

WANNI W. ANDERSON

Identities are always constructed and lived out on a historical terrain between necessity and choice.

—Angelika Bammer, *Displacements,* 1994

As one of the most recent Asian groups to arrive in the United States, Lowland Lao have received limited attention politically, educationally, and in public awareness. The perception that the Lowland Lao in Columbus, Ohio, have of themselves as the "forgotten refugees," as cited by Muir (1988, 8), is not far from the truth. Despite this apparent neglect, Lowland Lao from a variety of socioeconomic classes, levels of education, and past experiences are no less committed than other Asian groups to adapting to life in America—a new country with new socioeconomic and political environments, new cultures, and different value systems and expectations. Although a number of Lao adults have already obtained American citizenship and a new generation of young children is American-born, in 1991, the year of the main research study, a large number of Lao young men and women still held the status of permanent residents, eligible to apply for American citizenship in the years to come.

The present study is a psychological anthropological study of Rhode Island Lao female college students who are in the process of transforming themselves into a new group of Asian American women, the first-generation Lao American women. Although rapid social and technological changes in America have effected concomitant changes in American ethnic youth of all groups (see, for example, D. Sue 1973; S. Sue 1980; Spencer, Dobbs, and Swanson 1988; Burton 1997), this developmental process in the lives of Southeast Asian refugee youth, including the Lao adolescents and young adults, is further compounded by the trauma of the escalated Vietnam War and their flight from Laos (Tobins and Friedman 1984; Nguyen and Williams 1989; Trueba, Jacobs, and Kirton 1990; Nguyen-Hong-Nhiem and Halpern 1989). Once in the United States as members of displaced, refugee families, they face multiple adaptation contingencies as their families learn how to function effectively in the new society and restructure new lives. Theoretically significant for this study is Erikson's theory on the development of the self. Erikson's emphasis on the need of adolescents to achieve a balanced sense of self-identity, including gender identity and ethnic identity (Erikson 1968, 131) is regarded in this study as a developmental process that is as valid and critical for Lao youth living in the American sociopolitical environment as it is for other ethnic American youth. Self-identities, in the case of Rhode Island Lao young women who are becoming functioning adults in American society, are here defined to be strongly intertwined with individual expectations, future occupational identity, and their definition of what it means to be a woman. And as they are at the transitional stage, moving from refugee status to permanent resident status and to becoming American citizens, how they aim to negotiate their sense of displacement with the need to define their new ethnic identity, the Lao American identity, becomes part of this multifaceted self-formation and transformational processes.

Given that the Rhode Island female Lao college students under study were part of the Lao displaced population and were concurrently at the transitional points in several developmental aspects of the self, they provide a viable case study of the transitional, the emergent, and the transformation and formation processes. My focus on women college students follows my research interest on ethnic adolescents and young adults (Anderson and Anderson 1986). The theoretical and methodological approach of this study emphasizes processes. Self-formation is here conceived not as a static developmental process, accomplishable over a short period of time, but as a series of transformation processes, dynamic and ongoing. These processes are currently being formulated and reformulated by Lao adolescents, young men and women. Through these processes they are consciously and actively engaged in an ongoing self-formation and transformation while attempting simultaneously to adapt and restructure their new lives in America. Furthermore, as the Lao are what Espiritu (1989, 49–50) called "first-time minorities," that is a majority population in the home country who becomes minorities in the newly adopted country, ethnicity for the Lao is not a given. Being Lao American is neither traceable "primordial affinities and attachments" nor is it an identity acquired at birth (Isaacs 1975, 30), but it is an identity newly created in America where, for the first time, the Lao find themselves to be among the "minorities." The study on the Lao can shed significant light on ethnicization, defined on the group level (Espiritu 1989) as the coming together of members of a cultural group into an ethnic group and, on the individual level (Anderson: unpublished manuscript), as the process through which individuals are either socialized or self-select and identify themselves, each in his or her own way, as members of an ethnic group. The individual level is here distinguished from the group level to allow for differentiated individual formulation and self-invention. On the threshold of becoming a new Asian American group, the Rhode Island Lao are positioned at the historic moment, the moment when it is happening, for understanding ethnicization as processes.

Lao young women who are the focus of this study are college students in five colleges in Rhode Island: University of Rhode Island, Providence College, Rhode Island College, Rhode Island Community College, and Johnson and Wales College.[1] As of 1991 no Lao student had been enrolled at Brown University. The field research was carried out during the spring and summer of 1991, with Nalone Khammahavong, a Lao student at Rhode Island Community College, assisting to identify Rhode Island college students who were part of her college cohort.

Rhode Island Lao: Historical and Socioeconomic Contexts

The War and the Lao Immigration History

Laos suffered domino-like repercussions of the war in Vietnam. The fall of Saigon on April 12, 1975, and the withdrawal of the last of the American military forces in Vietnam, brought to the United States the first group of refugees of the war, the Vietnamese refugees. Five days later, on April 17, in neighboring Cambodia, the Khmer Rouge under Pol Pot entered Phnom Penh, the Cambodian capital. The Khmer Rouge's mass evacuation of the Cambodians, political indoctrination, the Cambodian genocide, starvation, and threatened survival (Yathay 1987; Ngor 1987; Him 2000) brought in another group of refugees, Cambodians via refugee camps in Thailand. A month later, the control of Laos fell to the pro-Viet Minh, Pathet Lao political faction under the leadership of Prince Soubhanouvong and Kaysone Phomvihane. The new government's mass political reeducation program, the dismantling of the former Western education system, and widespread economic hardship likewise forced the Lao to flee across the Mekong River into Thailand (Hua 2000). According to the statistics on Southeast Asian refugees (Office of the United Nations High Commissioner for Refugees 1991a), 10,195 Lao refugees arrived at the Thai refugee camps in the first year, 1975. The number increased to 19,499 the following year (Office of the United Nations High Commissioner for Refugees 1991b). The largest Lao exodus occurred in 1978, with 48,781 arrivals. The last exodus on record was in 1985, when 12,388 arrived at the camps. The refugee statistics of 1991, the year this research was conducted, enumerated 69,222 Southeast Asian refugees still waiting in the Thai camps for resettlement in a third country. Among them were 6,807 Lao. When most of the Cambodian refugees where repatriated, the number of Southeast Asian refugees in the Thai camps decreased significantly. Of the total 12,026 refugees in the Thai camps as of August 31, 1995, 1,079 were Lao (Office of the United Nations High Commissioner for Refugees 1995).

Between 1975 and 1991, the United States accepted 120,864 Lao refugees for resettlement. In accordance with the resettlement policies, they were at first, like other Southeast Asian refugee groups, scattered throughout the country in different cities and towns where families and agencies had offered sponsorships. The "scatter" approach was intended to facilitate the "assimilation" of refugees into American life as soon as possible and to minimize any negative impacts of refugees on American society that might arise from heavy concentrations of refugees in urban areas (Skinner and Hendricks 1979; Mortland and Ledgerwood 1987). Like other refugee groups, many Lao refugees later decided to make what Mortland and Ledgerwood called "a secondary migration," the process through which Southeast Asian refugees moved from their initial areas of resettlement to other locations (Mortland and Ledgerwood 1987, 296) to reunite with other family members or to a friendlier social environment and/or better job opportunities. Secondary migration was, however, not always the final resettlement move made by Lao refugees. Several Lao families I interviewed had settled in Rhode Island as a consequence of yet a third migration. These self-selected migrations placed large numbers of Lao, Hmong, Vietnamese, and Cambodians in Rhode Island, a state known among the refugees as having plentiful job opportunities in light, labor-intensive industries, especially the jewelry industry, where job performance requirements depended less on English-language proficiency than on the meticulous care and precision needed for the jewelry assembly line. They also regarded the social environment in Rhode Island to be fairly friendly. Rhode Island, with around 15,000 Southeast Asian refugees, became in 1991 a high-impact state with the third largest concentration of refugees in America. The increase was over 100 percent in the previous ten years.

Rhode Island Lao Community and Their Displacement

Approximately 3,500 Lao resided in Rhode Island in 1991. It was the second largest Rhode Island refugee group next to the Cambodians. The first Lao family arrived in the state in 1975, but the majority came at a much later date. Among the twenty-eight female Lao college students interviewed, the earliest to settle in Rhode Island came with her family in 1979; most of them arrived in the 1980s, and the most recent arrival of a member of this group was in 1989. The length of stay in the United States of the families in this study group thus varies from two to twelve years.

Eleven families came directly to Rhode Island from the Thai refugee camps. More, that is fourteen families, came as a result of secondary migration or third migration from the west coast (California, Oregon, Washington), the south (Tennessee), the Midwest (Arkansas), and from the neighboring New England states, Connecticut and Massachusetts. An example is a family who was at first placed in a city in Arkansas, not their own choice; they found themselves living a lonely existence as the only Lao family in town. When a relative who had earlier settled in Rhode Island was able to line up new job possibilities for them in Rhode Island a year later, the family chose to move in order to be closer to their relatives. Similarly, the only Lao family in a city in Oregon migrated to Rhode Island even though the father, university educated, had a fairly good position in Oregon as the interpreter for the Southeast Asian refugee community. As with other Southeast Asian refugee groups (Mortland and Ledgerwood 1987), secondary migration in all the Lao families interviewed was a personal choice, a self-selected adaptive response to initial resettlement situations over which they had no control and which did not work out. When some of these Lao refugees made the secondary migration but discovered, to their disappointment, that these new places of residence failed to meet their needs, they again took it upon themselves to locate other options. By then they had been in the United States for some time and had acquired more experience in adjusting and at selecting available options. I see their third migration as indicative of their accelerated self-reliance and a more advanced step in their adaptation to the new American societal contexts, ironically the very self-sufficiency that was the aim of the refugee resettlement policy.

Since the family is the most important social institution in Lao culture (LeBar and Suddard 1960, 62) and Lao family solidarity is, in practice, maintained through consistent, mutual support and close interpersonal relationships, their desires for family reunion and for economic self-reliance became decisive factors in the later stages of their resettlement. The traditional Lao extended family kinship networks and social support systems were reinvigorated and utilized in their diaspora to assist them, as they used to be in time of need in Laos. A friend helping another friend, a relative helping another relative to find a better job in a better location, as in the cases cited earlier, were characteristic of the group's problem-solving responses. These eventually functioned as viable cultural strategies of the Lao refugees for maximizing the family's chances of economic survival and for obtaining other social and psychological support from family members living close by. Muir (1988, 48) likewise found Lao mutual support, people helping each other, to be a strong reason for migration among the Lao of Columbus, Ohio. Through frequent and sustained economic and social interactions and participations in annual Lao cultural events, rituals, and family gatherings, the Rhode Island Lao have been able to maintain some measure of Lao cultural continuity and, when a critical number of Lao residents was reached, a Lao community in Rhode Island emerged.

Most Lao are Theravada Buddhists, as are all the Rhode Island Lao families in this study. Buddhism continues to be the spiritual focal point that brings all the Rhode Island Lao together both for annual Buddhist rituals and on a daily basis. Through strong leadership, Lao community members pooled their financial and human resources to support a Lao temple. By necessity, the first temple was a rented, converted two-storied wooden house in a Providence low-income area. And also by necessity, four Buddhist monks had to live on the second floor above the altar room with the big Buddha image, a practice that is dissonant with the tradition in Laos. Daily, the community organizes the preparation of the once-a-day meal for the monks, who do not beg for alms here as in Laos. The monks officiate at all religious rituals of the Lao community, and the temple serves also as the formal office of the Lao Association of Rhode Island and as the Sunday Lao language school for American-born children. In 1995, the Lao community pooled sufficient funds to move the temple to a more spacious and more tranquil neighborhood of suburban Warwick.

A Lao business community has also emerged in Providence. A few family-run small businesses—restaurants, grocery stores, video rental stores, and mechanic shops—catered at the beginning primarily to the needs of the Lao community. In the early 1990s their businesses could be characterized as being at the transitional stage, characteristic of an early stage of a diasporic group. Some were struggling to survive; a few went out of business within a year. Through time, many have succeeded as small business entrepreneurs and are known to other Rhode Island clientele beyond the Lao community.

Most Lao families who came to Rhode Island were at first resettled in rented apartments in south Providence, a mixed ethnic neighborhood of Irish, Italians, Latinos, Blacks, and Southeast Asians. The majority still reside in that area, although lately a number of families have been able to purchase homes in Woonsocket and, in smaller numbers, in Warwick. Their choices of the latter two cities were dictated by what they perceived to be safer, more peaceful living environments, manageable housing costs, proximity to the workplace, and in the case of Woonsocket, the positive attitude of the mayor. The mayor viewed the coming of Lao residents into the Woonsocket factory workforce as a positive potential for his city's economic growth. The current socioeconomic situation of the Lao in Rhode Island cannot, however, be generalized across the whole United States. Despite some evidence of upward mobility, it will be misleading to assume that Rhode Island Lao have already been successful as a group, for a large number of them are still struggling to make ends meet in low-skilled and low-paid jobs.

The 1990–1992 economic recession, the shrinking job market, and the decision of some companies to move their factories from Rhode Island to other states had drastic impacts on many Laotian factory workers, including both parents of one of the students in the study group, who were laid off from their jobs. They expressed feelings of insecurity and anxiety as they wondered what would happen to them next. "Life is hard and full of struggles here," said the father. He was acutely embarrassed of being on welfare. While waiting for new job openings, the father and son of this family of six tried to be self-dependent in other ways. Falling back on their former village subsistence skills, they went fishing every day to try to economize and maintain some measure of a stable diet for the family.

As in Laos, the Lao families in Rhode Island are bonded by close family relationship, strong loyalty to each other, and the sense of the family as a cooperative, interdependent economic unit. Many households are extended family households with an elderly grandparent or grandparents and/or other relatives, besides the nuclear family, living together. They work hard at their jobs. In 1991 a number of men held two or three jobs at the same time. Most Lao heads of household and their wives, if they could find employment, worked in factories as assembly-line workers, inspectors, or packers. Working husbands and wives with no relatives to baby-sit their small children frequently evolved an adaptive strategy of coordinating their work hours, taking on different work shifts, so that one of them at a time could take care of the family needs and other tasks. A concrete example was a family in which the wife worked on the 8:30 a.m. to 3:30 p.m. shift in one factory, whereas the husband worked on the afternoon shift, from 3:30 p.m. to midnight in another factory. The shift arrangement enabled the wife to maintain her multiple roles as daughter, wife, mother, and income earner. She was able to be back home in time to prepare dinner for the children and her aged father and had family time with them in the evening.

Pooling the family income was another economic survival strategy in the Lao displacement. Earnings of the husband and wife and grown-up, working children were pooled to take care of family expenses. Married children who lived in the same household also contributed part of their income to help defray expenses. Economic cooperation within the Lao family became a strong mechanism for attaining the family's self-reliance and economic independence. A family with multiple income earners and multiple pooled resources tended to fare better economically and were more self-sufficient than a family in which the father was the sole income earner, where the mother could not work because the children were still too young and needed her care, and the family size was too large.

All of the college students in the present study worked during the summers, mostly in factory jobs like their parents. A few worked in Lao or Thai restaurants. One student worked full-time on weekdays as a packer in the morning shift in a factory, then worked in a Thai restaurant on weekends as an assistant cook. Only one had a temporary summer job as a car salesperson. In her case, she was placed with a secondhand car dealer by the business management program of the college she was attending as part of her college's hands-on training requirement. In interviews on how they would use their summer income, some students said that they gave all of their earnings to their parents; others gave half to the parents and used the other half for their own clothing and pocket money. A few connected their earnings to their future education plans. They aimed to use the saved summer income toward their next year's college expenses, to lessen financial burden on their parents. One student in accountancy already put aside savings toward starting her own grocery store after her graduation.

College Student Study Group and Research Methods

In 1991, a total of twenty-nine Lao women attended colleges in Rhode Island as students. Within the same college cohort, only two students attended colleges elsewhere: one in Massachusetts and the other in California. Twenty-eight out of the twenty-nine students attending colleges in Rhode Island consented to participate in the study. Twenty-four were unmarried and four were married students, three with children. The unmarried students were nineteen to twenty-five years of age, with three pairs of sisters as part of the group. The four married students were twenty years old, thirty years old, and thirty-five years old (two students), respectively—all were part-time students.

None of the students in the group is American-born. Most are trilingual, speaking Lao, Thai, and English. Older students who graduated from high schools or colleges in Laos before coming to America speak four languages: Lao, Thai, French, and English. They arrived in America speaking better French than English because they had been studying French in the Lao public schools since third grade or, for those enrolled in private schools in Laos, since first grade. French, rather than English, was their second language and the principal foreign language in education and in other sociopolitical interactions. English-language courses were taught in Laos as elective courses, and not until high school. Unlike Southeast Asian refugees who migrated to France (Bousquet 1991; Dorais 1998) or to French-speaking Quebec (Chan and Dorais 1998), a lot of Lao refugees who came to America faced language setbacks. Also, regardless of previous college or vocational trainings in Laos, these high school graduates and college students found upon their arrival in America that their previous training was not accredited. All respondents in this study group had to start all over again to obtain high school certification, as in the case of Nalone Khammahavong, the research assistant on this research project, who was in her last year of her nursing college education when she left Laos. The loss of accreditation partly accounts for older-than-average ages of many students in the group. Several years of education were also lost during the transition period, while they were living in the refugee camps in Thailand. The third factor that has led to the older age of some of the students is that a number of them had to work to bring in income for the family and thus were enrolled in college as part-time students. This latter group of students tended to take classes in the morning and work in the afternoon, and therefore had to spend more years to finish college than the average full-time students.

Field research was conducted through a combination of participant-

observation, in-depth formal and informal interviews, and two sets of questionnaires. One set of questionnaires was on the history of the settlement of the
family in Rhode Island and demographic and educational data of the student
and her family, while the other set contained questions that investigated the
students' cultural values, attitudes, feelings, future goals, the formulation of the
self, and their definitions of self identities. In-depth interviews provided further
comprehensive and contextual data to cross-check and explore other dimensions in detail. I observed and participated in social interactions in Lao ritual
contexts, such as the Bune Pii Mai (the Lao traditional New Year celebration),
weddings, restaurant-work contexts, and the college context of interaction.

I carried out the interviews and other verbal interactions with the students
either in the Thai language (my native language, which is very close to the Lao
language, both being in the same Tai language family), or in English, or a combination of Thai and English, depending on which language the student preferred. In some interviews, all of the three linguistic strategies were used with
one student. As it turned out, the positive outcome of using such language
code-switching for conducting the research went beyond facilitating the language fluency of the students being interviewed. I was able to generate free-flow
responses from the students in the linguistic milieu they were most comfortable with in expressing their thoughts. Consequently, I was able to gain
increased semantic depth and precision to the issues under inquiry. For
example, the use of the Thai/Lao language enabled me to get at the exact Lao
words with the precise cultural meanings the students wanted to convey to
describe their values, attitudes, and feelings. Frequently proverbs or proverbial
expressions which the Lao and the Thai peoples share were cited by the students to elucidate and express what they wanted to convey more clearly. At
other times English words were used to discuss American concepts and values.

Self-Identities and Gender Constructs

Most students in the study group came from educated families in Laos. Fathers
of twenty-two of the twenty-eight students in the study group were educated in
Laos beyond the high school level. They were from the professional, government official group in the Lao class hierarchy: civilian government officials, or
police or military personnel. One was a college professor, another a government
official in the Ministry of Forestry, another a colonel in the army, and another
a captain in the police force. Only six were formerly blue-collar workers, such
as mechanics, a carpenter, and a taxi boat pilot. Unlike immigrants who came
from impoverished lives in their home countries in search of better lives, better job opportunities, and upward mobility in America, the fathers in the first
group of students, as government officials and military personnel turned factory workers, were underemployed in America. Their present occupational status
resulted from a "downward mobility" and a loss of their former socio-economic

status and prestige. They were professionally as well as spatially displaced. But as displaced persons, they recognized the long road ahead and the difficulties of having to start all over again in an uphill struggle. Like earlier immigrant groups, they were willing to work as long as the children were "healthy, study hard, work hard, and are good children," as one father said. One student remembered her father telling her, "As long as you are all happy here and are doing well, I can *odton* (endure it and be stoic about it)."

The fact that the students in the study group had succeeded in attending college, in contrast to other Lao women who dropped out of high school, entered the work force early, or got married right after high school graduation, categorizes them as high achievers. They are not, therefore, to be taken as a representative, randomly selected sample group. Lao women college students, not simply Lao women, were the focus of the study.

How do these Lao college students think about their displacement? The students had all experienced with their parents the wartime trauma of having to make the decision to leave their home country and leave other family members behind. They experienced the difficulties of the flight from Laos, and the uprooted, insecure life as refugees both in the Thai refugee camps and in their displacement in America. They shared their parents' vision of higher education as the key to success, a Lao cultural value that coincides with an adaptive strategy that other American immigrants have relied on to reconstruct a new future in the United States. Their American experiences also taught them that if they were to continue to live in America, they needed to create a more satisfying life and better prospects for their children and grandchildren. Because of these displaced lived experiences and what Safran (1991) called "diasporic consciousness," their top priority at this point in their life was to obtain after college graduation secure, well-paying jobs, not the factory jobs of their refugee parents who lacked better options. Despite their wishes for higher socioeconomic status and better income than those of their parents, they did not have the luxury of selecting the field of study that they "love the most" (Anderson 1996). The fields of study most of them were pursuing in the five colleges therefore cluster around service-delivery and technological-support professions: nursing, pharmacy, radiology technology, business administration, computer programming, and social work. What is also apparent from their fields of study is that, by necessity, most students opted for the prospect of immediate employment rather than selecting a field that requires long years of expensive postgraduate studies and/or uncertain employment prospects after graduation. One student confided that her personal career choice was medical school, but "for the sake of the family," she selected instead the field of medical technology, which requires fewer years of study and less financial burden on her family. Only one student aimed to get the additional teaching certificate to become a teacher. Personal decision as well Brown University's neglect to recruit at the high schools they attended account for the lack of Lao students at Brown University as of 1991, when Vietnamese, Hmong, and Cambodian students had been part of the Brown student body. When pressed in interviews for the reason for not applying on their own, a number of them cited the elitist image of Brown University, "up there on the hill" and their doubt of their family's financial capability to take care of the high tuition and other expenses. It was not until five years later that the first Rhode Island Lowland Lao student made it to Brown.

How, then, do the achievement motivations of Lao women students coalesce with the gender constructs of traditional Lao culture and with the cultural norms and demands of American society? To understand continuity and changes in female Lao students' values, behaviors, self-definitions, and the ways they are making selective choices for their future, one needs to step back in time and place to take a brief look at the cultural context and value orientation in Laos. There, when a young boy and a young girl get married, unless the boy's family is more financially well-off, he generally goes to live with the wife's parents until the couple is able to establish their own nuclear household. When the couple have their own home, it is usually within the property compound of the wife's parents. The choice of residence gives Lao culture a strong uxori-parentilocal emphasis, similar to what Keyes (1975) found as the pattern in the Thai-Lao community he studied. For married couples with children, property of all kinds is in principle divided equally among all, although in practice sons appear to be favored (LeBar and Suddard 1960, 68). But as in northern and in northeastern Thailand, a daughter often inherits the house and the house site. Beyond taking care of the household tasks and the children, the daughter who stays with the parents, married or unmarried, inherits the family home and is the person to take care of the parents in their old age. She also inherits the family shrine, and her house is the site of all familial ancestral rituals. As such, she becomes the organizer and a carrier of the family traditions and rituals. And eventually daughters rather than sons become the caretakers of elderly parents. Matrifocality as well as uxori-parentilocality are then the Lao cultural norms.

Men, on the other hand, tend to be the main income-earners, inherit the agricultural land, and have a stronger voice in other general decision-making domains, although in the case of family finance, the wife has some say in the decisions, since she takes care of the family purse (LeBar and Suddard 1960, 62). Lao men proudly regard this financial arrangement as a measure of trust of their wives (Phosamay Khammahavong, personal communication 1991). A Lao saying gives a metaphor of the marriage partnership as a *sampan* (a Lao/Thai paddle boat), in which "The wife paddles in the front seat while the husband paddles in the stern and mans the rudder." The saying underlines the interdependent roles of husband and wife in Lao culture and places the husband as the titular head of the family. As the metaphoric paddler in the front seat, the wife also has important role in the running of the family.

The fact that Lao social structure has codified prerogatives for women in postmarital residence, property inheritance, and family ritual rules as well as in family financial arrangements gives Lao women a relatively strong position within the society. The strength of this position has significant implications for their sense of self-identities and self-esteem beyond the material, monetary factors. They are not the passive, subservient women and wives commonly conceived to be the Asian stereotype. They provide additional examples of what Van Esterik (1982), Potter (1977), and Hoskin (1976) have pointed out as the high status and the structural significance of Southeast Asian women.

Lao cultural values place strong emphasis on family bonding, solidarity, politeness, avoidance of conflicts, respect for older people, and—as inculcated through the Buddhist philosophy "One is one's own refuge" (Rahula 1967, 1)— taking responsibility for one's own life and behavior. Family relationships, extending to consanquinal and affinal kins, are close. However, in terms of interpersonal relations between men and women, as LeBar and Suddard (1960, 98–99) pointed out, the norm of propriety guides formal behavior in all encounters in public, and defines the public display of affection between husband and wife as improper.

On the basis of ethnographic data on the social structure, inheritance rules, postmarital residence, cultural values, the cultural definition of gender, and my own familiarity with the Lao culture, I designed two sets of questionnaires, presented in Table 10.1 and Table 10.2, to locate the students' currently held values, attitudes, and behaviors, and to identify continuity and changes on these dimensions as they contribute to the formulation of the students' self-identities. The selection of the Lao cultural values, attitudes, and behaviors to query centered upon selected cross-culturally sensitive issues that are mostly likely to involve changes, whereby they might recede in significance or perhaps be abandoned because they are in direct conflict with American lifestyles and value orientations. Subsequent informal interviews of the students, following the ranking of the two sets of questionnaires, assisted in cross-checking, clarifying, and obtaining from the students contextualized, concrete instances and individual viewpoints that explained and gave deeper meanings to the Likert-scale rankings. At this point in the study, qualitative and quantitative methodologies went hand in hand. If one stumbles, the other is supposed to restore the balance. Or, as phrased by Miller (1997, 164), the two hold a "compatibility of alternative empirical methodologies."

For comparative purposes, four out of seven attitudes and values in Table 10.1 were taken from the 1986 social census research project carried out among the Lao in Murfreesboro, Tennessee (Blanchard 1992), with which I was involved at the initial stage. The four attitudes/values are: fifteen-year-olds should not date without a chaperone, opposite sexes should not hold hands in public, husbands have a decisive voice in the family, and a son is more valued than a daughter.

TABLE 10.1

List of the First Set of Attitudes and Values (N=28)

Attitude and Value	Agree		50/50		Disagree	
	No.	%	No.	%	No.	%
Young girl should not date without a chaperon	8	28.6	9	32.1	11	39.3
Boys and girls should not hold hands in public	5	17.8	11	39.3	12	42.8
My parents words are obeyed	22	78.6	4	14.3	2	7.1
Husband should have decisive voice in the family	6	21.4	0	0.0	23	82.1
A son is more valued than a daughter	9	32.1	10	35.7	9	32.1
It is difficult being a Lao woman	9	32.1	7	25.0	12	42.8
It's more difficult being a woman in America	15	53.6	4	14.3	9	32.1

Parents: From the Point of View of Daughters

The first six items in Table 10.1 are selected Lao traditional values, attitudes, and gender issues queried in the first set of questionnaires, rated by students on the five-point Likert scale (strongly agree, agree, fifty-fifty, somewhat, disagree). Since the number of students available for the study is small (twenty-eight students), in the analysis of the findings the numbers and percentages of the responses, "strongly agree" and "agree" were pooled and presented in the table as "agree." The pooled responses "somewhat disagree" and "disagree" are presented as "disagree." The "fifty-fifty" rating indicates a neutral position of the respondent on the issue.

Responses to the questionnaire show that the traditional Lao value of respect for older people, especially parents, was still strongly upheld by the respondents. Most (78.6 percent) saw being obedient to parents as part of the role of respectful daughters. Also consistent with the Lao cultural norm of daughters caring for parents in their old age, the consensus was unanimous on the care of aged parents. When asked in a separate interview about the options they now had in America of either putting aged parents in a home for the elderly or having them at home with them, no student selected the home for the elderly—even respondents who candidly professed to be somewhat rebellious, saying, "I obey my parents half of the time" or "I obey my parents only sometimes," and who might be regarded as more independent in the American societal context. One of these rebellious students explained, "It is not solely the parents' responsibilities to raise children, feed them, and send them to school. In Lao culture it's the children's duty to reciprocate with gratitude." Her attitude was not very different from that of another respondent who said she always obeyed her parents. She said, "Parents gave us life, so when they are old we should give them assistance and respect they deserve." Another respondent explained in more personal terms, "I want to take care of them like they take care of me." Two respondents with nursing school training from Laos who had work experience in Rhode Island homes for the elderly found the homes to be sadly deficient in appropriate care. One of them expressed in strong words, "I'll die first before I put them in a home."

It appears from this consensus that the Lao cultural expectation that daughters care for aged parents will continue to be honored in this group of female Lao college students. Blanchard's social census of 1986 (Blanchard 1992, 175) indicates almost as strong a response among 243 sampled Lao adults of Murfreesboro, Tennessee, to the question: Children should support their aged parents (mean = 1.787, with the responses given a scale value where one is always, and five, never).

"I Cook, You Wash": Reconstructing Gender

Both the 1991 Rhode Island Lao research and the 1986 Tennessee Lao research attempted to measure the impact of the American social environment on the Lao traditional behavioral norms in the domain of gender relations. For example: How did the dating behaviors as defined in Laos, with no hand-holding and with a chaperon, fare in America where few bars stand in the way of gender relations, in the Lao perception? And, when in Laos a woman was expected to be married and to take care of all the housework unless she was well-to-do with maids, how did Lao housewives in America and women college students view these traditional cultural expectations? The presence of both the single and married college students in the study group provided an opportunity for an intragroup comparison.

Blanchard's 1986 Tennessee Lao census data indicate a rather strong adherence to the traditional female Lao behavioral norm of fifteen-year-olds not dating without a chaperone (mean = 1.29) and the norm of opposite sexes not holding hands in public (mean = 2.19). Rhode Island Lao 1991 findings, in comparison, show more accelerated social change. The differences are most likely due to differences in the structure of the study groups (adults in the Tennessee study versus adolescent and young adult, female college students in the Rhode Island study) and in the year each research was conducted (1986 in the Tennessee research and 1991, five years later, in the Rhode Island research, when the young Lao had had longer exposure to American dating norms).

Behavioral norms of Rhode Island Lao women college students indicate definite changes. Whereas 28.6 percent of the students subscribed to the traditional behavioral rule of dating with a chaperon, a higher number (39.3 percent) indicated that they wanted the freedom of no chaperoning. Their preference for a more relaxed behavioral rules in male-female social interactions extended to the Western dating behavior of holding hands in public, 42.8 percent in comparison to 17.8 percent who wanted to maintain the traditional rule of no hand-holding. As adolescents and young adults, a large number appeared to want what was more consistent with the behavioral style they saw among their American peers. Individual Lao parents reacted differently on these behavioral changes. Some students admitted to having conflicts with their parents, especially in high school. But once in college, they appeared to have settled on a kind of truce. Although the parents recognized that they could not be too strict if they did not want to alienate their children, on the children's side there was a tacit acceptance that there was a line that should not be crossed. A student remembered her mother telling her, "Now that I allow you the freedom, use it wisely." Another student acknowledged, "I cannot let my family down." It must be noted again that the students in the study group had successfully entered college; they were not part of the school dropout group that reacted differently and is not the focus of this study.

One student in the study group not only subscribed to a more relaxed dating rule, she further crossed the racial boundaries in male-female social relationships. She was seriously dating a Euro-American. She showed up for the interview with her date. Her interracial relationship was not an isolated case. One student had a Swedish American brother-in-law, another a Jewish American brother-in-law, and the other an Italian American sister-in-law. Interracial marriage among the Lao group occurred even within the parents' generation, as attested by the marriage of a student's aunt to a Euro-American husband. Evidently, unlike the first-generation Chinese and Japanese immigrants, barred from interracial marriages because of the racist antimiscegenation laws (Spickard 1989), interracial and interethnic mixed marriages, in the case of the Rhode Island Lao, have occurred in the first immigrant/refugee generation, who have arrived in America at a period when societal attitudes toward interracial relationships have been more relaxed. They are also living in a period when the increasing trend in interracial marriages in America is demographically significant; the 1990 census reported two million interracially married couples (compared to 150,000 couples in 1960), and the 2000 census identified nearly seven million multiracials (Nash 1997, 18; Schmitt 2001). Among the Lao Americans, the trend is most likely to increase with time, with the more Americanized American-born generation and with increasing acceptance of intermarriage.

The Lao attitude toward interracial marriage is generally positive. One student cited her Swedish American brother-in-law as being her mentor for her American college life. He provided her with the know-how that her Laos-educated parents and older sister could not.

In the marriage domain, the traditional Lao social structure that allows women several key status and power positions, as previously discussed, gives Lao women a strong sense of self-worth. Further, arriving in America at the historic period of women's liberation, young Lao women college students were not unaware of the current feminist discourse and gender negotiations. It is not surprising therefore that they would prefer the husband-and-wife relationship to be on a more equal basis. Instead of husbands having the decisive voice in most family decisions, as in Laos, most perceived joint decision, with husband and wife discussing and deciding together, to be the desirable operating principle of marriage partnership in America. Fewer than one-fourth, that is only six respondents (21.4 percent), accepted the traditional male prerogative in decision making in the statement: Husband should have a decisive voice in the family. The majority, twenty-three respondents (82.1 percent), voted for equality in decision making. They totally rejected the idea that the husband should have a decisive voice in the family.

Consistent with the trend among the present generation of young American women, all respondents wanted to work after graduation and to continue working after marriage. When they were further asked in the in-depth interviews to project into the future as wives and as professional women, they indicated that they wanted equal sharing of family and household responsibilities, like American professional women.

> To me the pleasure of a married life lies also in sharing and helping each other out. To be married is not simply to have a woman in the house to take care of all the household chores and cook. (Twenty-year-old student)

> I like what I see in America as the equal rights of men and women. I disagree with men who think that women should take care of all the housework. I like the "I cook, you wash" formula. The shared responsibilities should be equal. After all, I work too. (Twenty-four-year-old student)

"I cook, you wash" is a succinct, new symbol of equal partnership in married life, advocated by Lao women students. Their attitude on this housework issue is not too surprising, considering that these are women who aim to function as professional women in American workplaces. Their view is shared by another group of Southeast Asian refugee women, the Vietnamese women. A growing number of Vietnamese women has been cited as experiencing upward mobility in America, while paradoxically their husbands are experiencing downward mobility (Kibria 1993). Vietnamese wives who had not worked in their home country and who now work to help bring in more needed income have been reported to likewise argue for more autonomy and equal partnership in the family, leading to family conflicts, wife abuse, and divorce in some cases (Luu 1989, 67). A similarly inverted shift of socioeconomic statuses has been found to occur among Vietnamese husbands and wives in Quebec (Dorais 1998, 302).

Despite the sense of empowerment and the desire for a new gender construct, Rhode Island women college students wanted to maximize the benefits of their bicultural worlds, American and Lao. In the future, when they were married, if their family was a double-career family and children came along, they hoped that they would be able to draw upon the traditional Lao social organization with its built-in family support system. They hoped that their parents or other relatives would not turn down child-care assistance. Their hope is not too far-fetched, as evidenced by married students with children in the study group whose triple responsibilities as student, wife, and mother were substantially eased by this strategic extended family support network. As of 1997, the built-in family support system was still at work. Their rootedness in the traditional Lao culture worked in this case to their advantage. All grandparents living with the family assisted in the care of their young grandchildren. Nalone Khammahavong, the research assistant on the project, now a nurse and a mother of two children, had her working-and-college-student husband and his parents taking turns babysitting her first child while she was finishing nursing school. When her husband's parents moved away from Rhode Island to be with their children working in North Carolina, another set of parents, Nalone's parents, arrived from Laos to temporarily take their place as caretakers of the grandchildren.

The cultural norm of having sons to continue the family line dies hard. In an interview of these students on the number of children they planned to have when they marry and the specific gender of the children, most wanted to have two to three children, which is a decidedly smaller family size than that of their parents. Still they wanted to have at least one son. Responses on the value of sons versus the value of daughters indicate a more slowly changing attitudinal trend in which some see the gender of children as not making any difference, whereas about a third of the respondents still value sons (32.1 percent) to continue the family line, the symbolic family name.

The keeping of maiden names after marriage, practiced by a number of American professional women, is not yet in practice among the Lao women. Nor is it, as yet, high on their priority list. Interestingly, when asked to compare their position with that of other women in America, over half (53.6 percent) see their difficulties as women as being not very different. Only about a third (32.1

percent) saw being female as well as being Lao as being difficult. It appears that at this point in their life, the students saw the gender variable, the issue of female liberation, and the shared struggles as "women" in America, more sharply in focus than their struggles as "ethnic women."

The result of the ranking on gender issues and the above-quoted views, in the students' own words, indicates, however, their positive view of American feminist discourse. Given their considerable status, power, and self-esteem codified by the Lao social structure, Lao women are strategically positioned to become increasingly liberated, with increasing autonomy. But, as on the issues of male-female behavioral norms, there are multiple voices. Caution and restraint are exercised by older, Laos-born students who want to accord their men the dignity and the respect they feel their husbands should have as the titular head of the family. Compared to students who arrived in America at a young age, their gender agenda is more restrained and more traditional. The relative age of the students' arrival in America thus becomes a decisive variable.

Transformation of the Self

The self is not a constant. As mentioned in the introductory section, I define self-formation as dynamic processes, not as a static state that can be achieved at a single, particular point or period in one's life. Self-formation is hence intricately interwoven with a series of transformations through which the self is formulated, reformulated, and tested. To bring more sharply into focus the formation of the self of Rhode Island Lao women college students and their emerging, new definition of womanhood in the American sociocultural context, specific American value variables were introduced into the research design of the second set of the questionnaires in addition to Lao values, here differently phrased to cross-check with the responses to the first set of questionnaires.

Table 10.2 is the second set of questionnaires on Lao and American values and behaviors rated on the five-point Likert scale (very important, important, fifty-fifty, sometimes, not important), and the result of the ratings, based on pooled "very important," "important" responses, presented as "important" in the table as compared to the pooled "sometimes," and "not important" responses, presented in the table as "not important."

As is apparent, knowledge has the top ranking (100 percent). The result of this total consensus can be explained by the respondents' parents' socialization. As mentioned earlier, most of the parents of these students were highly educated in Laos. In conversations and interviews, respondents made frequent references to how their parents, regardless of their level of education, have socialized them not to forfeit valuable opportunities for higher education in America. All respondents were on education scholarships of different types;

TABLE 10.2

List of the Second Set of Values and Behaviors (N=28)

Value and Behavior	Important		50/50		Not important	
	No.	%	No.	%	No.	%
Being rich is	15	53.6	5	17.8	8	28.6
Knowledge is	28	100.0	0	0.0	0	0.0
The family is	27	96.4	1	3.6	0	0.0
Helping around the house is	24	85.7	3	10.7	1	3.6
Helping brothers and sisters is	25	89.3	2	7.1	1	3.6
Financial support to old parents is	26	92.8	2	7.1	0	0.0
Earning my own salary is	26	92.8	2	7.1	0	0.0
In America competition is	18	64.3	8	28.6	2	11.4
Being married is	4	14.3	12	42.8	12	42.8

most prevalent for the study group were the Pell Grants, Rhode Island Scholarships for Higher Education, and various college scholarships. A number of juniors and seniors not working in factory jobs held their college's work/study grants.

Muir (1988, 106) found a similar parental emphasis on education among the Columbus, Ohio, Lao parents. Research on Vietnamese and Lao grade school and high school students carried out by Caplan, Choy, and Whitmore (1991, 1992) in Orange County, Seattle, Houston, Chicago, and Boston likewise found strong parental socialization. Such emphasis and the parents' and older siblings' willingness to tutor and work with them on their homework were deduced in the study as factors accounting for academic achievement of these Southeast Asian students in American grade schools and high schools. Through the research design of the present study, we have a finding on the academic directions of Lao students in college—beyond the high school level as reported by Caplan, Choy, and Whitmore. In the Rhode Island Lao college student group, another factor has earlier been identified, namely, the parent-student shared vision of education as the key to economic success and as a means for taking the family out of the blue-collar life and status. The students knew that earlier American immigrant groups have successfully utilized this adaptive strategy. This socioeconomic reality and their determination not to disappoint their parents' expectations, combined with their own desire to contribute to the family's well-being, become triple motivations. Success for Lao students is therefore defined not simply as individual achievement but concurrently in terms of the family, for the family.

Multiple indices (LeVine 1981; Anderson and Anderson 1986) built within the quantitative research methodology were used to measure further the significance of the family in an individual's life. In a series of questions where the place of the family was probed, phrased, and rephrased in diverse ways in terms physical, financial, or psychological support for family members, the findings point to the continuity of the Lao cultural emphasis on family in all of these domains. Topping the list of priorities is the place of the family as a whole (96.4 percent), followed by financial support of aged parents (92.8 percent), support for brothers and sisters (89.3 percent) and helping the family in household tasks (85.7 percent). The Thai/Lao word *chuaykan*, meaning helping and working together, was the word used in the responses of a number of students to convey the inherent Lao/Thai conceptual value and behavior connected with interdependence and solidarity within the family. The same attitude was held by the Columbus, Ohio, Lao community (Muir 1988, 82).

When three pairs of sisters in the Rhode Island study group were closely interviewed in terms of sibling relationship, it was discovered that the academic support provided by Lao older siblings to younger siblings as reported by Caplan, Choy, and Whitmore (1992) had increased both in kind and in scope in the Rhode Island case. These include economic, social, and academic support, including career counseling, critically needed by Lao siblings during their adolescent and college years. The three older sisters in the three paired sisters shared the income they had earned from their jobs with their younger sisters, drove them to classes, and mentored them on college life, dating, spouse selection, and career planning. More often than not, the older sister served as a surrogate parent to her younger sisters, since she knew more about these matters and could provide sounder advice than their parents, who had no experience in American college education and college life.

The American economic system, based on capitalism, is said to be built on the concept of economic success as measured by wealth. Klein (1992) sees "Greed is good" as being the ethos of the 1980s under Republican presidents. I tested that assumption on Lao students, where the data show that the capitalistic attitude has not been embraced by every segment of the population. Despite their future goal of being successful, the Lao students' definition of success at this point did not include a total absorption in becoming wealthy. Perhaps mediated by the philosophy of Buddhism, which negates materialism and accumulation of wealth, which is deemed impermanent, only slightly over half of the respondents (53.6 percent) ranked being rich as important. Over one-fourth, that is 28.6 percent, totally rejected it as an important goal in life. When queried differently in the in-depth interview about the constituents of a happy life, many Lao students stated that money is not important, money cannot buy everything. More important is having a happy, understanding family. Ong (2003, 7) similarly identified ambivalence about the American ethics of individualism and wealth among another new Southeast Asian American group, the Oakland and San Francisco Cambodian Americans.

The findings on this second set of questionnaires show convergent support in response to an open-ended question aimed at identifying the students' core values. Each student was asked early in the study to name five items she personally considered most important. The top priority with largest frequencies, and therefore most agreement among respondents, was the family. The other four items they valued, in consecutive ranking of importance, are: education, career (job), friendship, health, and wealth. Health came in a close fifth next to wealth.

While living in America, where competition is intense, how do Lao college students, coming from Lao society where cooperation and interdependence are the norms, negotiate what appear to be conflicting values? Besides the socializing effect of the Lao culture, it is likely that these students at this juncture in their lives had yet to compete in the job market. Also perhaps because they had intentionally chosen fields of study that could provide immediate employment after graduation, not all of them ranked competition as important, although the trend toward competitiveness or the recognition of the zero-sum game in the American societal context is there. Over half, that is 64.3 percent, regarded competition as significant. There is a strong correlation between the presence or absence of the competitive attitude and the kind of college the students were attending, as well as their educational achievement level. Those who ranked competition to be important tended to be enrolled in more competitive colleges or had higher academic achievement records than other students who ranked competition as unimportant. The finding points to individual variation in the achievement motivation of Lao students and to the critical role a college can play in inculcating competitiveness and scholastic drive in students.

What about marriage? Although being married is considered important for women in traditional Lao culture, most of the students did not see it as necessary in America. Only 14.3 percent considered it necessary. Two students frankly stated that they intended to remain single. Given what they had witnessed as marital conflicts, they preferred the freedom they can enjoy in America as single professional women. Marital status and personal experience turn out to be independent variables that have strong correlation with a positive or negative attitude toward marriage. Three out of the four students who rated marriage as important were happily married women. The fourth married student, a young twenty-year-old student who married against her family's wishes and was living with her husband's family (rather than having her husband come to live in her family, as is the Lao tradition) was rather ambivalent about marriage. Even though her husband's family was kind to her and helped take care of her baby during her class hours, she felt torn between class work and her wish to be with her child. The trend in culture change among the Lao women is definitely toward a decreasing significance of the marriage institution and the disappearance of the social stigma formerly attached to single women.

The Making of the Lao American Women

> I want a man who is honest and respects my parents. In our relationship I expect him to respect my viewpoints, to accept me for who I am. Of course he has to love me too. (Twenty-four-year-old student's view of an ideal husband)

James Clifford (1997, 258–259), who views diaspora experiences as always being gendered, asks: Do diaspora experiences reinforce or loosen gender subordination? Rhode Island Lao women college students, as can be seen from the above analysis, were retaining some of the Lao cultural norms and values. But in their cultural interaction with American culture, they had integrated American values, styles of behavior, and part of the American feminist discourse into their reinvented womanhood. Traits of professional American women's definition of womanhood were especially prominent in their discussions on economic independence and personal autonomy. Earning one's own salary became critical and very desirable. Since marrying a younger husband is acceptable in America, they were not as reticent about doing so as they would have been in Laos. And being single could now be a desirable choice. "If the marriage relationship doesn't work well," according to one student, "it's better not to be married at all." According to this same student, "Being single and being autonomous can be enjoyable. It's better to be single than to be unhappily married. When I work and earn my own salary, I don't need a husband to take care of me. I can take care of myself" (nineteen-year-old student). Compared with their mothers, these students had less aversion to divorce. As analyzed earlier, they expected a marital partnership in America to be on equal footing and both husband and wife to have equal voice in all family decisions, regardless of whether the husband is Lao or non-Lao. The processes of formulating, reinventing self-identities and future lives that would enable them to take better control of their own lives in America were being weighed, tested, and negotiated.

Beyond economic, gender, and marital aspects, other forms of Lao and American cultural syncretism had taken place and will continue to take place. I am using the terms "syncretism" and "hybridity" to convey the process of cultural change that accompanies acculturation and personal choices as distinguished from transculturation (Ortiz 1995; Hirabyashi 2002), the cultural changes that take place through conquest or colonial imposition. The dynamics of these cultural processes can be seen in the students' food consumption patterns, preferences, and their involvement with youth popular culture. In many instances not only the students and their young siblings, but also the whole family is involved in the changes. Every family that owns a private home has a vegetable and herb garden where hot pepper, sweet basil, coriander, *magrood*, and other Lao herbs are carefully tended during spring and summer. Meals in Lao homes are primarily Lao meals, and families shop for Lao grocery items in Lao grocery stores, facilitated by the growing globalization of Southeast Asian food exports. But fresh meat, vegetables, milk, and American snacks are generally purchased in American supermarkets. For the meals at school, the students have no choice, since they are served primarily American food. Meanwhile they have learned to enjoy certain American foods, the most frequently named of which are hamburgers and pizza. Perhaps a factor of American youth and fast-food culture, pizza has been named the favorite "American food" by both the Rhode Island and the Tennessee Lao youth.

Inasmuch as youth is the period when peer culture features most importantly in a young person's social life, I investigated the types of entertainment and popular culture that Lao women college students enjoyed as another measure of Lao cultural retention vis-à-vis the acceptance of an American lifestyle, leisure activities, and entertainment. In the realm of entertainment, Lao youth culture shows marks of cultural hybridity. Besides their access to American entertainment media, transnational economic and cultural networks link them to Asian globalized popular culture. They watched both American television programs and Thai or Chinese movie videos that their parents or grandparents had rented. Many of the Thai drama videos they were able to rent became the milieu through which they learned the shared, transnational Thai/Lao expressive culture while living here in America. Enculturation to Lao cultural performances came through diverse channels. A number of students named their grandparents or parents as culture bearers and tellers of Lao tales. In the music domain, they listened to Lao popular music, Thai popular music (in taped cassettes sold in Lao shops as well as through occasional performances of Lao and visiting Thai music groups), while simultaneously indulging in American rock music. A supportive Rhode Island Lao music environment is also responsible for the retention of Lao music appreciation among Lao residents. Two Lao popular music groups, Mungkorn Tong Band (The Golden Dragon Band) and Maitri Silpa Band (Art for Friendship Band) were the pride of Rhode Island Lao community in 1991. Musicians and singers of the two bands are Lao young adults, and the female singer on the Mungkorn Tong Band was a famed singer from Laos. Although some members of the two bands have moved to other states, three new bands have emerged. The music bands play at Lao social functions and serve the social needs of the community. Annually the Lao Traditional New Year celebration (Bune Pii Mai) starts with a religious ritual in almsgiving, a Soukhwan ritual, a communal feast, and ends with dancing to a Lao musical band in the evening, an event that is frequented mostly by the young crowd and parents who insist on chaperoning their young daughters.[2]

A Lao wedding ritual and celebration are likewise a syncretism of the East and the West, the Lao and the American. The traditional Soukhwan ritual, an offering of food and drink to the deceased ancestors, traditional Lao wedding costumes worn by the bride and the bridegroom, Lao food, and Western drinks are standard features of a Lao wedding. At a more elaborate wedding I attended, Lao music and Lao folk dances (*ramwong, phuthai* dance, and *pornsawan* dance) merged with Western dances as parts of the wedding celebration. While the older generation preferred the Lao dances, the young exuberantly participated in line dancing. A young man in his early teens performed what he called his "wedding present," a rap in Lao language that was an indication of his participation in and adaptation of the American hip-hop youth culture. The guests toasted the health and happiness of the wedded couple with French champagne, brought over from France by a French Lao cousin of the bride. Like the Viet Kieu (overseas Vietnamese) in Quebec, among whom transnational social networks and kinship ties play an important role in creating new forms of overseas Vietnamese social practices (Chan and Dorais 1998, 289), Rhode Island Lao transnational family ties and networks appear to function in the reinvented Lao culture within the new American homeplace.

The responsibility of women as important carriers of the Lao tradition continues in Rhode Island Lao community. Lao rituals and festive occasions cannot be accomplished without the communal work the women put in, especially in the preparations of Lao food and the *paakhwan* (the central flower-and-leaf arrangement with sacred threads) of the Soukhwan ritual, the core feature of all Lao rituals. Rhode Island Lao women have also formed a Lao Women Association of Rhode Island. One of their goals is the revitalization of Lao performance and aesthetic art forms. They train young Lao girls in traditional Lao dances and provide other logistic support to the Lao community. According to the current president of the Lao Association of Rhode Island, Lang Soupita, the retention of Lao cultural elements and of Lao language are critical for the maintenance of Lao identity. But Rhode Island Lao do not perceive their maintenance of Lao identity as exclusive, an all-or-nothing process. American festive occasions have lately found their way into Lao homes as welcomed additions to family festivities and gaiety. A number of families have adopted American Christmas gift-giving and Mother's Day gift giving traditions as part of the family's annual celebrations, in addition to Lao traditional religious rituals and rites of passage they celebrate. In another location, the greater Washington area, Krulfeld (1992, 7) has likewise identified the incorporation of new celebration events by the Lowland Lao group she studied.

Ethnographic interview data also reveal that a number of Lao women students have developed a strong sense of public and social consciousness and have become social activists. Two sisters were active members of a Lao youth organization that raised funds to support programs to keep young Lao from drugs and from being school dropouts. For another college senior, a series of deviant behaviors of Lao youth acted as a catalyst. Although she was scheduled to graduate in computer science with good job options, she felt that the Lao community and the Lao youth group need a Lao, an insider who understands Lao culture, to help solve the problems. She switched her field of study to social work, which required an additional year in college for her to pick up the social work courses she needed.

Ethnicity, Displacement, and the Homeplace

We're naming our son Gary after Gary Ley, the well-known meteorologist of Rhode Island Channel 10. My husband and I like him a lot. We hope that our son will grow up to be as successful as Gary Ley. (Nalone Kham-mahavong)

To this Khammahavong family of college-student husband and wife, Gary Ley represents a local symbol of success in America. Their choice of their son's name is also their way of expressing optimism for the future of their family, a personal symbolic act of forging their link to Rhode Island where they have resettled. As Gary Khammahavong, the son's name has a personal ethnic marker, signifying his dual identities as American and Lao from birth.

In 1991, ethnic identity as a facet of self-identity was not yet solidly defined and totally internalized among the college students studied. When they were asked how they identified themselves, "Lao" or "Laotian" were the answers. Similar self-identifications were voiced by the majority of the Lao in the greater Washington area (Krulfeld 1992, 17). When asked if they would apply for American citizenship when they become eligible, Rhode Island college students expressed ambivalence. They answered, "I am not sure" or "I'll wait and see." When queried further on how they would identify themselves if they decided to obtain American citizenship, the answers varied from "Laotian American," "Lao American," or just "Lao." One student who preferred the label "Laotian American" felt that the label "sounds nicer." In 1996, when ethnic consciousness among the Lao in America increased, the ethnic group label became a major issue. Opinions were expressed and passed on back and forth on the Lao internet on whether "Lao American" or "Laotian American" should be their ethnic group label (Sivilay S. Somchanhmavong, Cornell University, personal communication 1993). A strong argument was made in favor of the "Lao American" label. It was argued that the term "Lao" is linguistically the real native Lao label, a self-description, not the Western-imposed term "Laotian." The term "Lao" is there-

fore used in this study to refer to the Lao people and "Lao American" the ethnic label of the group.

James Clifford (1997, 246) posits: "Diasporas usually presuppose longer dis-
tances and a separation more like exile: a constitutive taboo on return, or its
postponement to a remote future." Clifford's view aptly captures the sense of
the diaspora and displacement of the Rhode Island Lao. At the turn of the
century, most of them had progressed from their initial "refugee" status to
"permanent-residence" status and have recently taken the decisive step of
embracing a new identity, becoming American naturalized citizens. Becoming
American citizens was an important turning point in their lives that forced
them to seriously reevaluate who they are. Rather than coveting U.S. citizenship
as the pinnacle of Americanness, they were ambivalent, and many resisted taking the step. As one Lao American woman put it:

> Even though we could apply for the American citizenship, for years we
> had been resisting it. Most of us were unsure about American identity.
> What does it really mean to be American? Others now feel that their
> dream of going back to live in Laos will never materialize. A large num-
> ber, on the other hand, feels that they have been living here in America
> for over a decade and they have more or less adjusted to American life.
>
> What about Laos? Of course, Laos will always be "home." We want to
> be able to go back there to visit in the future when the political situa-
> tion is more friendly. (Lao grocery store owner)

Memory about and longing for the homeland are what Safran (1991) also
links to diasporic consciousness. Nevertheless, America as the de facto homeplace, a displacement frame of reference, has gradually become part of the Lao
conceptual construct of their current life, their living community, and their living space. As a group, the Lao share with many displaced people the coexisting,
dual conceptualization of "home," that is, "home" as the living, physical space,
which may not be the same as "home" as the effective space, tied to their ancestral country (Maira and Srikanth 1996). For naturalized Lao Americans, America is now their "home," just as Laos is still "home." They are concrete replies to
Lesser's question: Does a person have multiple homes or just one? (Lesser 2003,
1). Most interviewed said that despite having obtained their American citizenship, this does not mean that they are no longer Lao in how they feel about
themselves. One student who selected "Lao" as her self-identity explained,
"Whatever I am legally, I know that deep down I am always Lao." Another who
has recently taken her American citizenship said, "I know that I am always Lao.
Every morning when I look into the mirror, I see a Lao." Only when filing an official document is American citizenship evoked. On other occasions, when asked
"What are you?" their answer generally is "I am Lao." The fact that all college

students in the study group were born in Laos, their Laoness is not only affective but also spatial and cultural. Every wedding, where food offerings are made to the deceased ancestors residing spiritually in Laos, is ritually a renewal and a marker of their ancestral and homeland ties. Their dual identities and conceptualization of belongingness, and the senses of the homeplace, take on the character of a displaced, transnational construct.

Like the Vietnamese Buddhists (Rutledge 1985) and the Cambodian Buddhists (Smith-Heffner 1999), who saw close identity between Buddhism and their ethnicity, the Lao students in this study saw the Lao part of the Lao American identity as being culturally connected to the retention of Lao language and the Buddhist religion. Both can be defined as Lao American ethnic markers, as are the Soukhwan ritual, the Bune Pii Mai (Lao traditional New Year) ritual, ancestral ritual, Lao food, being dressed in Lao traditional costume at the wedding, and other ritual observances and practices.

Except for a few students who will allow their children to select their own religious faith, most intended to raise them as Buddhists. All preferred to have their children become bilingual: English and Lao. All students speak Lao at home with their parents, older siblings, and other Lao, while English is used with Americans and American-born younger siblings. In peer-group interactions, language code switching has been observed to occur frequently. The students shifted from Lao to English, sometimes intermixing them in the same sentence. They explained that when they did not have the exact word in one language to express exactly what they wanted to convey, they switched to the other language. Their explanation suggests the use of this verbal pattern as a linguistic strategy for maximizing social interaction and levels of understanding. The equation of bilingualism among Latinos with the linguistic skill that makes Latinos more social, less ignorant, and less isolated (Shorris 1992) appears to apply linguistically and socially also to Lao students. Several of them stated that when they were in Lao settings such as at home or at Lao social and ritual gatherings, they behaved in Lao ways, and when they were in American settings they behaved like Americans. Bicultural, these students have utilized situational identity, that is using the role that is most appropriate to the situation that Nagata (1974, 343) considers a viable adaptive strategy for shifting contexts. Krulfeld (1993, 33) has likewise observed the use of situational identity among Lao men in the greater Washington area. The findings from Rhode Island indicates that situational identity among the young Lao is markedly heightened and takes several forms, both linguistic and behavioral, due to their constant exposure to diverse, intercultural interactional contexts. Hybridity, multilingualism, biculturalism, and the ability to shift identity according to the situation will be part of the characteristics of the Lao American identity of this first-generation Lao Americans.

As stated by Harding and Clement (1980, 5), cultural adaptation "occurs in response to pressures affecting the stability of a sociocultural system. The nature of its response, in turn, structures the potential for subsequent change so that the change is permitted, yet continuity is maintained." It is apparent that the sociocultural adaptation and changes among Rhode Island Lao women college students, as refugees, as displaced Lao, and as new ethnic Americans, are underscored by multiple forces, intricately linked in a web of pragmatic adaptation exigencies and selective choices. Lao cultural retention is, on the one hand, arbitrated by their adaptive strategy not to be in excessive discordance with American realities. Specific Lao cultural characteristics are, on the other hand, consciously guarded as the key to their group identity. As Romanucci-Ross (1996, 94–95) has stated, ethnic identity can be a conscious, selective process of choosing what ethnic members consider as accurately defining them and rejecting those that they feel do not define them.

Conclusions

The formulation of what it means to be a first-generation Lao American woman is indeed a series of transformation processes with observable shifts in attitudes, values, expectations, and commitments that were formerly held and codified in the traditional Lao social structure. For these Lao college students studied, to be able to achieve the transformation, the constant tug-and-pull of Lao culture versus American culture has made it necessary for them to weigh necessity and choices, to test new ones if they can, and to negotiate them if they must.

The multipronged study of multiple domains used in this study helps to identify and isolate how in each domain the process of transformation takes place. While increased autonomy is deemed desirable in the domains of marriage choice, family decisions, and self-earned income, the family continues to be defined in terms of traditional Lao cooperative and interdependent units, emotionally, socially, and economically. As is apparent in the above analysis, the primary importance of the family comes through in all the different types of indices used: the open-ended questions, the rank-scale questionnaires, ethnographic in-depth interviews, and participant-observations. Comparative research findings from other Lao communities in America indicate similar value orientations. Muir, in *The Strongest Part of the Family: A Study of Lao Refugee Women in Columbus, Ohio* (1988), likewise perceived the family to be their central concern. Caplan, Choy, and Whitmore (1992, 39), who studied Lao and Vietnamese children, reported that parents and children have a "mutual, collective obligation to one another and to their relatives."

The voices of Rhode Island Lao women college students are articulated from the position of displaced young individuals. Of the immediate future goals after graduation, besides having good jobs and good salaries, the first priority for students still living in inner-city Providence is to save their earning to help their parents purchase a house, "to live somewhere where we don't have to be afraid of theft, our car broken into, loud noises next door, and to be able to see many, many green trees," as one student put it. From their initial lack of choices, they want choices. To materialize their goals, most of these students have made a conscious decision to delay getting married and starting a family. The shift in class status, from blue-collar jobs to white-collar jobs of immigrants and ethnic Americans, and their residential migration from inner-city ethnic communities to suburban living have generally been analyzed as indicators of socioeconomic upward mobility. For Lao students whose fathers were formerly high-income or middle-income professionals in Laos, the desired move is a reclamation of the family's former class status and lifeways. Their definition of autonomy appears to be individualistic and at the same time intertwined with, not separate from, their family commitments and well-being. For them, autonomy and the sense of self-worth are therefore neither irreconcilable with family responsibilities nor deemed desirable as polarities.

The wish of Lao women college students to maintain some aspects of Lao cultural identity is an articulation of their need to maintain some cross-connections to their ancestral culture. As Americans, legally and psychologically, the bridge, for a number of them, had yet to be crossed in 1991. At this juncture, Lao American identity as an ethnic identity was not yet fully sensed and internalized. Label aside, one can nevertheless see from the above findings and analysis the emergence of Lao American women's self-identities—ethnic, social, and professional—that are not only different from but more liberated than those of their mothers. They are indeed more in keeping with the realities of their more American lives and expectations. The dynamic processes of their transformations as women, as wives, as mothers, and as professional women are not yet completed. They will go on as the meanings of womanhood, individual priorities, and self-identities are again and again redefined, reformulated, and restructured within the American sociopolitical contexts. Even at this point in time, one can nevertheless catch glimpses of the blossoming of Lao American womanhood, what the Lao American women themselves see as markers of their cultural and ethnic distinctiveness, and what may be chosen to characterize the Lao American community.

This study is conceptually also a study of the emergent. It has taken the Lao refugees beyond the highly traumatized, initial resettlement stage to the appearance of emerging trends. Both in time and space, future studies are needed. At another location, at another point in time, what will be the picture of the Lao American women? And when American-born Lao Americans reach womanhood, what will be their quest, professional and ideological? For comparison, what will be the picture of Lao American men? What will these be, say another twenty years from now?

NOTES

I appreciate the 1991 research grant of the Center for the Study of Race and Ethnicity in America, Brown University, under Acting Director John Ladd, which enabled me to engage a research assistant for the field research. Professor Beatrice B. Whiting kindly read my first draft and encouraged me to push my interpretation of the Lao gender construction further. I sincerely thank Lang Sopita, president of the Lao Association of Rhode Island; Nalone Khammahavong (research assistant); all the Lao students in the study group; and their families for their cooperation, patience, friendship, and for sharing their thoughts and feelings that has made this study possible.

1. The breakdown of the student numbers by college is: Rhode Island Community College (13), University of Rhode Island (8), Rhode Island College (3), Providence College (1), Johnson and Wales College (3).

2. The Soukhwan ritual, practiced both in Laos and in Thailand with certain variations in ritualistic details, is associated with the concept of the *khwan*, the life-force or vital spirit (Anuman Rajadhon 1961, 190). Sometimes referred to in English as "the soul" (LeBar and Suddard 1960, 47), the *khwan* resides, invisible, in the head of every individual. A person's health and happiness depends on his or her *khwan* remaining in situ. The Soukhwan ritual, literally the welcoming of the life force, is performed at transitional periods in life: birth, marriage, after a severe illness, after a period in the monkhood, and after a major journey such as study abroad and immigration to America. It is also held annually at the *Bune Pii Mai,* the Lao traditional New Year ritual. The origin of the *khwan* concept, part of popular religion, is not known. It was most likely in existence before the introduction of Buddhism.

REFERENCES

Anderson, Wanni W. n.d. "Ethnicity in action: Thai Muslim ethnicization in the Thai nation state." Unpublished manuscript.

———. 1996. "Ethnicity and the model minority reconsidered: Lao American college students." Paper given at the annual meeting of the Society for Asian American Studies, Washington, D.C.

Anderson, Wanni W., and Douglas D. Anderson. 1986. "Thai Muslim adolescents' self, sexuality, and autonomy." *Ethos* 14(4): 368–394.

Anuman Rajadhon, Phya. 1961. *Life and ritual in old Siam.* Translated and edited by William J. Gedney. New Haven: HRAF Press.

Bammer, Angelika, ed. 1994. *Displacements: Cultural identities in question.* Bloomington: Indiana University Press.

Blanchard, Kendall. 1992. "Sport, leisure, and identity: Reinventing Lao culture in middle Tennessee." *Play & Culture* 4: 169–184.

Bousquet, Gisele L. 1991. *Behind the bamboo hedge: The impact of homeland politics in the Parisian Vietnamese community.* Ann Arbor: University of Michigan Press.

Burton, Linda M. 1997. "Ethnography and the meaning of adolescence in high-risk neighborhood." *Ethos* 25(2): 208–217.

Caplan, Nathan, Marcella H. Choy, and John K. Whitmore. 1991. *Children of the boat people: A study of educational success.* Ann Arbor: University of Michigan Press.

——. 1992. "Indochinese refugee families and academic achievement." *Scientific American* (February), 36–42.

Chan Kwok Bun and Louis-Jacques Dorais. 1998. "Family, identity, and the Vietnamese diaspora: The Quebec experience." *Sojourn* 13(2): 285–308.

Clifford, James. 1997. *Routes: Travel and translation in the late twentieth century.* Cambridge: Harvard University Press.

Dorais, Louis-Jacques. 1998. "Vietnamese communities in Canada, France and Denmark." *Journal of Refugee Studies* 11(2): 107–125

Erikson, Erik E. 1968. *Identity, youth and crisis.* New York: W. W. Norton.

Espiritu, Yen Le. 1989. "Beyond the 'boat people': Ethnicization in American life." *Amerasia Journal* 15(2): 49–67.

Harding, Joe R., and Dorothy C. Clement. 1980. "Regularities in the continuity and change of role structures: The Ixil Maya." In *Predicting sociocultural change*, edited by S. Abbot and J. Van Willigen, 5–25. Athens: University of Georgia Press.

Him, Chanrithy. 2000. *When broken glass floats: Growing up under the Khmer Rouge.* New York: W. W. Norton.

Hirabayashi, Lane Ryo. 2002. "Reconsidering transculturation and power." *Amerasia Journal* 28(2): ix–xxii.

Hoskin, Marilyn W. 1976. "Vietnamese women: Their roles and their opinions." In *Changing institutions in modern Southeast Asia*, edited by D. J. Banks, 127–146. The Haque: Mouton.

Hua, T. G. 2000. *Land of smiles.* New York: Plume.

Isaccs, Harold R. 1975. "Basic group identity: The idols of the tribe." In *Ethnicity: Theory and experience*, edited by N. Glazer and D. P. Moynihan, 29–52. Cambridge: Harvard University Press.

Keyes, Charles F. 1975. "Kin groups in a Thai-Lao community." In *Change and persistence in Thai society*, edited by W. G. Skinner and A. T. Kirsch, 278–297. Ithaca: Cornell University Press.

Kibria, Nazli. 1993. *Family tightrope: The changing lives of Vietnamese Americans.* Princeton: Princeton University Press.

Klein, J. 1992. "Whose value?" *Newsweek*, June 8, 18–22.

Krulfeld, Ruth M. 1992. "Cognitive mapping and ethnic identity: The changing concepts of community and nationalism in the Laotian diaspora." In *Selected papers on refugee issues*, edited by P. A. Devoe, 4–26. Washington, D.C.: American Anthropological Association.

——. 1993. "Bridging Leviathan: New paradigm of method and theory in culture change." In *Selected papers on refugee issues II*, edited by M. C. Hopkins and N. D. Donelley, 29–39. Washington, D.C.: American Anthropological Association.

LeBar, Frank M., and Adrienne Suddard. 1960. *Laos: Its people, its society, its culture.* New Haven: HRAF Press.

Lesser, Jeffrey, ed. 2003. *Searching for home abroad: Japanese Brazilians and transnationalism.* Durham: Duke University Press.

LeVine, Robert A. 1981. "Knowledge and fallibility in anthropological field research." In *Scientific inquiry and the social science*, edited by M. B. Brewer and B. E. Collins, 172–193. San Francisco: Jossey-Bass.

Luu, Van. 1989. "The hardships of escape for Vietnamese Women." In *Making waves: An anthology of writings by and about Asian American women*, edited by Asian Women United of California, 60–72. Boston: Beacon.

Maira, Sunaina, and Rajini Srikanth. 1996. *Contours of the heart: South Asians map North America.* New York: Asian American Writers' Workshop.

Miller, Joan. 1997. "The interdependence of interpretive ethnographic and quantitative psychological methodologies in cultural anthropology." *Ethos* 25(2): 164–176.

Mortland, Carole J., and Judy Ledgerwood. 1987. "Secondary migration among Southeast Asian refugees in the United States." *Urban Anthropology* 16(3–4): 291–326.

Muir, Karen L. S. 1988. *The strongest part of the family: A study of Lao refugee women in Columbus, Ohio.* New York: AMS Press.

Nagata, Judith. 1974. "What is a Malay? Situational selection of ethnic identity in a plural society." *American Ethnologist* 1(2): 331–350.

Nash, Philip Tajitsu. 1997. "Will the census go multiracial?" *Amerasia Journal* 23(1): 17–28.

Ngor, Haing. 1987. *A Cambodian odyssey.* New York: Werner Books.

Nguyen, N. A., and H. L. Williams. 1989. "Transition from East to West: Vietnamese adolescents and their parents." *Journal of the American Academy of Child and Adolescent Psychiatry* 23(4): 505–515.

Nguyen-Hong-Nhiem, Lucy, and Joel Martin Halpern. 1989. *The Far East comes near: Autobiographical accounts of Southeast Asian students in America.* Amherst: University of Massachusetts Press.

Office of the United Nations High Commissioner for Refugees. 1991a. *Statistics and charts concerning Indo-Chinese in South East Asia for the month of October 1991.* Geneva, Switzerland.

——. 1991b. *Statistics of Indo-Chinese refugees in Thailand.* Geneva, Switzerland.

——. 1995. *Indo-Chinese refugees, asylum seekers and screened-out in Thailand.* Geneva, Switzerland.

Ong, Aihwa. 2003. *Buddha is hiding: Refugees, citizenship, the new America.* Berkeley: University of California Press.

Ortiz, Fernando. 1995. *Counterpoint: Tobacco and sugar.* Durham: Duke University Press.

Potter, Sulamith Hein. 1977. *Family life in a northern Thai village: A study in the structural significance of women.* Berkeley: University of California Press.

Rahula, Walpola. 1967. *What the Buddha taught.* Bedford: Gordon Frazer.

Romanucci-Ross, Lola. 1996. "Matrices of an Italian identity." In *Ethnic identity: Creation, conflict, and accommodation,* edited by L. Romanucci-Ross and G. DeVos, 73–96. Third edition. Walnut Creek, Calif.: Alta Mira Press.

Rutledge, Paul. 1985. *The role of religion in ethnic self-identity: A Vietnamese community.* Lanham, Md.: University Press of America.

Safran, William. 1991. "Diasporas in modern sciences: Myths of homeland and return." *Diaspora* 1(1): 83–99.

Schmitt, Eric. 2001. "For seven million people in census, one race isn't enough." *New York Times,* March 31.

Shorris, Earl. 1992. *Latinos: A biography of the people.* New York: W. W. Norton.

Skinner, Kenneth, and Glenn L. Hendricks. 1979. "The shaping of ethnic self identity among Indochinese refugees." *Journal of Ethnic Studies* 7(3): 25–41.

Smith-Heffner, Nancy J. 1999. *Khmer American: Identity and moral education in a diasporic community.* Berkeley: University of California Press.

Spencer, M. B., B. Dobbs, and D. P. Swanson. 1988. "Afro-Americans: Adaptational processes and socioeconomic diversity in behavioral outcome." *Journal of Adolescence* 11: 117–137.

Spickard, Paul R. 1989. *Mixed blood: Intermarriage and ethnic identity in twentieth-century America.* Madison: University of Wisconsin Press.

Sue, Derold Wing. 1973. "Ethnic identity: The impact of two cultures on the psycholog-
    ical development of Asians in America." In *Asian-Americans: Psychological analysis*,
    edited by S. Sue and N. N. Wagner, 140–149. Palo Alto: Science and Behavior Books.
Sue, Stanley. 1980. "Psychological theory and implications for Asian Americans." In
    Asian-Americans: Social and psychological perspectives, vol. II, edited by R. Endo,
    S. Sue, and N. N. Wagner, 288–303. Palo Alto: Science and Behavior Books.
Tobins, Joseph J., and Joan Friedman. 1984. "Intercultural and developmental stresses
    confronting Southeast Asian adolescents." *Journal of Operational Psychiatry* 15:
    39–44.
Trueba, Henry T., Lila Jacobs, and Elizabeth Kirton. 1990. *Cultural conflict and adapta-
    tion: The case of Hmong children in American society*. New York: The Falmer Press.
Van Esterik, Penny. 1982. "Lay women in Theravada Buddhism." In *Women of South-
    east Asia*, edited by P. Van Esterik, 55–78. DeKalb: Center for Southeast Asian Stud-
    ies, Northern Illinois University.
———. 1992. *Taking refuge: Lao Buddhists in North America*. Tempe: Program for
    Southeast Asian Studies, Arizona State University; and Toronto: Center for
    Refugee Studies, York University.
Yathay, Pin. 1987. *Stay alive, my son*. New York: Touchstone.

11

====================================

Mixed Desires

Second-Generation Indian Americans and the Politics of Youth Culture

SUNAINA MAIRA

One of the major questions driving the study on which this chapter is based is: What are the ways in which "being Indian" is (re)produced in the second generation, and how is national identity and culture recreated in the diaspora? My research intersedes with work on diasporic experiences in two ways; first, by using youth culture as a site in which to think about questions of cultural displacement, national reimaginings, and the politics of nostalgia in material contexts. Studies of Asian diasporic communities in the United States often view youth primarily through the lens of their reproduction of "ancestral cultures," the ways in which they recreate ethnic identities, and the by now well-worn debates on intergenerational conflict (Lowe 1996, 63). There is little attention to the complexities of Asian American youth experiences, such as the ways in which they are shaped deeply by local contexts and the rituals of American popular culture. Little attention is paid to the cultural productions of youth themselves, with the result that Asian American youth are considered agents mainly in the realm of subjective identity construction processes or in the arena of family relationships, rather than as active players in their own microcultural contexts. These have their own hierarchies of power, their own networks of affiliation, their own ideologies of authenticity, and are also constantly in interaction with wider social and economic structures. These local cultural productions are dialectically related to imaginings of the ancestral cultures through transnational links that are both ideological and material, making youth cultures an important site where local and global processes converge and also contradict one another.

I use the term "transnational" here deliberately, as a concept that has a somewhat different intellectual genealogy and disciplinary lineage from that of "diaspora." While acknowledging the experience of displacement and the ideological force of constructions of "homeland," the notion of transnationalism also forces us to think about the strategic ways in which immigrant communities "forge and sustain multi-stranded social relations that link together their societies of origin *and* settlement" (Basch, Glick Schiller, and Szanton Blanc 1994, 7; emphasis added). These social and material relationships are created in the context of global flows of capital, labor, media images, and ideologies—what Arjun Appadurai calls ethnoscapes, mediascapes, and ideoscapes (1996). Transnational "social fields" are created in these global scapes, but they are still mediated heavily by the structures and ideologies of nation-states and still deeply concerned with notions of "place" and processes of "localization." This is perhaps where some theorists of transnationalism and diaspora echo one other, acknowledging the ways in which locality remains a potent force, but one that does not connote the fixed, bounded opposite of "the global" and is itself "discursively and historically constructed" (Gupta and Ferguson 1997, 6). As James Clifford (1997, 287) argues, "the term diaspora is a signifier, not simply of transnationality and movement, but of political struggles to define the local, as distinctive community, in historical contexts of displacement." The larger study on which this chapter is based examines the ways in which second-generation youth culture becomes a site of struggles to define notions of authenticity that, while drawing on transnational imaginings of "India," also work to position these youth in relation to hierarchies of race, class, gender, and nationalism that mark them as "local."

On an analytic level, I am interested in the ways in which research on diasporas has contributed to the theorizing of essentialism and authenticity in cultural studies and anthropology, and I use my work on diasporic youth cultural production to rethink this framework, taking my cues from social experiences "on the ground." I am interested in the implications that different disciplinary and methodological approaches have for debates about cultural politics. Given that my own work occurs on the borders of several disciplines and their concomitant "nationalisms," I think that the forms that these understandings of diasporic cultural politics take are necessarily opened up, and also limited, by particular disciplinary perspectives, calling for a critical synthesis of interdisciplinary scholarship to address the complexity of diasporic cultural production.

Remix Youth Culture in New York

New York City is home to an increasingly visible youth subculture created by second-generation Indian Americans that centers on music and dance, specifically the fusion of Hindi film music and *bhangra* (a north Indian and Pakistani dance and music) with American rap, techno, reggae, and jungle music. This youth subculture has become a recognized part of New York City nightlife and popular culture, as heralded to the mainstream by concerts at the Summerstage series in Central Park, articles in the local news media, and documentaries by local independent filmmakers.[1] My research explores the tension between the production of a certain cultural nostalgia and the performance of "cool" in this subculture, and shows how the dialectic between these structures of feeling reveals the contradictory cultural politics of authenticity for Indian American youth (Williams 1961).

The music is remixed by Indian American DJs who perform at the parties hosted at local clubs, restaurants, and college campuses by party promoters, generally young Indian American men and women. Some of these are college students who do this as a source of part-time income and who have helped create an urban South Asian American youth subculture.[2] Every weekend, remix parties in Manhattan attract *desi* youth from New York, New Jersey, Connecticut, and even Pennsylvania—areas that have large concentrations of Indian, and South Asian, immigrant families as well as South Asian American student populations. Cover charges are steep but not atypical for New York parties, ranging from ten to twenty dollars, yet the parties draw hordes of youth from a range of class backgrounds who are willing to fork out money for leisure activities. Partygoers are for the most part second generation, although there are generally some first-generation South Asian youth in the crowd as well, who participate in the redefinition of desi "cool," in its urban, New York/Northeast incarnation, through the creative use of elements of popular culture.

The subculture that has sprung up in New York around Indian music remix includes participants whose families originate from other countries of the subcontinent, such as Bangladesh and Pakistan, yet these events are often coded by insiders as the "Indian party scene" or "desi scene." The word "desi" signifies a pan-South Asian rubric that is increasingly emphasized in the second generation, and literally means "of South Asia," especially in the context of the diaspora. Indian American youth describe desi parties as being spaces that support not just pan-Indian identification but also regional allegiances that extend beyond the party subculture to everyday social life, so that there are actually subcultures nested within the larger Indian American subculture. The invoking of regional identity through particular music mixes is most obvious in the passion aroused in many Punjabis and Sikhs by the sounds of the *dhol* drum used in bhangra, many of whom use remix parties as a stage to perform vigorous renditions of bhangra and claim the spotlight on the dance floor, as non-Punjabis look on. A flier for a bhangra remix party hosted by the United Sikh Association "proudly presents Mera Desh Punjab," which literally means "my country is Punjab" (although, testifying to the translocal nature of loyalties in the diaspora, the flier also describes the local DJs as "putting Queens on the map").

Furthermore, there are Indian American youth who are not in college and who also attend these parties, and there are "Indian parties" held outside Manhattan as well, such as on campuses in New Jersey and Long Island where there are large South Asian student populations.[3] Manhattan, however, provides a particular context for desi parties because of the presence of city clubs, such as the Madison, the erstwhile China Club, or S.O.B.'s (Sounds of Brazil), which draw large droves of South Asian American youth, who get down to the beats of bhangra. The party scene has created a social network of youth across the college campuses where I did my fieldwork, who gather regularly at these events and know others on the party circuit in Manhattan. The phenomenon of desi parties fits in with the larger structure of clubbing in New York and other cities, where clubs host different "parties" or nights that are ethnically, racially, and sexually segregated, and that feature DJs who can spin the right kind of mix for their target audience (Toure 1997, 98). This underscores ethnomusicologist Martin Stokes's (1994, 3) observation about the production of social spaces through music: "The musical event . . . evokes and organizes collective memories and present [sic] experiences of place with an intensity, power and simplicity. . . . The 'places' constructed through music involve notions of difference and social boundary. They also organise hierarchies of a moral and political order." It is this power of music, and dance, to evoke a sense of "place" in a social hierarchy as well as a spatial location that makes possible the collective nostalgia for India as well as the gauging of subcultural status at remix music parties.

In conjunction with the production of remix music, this subculture displays the construction of a culturally hybrid style, such as wearing Indian-style nose rings and bindis with hip hop fashion, and performing ethnic identity through dance, as in the borrowing of folk dance gestures from bhangra while gyrating to club remixes.[4] Indian American women were sporting bindis long before pop stars Madonna or Gwen Stefani did, but they now do so in the context of commodified ethno-chic; *mehndi* kits (Indian body art) and bindi packets (body jewels) have been sprouting in clothing stores, pharmacies, street fairs, and fashion magazines both in New York and nationwide in the years since I completed this research. The emergence of Indo-chic in the late 1990s is a charged issue, especially for young desi women. Elsewhere, I demonstrate the ways in which the commodification of Asian signifiers becomes a frame used by women who have grown up in different parts of the South Asian diaspora to negotiate contests of ethnic authenticity and critique the unevenness of global capital (Maira forthcoming). Underlying these debates about youth popular culture is always the problematic of consumption and the relationship of youth to the labor market, for there are Indian Americans who are not in college and who attend these parties, and there are strains of materiality and class mobility that are mixed with the vibes of nostalgia in this subculture.

Indian Remix Music and the Manhattan "Desi Scene"

The creation of this Indian American, and South Asian American, youth culture in Manhattan has, in part, been made possible by the presence of a large local

Indian immigrant community. New York City currently has the "largest concentration of Indians [of any metropolitan area] (about 10 percent of total 1990 population in the country)" (Khandelwal 1995, 180). According to the 1990 census, New York City had 94,590 Indian residents out of a total of 815,447 in the United States. Whereas the earlier wave of Indian immigrants, who arrived in the late 1960s and 1970s and spread to the suburbs of America, were mainly professionals and graduate students, New York City and New Jersey have seen an influx of South Asian immigrants in the 1980s and 1990s who are less affluent and less highly educated.[5]

Madhulika Khandelwal (1995) suggests that while the earlier immigrant elite primarily founded pan-Indian organizations and sponsored public performances of classical Indian arts, later immigrant waves have spawned the growth of regional organizations and sectarian religious institutions that cater to specific subgroups within the Indian American community. Their definitions of "Indian culture," whether based on classical or popular visions, exemplify the repertoire of meanings that are attached to "tradition" in diasporic communities and the selective use of certain kinds of cultural production to represent national identity.[6] In the 1990s, multiculturalism provided the context for officially sanctioned displays of national culture that coexisted with popular recreations of tradition, as in the case of different kinds of cultural production by desi youth. There is sometimes a tension between the two versions that suggests the contradictory workings of the politics of nostalgia.

In his collection of incisive essays on Latino popular culture and politics, *From Bomba to Hip Hop* (2000), Juan Flores suggests that popular culture expresses "the problem of contemporaneity," the simultaneous "coexistence of tradition and modernity" (21), a temporal dialectic that is deeply embedded in second-generation youth cultures that are always wrestling with notions of presumably vanishing "traditions" and derivative or threatening practices of the present. This popular culture is a critical site for understanding the ways in which second-generation youth are positioning themselves in the landscape of ethnic and racial politics, because it showcases performances of ethnic authenticity, cultural hybridization, racialized gender ideologies, and class contradictions. I argue that in remix youth culture, the politics of nostalgia is infused into the production of "cool," a dialectic that has revealing implications for understanding processes of ethnicization and racialization for second-generation youth in the United States. In the rest of this chapter, I use subcultural theory to outline some of the cultural contradictions mediated through music and dance for second-generation youth and then explore their implications for racialized and gendered constructions of authenticity and subcultural "cool" in remix youth culture's sampling of hip hop.

Subcultural Theory and Second-Generation Youth Culture

Viewing this Indian American music and style as elements of a youth subculture draws on the particular tradition of cultural studies associated with neo-Marxist theorists in the United Kingdom, who developed a materialist ethnography of post-World War II youth (Kirschner 1998; G. Turner 1996).[7] According to Stuart Hall and other theorists of the Birmingham school (Clarke et al. 1976, 47), individuals belong to a shared subculture when there is "a set of social rituals which underpin their collective identity and define them as a 'group' instead of a mere collection of individuals. They adopt and adapt material objects—goods and possessions—and reorganize them into distinctive 'styles' which express the collectivity . . . [and] become embodied in rituals of relationship and occasion and movement."[8]

Popular culture is laden with existing ideologies about youth that are racialized, gendered, and classed, but it also offers an arena for youth to re-appropriate or symbolically transgress existing racial, gendered, and class boundaries. This provides the basis for the Birmingham school's central argument, which has had a significant influence on cultural studies, that youth subcultures are based on rituals that resist the values inherent in the dominant culture. The creation of a subculture is understood as a response to the personal, political, and economic contradictions or crises that youth confront on the brink of adulthood (Clarke et al. 1976). The Birmingham school's structuralist and semiotic approach to subcultures has met with some criticism from cultural studies theorists and sociologists who point out that this school of subcultural theory often overinterpreted social action in terms of resistance and symbolic resolution (Cohen 1997).[9] Contemporary subcultural theorists and researchers have a more complex vision of subcultures, but acknowledge that the basic tenets of subcultural theory, reaching back to its early Chicago school roots, are still useful (Duncombe 1998; Leblanc 1999; Sardiello 1998). As Sarah Thornton (1997, 201) observes, "Subcultural ideologies are a means by which youth imagine their own and other social groups, assert their distinctive character and affirm that they are not anonymous members of an undifferentiated mass."

The early Birmingham theorists viewed youth subcultures as attempts to symbolically resolve the tensions between the larger group culture, or "parent culture," to which they belong and their own generational concerns. In the case of the desi party scene, one can read this diasporic subculture as an attempt to mediate between the expectations of immigrant parents and those of mainstream American peer culture, by using musical remixes and urban fashion as materials with which to construct and display a seemingly hybrid "cut n' mix" style. One of the themes running through the findings from the larger study is that the immigrant generation's desire to preserve an authentic ethnic identity lingers in the second generation, for whom being essentially Indian becomes a marker of cultural and even moral superiority. Yet Indian American youth are, simultaneously, positioning themselves in the racial and class hierarchies of the United States and coming of age in contexts shaped by public institutions such as schools, colleges, and the workforce. A uniquely Indian American subculture thus allows second-generation youth to socialize with ethnic peers while reinterpreting Indian musical and dance traditions using the rituals of American popular culture. As Jean Comaroff suggests, "Syncretistic ritual . . . movements are . . . 'at once both expressive and pragmatic, for they aim to change the real world by inducing transformation in the world of symbol and rite'"—"a world," Nicholas Dirks adds, "in which representation is itself one of the most contested resources" (Comaroff, cited in Dirks 1994, 487). For Indian American youth who are in college, and who participate in the ethnically demarcated club culture of New York, representation through campus organizations and popular culture rituals becomes a way to stake a claim in local spaces, but it is a claim with limited potential for changing the categories that define them.

The "subcultural solution," as conceptualized by the Birmingham school, remains a representational solution to the crises of youth, and one enacted only in the realm of the social and symbolic. Using the notion of ritual as a site for reimagining the social order, Phil Cohen argues that such a subculture is seductive to youth because it helps to ideologically resolve the paradoxes between the different social spheres that they occupy, by enacting an option that may not be possible in actuality (in Clarke et al. 1976). The performances made possible by remix youth culture in New York, although not enabling wider systemic change, do, however, fulfill an immediate social and affective need for desi youth. Les Back (1994), analyzing the "intermezzo culture" produced in the fusion of bhangra and reggae by Asian musicians in Britain, suggests that "in the alternative public sphere of the dance, liminal ethnicities are produced which link together different social collectivities" (cited in Sharma 1996, 36).

However, after the party is over, youth must return to the constraints of interacting with their parents, peers, and communities (Cohen 1997; Gelder 1997). Hybridity, though fashionable in cultural theory and also literally in "ethnic chic," is not always easy to live, for social institutions and networks continue to demand loyalty to sometimes competing cultural ideals that may be difficult to manage for second-generation youth. For many, liminality is an ongoing, daily condition of being betwixt and between cultural categories (V. Turner 1967; 1987, 107) that is symbolically expressed in remix culture. The performance of a visibly hybrid ethnicity is not always optional; some social contexts elicit a more bounded, fixed notion of Indianness. Indian American youth still find themselves having to switch between multiple identities, as they did when moving between high school and family (Agarwal 1991; Bacon 1996; Gibson

1988; Maira 2002; Wakil, Siddique, and Wakil 1981), only now perhaps they change from baggy pants and earrings that they wear among peers to conservative attire on the job, or from secret relationships at college to dutiful daughters on visits home. These transitions clearly have a gendered dimension, for the tension between ethnic identity and national culture is embodied differently by women than men. Furthermore, the relationship between the categories "Indian" and "American" is closely intertwined with the racialization of Indian Americans in the second generation. The symbolic role played by youth subcultures can no longer simply be a mediation of generational or class conflict, as imagined by the Birmingham school, but in the case of this Indian American youth culture, it also provides an "expressive and pragmatic" negotiation of racialization and nationalism. Race politics is deeply implicated in the question of what it means for a young woman or man to become an (In-dian) American subject and, for second-generation youth, the question of what it means to participate in performances of urban "cool" or of collective nostalgia.

Masculinity, Racialization, and Subcultural Capital

Dharmesh, a young man whose family lives in New Jersey, remarked that Indian American youth who grew up with blacks and Latinos, and even some who did not, often acquire "the style, and the attitude, and the walk" associated with these youth on coming to college. Hip hop is not just "the Black CNN," but has become the channel for youth culture information in general, defining "coolness" and "peer status" for suburban as well as urban American youth (Christenson and Roberts 1998, 111). Hip hop culture is resignified by Indian American "homeboys" when it crosses class boundaries, as Sujata, a woman who grew up in Connecticut, pointed out: "A lot of them are like total prep school, but they put on a, like, it's this preppie boy-urban look, you know, it's like Upper East Side homeboy, you know. Huge pants, and then, like, a nice button-down shirt, you know." However, while many desi youth identify with hip hop music and style, there are rarely any African American DJs spinning at "Indian parties" that draw an almost exclusively South Asian crowd.

The music and media industries have helped make hip hop a language increasingly adopted by middle-class/white/suburban youth (Giroux 1996; Roediger 1998), and Asian American, Latino, and white youth from urban as well as suburban backgrounds have claimed the hip hop look and dialect. David Roediger, in his writing on "wiggers," or "white niggers," observes that: "The proliferation of *wiggers* illuminates issues vital to the history of what Albert Murray has called the 'incontestably mulatto' culture of the United States. From minstrelsy through Black Like Me, from the blackfaced antebellum mobs that victimized African Americans to the recent film *Soul Man*, the superficial notion that Blackness could be put on and taken off at will has hounded hybridity" (1998, 361–362). The question of hybridity is doubly complicated for desi youth in New York, for not only are they reworking hip hop into their own youth culture but into a *remix* youth culture, one that expresses the cultural imaginaries of second-generation youth from an immigrant community of color. Desi youth turn to hip hop, most fundamentally, because it is key to marking their belonging in the multiethnic, urban landscape of New York City (for more on the racial politics of this youth subculture, see Maira 1999, 2000).

For women in this subculture, however, many youth noted that a "'hoody," or streetwise hip hop, image was not considered as appealing as it was for men, and the pervasive image of desirable femininity rested on designer-inspired New York fashion. Manisha, whose friends were mainly African American and Latino, thought that this was because a 'hoody, or urban, hip-hop-inspired style was seen as not feminine enough for women, and it was also interpreted as indicating identification with African American or Latino youth. She observed that a 'hoody style lead to marginalization for women within the Indian American subculture, but not for men: "I think that the guys are actually intimidated by people like me, who sometimes dress like a guy, I guess maybe it shows a different identity and they think that they might not be strong enough for that . . . but the guys that are part of the Indian cliques that dress like that, like 'hoody and all that, they usually go out with the girls that dress not like that."

Women are expected to embody a certain kind of ethnic affiliation through style and through the performance of an appropriate Indian American femininity. There seemed to be two other kinds of heterosexual femininities idealized within this second-generation subculture that contradicted not only the "gangsta girl" image of black-identified femininity but also were in opposition to each other, evoking the tensions between desires for nostalgia and "coolness." Many women noted that the sexually provocative style of women at remix parties—the "hoochy mamas"—was more alluring than the androgynous hip-hop look, but fitted into the virgin/'ho (whore) dichotomy when read against chaste Indian womanhood. Women can derive great pleasure from dressing in a way that allows them to assert their sexuality, yet these same women are considered "loose," that is, not the type of Indian American woman a man would like to marry. I argue elsewhere that the chastity of second-generation women becomes emblematic of not just the family's reputation but also, in the context of the diaspora, of the purity of tradition and ethnic identity, a defense against the promiscuity of "American influences" (Maira 1998, 1999), as suggested by feminist and postcolonial analyses of the gendering of nationalism, or "the woman question" (Bhattacharjee 1992; Chatterjee 1989; Dasgupta and Das Dasgupta 1997; Mani 1993). However, images of heterosexuality and style for Indian American men are seemingly not used to index issues of ethnic authenticity, as they are for women. In this chapter, I focus on the production of a particular masculinity that mediates the tensions of racial positioning and class aspirations for second-generation youth, by drawing on both the local codes of "hipness" in urban youth culture and the immigrant mythologies of class mobility that rationalize the family and community's displacement.

Sharmila, a young woman at NYU who had helped organize remix parties, noted that for many second-generation men, hip hop style connotes a certain image of racialized hypermasculinity that is the ultimate definition of "cool": "South Asian guys give more respect to African Americans than to whites because they think the style is cool. The guys look up to them because it's down [fashionable]. They think, 'I'm kinda scared of them but I want to look like them because they're cool." Ravi, who began going to Indian parties while in high school in California and has continued to do so in New York, reflected, "The hip hop culture has just really taken off. It's really appealed to the Indians, maybe just listening pleasure, the way it sounds, I guess. Maybe the toughness it exudes." Black style is viewed as the embodiment of a particular machismo, the object of racialized desire, and simultaneously, of racialized fear.[10]

In his work on (East) Asian American hip hop artists, Oliver Wang (1997) points out that "the authentic black subject in hip hop" is rendered hypermasculine in the context of wider racist constructions of Black and Latino men as hypersexual or macho and Asian American men as historically emasculated.[11] Yet very few of the young desi men resonated with arguments about emasculated Asian American men. Rather, Sunil, a member of an Indian American fraternity, was concerned about class-coded images of Indian American men as "convenience store owners" or innately nerdy students. Sunil traced these images to the two major waves of post-1965 Indian immigration to the United States: "Like toward the lower middle class, they say, 'You're the shopkeeper,' the upper middle class, they'd say, 'Oh, you're this intellectual.'" The fact that the critique of emasculation did not explicitly resonate with these Indian American men does not mean that they were unconcerned with the particular overtones of masculinity that are available to them through hip hop. Listening to what these Indian American men have to say, it is apparent that it is also the powerful appeal of hip hop music and youth style, not to mention the sheer pleasure of the music, as Robin Kelley (1997) and Tricia Rose (1994) remind us, that draw them to hip hop—the resonance is "rhythmic" and not just "symbolic" (Christenson and Roberts 1998, 111).

It becomes apparent, as I draw out more fully elsewhere (Maira 1999), that this subculture is not only engaged with essentialized definitions of what it means to be truly Indian but also reacts against this ideal by adopting an essentialized definition of what it means to be "cool" (that is, the antithesis of unfashionable or traditional) which draws on urban black and Latino youth style (Banerjea and Banerjea 1996). The production of nostalgia clearly involves reified understandings of ethnicity, but it is in dialectical relation with a cultural complex of ideas about being "young," "urban," and "hip," that is not without its own notions of authenticity. The construction of subcultural "cool" is rooted in the nuances of style and dialect, in connections to a social network, and in knowledge of urban space that have their own contests of power and codes of belonging. The cultural production and consumption of diasporic youth culture is a "moral project," in Daniel Miller's words, for the use of commodities offers possibilities to reimagine cultural ideologies, such as those of "self" and "other," and to construct and negotiate social boundaries.

In addition, as Miller observes, "material culture is often the concrete means by which the contradictions held within general concepts such as the domestic or the global are in practice resolved in everyday life (Miller 1998, 19). In the case of hip hop, the globalization of mass media in the era of late capitalism has resulted in the seeping of black-identified American popular culture and fashion into remote corners of the world. Indian youth living in rural areas can now listen to American rap or Indian remixes from the United States as a result of media channels and family networks that span national borders. There may be no "authentic" reading of the consumption of hip by desi youth, but there is indeed a politics of authenticity that has meaning in the lives of these youth at this particular moment in New York City, and that is constantly being negotiated with reference to their positionings in a larger Indian diaspora and to global flows of culture.

The Racial Politics of "Cool"

The meanings of this appropriation of black style obviously have different implications for youth, depending on the particular racial and class locations they occupy; an understanding of the politics of cool is necessarily conjectural. Codes of hipness at work in Asian American youth subcultures are always in relationship to the racialization of Asians and to their negotiation of the black-white racial paradigm of the United States. Dorinne Kondo (1995, 53), commenting on urban Asian Americans who identify with African Americans and borrow their dialect, observes that this reflects "the persistence of the black-white binary in the dominant imagery and the in-the-middle position of Asian Americans and Latinos on that unidimensional hierarchy. If you are Asian American or Latino, especially on the East Coast, white and black are the poles, and if you don't identify with one, you identify with the other." Gary Okihiro (1994) probes more deeply into the positioning of Asian Americans within this racial binary by addressing the political implications of the question, "Is yellow black or white?" Or, if you will, is brown black or white? Okihiro (1994, 34) notes that Asian Americans, Native Americans, and Latinos are classified as either "near whites" or "just like blacks" depending on the operation of model minority myths or their subordination as minorities. Okihiro concludes that the question, as posed, is a false proposition because it reinscribes the bipolar racial framework of the United States, disciplining ethnic minorities and erasing histories of alliances (62).

Yet like the very notion of racial formation, racial polarity is a system of representation that still plays a role in shaping social structures and individual experiences (Omi and Winant 1994, 55). The work of hip hop for Indian Americans is similar to the use of images of blacks in Japanese mass culture, which John Russell (1995, 299) explains as a "tendency to employ the black Other as a reflexive symbol through which Japanese attempt to deal with their own ambiguous racial status in a Eurocentric world, where such hierarchies have been largely (and literally) conceived in terms of polarizations between black and white and in which Japanese as Asians have traditionally occupied a liminal state." The black/white binary exerts a pull on some second-generation Indian Americans who feel that they straddle the monochromatic racial boundaries of the United States. In some instances, Indian American youth seemed to show an acceptance, or more of a passive nonrejection, of the racial status quo, but in other contexts, they explicitly identified as nonwhite and resisted antiblack racism. What makes these responses complex and contingent is that the particular youth culture I am discussing here is not simply hip hop but an Indian remix youth culture that samples hip hop, and, therefore, is an overt expression of ethnicity. The emphasis on an ethnic identity in response to racial ambiguity is perhaps a reflexive strategy, as described by Russell, but one that contains within it some degree of distancing from, or solidarity with blacks, or both.[12]

The discourse of ethnic identity, according to some youth as well as scholarly commentators, is a way to resolve, or perhaps deflect, the question of racial positioning for Indian Americans. Chandrika, who was actively involved with Asian American student activism on her campus, commented, "No matter what it is, if you haven't been accepted, you're not going to be black, like all your friends, or white, like all your friends, it's not going to happen. You seek refuge." Second-generation Indian Americans who search for a category of belonging often find it is provided by ethnicity in the context of the ethnic student organizations and ethnic identity politics prevalent on American college campuses. Chandrika thought this explained why some of her peers began flaunting Indian symbols of dress and jewelry and literally performing their ethnic identity with "bhangra moves" on the dance floor, using these symbolic markers to assert their ethnic identity. Although there are small groups of youth within most of these South Asian student organizations in New York who are more politicized and interested in building alliances with other minority student groups, I found that what most of these South Asian student organizations share is an emphasis on performing a strictly cultural Indian/South Asian American identity in an exclusively Indian/South Asian American social space.

These "ethnicizing" moves reflect broader patterns of emphasizing ethnic identity by some segments of the Indian American community, which are viewed by critics as attempts to position Indian Americans outside the racial classification in the United States and deflect identification with less privileged minority groups of color (George 1997; Mazumdar 1989; Visweswaran 1997). Toni Morrison writes in her incisive essay, "On the Backs of Blacks" (1994, 98): "Although U.S. history is awash in labor battles, political fights, and property wars among all religious and ethnic groups, their struggles are persistently framed as struggles between recent arrivals and blacks. In race talk the move into mainstream America always means buying into the notion of American blacks as the real aliens. Whatever the ethnicity or nationality of the immigrant, his [or her] nemesis is understood to be African American."

Second-generation performances of ethnicity are motivated by needs that are perhaps more complex than a simple evasion of racial classification. Having grown up as youth of color in the United States, unlike their parents, their search for categories of belonging are necessarily shaped by the ethnic identity frameworks available to them in the United States and by their experiences of growing up as minorities; the category of "Asian American" is a racial project now available to Indian Americans as a panethnic identification, as are multiculturalist constructions of ethnicity, particularly on college campuses. The question is, of course, whether these youth can build a racial politics that would allow them to participate in both spheres, those based on ethnicity and those supporting alliances with youth of color, and whether they can resist the ethnic chauvinism of South Asian student organizations that view other group allegiances with suspicion. Remix youth culture's sampling of hip hop allows desi youth to hold the two impulses, of ethnicization and also of participation in the U.S. racial formation, in a somewhat delicate balance; as a racial project, perhaps it defers the question of "black or white" through the ambiguity of adopting Black style in an ethnically exclusive space.

The emulation of urban African American style has more subtle implications if situated in differentials of privilege and generational divides over racial politics. Sunita, who has been going to "Indian parties" since she was in high school, commented that for her Indian American peers "identifying with hip hop is a little more rebellious" than adopting other youth styles "because it's not the norm associated with white culture." She pointed out that the adoption of hip hop sometimes becomes a gesture of defiance against parents, such as her own, who belong to the wave of Indian immigrants who came to the United States in the mid-1960s and 1970s and were highly educated professionals and graduate students.[13] For several lower-middle-class as well as upper-middle-class youth, identification with African Americans is often fraught with conflicts with immigrant parents on issues of race politics. Perhaps the most emotional critique of the antiblack prejudices of immigrant parents was expressed by women who had dated African American men and struggled with parental disapproval.

Amritjit Singh (1996, 98) suggests that the turn to hip hop among desi youth is explained in part by the alienation of second-generation youth from the model minority leanings of their parents, including its manifestations as antiblack racism. Rebellion through popular music, moreover, is a familiar rite of youth culture—often a particularly masculinized one (Whitely 1997)—that perhaps offers Indian American youth a cultural form to express their distancing from parents. However, for some Indian American youth there seems to be a convergence between both kinds of responses; a style that subverts their parents' expectations and racial prejudices may also be an expression of their own critique of the racialized caste stratification of U.S. society. The turn to hip hop by desi youth in the 1990s is rooted in larger histories of appropriating black music by non-African Americans as part of the reinvention of ethnic identity by various groups.

The resonant connections between the work of cultural studies theorist George Lipsitz (1994) and anthropologist Michael Fischer (1986) provide interesting insights into the implications of Indian American hip hop. Lipsitz, commenting on white American artists who were drawn to African American and Latino musical traditions, writes: "Black music provided them with a powerful critique of mainstream middle-class Anglo-Saxon America as well as with an elaborate vocabulary for airing feelings of marginality and contestation. They engaged in what film critics Douglas Kellner and Michael Ryan call "discursive transcoding"—indirect expression of alienations too threatening to express directly" (Kellner and Ryan 1988, cited in Lipsitz, 1994, 55). This alienation, for Indian American youth, may arise partly as a result of what Fischer calls "ethnic anxiety," a deep desire to maintain a sense of difference in the face of homogenization and to redefine the relationship between self and community (1986, 197). In part, as for the musicians of Greek, German, or Jewish descent that Lipsitz discusses, this anxiety sometimes emerges from a political understanding of relationships of racial dominance and subordination, and the engagement with black music may signal the recreation of a "moral vision" of the meanings of community and tradition (ibid.). For Indian American youth, the turn to hip hop is not always based on clearly articulated political dissent or moral outrage, but it may at least provide a discourse for coding an alienation from parents that is bound up with struggles over what it means to be Indian in the United States. Their alienation is not simply a rejection of their parents' racial ideologies but also perhaps expresses an ambivalence toward the upwardly mobile path that their parents have attempted to carve out for them, with its burden of suitable educational fields and careers (Maira, forthcoming). This analysis echoes the Birmingham school's theory of youth subcultures, but it, too, does not presume that the appropriation of black popular culture is an intervention with lasting social or material impact. As suggested by Peter Stallybrass and Allon White's analysis of carnival, it is but "one instance of a general economy of transgression and of the recoding of high/low relations across the whole social structure" (1986, 19).

The context of bhangra/remix youth culture in New York, or more generally in the United States, stands in contrast to that in Britain, where the late 1970s and early 1980s saw a "new symbolic unity primarily between African-Caribbean and Asian people" through identification with the category "Black" (Sharma 1996, 39). This identification, Sanjay Sharma notes, was a political project involving "autonomous, anti-racist community struggles in Britain." However, he also points out that the coalitional label, Black, "had a certain way of silencing the very specific experiences of Asian people" (Hall 1991, cited in Sharma 1996). Bhangra remix emerged as a "new Asian dance music" that offered an Asian identity as a possible racial location, but still one that, in Sharma's view, "continues to be intimately tied to rethinking the possibilities of the Black anti-racist project" (1996, 34). Keeping this contrast in mind is instructive, because it is a reminder that South Asian dance music is not inherently subversive, but is differentially politicized depending on the historical, economic, and national context of particular immigrant communities.

SUCH ARE THE contradictions that constitute the textures of cultural practices that youth use to position themselves in relation to ethnic community, racial formations, and nation-states. Using youth culture as a focal point, I argue, demonstrates that the cultural forms that responses to diasporic or transnational experiences take cannot be understood only in terms of the nature of migration but must also be understood in terms of relationships to local cultural and political economies. Perhaps this analytic emphasis is more easily highlighted in the case of youth, because a common trope in immigration studies is that the second generation is where the politics of national allegiance and cultural displacement becomes most fraught—a debatable point, but certainly one that forces attention to Clifford's "political struggles to define the local," struggles that are readily apparent in the collision of Indian remix music and hip hop.

How useful are notions of diaspora and displacement for second-generation youth with the kinds of concerns discussed here? What does continuing to think about these concerns within the framework of diaspora, however broadly, allow us to do and also *not* allow us to see? The specificity of the term "transnationalism," and its attempted intervention in immigration studies, as I mentioned at the outset, may offset the diffuseness of a loose notion of diaspora or an overdetermined notion of "displacement as a theoretical signifier, a textual strategy, and a lived experience" (Bammer 1994, xiii). Yet in the late capitalist economy of the United States, where hyperbolic stories of the "new rich" and young "dot.com" millionaires share the front pages with ongoing accounts of the scapegoating of the poor, abuses of immigrant labor, and relentless police attacks on black immigrant and American men, we need to think carefully about the national contexts, racial groups, and class strata that immigrant communities imagine their relationships to, and the kinds of theoretical interventions we wish to make. Perhaps the term "diaspora" is still necessary, but I think for many it is no longer sufficient.

NOTES

1. For example: *Gimme Something to Dance To*, directed by Tejaswani Ganti, New York, 1995; *Desi Dub*, directed by Swati Khurana and Leith Murgai, New York, 1997. A full-page article in the *New York Times* by Somini Sengupta (1996), titled "To be young, Indian, and hip," sparked much debate among South Asian American youth in the city who were confronted, many for the first time, with a public representation of their subculture in the mainstream media.

2. Nearly all the DJs that I met or heard about were Indian American, a point that deserves further reflection.

3. S.O.B.'s has been home to one of the most well-known regular bhangra parties since March 1997, when DJ Rekha launched Bhangra Basement, the first Indian remix music night to be featured monthly on the calendar of a Manhattan club— and the first to be hosted by a woman DJ.

4. Bindis are, traditionally, powdered dots, and more commonly today, small felt or plastic designs, worn by women between the eyebrows.

5. New York City is one of the primary receiving areas for Indian immigrants to the United States because of two major factors: first, the local labor market offers a range of employment opportunities, from engineering jobs in industries in New Jersey and Connecticut to employment in hotels, motels, banking, insurance, public health, and garment and jewelry businesses, including import/export trade (Lessinger 1995). Working-class Indian immigrants, or middle-class Indians who could not find the jobs they had hoped for, sometimes find employment in the service sector or unskilled labor market (Lessinger 1995). In 1992, the Taxi and Limousine Commission of New York City reported that 43 percent of Manhattan-based yellow cabs were driven by South Asians, equally represented by Indians, Pakistanis, and Bangladeshis (Advani 1997). The second factor that has motivated many Indian immigrants to settle in New York City, at least initially, is that many have immigrated through family reunification categories, especially in the 1980s and 1990s, and have chosen to live close to relatives already settled in the area or in localities where there they know there are other Indian families.

6. 1997, one of the years I was doing my field work, was coincidentally the fiftieth anniversary of India's independence and saw the flourishing of several well-publicized events in New York City that showcased Indian classical music and traditional arts. Concerts featuring lineups of Indian classical music maestros were held at elite arts institutions such as Lincoln Center and Carnegie Hall, and the Asia Society organized several art exhibits on the Upper East Side. Members of the Indian immigrant elite flocked to these events, and to a host of others that were held through the year, demonstrating that there continue to be different, some-

times competing, strands of Indian art and "culture" that are selectively imported by Indian immigrants to define "tradition" and represent the nation.

7. Thornton (1997, 3) traces the intellectual genealogy of British subcultural studies of the 1970s to two earlier schools of thought: the Chicago school of sociology, which was interested in the particularity of urban life as manifested in "subcultures"; and the Frankfurt school's Marxist theory of mass society. Both perspectives were fused in the Birmingham tradition that focused on the "relationship of subcultures to media, commerce, and mass culture."

8. Theorists of youth subcultures also note that the category of "youth" is one that is socially and culturally constructed, and has often been the focus of debates over social control as well as a marketing principle for the music and fashion industries (Clarke et al. 1976). The Birmingham theorists strategically chose to use the term "subculture" rather than "youth culture," because they argued that the latter descriptor obscured the links between the cultural construction of youth as a distinct category and the creation of a "teenage [consumer] market"; the concept of a "subculture," in their framework, was embedded in a deeper structural explanation of the dialectic between "youth" and youth industries (Clarke et al. 1976, 16).

9. Simon Frith argues that subcultural theorists have sometimes been guilty of "a relentless politicizing of consumption, . . . the constant misreading of the mainstream as the margins" (1992, 180). Overestimating the political significance of popular culture and underestimating the complexity of the aesthetic aspects of youth culture, these theorists have in fact projected their own myths onto youth culture. Angela McRobbie, while emphasizing the value of the "structural, historical, and ethnographic" approaches of early cultural studies research, cautions against the "dangers of pursuing a kind of cultural populism to a point at which anything which is consumed and is popular is also seen as oppositional" (1994, 39). Other contemporary cultural studies theorists have, similarly, argued that early subcultural studies privileged politicized interpretations of youth style and glossed over the contradictions and conflicts within these subcultures (Clarke 1997; Thornton 1997). Feminist critiques have also pointed out that this early research deemphasized, or even misinterpreted, the role of women and girls, focusing instead on male, working-class youth and portraying females as more passive or identified with the "mainstream" (McRobbie 1994; Pini 1997; Thornton 1996).

10. Roediger points out that "in a society in which the imagination of Blackness so thoroughly frames what both attracts and repulses whites," American male youth often "identify with violence, scatology, and sexism in rap rather than with Black music and culture more broadly" (1998, 359, 361).

11. In turning to hip hop to challenge representations of Asian American masculinity, Wang points out that these rappers reinscribe a "hegemonic ideology" of "ideal masculinity and sexuality" that rests on a stereotypical notion of "the authentic black subject in hip hop," and that ultimately uses an "idealized white masculinity" as its normalizing frame of reference (1997, 14–15, 17).

12. An example of Asian American youth cultural production using hip hop to resolve the perception of racial ambiguity while asserting solidarity with youth of color is the progressive zine *Native Tongh*, by the hip-hop artist identified as MaddBuddha, whose credo is: "A yellow shade in a black and white world." Key Kool, a Japanese American hip hop artist, expressed a similar view at the plenary

session of the conference, "FreeZone," on Asian/Pacific/American youth culture and argued that rather than speaking of Asian American hip hop, which implies that hip hop is ethnic-specific, he preferred to speak of Asian Americans in hip hop, a common language and youth movement. For other examples of Asian American musicians in hip hop taking similar positions, see Wang (1997).

13. The more recent wave of South Asian immigrants that has been arriving since the 1980s, partly as a result of sponsorship by relatives who had emigrated earlier, has generally been less economically privileged and educationally qualified than the earlier cohort and more concentrated, at least initially, in multiethnic urban neighborhoods (Khandelwal 1995; Lessinger 1995).

REFERENCES

Advani, Anuradha G. 1997. "Against the tide: Reflections on organizing New York City's taxicab drivers." In *Making more waves: New writing by Asian American women*, edited by E. H. Kim, L. V. Villaneuva, and Asian American United Women of California, 215–222. Boston: Beacon.

Agarwal, Priya. 1991. *Passage from India: Post-1965 Indian immigrants and their children: Conflicts, concerns, and solutions*. Palos Verdes, Calif.: Yuvati.

Appadurai, Arjun. 1996. "Disjuncture and difference in the global cultural economy." In Appadurair, *Modernity at large: Cultural dimensions of globalization*, 27–47. Minneapolis: University of Minnesota.

Back, Les. 1994. "X amount of sat sri akal: Apache Indian, reggae music and intermezzo culture." South Asia seminar series, ICCCR, Universities of Manchester and Keele, United Kingdom.

Bacon, Jean. 1996. *Lifelines: Community, family, and assimilation among Asian Indian immigrants*. New York: Oxford University Press.

Bammer, Angela. 1994. "Introduction." In *Displacements: Cultural identities in question*, edited by A. Bammer, xi–xx. Bloomington: Indiana University Press.

Banerjea, Koushik, and Partha Banerjea. 1996. "Psyche and soul: A view from the 'South.'" In *Dis-orienting rhythms: The politics of the new Asian dance music*, edited by S. Sharma, J. Huntyk, and A. Sharma, 105–124. London: Zed Press.

Basch, Linda, Nina Glick Schiller, and Cristina Szanton Blanc. 1994. "Transnational projects: A new perspective." In Basch, Glick Schiller, and Szanton Blanc, *Nations unbound: Transnational projects, postcolonial predicaments, and deterritorialized nation-states*, 1–19. Amsterdam: Gordon and Breach.

Bhattacharjee, Annanya. 1992. "The habit of ex-nomination: Nation, woman, and the Indian immigrant bourgeoisie." *Public Culture* 5(1): 19–44.

Chatterjee, Partha. 1989. "Colonialism, nationalism, and colonialized women: The contest in India." *American Ethnologist* 16(4): 622–633.

Christenson, Peter G., and Donald F. Roberts. 1998. *It's not only rock & roll: Popular music in the lives of adolescents*. Cresskill, N.J.: Hampton Press.

Clarke, John, Stuart Hall, Tony Jefferson, and Brian Roberts. 1976. "Subcultures, cultures, and class." In *Resistance through rituals: Youth subcultures in post-war Britain*, edited by S. Hall and T. Jefferson, 9–74. London: Hutchinson, in association with Centre for Contemporary Cultural Studies (University of Birmingham).

Clifford, James. 1997. "Diasporas." In *The ethnicity reader: Nationalism, multiculturalism, and migration*, edited by M. Guibernau and J. Rex, 283–290. Cambridge: Polity.

Cohen, Stanley. 1997. "Symbols of trouble." In *The subcultures reader*, edited by K. Gelder and S. Thornton, 149–162. London: Routledge.

Dasgupta, Sayantani, and Shamita Das Dasgupta. 1997. "Women in exile: Gender relations in the Asian Indian community." In *Contours of the heart: South Asians map North America*, edited by S. Maira and R. Srikanth, 381–400. New York: Asian American Writers' Workshop.

Dirks, Nicholas. 1994. "Ritual and resistance: Subversion as a social fact." In *Culture/power/history: A reader in contemporary social theory*, edited by N. Dirks, G. Ely, and S. Ortner, 483–503. Princeton: Princeton University Press.

Duncombe, Stephen. 1998. "Let's all be alienated together: Zines and the making of underground community." In *Generations of youth: Youth cultures and history in twentieth-century America*, edited by J. Austin and M. Willard, 427–451. New York: New York University Press.

Fischer, Michael. 1986. "Ethnicity and the post-modern arts of memory." In *Writing culture: The poetics and politics of ethnography*, edited by J. Clifford and G. Marcus, 194–233. Berkeley: University of California Press.

Flores, Juan. 2000. *From bomba to hip hop.* New York: Columbia University Press.

Frith, Simon. 1992. "The cultural study of popular music." In *Cultural studies*, edited by L. Grossberg, C. Nelson, and P. Treichler, 174–196. New York: Routledge.

Gelder, Ken. 1997. "Introduction to Part Three." In *The subcultures reader*, edited by K. Gelder and S. Thornton, 145–148. New York: Routledge.

George, Rosemary M. 1997. "'From expatriate aristocrat to immigrant nobody': South Asian racial strategies in the southern Californian context." *Diaspora* 6(1): 31–60.

Gibson, Margaret A. 1988. *Accommodation without assimilation: Sikh immigrants in an American high school.* Ithaca: Cornell University Press.

Giroux, Henry A. 1996. "White panic and the racial coding of violence." In *Fugitive cultures: Race, violence, and youth*, edited by H. Giroux, 27–54. New York: Routledge.

Gopinath, G. 1997. "Nostalgia, desire, diaspora: South Asian sexualities in motion." *Positions: East Asia Cultures Critique* 5(2): 468–489.

Gupta, Akhil, and James Ferguson. 1997. "After 'peoples and cultures.'" In *Culture, power, place: Explorations in critical anthropology*, edited by A. Gupta and J. Ferguson, 1–29. Durham: Duke University Press.

Kelley, Robin D. G. 1997. "Looking to get paid: How some black youth put culture to work." In Kelley, *Yo' mama's disfunktional! Fighting the culture wars in urban America*, 43–77. Boston: Beacon.

Khandelwal, Madhulika S. 1995. "Indian immigrants in Queens, New York City: Patterns of spatial concentration and distribution, 1965–1990." In *Nation and migration: The politics of space in the South Asian diaspora*, edited by P. van der Veer, 178–196. Philadelphia: University of Pennsylvania Press.

Kirschner, Tony. 1998. "Studying rock: Towards a materialist ethnography." In *Mapping the beat: Popular music and contemporary theory*, edited by T. Swiss, J. Sloop, and A. Herman, 247–268. Malden, Mass.: Blackwell.

Kondo, Dorinne. 1995. "Bad girls: Theater, women of color, and the politics of representation." In *Women writing culture*, edited by R. Behar and D. A. Gordon, 49–64. Berkeley: University of California Press.

Leblanc, Lauraine. 1999. *Pretty in punk: Girls' gender resistance in a boys' subculture.* New Brunswick, N.J.: Rutgers University Press.

Lessinger, Johanna. 1995. *From the Ganges to the Hudson: Indian immigrants in New York City.* Boston: Allyn and Bacon.

Lipsitz, George. 1994. "'The shortest way through': Strategic anti-essentialism in popular music." In Lipsitz, *Dangerous crossroads: Popular music, postmodernism, and the poetics of place*, 49–68. London: Verso.

Lowe, Lisa. 1996. "Canon, institutionalization, identity: Asian American studies." In Lowe, *Immigrant acts: On Asian American cultural politics*, 37–59. Durham: Duke University Press.

Maira, Sunaina. 1998. "Chaste identities, ethnic yearnings: Second-generation Indian Americans in New York City." Ph.D. dissertation, Harvard Graduate School of Education.

———. 1999. "Identity dub: The paradoxes of an Indian American youth subculture (New York mix)." *Cultural Anthropology* 14(1): 29–60.

———. 2000. "Ideologies of authenticity: Youth, politics, and diaspora." *Amerasia Journal* 25(3): 139–149.

———. 2002. *Desis in the house: Indian American youth culture in New York City.* Philadelphia: Temple University Press.

———. Forthcoming. "Henna and hip hop: The politics of Indo-chic and the work of cultural studies." *Amerasia Journal.*

Mani, Lata. 1993. "Gender, class, and cultural conflict: Indu Krishnan's *Knowing her place.*" In *Our feet walk the sky: Women of the South Asian diaspora*, edited by Women of South Asia Descent Collective, 32–36. San Fransisco: Aunt Lute Books.

Mazumdar, Sucheta. 1989. "Racist responses to racism: The Aryan myth and South Asians in the United States." *South Asia Bulletin* 9(1): 47–55.

McRobbie, Angela. 1994. "New times in cultural studies." In McRobbie, *Postmodernism and popular culture*, 24–43. London: Routledge.

Miller, Daniel. 1998. "Why some things matter." In *Material cultures: Why some things matter*, edited by D. Miller, 3–21. Chicago: University of Chicago Press.

Morrison, Toni. 1994. "On the backs of Blacks." In *Arguing immigration*, edited by N. Mills, 97–100. New York: Touchstone.

Okihiro, Gary Y. 1994. "Is yellow Black or White?" In *Margins and mainstreams: Asians in American history and culture.* edited by G. Okihiro, 31–63. Seattle: University of Washington Press.

Omi, Michael, and Howard Winant. 1994. *Racial formation in the United States: From the 1960s to the 1990s.* New York: Routledge.

Pini, Maria. 1997. "Women and the early British rave scene." In *Back to reality: Social experience and cultural studies*, edited by A. McRobbie, 152–169. Manchester: Manchester University Press.

Roediger, David. 1998. "What to make of wiggers: A work in progress." In *Generations of youth: Youth cultures and history in twentieth-century America*, edited by J. Austin and M. N. Willard, 358–366. New York: New York University Press.

Rose, Tricia. 1994. "A style nobody can deal with: Politics, style and the postindustrial city in hip hop." In *Microphone fiends: Youth music and youth culture*, edited by A. Ross and T. Rose, 71–88. New York: Routledge.

Russell, John. 1992 (1995 edition). "Race and reflexivity: The Black Other in contemporary Japanese mass culture." In *Rereading cultural anthropology*, edited by George Marcus, 296–318. Durham: Duke University Press.

Sardiello, Robert. 1998. "Identity and status stratification in deadhead subculture." In *Youth culture: Identity in a postmodern world*, edited by J. Epstein, 118–147. Malden, Mass.: Blackwell.

Sengupta, Somini. 1996. "To be young, Indian and hip: Hip-hop meets Hindi pop as a new generation of South Asians finds its own groove." *New York Times*, June 30, Section 13: 1.

Sharma, Sanjay. 1996. "Noisy Asians or 'Asian noise'?" In *Dis-orienting rhythms: The politics of the new Asian dance music*, edited by S. Sharma, J. Huntyk, and A. Sharma, 32–57. London: Zed.

Singh, Amritjit. 1996. "African Americans and the new immigrants." In *Between the lines: South Asians and postcoloniality*, edited by D. Bahri and M. Vasudeva. Philadelphia: Temple University Press.

Stallybrass, Peter, and Allon White. 1986. *The poetics and politics of transgression*. Ithaca: Cornell University Press.

Stokes, Martin. 1994. "Introduction: Ethnicity, identity, and music." In *Ethnicity, identity, and music*, edited by M. Stokes, 1–27. Oxford: Berg.

Thornton, Sarah. 1996. *Club cultures*. Cambridge: Polity.

———. 1997. "General introduction." In *The subcultures reader*, edited by K. Gelder and S. Thornton, 1–15. New York: Routledge.

Toure. 1997. "Members Only." *New York Times Magazine*, October 19: 98–99.

Turner, Graeme. 1996. *British cultural studies: An introduction*. Second edition. London: Routledge.

Turner, Victor. 1967. *The forest of symbols: Aspects of Ndembu ritual*. Ithaca: Cornell University Press.

———. 1987. *The anthropology of performance*. New York: Performing Arts Journal Publications.

Visweswaran, Kamala. 1997. "Diaspora by design: Flexible citizenship and South Asians in U.S. racial formations." *Diaspora* 6(1): 5–29.

Wakil, S. P., C. M. Siddique, and F. A. Wakil. 1981. "Between two cultures: A study in socialization of children of immigrants." *Journal of Marriage and the Family* 43(4): 929–940.

Wang, Oliver. 1997. "Big yellow knuckles: The cultural politics of Asian American hip hop." Paper presented at the annual meeting of the Association for Asian American Studies, Seattle, Wash., April.

Whitely, Sheila. 1997. "Introduction." In *Sexing the groove: Popular music and gender*, edited by S. Whitely Routledge, xii–xxxvi. London:. Routledge.

Williams, Raymond. 1961. *The long revolution*. London: Penguin.

PART FOUR

===========================

Opening the Dialogue

12

=======================================

Crossing Borders of Disciplines
and Departments

ROBERT G. LEE

The admonition to "think globally, act locally" has become something of a cliché over the past decade. Yet the current crisis, the putative "global war on terrorism," is a sharp reminder that the experiences of displacement examined in the preceding chapters continue to take place on a terrain of intense struggle. The two chapters introduced here, Nancy Abelmann's "Anthropology, Asian Studies, Asian American Studies: Open Systems, Closed Minds" and Epifanio San Juan Jr.'s "The Ordeal of Ethnic Studies in the Age of Globalization," explore the epistemological, ethical, and political implications of displacement and transnational studies for our intellectual commitments and institutional arrangements. They both ask, in quite different registers, "What is to be done?"

Shortly after the symposium at Brown University in Providence, Rhode Island, that was the impetus for these essays, terrorists from the Third World (to resurrect an appellation prematurely discarded) brought down the twin towers of the World Trade Center in a dagger thrust to the beating heart of globalization. Their weapon of choice was itself another instrument of globalization, the jumbo jet full of fuel and travelers. Two days later, an Amtrak train from Boston to New York was stopped in Providence, where Sher Singh, a Sikh American, was taken from the train and arrested. To some of his fellow passengers, conductors, and the local police, Singh's turban and beard had marked him as a likely terrorist. A lynch mob quickly gathered at the train station as the local news media, always anxious to find some local connection to the national news, trumpeted the quick, albeit false arrest of one of the evildoers of the September 11 attacks. Fortunately the state police were successful in hustling Sher Singh through the mob, but he languished in the local jail until he was cleared of any involvement in the World Trade Center attacks. Although he was able to prove that he was returning from a business trip to Boston to his home in New Jersey, Singh was charged nevertheless with carrying a concealed weapon—his three-inch *kirpani*, the sacred knife that all religiously observant Sikh men are required to carry at all times. Although Singh's arrest did not lead to his bodily harm and, in hindsight, seems to have had a slightly Gilbert and Sullivan quality about it, events in other states had far grimmer consequences. Within a few days of the 9/11 attacks, Balbar Singh Sodhi was shot to death in front of his gas station in Mesa, Arizona, and Waqar Hasan, an immigrant from Pakistan, was found shot to death in his grocery store in Dallas.

Like Quan Nguyen from Vietnam and Fu Lee from China, whose voices began this volume, Sher Singh, Balbar Singh Sodhi, and Waqar Hasan were among the hundreds thousands of Asian immigrants who have arrived on these shores in the past three decades in the wake of late-twentieth-century globalization. The current wave of globalization reflects the practice of everyday life. That it is now possible to watch television programs in Hindi even in such outposts as Providence, Rhode Island, or in Tamil or Malayam in large TV markets such as the New York/New Jersey area should not obscure the brute reality of the displacements and dislocation that mark globalization. Globally and locally, multiculturalism, the celebration of hybridity as a commercialized lifestyle, has become the ideology for managing the increasingly deep class and racial cleavages brought about by neoliberal economic policy. Shortly after the murders of Balbir Singh Sodhi and Abdul Hasan, President George W. Bush rushed to reassure the world that multiculturalism remained the official ideology of the imperial state, and he criticized those who took the law into their own hands by targeting Muslim Americans (or those who were assumed to look like Muslim Americans) for retribution. At the same time, his attorney general John Ashcroft went about authorizing the arrest and secret detention of thousands of Muslim Americans and immigrants.

It is a media commonplace to say that everything has changed since 9/11. For immigrants, European and non-European (though not in equal measure), legal residents as well as the undocumented, life has simply gotten more difficult; the state is more intrusive and hostile; decent housing, education, and healthcare have been placed out of reach; exploitation has risen along with unemployment; and the social safety net is virtually nonexistent. Beginning in the 1990s, well before 9/11, a wave of anti-immigrant legislation stripped undocumented immigrant workers and their families of the most basic social services and protection and placed increasing restrictions on immigration from Latin America and Asia. Whereas the anti-immigrant wave of the 1990s was marked by a discourse about a "loss of control" over America's southern borders and a "Latinization" of American society, the immigration "reforms" have had an equally adverse impact on thousands of Asian immigrants and their families. For example, in 1996 Congress authorized the Immigration and Naturalization Service to deport any immigrant who had any conviction (violent or nonviolent, felony or misdemeanor) in her or his past. Thousands of immigrants have been deported to "home" countries where they may not have lived since early childhood for such past violations as shoplifting or traffic tickets, "crimes" for which penalties had already been exacted and paid. The resulting arrests and deportations have had devastating effects on immigrant deportees and their families.

Since the attacks on the Pentagon and the World Trade Center, the attack on immigrants has intensified. In addition to the intense surveillance of certain immigrant communities, and the secret detention of hundreds of Arab and Muslim immigrants, all immigrants, including those with permanent resident status, have had to register with the Immigration and Naturalization Service, now an arm of the ministry of homeland security. Hundreds have been detained and deported on the basis of technical violations of their visa status.

The empire has struck back, exposed in all its ferocity by the attack of its renegade agents. The surveillance, mass arrest, and deportations of immigrants, the concentration of police powers in the central government, the massive policing of civil society, and the punitive expeditions into Afghanistan and Iraq remind us of the brute reality of power of the American state and its monopoly on the power of regulation and coercion. The state, its demise prematurely proclaimed, has returned with a vengeance indeed.

The chapters in the preceding two sections have demonstrated the historical character of the Asian migration and the present diversities of the transnational Asian experience in the Americas. The two chapters that conclude this collection pose the questions: What are the epistemological, political, and institutional implications for our recognition of what Alejandro Portes (2000) has called "globalization from below"? How does our understanding of the Asian experience in the Americas as a transnational or translocal experience of displacement shape our understanding of the processes of globalization, of empire, of identities? And what are the disciplinary frameworks and institutional arrangement that will need to be built in order to accommodate that understanding? The two chapters in this section take up these questions in different contexts and registers. Abelmann's and San Juan's teaching careers straddle several disciplines. As academic insiders, they provide sharp insights into and critiques of tensions in academic departmental and university politics, existing both in single disciplines and in multidisciplinary departments.

Nancy Abelmann, who has teaching appointments in Anthropology, East Asian Languages and Culture, and Asian American Studies, shows in broad epistimological terms how the transnational experience challenges the disciplinary boundaries of anthropology and the geographically defined borders of her East Asian Languages and Cultures department, and finally how different transnational experiences between international and immigrant students shapes the communication between Korean nationals, and Korean American immigrant students, and herself. She shows how accounting for the translocal presents an anomaly to anthropological paradigms, calling into question the status of informants, of the native, and the legitimacy of culture-bound research in a discipline deeply invested in the local. Abelmann writes about the complications she encountered when attempting to offer a course entitled "The English Language Ethnography of Korea." The title of her course exposes the inherent bias and limitations of the scholarly literature, troubling her academic administrators. Finally, she shows how the disparate class experiences of international students and immigrant students of Korean ancestry shape the ways in which they evaluate their own and each other's "Koreanness." Abelmann, as an anthropologist and a teacher, underscores the importance to close listening for the different registers of the transnational experience. To establish a dialogue among disciplines, Abelmann raises the issues of interdisciplinary borderlands and the closed academic system of some disciplines that penalize scholars who trespass the borders. She sees Appadurai's call for academic border-crossing, learning from other scholars of other nations where the lines are not as sharply drawn, as a necessary and critical call for the opening of localities.

In revising his essay for this volume, Epifanio San Juan Jr., a long-time veteran of the Ethnic Studies movement and recent chair of an Ethnic Studies department, takes up the crisis in racial formation in the wake of the 9/11 attack on the World Trade Center. The attacks reveal the sharpening contradictions of class and race on a global scale. These in turn expose the shortcomings that he sees in the field of Ethnic Studies as a tool for mobilizing the new racialized transnational working class.

What is the way out? San Juan reminds us that the transnational experience of contemporary Asian immigrants must be understood in the context of a globalization that has produced the savage inequalities that drive the dynamics of dislocation. He provocatively questions whether Ethnic Studies continues to be a useful intellectual construct or institutional platform for scholars who remain committed to a vision of social justice in the age of globalization. He argues that Ethnic Studies as practiced in the U.S. academy has been caught in the parochialism of American exceptionalism and that the radical critique that had engendered Ethnic Studies has been undermined by its long struggle for legitimization in the halls of the academy. Ethnic Studies, in his view, has too often succumbed to the managerial ethos of official multiculturalism. San Juan sees a critique of racism, class formation, community participation, the studies of cultural productions, cultural practices, and group relations, understood as a function of global capitalist relations, as a necessary strategy for revivifying the discipline. The point, San Juan insists, is not to build an Asian American Studies through which to understand American society but rather to build an Asian American Studies with which to change the world.

REFERENCE

Portes, Alejandro. 2000. "Globalization from below: The rise of transnational communities." In *The ends of globalization: Bringing society back*, edited by D. Kalb et al., 253–272. Lanham, Md.: Rowman and Littlefield.

13

Anthropology, Asian Studies, Asian American Studies

Open Systems, Closed Minds

NANCY ABELMANN

A series of papers written in 1957 and 1958 culminated in prominent British anthropologist Max Gluckman's 1964 edited volume, *Closed Systems and Open Minds: The Limits of Naivety in Social Anthropology.* The subtitle of this chapter inverts that title: open systems and closed minds. That early volume's methodological interest in how anthropologists define and delimit their "field"—both in the disciplinary and ethnographic sense (that is, field site)— was indeed prescient of debates to come in anthropology (for example, Gupta and Ferguson 1992; Lavie and Swedenburg 1996). Gluckman and collaborators (Devons and Gluckman 1964a, 15) champion naiveté—the treatment of complex social phenomena "as simple, crude, or gross"—so as to "get on with the job." In parallel, they defend interdisciplinary naiveté or "artlessness" in order to be disciplined—as anthropologists, that is. They explain: "We have confined naiveté to the situation where the anthropologist disregards the researches and conclusions of other disciplines about aspects of the events he is studying, as irrelevant to his problem" (Devons and Gluckman 1964b, 212). Both the introduction and conclusion to the volume assert that one of the essays, although included, is in fact outside of their venture: namely, that of William Watson (on social mobility and social class in industrial communities), who became overly entangled in bordering social processes (in a disciplinary sense). Devons and Gluckman (1964b, 211) matter-of-factly declare, "In short, he ceased to be a social anthropologist and became himself a sociologist." That is, they defended an eyes-open and humble eschewal of geographic, processual, and disciplinary borderlands.[1] Eyes-open humility refers, then, to the "open minds" in the equation: namely, that while necessarily "closing his [*sic*] system" the anthropologist nonetheless recognizes the "entanglements" of the "web of reality" and by extension the necessary artifice and arbitrariness of closed systems (ibid., 185). In this chapter, I consider the costs of that artifice and arbitrariness, both in the institutional life of the academy and in our classrooms.

In another vein, the final passages of *Closed Systems and Open Minds* turn to the divisions between "poetry and prose," and the human and social sciences, cautioning, "in [t]hose borderlands trespass is dangerous save for the genius" (Gluckman 1964b, 261). Thus they argue that the anthropologist must opt for the secure bounds of the social sciences generally (as against the human sciences), of anthropology (as against other disciplines), and of the particular closed systems of analysis. These options refer in parallel to "discipline" (for example, anthropology), "area or site" (for example, closed systems), and literary conventions (for example, prose over poetry). This single classical anthropological volume thus reveals (as would many others) the intellectual constellations implicated in anthropology, fieldwork, and the social sciences. In this chapter, I consider the ways in which divisions such as these have been drawn and sustained in the academy (in research, writing, and teaching). In so doing, I challenge the sort of naiveté promoted in the Gluckman et al. volume.[2]

Arjun Appadurai (1999, 237), one of contemporary anthropology's most important thinkers on diaspora and displacement—the terms around which the conference that inspired this book was organized—makes a compelling argument about the workings of these homologously closed systems. Like Gluckman and collaborators, he takes up the very nature of research, noting that it represents a particular Western set of techniques, requirements, and expository conventions. In a sense, Gluckman's work, if ironically, prefigures Appadurai's precisely by underscoring the active naiveté entailed in closing systems. But these anthropologists' projects run counter to one another: Gluckman sets out to close systems, Appadurai's to open them. Appadurai's writings argue that locality (here I take "systems" to be localities of a sort) is itself a *work*, something produced, "not a fact but a project" (231). And again, paralleling, but opposing, Gluckman et al. on prose and poetry, Appadurai (1999, 237, emphasis added) asks: "Is there something for us to learn from colleagues in other national and cultural settings whose *work* is not characterized by a sharp line between social scientific and humanistic styles of inquiry?" Thus, contra Gluckman, he invites the non-geniuses among us to blur those lines, to allow for "undisciplined" voices. In this chapter, I will offer examples of what I call "culture" talk that both disrupt received ideas of locality and demand "humanistic styles of inquiry."

Indeed, contra the rules of naiveté of Gluckman et al, trespassing of all the borders sketched in that volume has become quite commonplace in research and writing today, in anthropology and beyond.[3] In this chapter, I am primarily interested in the trespassing within the academy, and in that entailed in our students' lives.[4] I mean to think about the ways that some of this trespassing takes place, takes shape, and makes trouble.

Chapters of this length lend themselves to the anecdotal, a comfortable space for many ethnographers.[5] Note that the anecdotal is neither the incidental nor the accidental.[6] I introduce here two clusters of anecdotes: the first about the micropolitics of academic localities (departments, disciplines, and the like); the second, on (mis)communication in those localities, and particularly on the student body at the millennial fin de siècle.

In making the connection between academic politics and student worlds (and classrooms) I mean to assert that parallel occlusions and elisions mediate against effective communication and understanding among and within these academic spaces. For both contexts, Appadurai's notion of the "work" of locality reviewed above is helpful. Fields, departments, and classrooms are all "works" of locality; that is, they have their own rules, their own systems of naiveté—rules and systems that I argue have become increasingly untenable. Thus this chapter first examines the way that academic localities beyond the classroom are maintained and policed, just as that very work is rendered invisible; it then turns to the classroom and the lecture hall, to the ways in which talk, students' talk, manages to disrupt comfortable boundaries. For each case, I suggest that the work entailed in locality making is disrupted, or revealed.[7]

The Politics of English

In February 2000 I received a formal letter from the chair of our Anthropology Department's Courses and Curriculum Committee indicating that the committee "enthusiastically supports" my efforts to cross-list "The English Language Ethnography of Korea," a new course that I developed for East Asian Languages and Cultures (EALC).[8] The letter then goes on to ask, "Will you reconsider your decision to *limit* the course by design just to the English literature (specifically, the "English Language" qualification in the course . . .)? Given that the medium of instruction at UIUC [the University of Illinois], in all but the language training courses, is English, it follows that the bias of this medium is *inherent* in everything we teach" (emphasis added). These two sentences (a query and a mandate) are fascinating in juxtaposition. The first seemed to suggest that I might reconsider my decision to limit the course to English-language materials; the second, on the other hand, makes it entirely clear that the objection is not to the limits that I had imposed but rather to my having explicitly referred to those limits in the course title. In Gluckman's idiom above, my insertion of "English language" in the course title had broken, I think, with the department's (the field's?) unstated (or "inherent") naiveté—about the "closed system" of many (most?) of the syllabi (works) we teach.

I do not in any way offer this anecdote as a personal hardship tale of university administrivia, but rather because I think it is substantively revealing of larger issues. By underscoring implicit rules, marking the inherent naiveté of our pedagogy, I had transgressed the rules by which we name or mark our practices. I decided to name the course that way in appreciation of the English-language anthropological academy as but one academic circle among many, including importantly the South Korean anthropological community. Syllabi are implicitly constructed to "cover" topics, to delimit fields. Although in my teaching I always insist that coverage (of this or that topic) is not my aim (some syllabi lend themselves more easily to those caveats; it is more difficult to make such claims for those with ethnic-national signifiers such as "Korean" or "Korean American"), I think that syllabi nonetheless imply such coverage. In this small example even a symbolic attempt (I acknowledge that it was nothing more than that) to suggest the confines, the work of locality, of our (my) pedagogy was refused. I do not, however, mean to single out anthropology or, by omission, to praise EALC. Generally, the politics of language in area studies programs are of a very different variety: in such areas, materials in the vernacular are often prized, if not fetishized, as "authentic," nearer to the source.[9]

In the university culture I know, faculty are encouraged to put their courses "on the books"; formal course numbers make for easier accounting (in all senses of that word). In the era of so-called responsible budgeting (in which student numbers—at my university we frequently hear about "student feet"—are the bottom line), "the books" matter. Putting things on the books is clearly a disciplinary practice; one must, then, play by the books or rules. It is in these sorts of details that we can observe the boundary making and maintenance work of our institutions.

I turn now to another locality, one where the boundaries of knowledge and fields are quite obviously policed: an encyclopedia (*The International Encyclopaedia of the Social and Behavioral Sciences*). The anecdote I offer in this vein is one that again takes up questions of language and of "national" academies.

Just as the letter cited above arrived from the Department of Anthropology, I was agonizing over an encyclopedia article on the anthropology of Korea (Abelmann 2001); limited to 2,500 words, English-language citations,[10] and fifteen bibliographic entries, the article was becoming moment by moment more political as I wrestled over who and what to include or exclude; the assertion of genealogies or fissures; and how to best refer to the anthropology beyond English. A number of generous readers, among them a number of South Korean anthropologists of South Korea in training in the United States, were quick to note very critically the many silences and contradictions in my drafts: that while I sought to tell at least partially the story of an anthropology beyond English and the United States, the allotment of my sentences—most of them devoted to the works of white anthropologists working in the United States—

told another story; that while I sought to document the coordinates of a transnationally shared anthropological history of the portrayal of "Korean" "culture" (while problematizing both terms), I had in fact conflated distinct histories and subjectivities. My point here is that a community of "diasporic" scholars[11] was insisting that my own attempts at exposing the naiveté (in Gluckman's sense) of my article and of the prescribed narrative conventions were neither loud nor bold enough. They were right.

I eventually submitted the article, running over by some 500 words and eight citations. Caught, I was asked to cut the 500 words and the extra citations; I did. It felt as if I had been asked to erase the very traces of my feeble attempts to broaden the article's scope and stretch. I do not mean to dismiss my own responsibility; we are, as is so often repeated in acknowledgments, solely responsible for our writings (including our syllabi). In fact, I am complicit in the limitations of the "English language" in both instances: my naiveté is, in the final analysis, my own work, much as Gluckman et al. suggest. Efforts to the contrary, I am nonetheless party to the localities I have been sketching here.

I will close this discussion of university localities with another instance of the mechanics of cross-listing, this time an anthropology course with the EALC. In the same semester that the Anthropology Department tinkered with my EALC offering, EALC decided against cross-listing a new course I was developing for the Anthropology Department, "The Ethnography of Asian America." The departmental letter explained that if the department cross-listed this course, where would it "draw the line?" (for other courses into the future). Along other bureaucratic trails (and trials), "The Ethnography of Asian America" was rejected five (!) times by the College (Liberal Arts and Sciences) Courses and Curriculum Committee because they failed to see how this course differs sufficiently from an existing course that introduces Asian American communities. Although the proposed new listing aimed to situate the ethnographic literature on Asian America in the context of theoretical and textual developments in anthropology, the "University" could not see beyond the overlap of ethnic domain or geography, hence the assertion of redundancy.[12] (It was eventually accepted and has to date been taught twice.) In each case, university localities are at work. In the first instance, an area studies program decides that an ethnic studies offering (although one with an explicitly transnational approach) is beyond its purview. In the second case, it becomes apparent that college committees exercise their own understandings of "ethnic" when it comes to anthropology offerings: that, in this case, Asian American ethnography is somehow not entirely viable as a literature through which to interrogate anthropological theory and practice, but that anthropology can be comfortably mobilized to portray Asian America.[13]

What these ever so micropolitics reveal, I think, is a university—and I do not take ours to be exceptional or uniform—*closing its systems*, and not necessarily *open-mindedly.* In the letter from the Anthropology Department, the apt criticism from my readers, and the mechanics of the Asian American Studies course offering, we can see people (myself included) struggling over fuzzy borders, wanting to retreat to their own naiveté. It is, it seems, unsettling when the bounds of regional studies, ethnic studies, the social sciences, or English (-only!) academia, are unsettled. This said, however, I want to emphasize that these comments are not meant to vilify departments (my own), university committees, or particular individuals. It is unreasonable and unproductive to point the finger of blame narrowly. Rather, I mean to suggest that the practices mentioned here are implicated in long-standing organizational, institutional, and ideological configurations.

Talking "Culture": In and Beyond the Classroom

I turn now from the politics encircling disciplinary and pedagogical spaces to the communication therein, and particularly to that of students. I am especially interested in the myriad miscommunications that take place in classes and forums devoted to the presentation of nationally or ethnically circumscribed knowledge (such as area and ethnic studies). Here I am necessarily an interested observer because of the teaching I do on Korea and Korean America, domains that are increasingly blurring in my own research and teaching life. In this section I am interested in the articulation between ethnic and area studies—between the ethnic and the national. In parallel with the above discussion of institutional localities in the academy, I will suggest that culture talk disrupts and decenters received configurations of knowledge. Chakrabarty (1998, 474) writes of the effects of "diasporic life-forms" in a similar vein: "They move us away from all conceptions of centers. Area studies scholarship has been focused on centers—cultural, statist, bureaucratic, familial. Diasporic studies lead us away from the imagination of centralizing structures." A similar logic or observation is revealed in the comment that I have heard repeated by older white, male scholars of East Asia over the last few years: namely, that with the large numbers of Asian Americans in their classes, they can no longer teach the way they always have. I choose a sympathetic reading of such comments: that the changing demography of these professors' classes has made them aware of problems (that have always been there) in the way they parsed and packaged knowledge on East Asia, problems with the "closed systems" in which they have long worked.[14]

Although I appreciate the many sensible critiques of transnationalism run wild,[15] I nevertheless think that the complex social networks and spaces inhabited by immigrant or second-generation Asian Americans in our classes *do* demand new pedagogy and disallow facile assumptions about the transparency of knowledge transmission; of course, it never has been transparent. As mentioned (see note 4), I think that these disruptions can be highlighted for the student body at large, not just for its ethnic or immigrant members.

I turn now to an exchange from a conference on Korean and Korean American Christianity held at the University of Illinois in the fall of 1999. At the conference, a Korean American Christian student in the audience posed a somewhat rhetorical question to a senior Korean immigrant sociologist (a practicing Catholic, secular in his scholarship—subject positions that he had made clear) who had noted in his remarks that because Confucianism is a system of social ethics, not a religion (that is, that there is nothing divine or transcendent about it), it is entirely compatible with Christianity—and indeed has, as such, in turn facilitated Korea's Christianization. The clearly devout student queried, "Isn't Christianity also a system of social ethics?" and he proceeded to talk briefly about the guiding idea of the "self as servant" in his own church; unstated was the implication (my read of this moment) that a Confucian social ethics might be a odds with a (his) Christian one. The senior scholar responded with great interest and empathy that *indeed* Confucianism and Christianity comprise radically different world views in that Confucianism is always about the self immersed in, and inextricable from, collectivities.[16] He went on to elaborate in some detail his own more collectivistic identities in spite of his many decades living in the United States. Implicit in this senior scholar's response was his understanding of particular lines of contrast between "collectivistic" Confucianism and "individualistic" Christianity.[17]

Further exchange, however, clearly revealed that the student had wanted to contrast the self-abnegation of his Christian practice with the self-aggrandizement of what he understands as the Confucian-inflected Christianity of his parents. I understand this exchange as a moment of profound confusion across a generational (and perhaps religious, and other) divide: the professor spoke of compatibility; the student alluded to more fundamental difference. The professor acknowledged difference, and in so doing stood on its head the students' sense of Christian differences of selfhood, instead assigning himself to collectivistic norms he considered generational.[18] This is a very partial ethnographic vignette, sketched through the lens of my ongoing research on Korean American students, among them evangelical Christians.[19] Elsewhere I have sketched some of the elements at work in this failed communication.[20] It would take further ethnographic exploration to really understand this particular conversation and the specificity of its interlocutors. I think that to really trace what was happening in this moment would be quite complicated indeed, and would no doubt extend to the student's culturally inscribed sense of intergenerational difference, to the particularity of the immigrant life and trajectory of the émigré scholar, to the heterogeneity of Korean American Christiani*ties*, and so on.[21] I take this moment to be illustrative of how complicated it is to locate or fix "culture" or cultural discourse. In this example the cultural signifiers—

Korean, Korean-American, Christian, Confucian—are disruptive in their work. In the terms of this chapter, they disrupt localities. I call particular attention to the student in this communication because I think that in this exchange his words go furthest in the work of disruption—against locality.

I submit that *all* cultural representations (be they in traditionally configured Asian studies or Asian American courses or in ones more transnationally organized, or in all courses, for that matter) begin in the middle for most students.[22] Unraveling the maze of received understandings, moored to the specificities of students' lives and histories, is not a simple matter; beyond that, trying to have a conversation is quite a feat.

In a fascinating critique of the university—arguing that its enlightenment mission is entirely out of synch with today's society—Bill Readings (1996, 12–13) suggests that the university must be rethought in a transnational framework (no longer the voice of "national culture in the modern nation-state"). Readings (1996, 19) champions the notion that the pedagogical exchange "*hold open* the temporality of questioning so as to resist being characterized as a transaction that can be concluded, either with the giving of grades or with the granting of degrees."[23] I appreciate this line of argument because I think that the "temporality of questioning" in today's classrooms must, as Readings suggests, be "held open." Gluckman and collaborators' comfortable (comforting?) closed systems and naiveté fly in the face of students' lived realities.[24]

Readings's critiques of the university and the complexity of student networks and movement aside, there is no question that there remain, in Gluckman's sense, meaningful "systems" that constitute students' worlds. Smith and Guarnizo (1998, 7) aptly note that "nationalist projects and identities" remain salient and that "Transnational practices, while connecting collectivities located in more than one national territory, are embodied in specific social relations established between specific people, situated in unequivocal localities, at historically determined times" (11). In this vein, I can also appreciate the "corrective" voice of senior anthropologist Sidney Mintz (1998, 131) who explains that contra transnationalism, the teaching anthropologist will meet (in her classroom) "some unruly [i.e., against disciplinary fashion] youngster [who] wants to know where the folks we contemplate come from, what they speak, when they began traveling, what they prefer to eat, and how one may elicit information from them." A long-time champion of transnational realities and techniques in anthropology, it is interesting that Mintz closes his article with warnings: "The new theories of transnationalism and globalization are not respectful enough of history, especially of the history of exploration, conquest and the global division of labor. . . . Anthropology has traditionally aspired to get its information in a manner other than *by imagining it*, and its traditional methods still work" (emphasis added). I, too, subscribe to the empirical bias of the ethnographic method—and continue to live and work with/through it—but

I think that it is critical that we pay attention precisely to the *imaginations* of our students and anthropological interlocutors, like those at the heart of the intergenerational exchange I introduced above. And, in this spirit, I continue to admire the writings of Arjun Appadurai (1999, 231) and others on the imagination (such as Rushdie 1991), that "faculty which informs the daily lives of ordinary people in myriad ways . . . which allows people to consider migration, to resist state violence, to seek social redress, and to design new forms of civic association and collaboration, often across national boundaries."[25] Here we can recall Gluckman et al. on poetry and prose—the warning to not trespass across those divides. The social world, though, demands such trespass.

So, then, how does that imagination render its effects on our classrooms and on our disciplinary lives? It is constitutive of the identities and identifications of our students; it demands of us an *open mind* about what is taking place between the lines and lives of our students. Two anecdotes come to mind. The first comes from the first time I taught the aforementioned "English Language Ethnography of Korea." Over the entire course of the semester a number of South Korean international graduate students (from Anthropology and other departments) struggled to understand the heightened emotional responses to the readings of a Korean American first-year graduate student; likewise, the Korean American student struggled to understand their seeming dispassion. This came to a head when the Korean American student finally threw up her arms and wondered aloud how she or anyone—and especially the South Korean "nationals" in the class—could themselves take part in *any* representation of the Koreas. I would be hard pressed to summarize or neatly package this semester-long unfolding exchange. I would submit that this exchange can not be thought of independently of the limits of the "*English language* ethnography of Korea." But, this sort of exchange challenges the sorts of closed systems according to which many of us divide our lives, syllabi, and so on. As with the earlier anecdote (on the Korean American Christianity conference), it would be no small feat to closely analyze these relations. In brief, however, let me suggest that here too the complexity of the work of the signifiers "Korean," "Korean American," "diasporic," and so on would disrupt the received boundaries of ethnic studies, area studies, and anthropology. Such disruption is entirely necessary, I argue, if we are to make sense of, or do justice to, our students and classrooms.

The final anecdote is one I learned of secondhand through Hyunhee Kim, a graduate student anthropologist from South Korea in my department, who has been assisting me with my research on Korean Americans in Illinois public higher education. Recently, Ms. Kim has spent some time with South Korean international student undergraduates (a relatively new and still very small group on our campus) who often spend dormitory and dorm cafeteria time with so-called 1.5 Korean immigrants (typically high-school-age immigrants who remain more comfortable speaking Korean than English). The international students complained to Ms. Kim that these immigrant students have no *yôyu*—space of mind, largesse of spirit—most particularly because of their stinginess with food, their unwillingness to open their parents' Chicagoland homes to them (particularly when they travel to and from Chicago), and their narrow career and intellectual focus. The immigrants, on the other hand, remarked that the cosmopolitan futures of the elite international students are secured (by their class privilege) and that they have little understanding of the struggles and insecure futures of immigrant students. No doubt the immigrant students, if confronted with the allegations about *yôyu*, would answer that they do not have that privilege. Although these groups of students find each other because they can talk together, and because they enjoy eating together (and supplementing dorm fare with Korean foods), they are divided by diasporic diversities—diversities that constitute our classrooms. And these diversities have everything to do with diaspora and displacements, and with thinking anew the university and its boundaries.

THIS CHAPTER HAS discussed in turn institutional (micro-) politics in the academy (research, publication, and pedagogy) *and* the social /discursive worlds of students at a large public university. My aim has been, following Appadurai, to call attention to the ways in which everyday practices in the academy elide or obscure the *work* of locality: the necessary, and quite constant, policing that a conviction about local autonomy (of disciplines, of departments, of national academies etc.) entails. Through the anecdotal, I have considered how localities are produced, policed, and maintained in the academy. It seems fair to issue a call for *open minds* to contend with *open systems*.

I would like to end with some practical considerations for institutional practice in the academy. The calls I make here are ones that are, I think, already being considered or implemented at many colleges and universities, including my own. We all know that universities necessarily classify (as do all institutions) in order to create course catalogues, to delineate requirements, and so on. There are times, however—and today is one of them—in which some of the categories need to be reconsidered. Dichotomies such as the "West" and "non-West," for example have become problematic, as have those between the "homeland" or "nation" and its "diaspora"; these dichotomies remain ones that count and are counted at my university—although happily there is movement afoot to disrupt them (much need in anthropology, area studies, and ethnic studies). Faculty and administrators, regardless of disciplinary home and/or training, need to be able to transgress these sorts of neat dichotomies as they configure their programs, courses, degree requirements, and so on. In a related vein, faculty need to continually consider anew their student body and to appreciate the often boundary-crossing nature of their backgrounds, be it the remarkably cosmopolitan life-course of a so-called international student or the active ties to the homeland of the so-called ethnic student. Similarly, faculty need to appreciate the local complexity of the culture talk of one or another student population so as to understand the complex, and often surprising, valence of one or another matter. These calls have implications for the day-to-day work of our universities: work that constantly assesses worth, determining, for example, who is well trained, who deserves to be admitted, funded, celebrated, hired, tenured, and so on. It is, I submit, in the smallest of our practices that we exercise the institutional logics that we need to continuously reassess; this is very hard work—it is always easier to parse the world, to classify, in just the way that we have always done.

Finally, I would like to make a plea for college and university practices that foster faculty and administrator learning. If it seems absurd to make a call for institutions of higher education that allow its nonstudent constituents to learn, I submit that it is not. It is costly and time consuming, not to mention often frightening, to learn. This means that professionals need to be given the time, safe spaces, and collaborative settings in which to collectively rethink—with open minds—the transforming systems of our times.

NOTES

I am deeply grateful to Hyunhee Kim and Martin Manalansan for having read and commented on several drafts of this chapter. I am also appreciative of several colleagues who offered insightful readings of an encyclopedia article that I discuss in this chapter (Abelmann 2001): Roger Janelli, Laurel Kendall, Soo-Jung Lee, and Laura Nelson. Finally, this paper benefited greatly from the research assistance of Hyunhee Kim, Hye-Young Jo, and Katherine Wiegele.

1. I use the word "borderlands" with caution, recognizing that academic borders, and their policing, are of an entirely different sort from those on which lives and well-being turn. I have learned a great deal from scholars who suggest caution in using these terms so that we do not inadvertently equate all social barriers with those that impose greater political costs (such as national borders) (Lugo 2000, Manalansan 2000).

2. To those who charge that I make straw men of Gluckman and collaborators in this paper, I plead guilty. I do, however, mean also to pay tribute to that work for its eloquent articulation of the more often unarticulated conventions of the field of anthropology and of anthropological fieldwork and field sites. Furthermore, my arguments are meant to serve as critiques not of their work but rather of ongoing academic practices that were articulated interestingly in that early work.

3. See note 1 with regard to this use of "trespassing."

4. Although the examples I take up here are limited to Asian American and Asian international students, I would be willing to make this argument more broadly for all students.

5. This chapter was initially drafted for a round-table discussion of pedagogical issues. This revised version is still meant as a discussion piece.

6. As Dipesh Chakrabarty (1998, 475) writes, "I use anecdotes merely to present the ethnographic evidence one inevitably collects from life."

7. Before proceeding I will briefly outline my own disciplinary homes and allegiances, as these are the locations, the localities, from which I experience the university. I have a split appointment—we are always reminded to say "joint" appointment—between the departments of Anthropology and East Asian Languages and Cultures. I also have a so-called zero-time appointment in Women's Studies (zero refers finally to money, I think). And I have been a member of the UIUC Asian American Studies Executive Committee since its inception in 1997. It is only very recently that Asian American Studies has become a "program." Before becoming a program, let alone a department, although there was a group of us that presided over seven hires, our work there remained quite invisible, while its locality was not yet firmly established. This sort of invisibility, of course, has real implications for Asian American (and ethnic) studies generally, and for untenured faculty in particular. Today I am happily a teaching faculty member of our Program in Asian American Studies.

8. Although this book (and the conference on which it was based) focuses on the research and teaching of the diaspora, a number of the examples I draw on here take up the politics of Asian studies and anthropology. I do this in the confidence that the production of academic locality is necessarily dialogic: a co-production in dialogue with other academic localities.

9. See Harootunian (2000; see especially p. 25–42, second paragraph, notes 160–161) for an illuminating discussion of this notion of authenticity and particularly of the "field" in the study of East Asia. See also Rafael (1994) for a discussion of a similar logic.

10. This was recommended, not required.

11. See Rafael (1994) for an important discussion of the problematic concept of "indigenous intellectuals."

12. The quotes are meant to underscore the fact that the university is not a monolith, nor is it populated by like-minded people.

13. It is the determination of this committee against approving these offerings that has led me to postulate (perhaps unfairly) that such is the logic at work. Please note, however, that the Anthropology Department has been entirely supportive of these two listings.

14. The matter of the professoriate adjusting to the changing demography of their student body would make for very interesting ethnographic exploration.

15. Critiques made, for example, in response to declarations of the demise of the nation-state or of national culture (Portes, Guarnizo, and Landolt 1999, 219; Smith and Guarnizo 1998, 7) or of free movement and border crossing (see note 1).

16. See Dirlik (1995) for an interesting discussion of critical transformations in the transnational apperception of Confucianism. See Sharf (1995) for a brilliant discussion of ethnographic, historical, and philosophical naiveté in the long-standing Western perception of Japanese Zen Buddhism. I take these as exemplary of the sort of archaeology or genealogy demanded by transnational analyses.

17. Needless to say, these are well-worn tropes in anthropology and cross-cultural study generally (e.g., Markus and Kitayama 1991). See Abu-Lughod (1991) for an anthropological critique of this sort of "culture" concept.

18. See Leonard (2000, 186) for a fascinating discussion of "culture" (and religion) talk in the Hyderabad diaspora that makes points similar to those I make here.

19. I was assisted in my research on Korean American Christianity by Katherine Wiegele.

20. See Abelmann and Wiegele 1999.

21. Lisa Lowe (1996) cautions importantly that we not collapse "incommensurabilities of class, gender, and national diversity among Asians" to those of generation.

22. I am grateful to campus workshops on teaching for making this point about pedagogy generally: that the teacher encounters students (that is, persons), not blank slates.

23. In what I take to be a similar spirit, Fredric Jameson (1996, 358) remarks, "I propose a notion . . . of what I call 'cognitive mapping' . . . to . . . suggest that our task today as artists or critics or whatever is somehow to reach some way in which we recapture or reinvent a new form of representation of this new global totality."

24. Nowhere is this more apparent than in the ethnography presented in Hye-Young Jo's (2000) dissertation on Korean Americans in college Korean-language classrooms.

25. I appreciate the balanced position taken by Lavie and Swedenburg (1996, 13, see also 17): "We wish to stake out a terrain that calls for, yet paradoxically refuses, boundaries, a borderzone between identity-as-esssence and identity-as-conjuncture, whose practices challenge the ludic play with essence and conjuncture as yet another set of postmodernist binarisms. This terrain is old in experience and memory but new in theory: a third time-space."

REFERENCES

Abelmann, Nancy. 2001. "3.1.201 Asia, sociocultural overviews: Korea." In *International encyclopaedia of the social and behavioral sciences*, 8,152–8,162. New York: Elsevier Science.

Abelmann, Nancy, and Katherine Wiegele. 1999. "Competing regimes and rhetorics of time and personhood in Korean American college student bible study groups." Paper presented at the Annual Meeting of the American Anthropological Association, Chicago.

Abu-Lughod, Lila. 1991. "Writing against culture." In *Recapturing anthropology: Working in the present*, edited by R. G. Fox, 137–162. Santa Fe, N. M.: School of American Research Press.

Appadurai, Arjun. 1999. "Globalization and the research imagination." *International Social Science Journal* 51(2): 229–238.

Chakrabarty, Dipesh. 1998. "Reconstructing liberalism? Notes toward a conversation between area studies and diasporic studies." *Public Culture* 10(3): 457–481.

Devons, Ely, and Max Gluckman. 1964a. "Introduction." In *Closed systems and open minds: The limits of naivety in social anthropology*, edited by M. Gluckman, 13–19. Chicago: Aldine.

––––. 1964b. "Conclusion: Modes and consequences of limiting a field of study." In *Closed systems and open minds: The limits of naivety in social anthropology*, edited by M. Gluckman, 158–261. Chicago: Aldine.

Dirlik, Arif. 1995. "Confucius in the borderlands: Global capitalism and the reinvention of Confucianism." *Boundary 2* 22(3): 229–273.

Gluckman, Max, ed. 1964. *Closed systems and open minds: The limits of naivety in social anthropology.* Chicago: Aldine.

Gupta, Akhil, and James Ferguson. 1992. "Beyond 'culture': Space, identity, and the politics of difference." *Cultural Anthropology* 7(1): 6–23.

Harootunian, Harry. 2000. "Tracking the dinosaur: Area studies in a time of 'globalism'" (selection). In Harootunian, *History's disquiet: Modernity, cultural practice, and the question of everyday life.* New York: Columbia University Press.

Jameson, Fredric. 1996. "South Korea as social space: Fredric Jameson interviewed by Paik Nak-chung, Seoul, 28 October 1989." In *Global local: Cultural production and the transnational imaginary,* edited by R. Wilson and W. Dissanayake, 348–371. Durham: Duke University Press.

Jo, Hye-Young. 2000. "Negotiating ethnic identity: Korean Americans in college Korean language classes." Ph.D. dissertation. University of Illinois at Urbana-Champaign.

Lavie, Smadar, and Ted Swedenburg. 1996. "Introduction: Displacement, diaspora, and geographies of identity." In *Displacement, diaspora, and geographies of identity,* edited by S. Lavie and T. Swedenburg, 1–25. Durham: Duke University Press.

Leonard, Karen. 2000. "Identity in the diaspora: Surprising voices." In *Cultural compass: Ethnographic explorations of Asian America,* edited by M. F. Manalansan IV, 177–198. Philadelphia: Temple University Press.

Lowe, Lisa. 1996. *Immigrant acts: On Asian American cultural politics.* Durham: Duke University Press.

Lugo, Alejandro. 2000. "Theorizing border inspections." *Cultural Dynamics* 12(3): 353–373.

Manalansan, Martin. 2000. "Introduction." In *Cultural compass: Ethnographic explorations of Asian America,* edited by M. F. Manalansan IV, 1–13. Philadelphia: Temple University Press.

Markus, H. R., and S. Kitayama. 1991. "Culture and the self: Implications for cognition, emotion, and motivation." *Psychological Review* 98: 224–253.

Mintz, Sydney W. 1998. "The localization of anthropological practice: From area studies to transnationalism." *Critique of Anthropology* 18(2): 117–133.

Portes, Alejandro, Luis E. Guarnizo, and Patricia Landolt. 1999. "The study of transnationalism: Pitfalls and promise of an emergent research field." *Ethnic and Racial Studies* 22(2): 217–237.

Rafael, Vicente L. 1994. "The cultures of area studies in the United States." *Social Text* 41: 91–112.

Readings, Bill. 1996. *The university in ruins.* Cambridge: Harvard University Press.

Rushdie, Salman. 1991. *Imaginary homelands.* New York: Viking.

Sharf, Robert H. 1995. "The Zen of Japanese nationalism." In *Curators of the Buddha: The study of Buddhism under colonialism,* edited by D. S. Lopez, Jr., 107–160. Chicago: University of Chicago Press.

Smith, Michael P., and Luis Guarnizo. 1998. *Transnationalism from below.* New Brunswick, N.J.: Transaction.

14

The Ordeal of Ethnic Studies in the Age of Globalization

E. SAN JUAN JR.

> When I look back now from this high hill of my old age, I can still see the
> butchered women and children lying heaped and scattered all along the
> crooked gulch as plain as when I saw them with eyes still young. And I can
> see that something else died there in the bloody mud, and was buried in
> the blizzard. A people's dream died there. . . . [T]he nation's hoop is broken
> and scattered. There is no center any longer, and the sacred tree is dead.
>
> —Black Elk of the Oglala Sioux

After September 11, 2001, reflections on ethnic and racial conflicts in the
"homeland" have automatically undergone surveillance and security checks.
But is this a new situation? Have we, people of color in the racial polity, ever
been truly released from such emergency measures? In any case, I want to frame
the following discourse in the context of what precedes it: the killing of Filipino-
American Joseph Ileto by a white supremacist in 1999 and the trial of Chinese-
American scientist Wen Ho Lee, and what occurred after the destruction of the
World Trade Center—the murder, ostracism, and continuing harassment of
thousands of South Asians and Arab Americans, coupled with the imprisonment
by the government of hundreds of unnamed suspects who might be tried before
military tribunals.

The "war on terrorism" threatens to preempt all agendas. With the persistence of the neoconservative tide and the accelerated rollback of civil rights
gains and initiatives throughout the country, it might be superfluous if not an
otiose imposition to rehearse at this time the predicament of ethnic studies in
the academy today. What can be more droll for besieged scholars, or even dangerous for community activists and partisans of social justice? It might be the
"changing same," as Amiri Baraka puts it. But history never repeats itself in
exactly in the same manner—because we intervene through collective praxis,
memory, reinscriptions, and other transformative ways. And often the past, the

repressed has had a way of returning without consulting us in order to make us aware that history is what hurts. The cases of Mumia Abu-Jamal, Leonard Peltier, and Assata Shakur, not to speak of Wen Ho Lee and who knows how many undiscovered cases of enslaved migrant workers in Los Angeles, New York, Miami, and the new global cities—all these remain "hurts" left for us to discover. They are not Baudrillard's simulacras or counterfactual simulations regurgitated by cyborgs. George Lipsitz (1998) has cogently warned us of the "ruinous pathology of whiteness" that continues to sustain the "absence of mutuality," responsibility, and justice in our society, while David Harvey (2000) reminds us how Marx long ago taught us that the constructions of race and ethnicity are implicated in the ongoing circulation process of variable capital—labor power as commodity is now racialized in the global marketplace policed by the World Trade Organization (WTO), the International Monetary Fund (IMF), and the World Bank.

With the changed global/local conditions, a reassessment of our critical tools and paradigms is needed. The conversation on the situation of Ethnic Studies today is always an act of historicizing, a process of articulation in the moments of passage from one crisis to another. Every interruption of "business as usual," no matter how minor, opens up the space for strategic interventions. Crisis not only implies danger but also provides the break for seizing opportunities to intervene in refashioning our life-world.

Whether before or after September 11, the discourse on race and ethnicity—both dynamic sociopolitical constructs—remains as politically charged as before. The terrain of controversy is sedimented by objective contradictions that cannot be flattened by the customary pedagogical formula of either "teaching the conflicts" or replaying the "intersections of class, race, and gender" in the classroom. Less insistent now is the debate over terminologies: race vis-à-vis racial formation, race versus ethnicity, and so on. The predicament I address may lie in the forgetting of origins and concomitantly in the loss of purpose. The program brochure I revised three years ago for Washington State University's Department of Comparative American Cultures (CAC) features its beginning in the mid-seventies with the setting up of individual programs and their gradual if contentious coalescence: Chicano Studies, Black Studies, Native American Studies, Asian American Studies. Aside from the tasks of improving ethnic representation in body counts of students and faculty, one of the tasks CAC has tried to address is that of "investigating and criticizing the traditional ways of understanding U.S. society and history that deny the centrality of 'race' and ethnicity to the American experience."

The CAC (which I chaired then) has had to reinvent itself anew every year amid budget cutbacks, downsizing, and retrenchment (Nash 2001). Across the country in the last two decades, the field of Ethnic Studies as a whole has found itself placed on trial and besieged by its enemies, with foes often masquerading as friends. Paradoxes and antinomies afflict our horizon of thought, making necessary a retreat for self-reflection, regrouping, and renewal. What follows are remarks needed to situate ourselves historically, to project ourselves as sharing the plight of Others, in order to make what we do analytically comprehensible and thus open to reconstitution and renewal.

Paradox Unbound

In 1995, Evelyn Hu-DeHart wrote a wake-up piece for the *Chronicle of Higher Education* entitled "The Undermining of Ethnic Studies." She reflected on the paradoxical situation of Ethnic Studies as an academic discipline—paradoxical because it is both widely endorsed and universally ignored, long established but still marginalized (Butler 1991). Why this ambivalent position of being both blessed and maligned? It may be that the paradoxical condition of the field is a symptom of the crisis of pluralist transnational capitalism, more specifically a crisis of political legitimation (San Juan 1995). That is, the cooptive maneuvers to contain this emergent discipline reflect the systemic contradictions of the social and global formation we inhabit. The latest attempt to neutralize this challenge to received ideology is by way of postcolonial nostrums of hybridity, ludic body politics, transmigrancy, and chic populism ascribed to diasporic, transnational intellectuals in First World academies and their neoliberal "fellow travelers."

All departments of Ethnic Studies, to be sure, have experienced the anxieties of in-betweenness and contingency, haphazard "trips" of indeterminacy. Their survival is nothing short of a miracle—except that this miracle, seen in historical perspective, involves secular agents: the ordinary and daily acts of resistance by people of color against exclusion, genocide, exploitation, and various forms of oppression. I have in mind the mobilization of popular energies against discrimination and racist violence throughout United States history—a dialectic of forces that have constituted this white-supremacist polity from its founding as a settler formation. The birth of Ethnic Studies in the fury of emergencies, in the fires of urban rebellions and national liberation struggles inscribed within living memory, has marked its character and destiny for better or worse, perhaps to a degree that explains the risks and the stakes in this peculiar (to use Wittgenstein's term) "form of life."

All the bad ways of "using" or, more precisely, manipulating Ethnic Studies described by Hu-DeHart persist, including the way its singular virtue—as an "integral part of multicultural education" (Banks 1991)—is harnessed to conceal existing inequalities. Could there be a more instructive specimen of bourgeois hegemonic strategy in action? This shows that the field (I hesitate to call it "discipline" because I and my colleagues are products of various disciplinary formations) is susceptible of being utilized by forces inimical to its emancipatory vocation. One might retort: So what else is new? Neither subsumed within area studies, minority studies, panethnic diasporic studies, nor an adjunct of American Studies of Cold War provenance, a species of Ethnic Studies has in practice become a means to an end: to promote a version of cultural diversity required by equal opportunity and affirmative action laws. Now that this requirement—part of the "fire insurance program"—is gone, a substitute rationale has appeared: multiculturalism and global studies. This ties in with student service demands, altered demographics, and the multiethnic marketing niches of globalization.

We are witnessing today a fateful turn of events in the politics of local/global cultures as we enter the first half of the twenty-first century. Although its viability and provocativeness still draws sustenance from the historical conditions at its advent, the plight of Ethnic Studies also depends on the current conjuncture of circumstances. It depends chiefly on the sense of responsibility of "organic" intellectuals to their communities. Everyone recognizes that this discipline would not have been possible without the radical democratic engagements of women, youth and people of color in "internal colonies" and overseas dependencies—in projects to achieve cultural autonomy, sovereign rights, and self-determination. Today, it is allied to the struggle against the endemic racial profiling of Arabs and Arab Americans targeted by the "homeland" security state. One might say that our field is concerned with theorizing such variegated praxis (for historical background, see Bennis and Moushabeck 1993; Steinberg 1995; Featherstone, Lash, and Robertson 1995) and corollary projects.

With the neoconservative counterrevolution of the eighties, such conditions of possibility may have been extinguished, hence the ambivalent mapping of this field. Hu-DeHart is sorely pressed to argue for its scholarly legitimacy and respectability, so she tries to reinvent its reformist "contract" with society by invoking the triumphalist claim that Ethnic Studies is here to stay because "it is an integral part of multicultural education." I do not mean to ascribe a naive optimism to Hu-DeHart; her view is partly substantiated by demographics and revitalized opposition to the neoconservativism of the last two decades. Ethnic Studies will stay so long as its practitioners adhere chiefly to the power/knowledge regime of the "role model" and regard this subject-position as the pedagogical transcoding of the chameleonic politics of identity (otherwise known as "border," hybrid, and cyborg lifestyles). The routine slogan for these role models, I believe, goes like this: "Look, marvel at our inimitable crafts, performances, apparel, idioms—we contribute to making America a colorful saladbowl of differences!"

The disjuncture between civil society, the realm of difference, and the bourgeois state that commands the abstract unitary citizen, explains the limits of liberal multiculturalism—a permanent contradiction in capitalism diagnosed by Marx in "On the Jewish Question" and his critique of Hegel's *Philosophy of*

Right (Marx 1968, 1970). In "On the Jewish Question," Marx located ethnic distinctions (such as religious belief) in civil society dominated by egoistic individualism, in the bourgeois world where rights of private, fragmentary interests competed against one another. In contrast, the right of citizens (*citoyens*) guaranteed by the state exists in an abstract, "spiritual" community that ignored cultural differences. For genuine human emancipation (species-being/*Gattungswesen*) to be realized, the political abstract citizen needs to coincide with the self-interested individual to discover the socialized powers that sublate cultural and other particularistic differences. This coincidence of the citizen and the actual individual has been displaced by the liberal program of cultural pluralism. Angela Davis rightly objects to this cooptative management of diversity for corporate profit making, making it incapable of challenging the gender, ethnic, and race hierarchies framed by the class/property dynamics that structure the major institutions: "A multiculturalism that does not acknowledge the political character of culture will not . . . lead toward the dismantling of racist, sexist, homophobic, economically exploitative institutions" (1996, 47).

Meanwhile, I want to provoke here an exploratory reflection on these themes of telos and commitment in this time of cynical reaction by posing the following questions: If multicultural education (for some, the "cult of literacy") has displaced the centrality of mass social movements, does this signify that we have again been subtly recolonized? Has the "power elite" (to use C. Wright Mills's old-fashioned term) succeeded in obscuring fundamental inequalities grounded in social production relations by shifting the attention to cultural differences, lifestyles, and the quest for authentic selves? Has ethnic pluralism and liberal tolerance (Walzer 2000) erased racism? Is the generic brand of Ethnic Studies and its discourse of diversity not culpable of problematizing Others of its own invention? Is it now simply used to manage and harmonize differences by refurbishing the trope of the "melting pot"? Has it been retooled to perform what Marcuse once called "repressive desublimation" under the guise of civic republicanism or communitarianism? Or is it deployed as prophylaxis to service the aspirations of the comprador intelligentsia of the subalterns and ultimately pacify the populace?

In Search of a New Problematic

Ethnicism, the absolutizing of ethnicity in the agenda of liberal multiculturalism, occludes racism and delegitimizes resistance to it. We need to engage in a research program of systematic demystification in order to clarify the complex articulation of ethnicity and racialization in the capitalist world system. Our goal is to avoid reifying cultural traits and show how such allegedly fixed and static attributes change under the pressure of circumstances and the transformative force of people's actions. What is imperative is to historicize the so-

called ethnic predicament—the salience of cultural practices, customs, traditions, religion, languages, and so on, in situations of collective uprooting, surveillance, alienation, exclusion, violence. This is achieved by inscribing the
racial marking of bodies of color and their labor power in the unevenly syn-
chronized but universalizing narratives of the growth, consolidation, and
expansion of U.S. capital in the continent and around the world (Applebaum
1996; Ong, Bonacich, and Cheng 1994).

Taking into account the altered character of working-class struggles made
more complicated by ethnic, gender, regional, and other contingencies, neo-
Marxists have now formulated a new approach that focuses on the flexible,
more genuinely dialectical articulation of "superstructures" and "base," of various modes of production that constitute a given social formation. Ethnicity is
factored into class in a social totality "structured in dominance." Influenced by
Gramsci and Althusser, Stuart Hall and his followers—formerly centered around
the Center for Contemporary Cultural Studies, University of Birmingham—
reconstruct the Marxist problematic by allowing ethnicity and "race" to exert a
relatively autonomous impact on class consciousness and class antagonisms in
historically specific situations. What is important is to analyze the concrete
articulation among race, ethnicity, and class in specific historical conjunctures
and geopolitical formations.

Within a milieu characterized by authoritarian statism and popular racism
in Britain, Hall argues that the regime of late capitalism structures the labor
force through differentiation by ethnic, gender, and national characteristics
(1986, 24). Since identity is socially and discursively constructed, Hall sees a
renewed contestation over the term "ethnicity" in the politics of representation. Ethnicity has been used before to disavow racist repression, but the term
needs to be dissociated by people of color from the liberal discourse of "multiculturalism" and transcoded into the over-determined field of sociopolitical
differences: "The term ethnicity acknowledges the place of history, language
and culture in the construction of subjectivity and identity, as well as the fact
that all discourse is placed, positioned, and situated and all knowledge is contextual" (1992, 257). Hall envisages the "return of ethnicity" as diasporic communities in Europe and elsewhere question the hegemonic nationalisms of the
old nation-states and in the process generate syncretic identities out of diverse
ethnic properties. Ethnicity is thus reconceptualized as relatively autonomous
within the overarching process of multiform struggles involving sexuality, gender, nationality, and so on in class-determinate specific formations.

The postmodern tendency toward space-time compression (Harvey 1989)
has led some observers to postulate the ongoing globalized homogenization of
cultures, even as aspects of ethnicity/otherness become consumer objects for
an international market. Because of unequal relations of power between the
West (including Japan) and "the Rest," globalization remains basically the

export of Western commodities, priorities, and values. At best an uneven process, globalization allows for a new articulation between the "global" (Western capitalist domination) and the "local," now subject to relativization. Ethnic and racial markers become "floating signifiers" with meanings dependent on who articulates them, for what purpose, under what circumstances of production and reception, in what place and at what time.

Although the term "multiculturalism" has been used by liberals to describe the coexistence of diverse cultures, it is best for analytical purposes to evaluate the politics implied by this terminology. Claude Meillassoux, for example, has proposed the term "social corps" to incorporate nonclass features into "bodies serving the social classes" (1993, 3). When previously closed, unified national cultures come under the influence of globalization and the migrant influx, there are two major effects: first, there is a rise of ethnic absolutism and a turn to the homogenizing concept of "tradition" in nationalist, local-centered movements among the majority (Solomos and Back 1996); and, second, there is a strategic return to a defensive ethnic identity among minority communities. Creative alternatives also exist. Within the category "black," for example, Afro-Caribbeans and Asians in the United Kingdom construct a coalitional political identity at the conjuncture of other cultural and social differences. Ethnicity, in this case, becomes an articulation of identity and difference, a problem of translation and negotiated self-interpretation, within milieus exposed to the transformative pressures of diversity and otherness brought about by the profound global crises of late "transnational" capitalism.

Now liberals have proposed that we need multicultural education to solve the contemporary crisis, one that would get rid of the basis of institutional racism and any form of "ethnic cleansing" such as the lynching and murder of targeted populations. Everyone knows that the movement to revise the Eurocentric canon and curriculum in order to allow the teaching/learning of our society's cultural and racial diversity has been going on since the introduction of "Third World" and Ethnic Studies in the sixties. But one may ask: Has the formula of adding and subtracting texts, or even deconstructing the canonical discourses and hegemonic practices, really succeeded in eliminating chauvinist stereotypes and covert discrimination, not to speak of institutional racism and genocidal policies? Do we really need a pedagogical strategy of commodifying cultural goods and knowledges that consorts well with de facto apartheid in cities such as Los Angeles, Atlanta, Detroit, Chicago, Miami, and others?

Like the nativists of old, present-day advocates of immigration reform and assorted neoconservatives contend that multiculturalism is precisely the problem. They believe that the "large influx of third-world people . . . could be potentially disruptive of our whole Judeo-Christian heritage." Multiculturalism even of the liberal variety is considered politically correct terrorism. It allegedly undermines high academic standards. Above all, like feminisms, multiculturalism and its agents, Ethnic Studies scholars, are suspected of threatening Western civilization and its legacy of free enterprise, rationality, free speech, and so on.

The guardians of the "homeland" now suspect cultural pluralism as a danger to national security. They are prescribing a return to the ideal of assimilation or integration couched in terms of civic duty, a citizen cosmopolitanism, a refurbished "melting pot" notion that would by some magical gesture of wishfulfillment abolish exploitation, gender and racial inequality, and injustice. The renewed call by patriotic fundamentalists to rally behind the flag—a nationalism coded in terms of fighting for freedom, democracy, human rights, and so on—is presented as a substitute for the comfort of ethnic belonging. Whatever its merits, I think this can only restore the paranoia of alienation and the scapegoating of the last half century. It is also problematic to claim simply that we all benefit or suffer equally unless we see the mutual dependence of victimizer and victimized—the proverbial moralizing, cosmopolitan nostrum of tolerance and love for one another pronounced at the conclusion of this weekend's sermon.

Multiculturalism and Globalization

Given this background of systemic contradictions, the production of knowledge in Ethnic Studies reflects the tensions of colliding lines of sociopolitical forces in national and world history. It is not a scandalous gesture to observe that the contentious and contestatory situation of the field—to echo my initial assertion—mirrors the systemic contradictions of globalized, late capitalism headquartered in the metropolitan centers of North America, Japan, and Europe. Now with the increase of postmodernist and ludic academics, together with the flourishing of the postcolonialist industry, Ethnic Studies has acquired a new orientation more adapted to the imperatives of globalization. The university itself has become a conduit if not an apparatus for transnational business schemes such as the emphasis on "brand" marketing, distance learning, and other flexible transactions lauded as cosmopolitan humanism and transcultural excellence.

Globalization is, simply put, the "formalization of neoliberal ideology" (Lazarus 1998–1999, 95). It is the triumphalist rhetoric of the centralized free market, privatization, deregulation, a return to an administered technocratic Taylorism. Of course, it's not just rhetoric but actual practices that generate concrete, substantive effects. This is not the occasion to delve deeper into this challenging field of research. Suffice it to ask: What are its implications for our work?

Let me take first the issue of official multiculturalism as the new rationale for the renewed interest in ethnic, as well as gender and sexual, differences from a globalizing perspective. Slavoj Zizek (1997), the Slovenian philosopher, calls multiculturalism "the cultural logic of multinational capitalism." Like any cultural turn, this has elicited its antithesis in the form of what is called "the new racism," in which cultural differences become reified, fixed, immutable (Hoogvelt 1997). In spite of this multiculturalist syndrome, William Greider and others refer to a "prefascist situation" here and in Europe where populist, demagogic politics exacerbates ethnic suspicions and hostilities (Martin and Schumann 1997). Others have referred to this way of conceiving Ethnic Studies as "a peaceful management of differences," a way of doing identity politics without tears (San Juan 1998)—so long as "difference" and civil-society identity function as covers for foundational inequality. Has the vogue of identity politics ever questioned private property or the surplus value created by unpaid labor?

The politics of difference within the globalized political economy complicates the analysis of ethnic processes. In the light of the historical conflicts surrounding the emergence of Ethnic Studies, Ramon Gutierrez emphasizes certain "methodological principles" of the field derived from the intensive study of the histories, languages, and cultures of America's racial and ethnic groups in and among themselves. Aside from the situated and partial nature of all knowledge claims, Gutierrez assumes a postmodernist stance in upholding the principle that "culture was not a unified system of shared meanings, but a system of multivocal symbols, the meanings of which were frequently contested, becoming a complex product of competition and negotiation between various social groups" (1994, 163). Although I would agree that the focus of our discipline is comparative and relational—we explore commonalities and divergences in the experiences of racial and ethnic groups domestically and worldwide—this does not imply a thoroughgoing relativism or nominalism that would reduce history to a matter of equally suspect points of view or subject positions. Such would be the ethnicist "insider's" approach. In analyzing the historical dynamics of race in the United States situated in global and comparative grids, we are precisely grounding interpretations and judgments based on a consensus of historians that is open to falsifiability. Otherwise, the "culture wars" based on identity politics would rule out not only dialogue but also all rational communicative action.

Gutierrez extols the University of California (San Diego)'s program in its replacement of the vertical model of single ethnic-based programs with "a horizontal model that focused on common trends and experiences among social groups," that is, a comparative culture approach. Boundaries of disciplines supposedly erode when processes of ethnogenesis, the construction of borderland identities, and hybridization are examined, as Johnella Butler (1991) earlier surmised. But frankly I haven't witnessed this change. It may be a chimerical ideal to pacify subalterns.

Now, can the refinement of Ethnic Studies as comparative cultural studies, including research into diasporas, immigration, transcultural or border-crossing phenomena, insure us against cooptation? Can a repackaging of Ethnic Studies as transcultural or transmigrant studies do the trick of producing knowledge useful for an oppositional, not to say emancipatory, project true to its original plebeian grassroots inspiration? Do we abandon these narratives and make do with local stories and pragmatic opportunist tactics espoused by De Certeau and Lyotard? The sacred doctrine of "American exceptionalism" is supposedly challenged, but American Studies internationalized simply resuscitates the canonical texts, this time read in the ludic postmodernist and postcolonial way. Addition of the excluded others in the canon without structural change does not alter the hegemony of "possessive whiteness," just as the multiplication of difference—"recognition politics," as Nancy Fraser (1997) formulates it—does not translate into achieved equality or fairness in the redistribution of social wealth.

A replay of the culture wars, focusing on issues of American exceptionalism and identity politics, occurred recently in the *Chronicle of Higher Education*. Sean Wilentz (1996), professor of history at Princeton University, bewailed the celebration of fragmentation and difference ascribed to provincial scholars in ethnic studies. He called for their incorporation into orthodox American Studies with a cosmopolitan dressing. Wilentz celebrates in turn American culture's "cosmopolitan roots and global impact." American Studies will concentrate not just on a multicultural society but on "multicultural individuals" integrated together in a new all-encompassing commonality. Cosmopolitan individualism supplements multiculturalism to glamorize the way things are and vindicate American ascendancy—to which some Ethnic Studies stalwarts, among them Jesse Vasquez and Otis Scott, responded by denouncing Wilentz's imperial and elitist presumptuousness.

Remappping Transitions

Clearly, we need to reassess the fundamentals of our intellectual project. Manning Marable (2000) summed up the case for a renewal if not revitalization of the field by calling attention to the way international power relations have reconfigured racialized ethnicities in the light of capital's attempt to shore up declining profit margins. Marable appropriately reviews the separate genealogies of the categories of "race" and "ethnicity" against the background of the political economy of the United States from the period of slavery to the epoch of immigration in the nineteenth and twentieth centuries. Marable rehearses the debate between Ronald Takaki, now ranked among the multiculturalists who champion the cause of racialized ethnicities, and Nathan Glazer, who (together with Daniel Patrick Moynihan) represents the "cultural universalists," a rubric that I think does not capture their drive for reimposing a diehard white-supremacist world outlook.

Exponents of the latter view, from Wilentz to Werner Sollors and postethnics like Richard Rorty and David Hollinger, have shifted the discourse of racism and inequality to the matter of citizenship and the politics of recognition (see Perea 1998). Ultimately, Marable believes that the ordeal of the practitioners of "Ethnic Studies" pivots around negotiating the binary opposites or "twin problems," in his words, of "cultural amalgamation" and "racial essentialism" (also known as cultural nationalism). Lost in this dualistic schematization is the dialectics of the global and local, of the logic and rhetoric of the relationship between power and knowledge, as delineated by Stuart Hall (1992), Arif Dirlik (2000), Arnold Krupat (1996), and others.

Whatever the vicissitudes of his problematization of the field, Marable has sharply diagnosed the urgency of revaluation, of synchronizing theory and practice. He feels that we, experts in the critical study of racialized ethnicities, should gear up to meet the challenge of analyzing the new globalized reality of capital: that it is mobilizing racial and ethnic categories for its aggrandizement. The color line has assumed a metamorphosis—the understanding of which requires a recasting of speculative, analytic instruments: "A new racial formation is evolving rapidly in the United States, with a new configuration of racialized ethnicity, class, and gender stratification and divisions. . . . Traditional white racism . . . is being [replaced] by a qualitatively new color line of spiraling class inequality and extreme income stratifications, mediated or filtered through old discourses and cultural patterns more closely coded by physical appearance, legal and racial classification, and language" (Marable 2000, B7). Hence we need to revise and renew the critical thrust of our evolving discipline if we want to confront such realities in the United States—not to mention such facts of the political economy of globalization as, for example, the horrendous exploitation of seven million Filipino migrant workers (most of whom are female domestics) in the Middle East, Europe, Asia, and North America (Aguilar 2000).

Aside from the multiple diasporas occurring around the planet, the intensity of ethnic and racialized conflicts after the end of the Cold War has signaled the onset of a new stage of the historical "long period" we are living in. Works like Evelyn Hu-DeHart's *Across the Pacific: Asian Americans and Globalization* (1999), Hans-Peter Martin and Harald Schumann's *The Global Trap* (1997), Mike Featherstone's *Global Culture* (1990), David Harvey's *Spaces of Hope* (2000), and others have decentered the influential paradigm of a flexible "racial order" that proponents of a postmodernist racial-formation theory believe still prevails. Racialization has assumed new forms and functions in a technologically mediated accumulation process. A world-systems analysis needs to be supplemented by what Peter Gran (1993) calls a Gramscian analytic of hegemony, in which race and racism operates as a crucial variable. The analysis combines culturalist and political-economic approaches to ascertain the new logistics of racism in late capitalism.

We still inhabit a regime of intense commodification, not a postcapitalist or postliberal ecosystem. What has happened is, I think, a profound, radical disaggregation of the nation-state system and reconstitution of world hegemony; these trends have encouraged the postmodernist assertion that the Enlightenment metanarrative, among others, has come to an end. Race and ethnicity have thus to be reconceived in the light of a universal "dereferentialization" and the collapse of the old capitalist logic—which argues for a return to applying the methods of Marx and Lenin to the new flexible, cyborg-like, even performative imperialism.

A response to the postmodernist argument may clarify my position here. In his brief for inventing a new community of dissensus and singularities in the wake of the end of the nation-state and its ideals of autonomy and of citizenship, Bill Readings contends in his book, *The University in Ruins* (1996), that we should abandon the old notions of identity, consensus, and so on. Although I disagree with his premature thesis of the end of the nation-state and with the instrumental cult of Otherness, Thought (with a capital T), and singularities, Readings can provoke and perhaps infuriate those not already convinced. His thesis presupposes a historicist reading of structural mutations:

> It is the desire for subjective autonomy that has led North Americans, for example, to want to forget their obligations to the acts of genocide on which their society is founded, to ignore debts to Native American and other peoples that contemporary individuals did not personally contract, but for which I would nonetheless argue they are *responsible* (and not only insofar as they benefit indirectly from the historical legacy of those acts). In short, the social bond is not the property of an autonomous subject, since it exceeds subjective consciousness and even individual histories of action. The nature of my obligations to the history of the place in which I live, and my exact positioning in relation to that history, are not things I can decide upon or things that can be calculated exhaustively. No tax of "x percent" on the incomes of white Americans could ever, for example, make full reparation for the history of racism in the United States (how much is a lynching "worth"?) Nor would it put an end to the guilt of racism by acknowledging it, or even solve the question of what exactly constitutes "whiteness." (1996, 186)

Despite his adherence to a ludic posteriority—posthistorical, postcultural, postnational—and a neopragmatism that refuses alibis, Readings can only offer a hope that by thinking together within the ruins of the university academics may construct the community of singularities, the ersatz utopia, that will be the only alternative. How that goal can be achieved by a gestural negation of the capitalist logic of accounting and exchangeability that legitimizes the university as a transnational corporate machine in our era remains to be seen. Despite gestures of resistance, the task of revolutionary transformation is shirked; academic quietism and resignation supervene.

From Alterity to Alternatives

Meanwhile, we toil in the shadow of the university's ruins, far from the aura of Plato's cave or the Socratic forum. Former fellow-travelers have resigned themselves to "cultivating their garden," acquiescing to the still pervasive hold of utilitarian individualism, the neoliberal ideology of the market, that justifies the operations of the World Bank, IMF, and the WTO. Education in the United States remains racialized in open and covert ways (Bonacich 2000). And formerly oppositional educators like Henry Louis Gates Jr., it seems, have made their peace with the Establishment. Gates believes that we cannot escape the complicity of self and other, the antinomies of center and periphery "where the center constructs the margin as a privileged locale, [where] you assume authority by representing yourself as marginal, and, conversely, you discredit others by representing them as central" (1992, 298). The threat to alterity is not assimilation or dissolution, Gates pontificates, but its preservation by the center, homogenizing the other as simply other. Hence literary culture proves its worth once again in its ideological service to the nation-state (Shumway 1994) which, in this post-Kosovo period, has experienced a fitful revival despite claims that it is not ethnic but civic nationalism of republican vintage that we find in the United States. In the current crisis, the settler mentality revives the circle of wagons to prevent ethnic intruders and internal aliens from destabilizing the polity.

Well before the end of the millennium of *pax Americana*, we are asked to resurrect a convivial or consensual society committed to egalitarian principles. With the end of ideology and of history as well, the system in crisis does not need to establish its legitimacy. There is no alternative—TINA, to cite an old Thatcherism. Culturalism sanctions the apparent equality of cultures, of relativism and nominalism premised on a hierarchical division of social labor. But contradictions persist, as well as manifestations of good old "institutional racism." Samir Amin observes that with the triumph of the "free market," "this neoliberal utopianism [of global capital] . . . is forced to cohabit with its opposite: ethnic communalism, the spread of irrationality, religious cultism, the rising tide of violence, and all sorts of fanaticism (1998, 119). Within the corporatized academy, the cry for accountability reverberates. Richard Ohmann (2000) considers this imperative of accountability—that is, accountability to the elite, not to the disempowered citizenry—the project of the right with two aims: to contain social movements that date back to the sixties, and for global capital to recompose itself internationally. A kind of burlesque parody of the corporatized university may be found in the acts of the intelligentsia who compete to update Gunnar Myrdal's schizoid metaphors and perform as gadfly publicists funded by corporate money in order to urge the humanities to "restore the public rigor of the metanarratives" (Miyoshi 2000, 49).

Are the fields of pedagogy and Ethnic Studies the new frontier to be conquered? It would be useful to conduct a massive assault on the academic bureaucracy responsible for the commodification of education, but this would be ill-conceived. It would be a mistake of taking the part for the whole. Although embedded in concrete institutions and agencies, market forces are systemic and structural, enabling individual and collective agencies to exercise their instrumentalities everywhere. The indicator of commodification here is the theory and practice of multiculturalism. What can a department or program of Ethnic Studies offer as a means of resistance when it has become transformed into an instrument to camouflage, if not directly advance, the interest of universal commodification?

Permit me to hazard some proposals. One strategy is frontal assault by polemic and mass mobilization of students and faculty to expose institutional racism. Knowledge about class conflict and the political economy of culture can be translated into practice by a critique of education and of the university as agencies of the ideological state apparatus. Reciprocally, these extra-class activities (with community and neighborhood participation) can invigorate classroom discussions and inquiry, testing hypotheses, theories, and so on. The other mode of integrating ethnic studies pedagogy and social practice can supplement the first. It involves the Gramscian "war of position" favored by "armchair guerillas" who are engaged in critique of ideology, deconstruction of discursive racism, and counterhegemonic programs to dissolve boundaries and other sociopolitical constructs.

Culture in its various guises (performance, popular practices, transmigrancies, family rituals) thus becomes the key topic if not the site of ideological and political battles. If culture is a relational site of group antagonisms—culture is what enables the thought of the Other in the form of belief, of stereotypes, and so on—then the ideal object of inquiry is cultural production and practice. (Here the works of Pierre Bourdieu, Jean-Paul Sartre, Erving Goffman [1963], and others, as well as George M. Fredrickson's [1997] comparative histories of racism are extremely relevant.) Our field would then engage the study of group relations and the dichotomous processes they enact, processes that symbolically replay versions of Gramscian hegemony and historic blocs. Ethnic struggles can be clarified by the investigation of class formation and the political economy of cultural process and habitus. Students might be encouraged to engage in internships and actual investigations of community problems so as to critique state policies, corporate operations, and other institutional agencies that affect the everyday lives of people of color. This will reorient Ethnic Studies curricula, often designed to perform morale boosting for students of color, toward a more interventionist direction while maintaining a rigorous scholastic research program. Without such "reality checks," Ethnic Studies would reconfirm the suspicion that it is simply a site for careerists willing to apologize for the racial polity, or a cheap scheme to foist on naive taxpayers the illusion of genuinely representing its ethnically heterogeneous clientele.

At this point, we might pause to see if we can learn something from Fredric Jameson's project of recasting the agenda of Cultural Studies as an inquiry into the dialectics of class and group-in-action:

> whatever group or identity investment may be at work in envy, its libidinal opposite always tends to transcend the dynamics of the group relationship in the direction of that of class proper. . . . In general, ethnic conflict cannot be solved or resolved; it can only be sublimated into a struggle of a different kind that *can* be resolved. Class struggle, which has as its aim and outcome not the triumph of one class over another but the abolition of the very category of class, offers the prototype of one such sublimation. . . . "American democracy" has seemed able to preempt class dynamics and to offer a unique solution to the matter of group dynamics. . . . We therefore need to take into account the possibility that the various politics of difference—the differences inherent in the various politics of "group identity"—have been made possible only by the tendential leveling of social identity generated by consumer society; and to entertain the hypothesis that a cultural politics of difference becomes feasible only when the great and forbidding categories of classical Otherness have been substantially weakened by "modernization" (so that current neoethnicities may be distinct from the classical kind as neoracism is from classical racism). (1995, 275–76)

What Jameson's insight into the submerged problematic of Cultural Studies suggests is a need to reorient the field of ethnic studies, first, within the parameters of the hitherto proscribed matter of social totalities—the dreaded "totality" exorcized by Lyotard cannot be evaded—and second, more important, within the arena of antagonisms of all kinds (not just the Weberian conflict of tradition and rationality) underpinned by class relations of production and social reproduction in history. This will also put in center stage the issues of "internal colonialism" and neocolonialism underlying contemporary diasporas, putative transmigrations, and other enigmatic but ubiquitous phenomena in the international division of labor.

Toward an Inventory

Lest my argument be misconstrued, I am not advocating the outright abolition of ethnic studies as a discipline, for how can one abolish by fiat the sociohistorical conditions that enable its persistence? Rather, I am proposing a new function for its cadre of teachers-scholars to enhance its efficacy as a social agent of change within and outside the university. Meanwhile, one can ask: Has progress in refining the theory and practice of Ethnic Studies been achieved?

No doubt more people are aware, even appreciative, of cultural differences. But this new knowledge or information merely functions as an addition to the conventional furniture of suburban lifestyle. It does not alter the political and economic structures of the status quo. Although I generally agree with the historical and structural approach of a reconstructed Ethnic Studies—an inquiry into the dynamics of race and ethnicity in global and comparative contexts, including the dynamics of diaspora and immigration—I am skeptical whether this new retooling can give a pedagogically sharper analysis and more socially effective critique of racism, ethnic conflict, nationalism in its various modalities, and exploitation in its late-capitalist disguise. Given the absorption of innovative schemes by a market-oriented logic of equivalence, no amount of multidisciplinary analysis and border crossing, I am afraid, can grasp the material processes that condition our epistemological apparatus, our frames of intelligibility, and especially the nature of the contradictions inherent in the racial polity. Unless we factor in the dialectic of social institutions and collective agencies that constitute the history of social formations within the world system of accumulation, and especially the need to transform the totality for the sake of saving lives and our environment, Ethnic Studies will continue to be a futile academic exercise. However, I am hopeful that the post-Battle of Seattle generation will cultivate a fresh revolutionary sensibility that will not fear the prospect of radical transformations of our communities and regenerative, even utopian, visions of the future.

After more than ten years in Ethnic Studies and comparative literature departments, and three years as chair of a Comparative American Cultures Department, what have I learned? (An autobiographical note: For over twenty years I was a professor of English and American literature engaged in traditional formalist aesthetic criticism. In the early 1990s, when I joined the Department of Ethnic Studies at Bowling Green State University, my work shifted gradually from comparative literary inquiries to "Third World" cultural and ethnic studies, culminating in my 1992 book *Racial Formations/Critical Transformations*.) Nothing earth-shaking. One thing, perhaps: that people of color can victimize themselves by the successful exploitation of liberal guilt, and by various compensatory rituals of self-affirmation. If we want to avoid being tokenized,

exoticized, or used to sell multicultural commodities and legitimize the ideological rationale of the university—and by extension the neoliberal state—we
need to begin a critique of institutions (among them the university) in their
historical matrix and trajectory. We need to abandon again the methodological
individualism of our distinct ethnicities and forge alliances against what is proclaimed to be the objective necessity of the privatized market, the forces of
deregulated Taylorism and of a populist/elitist brand of Social Darwinism. We
need solidarities and coalitions that will release humanity's and also nature's
potential for overcoming the wreckage and destructive havoc inflicted by capital
since Columbus started the genocide of indigenous peoples; their contemporary
struggles for land and sovereignty measure our advance toward planetary, ecosys-
temic emancipation.

Clearly we need to distance ourselves from complicity in neoliberal
schemes of recuperation either by reforming citizenship standards or by
indulging in an antistatist, anarchist culturalism. Pretending to resist assimilation, some of our colleagues have succumbed to enchanting varieties of philosophical idealism. Even a cursory study of T. H. Marshall (1950) on the paradox
of democratic citizenship premised on class inequality could have saved us all
those vacuous texts on citizenship within the U.S. nation-state, immigrant acts
of representation, consent, "double consciousness," and so on, that litter the
archives of Asian American scholarship. In truth, the mutual recognition of
rights to property and the formal equality of individual citizens (already adum-
brated by Marx in "On the Jewish Question") are the key precondition for economic exploitation regulated and supervised by the liberal-democratic state
(Jessop 1982). In short, representative democracy thrives precisely on the spoils
of wage slavery.

It is therefore imperative that we attend to the political economy of differences inscribed in the material histories of interlocked groups, classes, and sectors within a global arena of conflicting political forces. I would propose that
instead of accentuating cultural difference and its potential for *bantustans*, turf
wars, liberal apartheid, and—even worse—"ethnic cleansing" in practice and
discourse (a cliché that has portentous resonance for the field), we need to
attend to the problem of power. This would include the knowledge it produces
and that legitimates it, the uses of such knowledge in disciplinary regimes, and
its mutations in history. We need to examine not only the diverse cultures of
ethnic groups vis-à-vis the dominant society, the solidarities and conflicts
among them, but also more fundamental problems: how ethnicity itself is
linked to and reproduces the market-centered competitive society we live in;
and how ethnic particularisms or selected cultural differences are mobilized
not only to hide systemic contradictions but also to defuse the challenges and
resistances integral to them. As Stephen Steinberg argues, no amount of glori-
fying ethnic myths and other cultural symbols of identity can hide or downplay

the inequality of wealth, power, and privilege in our society that underpins the production of knowledge and the claims to objectivity and transcendent universalisms (Steinberg 1981). Such an insight into foundations should not be taken as dogma but simply as a heuristic guide to counter the formalist essentializing of identities or utopianization of ethnicity. We cannot theorize the uneven terrain of contestation without conceptualizing the totality of trends and tendencies. Privileging neither the global nor the local, our approach should be dialectical and praxis-oriented so as to take up the inaugural promise of ethnic studies: to open up a critical space for enunciation by those who have been silenced—Paolo Freire's speechless subalterns, or Frantz Fanon's *Les Damnés de la Terre*—within the horizon of a vision of a just society accountable to all. The question is: Can we imagine a different and better future for all?

Such a consensus on common purpose should not foreclose disagreements or differences. What it safeguards in this period of nihilism or pragmatic relativism is the temptation to indulge in playful self-irony, infinite ambiguity, or fluid polyvocality with the pretense that this is the most revolutionary stance against reaction and all forms of determinisms. In this time of chauvinist and persecutory backlash, when the politicizing of citizens has been unleashed by the really "politically correct" officials and corporate philosophers, it is incumbent on us not to forsake the "grand narratives" even while appreciating the local and familiar. We need to recognize the dialectics of apartheid racism and cosmopolitan consumerism, of local ethnocentrism and global charity. We need to grasp the fact "that glorification of local systems of knowledge which are rooted in racial, religious, and ethnic distinctions, [is] fundamentally tied to the globalization, commodification, and massification of social life" (Gutierrez 1994, 165).

We need to investigate above all the reality of racism and the accompanying racial politics embedded in the everyday practices of business society, the interaction of racial ideologies with other categories (such as gender, sexuality, locality, nationality, and so on) in order to cross the boundary between academic theory and practice in the real world. Unless we simply want to be used to manage peacefully the crisis of differences among the "natives" and reinforce the status quo ethos of liberal tolerance, "business as usual," then the practitioners of Ethnic Studies need to be self-critical of received ideas and be not just adversarial but also oppositional, in accord with the field's revolutionary beginnings, performing the role of, in James Baldwin's words, unrelenting "disturbers of the peace" (Baldwin 1988, 11).

Finally I want to say something outrageous, not a proposal but a thought-experiment. We may need to phase out eventually, or sublate into some other form, the Ethnic Studies program and relocate the focus of our energies elsewhere, in teach-ins outside and inside the university, in various organizing movements in diverse neighborhoods and in constituencies abroad. We then ought to disperse our faculties to the traditional departments that meanwhile have become entrenched bastions of "white supremacy," given the fact that Ethnic Studies has become the monopolistic agency of cultural diversification. And we may need to intervene directly in the "culture wars," in the controversies over the revamping of Cultural Studies and the reconfiguration of American Studies here and internationally. At any rate, I foresee Ethnic Studies as submitting to the unrelenting labor of the negative, settling accounts with the aborted promise of the civil rights struggles of the sixties, and launching forth into areas once the preserve of scholastic, quarantined regimes of reaction and neofascist repression.

Otherwise, the alternative is paralysis, desuetude, and impotence. We might resemble the three dead Chinese recently found inside a cargo container aboard a ship from Hong Kong by Seattle immigration officials (Zalin 2000, 4). Eighteen other immigrants survived the three-week ocean journey inside a forty-foot-long container, twelve feet high and ten feet wide, customarily used for shipping electronic goods. There is a cautionary parable inscribed here. Do we need to redesign our academic Trojan horse to insinuate the tidings we carry, delivering our messages from the "belly of the beast" into the Empire's heartland? Or do we need to invent new weapons that will harness the energies of the world proletariat, of women and indigenous peoples, and all the pariahs and outcasts of the earth, in order to overcome the Leviathan of capital whose most seductive and impregnable masquerade is white supremacy, "the possessive investment of whiteness," the Moby Dick of Euro-American racism that has haunted the prehistory of the world as have known it so far? May the prophecy of Black Elk be reversed, if not altogether redeemed, in our common struggle for a better life for all.

REFERENCES

Aguilar, Delia D. 2000. *Globalization, labor and women.* Bowling Green, Ohio: Department of Ethnic Studies, Bowling Green State University.

Amin, Samir. 1998. *Spectres of capitalism: A critique of current intellectual fashions.* New York: Monthly Review Press.

Appelbaum, Richard P. 1996. "Multiculturalism and flexibility: Some new directions in global capitalism." In *Mapping multiculturalism*, edited by A. Gordon and C. Newfield, 297–316. Minneapolis: University of Minnesota Press.

Baldwin, James. 1988. "A talk to teachers." In *The Graywolf annual five: multicultural literacy*, edited by R. Simonson and S. Walker, 3–12. St. Paul, Minn.: Graywolf Press.

Banks, James A. 1991. *Teaching strategies for ethnic studies.* Boston: Allyn and Bacon.

Bennis, Phyllis, and Michel Moushabeck. 1993. *Altered states: A reader in the new world order.* New York: Olive Branch Press.

Black Elk and John Gneisenau Neihardt. 1972. *Black Elk speaks: Being the life story of a holy man of the Oglala Sioux.* New York: Pocket Books.

Bonacich, Edna. 2000. "Racism in the deep structure of U.S. higher education: When affirmitive action is not enough." In *Structured inequality in the United States*, edited by A. Aguirre and D. Baker. Upper Saddle River, N.J.: Prentice Hall.

Butler, Johnella. 1991. "Ethnic studies: A matrix model for the major." *Liberal Education* 77(2): 26–32.

Davis, Angela. 1996. "Gender, class, and multiculturalism: Rethinking 'race' politics." In *Mapping multiculturalism*, edited by A. Gordon and C. Newfield, 40–48. Minneapolis: University of Minnesota Press.

Dirlik, Arif. 2000. *Postmodernity's histories: The past as legacy and project.* Lanham, Md.: Rowman and Littlefield.

Featherstone, Mike. 1990. *Global culture: Nationalism, globalization, and modernity.* London: Sage.

Featherstone, Mike, Scott Lash, and Roland Robertson. 1995. *Global modernities.* London: Sage.

Fraser, Nancy. 1997. *Justice interruptus: Critical reflections on the "postsocialist" condition.* New York: Routledge.

Fredrickson, George M. 1997. *The comparative imagination: On the history of racism, nationalism, and social movements.* Berkeley: University of California Press.

Gates Jr., Henry Louis. 1992. "Ethnic and Minority Studies." In *Introduction to scholarship in modern languages and literatures*, edited by J. Gibaldi, 288–302. New York: Modern Language Association of America.

Goffman, Erving. 1963. *Stigma: Notes on the management of spoiled identity.* Englewood Cliffs, N.J.: Prentice-Hall.

Gran, Peter. 1993. "Race and racism in the modern world: How it works in different hegemonies." *Transforming Anthropology* 5(1 and 2): 8–14.

Gutierrez, Ramon. 1994. "Ethnic studies: Its evolution in American colleges and universities." In *Multiculturalism: A critical reader*, edited by D. Goldberg, 157–167. Cambridge, Mass.: Blackwell.

Hall, Stuart. 1986. "Gramsci's relevance for the study of race and ethnicity." *Journal of Communication Inquiry* 10(2): 5–27.

———. 1992. "New Ethnicities." In *Race, culture and difference*, edited by J. Donald and A. Rattansi, 260–270. London: Sage.

Harvey, David. 1989. *The condition of postmodernity: An enquiry into the origins of cultural change.* Oxford: Blackwell.

———. 2000. *Spaces of hope.* Berkeley: University of California Press.

Hoogvelt, Ankie M. M. 1997. *Globalisation and the postcolonial world: The new political economy of development.* Basingstoke: Macmillan.

Hu-DeHart, Evelyn. 1995. "The undermining of Ethnic Studies." *Chronicle of Higher Education*, October 20.

———. 1999. "Introduction." In *Across the Pacific: Asian Americans and globalization*, edited by E. Hu-DeHart, 1–29. New York: Asia Society.

Jameson, Fredric. 1995. "On cultural studies." In *The identity in question*, edited by E. Rajchman. New York: Routledge.

Jessop, Bob. 1982. *The capitalist state: Marxist theories and methods.* New York: New York University Press.

Krupat, Arnold. 1996. *The turn to the native: Studies in criticism and culture.* Lincoln: University of Nebraska Press.

Lazarus, Neil. 1998–1999. "Charting globalization." *Race and Class* 40: 91–110.

Lipsitz, George. 1998. *The possessive investment in whiteness: How white people profit from identity politics.* Philadelphia: Temple University Press.

Marable, Manning. 2000. "We need new and critical study of race and ethnicity." *Chronicle of Higher Education*, February 25.

Marshall, T. H. 1950. *Citizenship and social class and other essays*. Cambridge: Cambridge University Press.

Martin, Hans-Peter, and Harald Schumann. 1997. *The global trap: Globalization and the assault on prosperity and democracy*. New York: Zed Books.

Marx, Karl. 1968 (1843). "On the Jewish question." In *Marxist social thought*, edited by R. Freedman. New York: Harcourt, Brace, and World.

———. 1970 (1843). *Critique of Hegel's "philosophy of right."* Translated by Joseph O'Malley. Cambridge: Cambridge University Press.

Meillassoux, Claude. 1993. "Toward a theory of the 'social corps.'" In *The curtain rises: Rethinking culture, ideology, and the state in Eastern Europe*, edited by H. De Soto and D. Anderson. Atlantic Highlands, N.J.: Humanities Press.

Miyoshi, Masao. 2000. "Ivory tower in escrow." *boundary 2* 27(1): 7–50.

Nash, Phil Tajitsu. 2001. "WSU, San Juan, and the future of Ethnic Studies." *Asianweek*, 4.

Ohmann, Richard. 2000. "Historical reflections on accountability." *Academe* 24–29.

Ong, Paul M., Edna Bonacich, and Lucie Cheng. 1994. *The new Asian immigration in Los Angeles and global restructuring*. Philadelphia: Temple University Press.

Perea, Juan. 1998. "Am I an American or not? Reflections on citizenship, Americanization, and race." In *Immigration and citizenship in the twenty-first century*, edited by N.M.J. Pickus, 49–76. Lanham, Md.: Rowman and Littlefield.

Readings, Bill. 1996. *The university in ruins*. Cambridge: Harvard University Press.

San Juan, E. 1992. *Racial formations/critical transformations: Articulations of power in ethnic and racial studies in the United States*. Atlantic Highlands, N.J.: Humanities Press.

———. 1995. *Hegemony and strategies of transgression: Essays in cultural studies and comparative literature*. Albany: State University of New York Press.

———. 1998. *Beyond postcolonial theory*. New York: St. Martin's.

Sassen, Saskia. 1998. *Globalization and its discontents*. New York: New Press.

Shumway, David R. 1994. *Creating American civilization: A genealogy of American literature as an academic discipline*. Minneapolis: University of Minnesota Press.

Solomos, John, and Les Back. 1996. *Racism and society*. New York: St. Martin's.

Steinberg, Stephen. 1981. *The ethnic myth: Race, ethnicity, and class in America*. New York: Atheneum.

———. 1995. *Turning back: The retreat from racial justice in American thought and policy*. Boston: Beacon.

Walzer, Michael. 2000. "What does it mean to be an American?" In *Race and ethnicity in the United States*, edited by S. Steinberg, 186–196. Malden, Mass.: Blackwell.

Wilentz, Sean. 1996. "Integrating ethnicity into American Studies." *Chronicle of Higher Education*, November 29.

Zalin, Larry. 2000. "Three illegal immigrations found dead in cargo container at port." *Daily Evergreen* (Pullman, Washington).

Zizek, Slavoj. 1997. "Multiculturalism, or, the cultural logic of multinational capitalism." *New Left Review* 225(September–October): 40–47.

CONTRIBUTORS

NANCY ABELMANN is an associate professor in the Department of Anthropology and East Asian Languages and Cultures, and Asian American Studies program at the University of Illinois at Urbana-Champaign. She has published on social movements in contemporary South Korea, *Echoes of the Past, Epics of Dissent: A South Korean Social Movement*; on Korean America, *Blue Dream: Korean Americans and the Los Angeles Riots* (with John Lie); and on South Korean women and social mobility, *The Melodrama of Mobility: Women, Talk and Class in Contemporary South Korea*. She is coeditor of the forthcoming book *Gender, Genre, and Nation: South Korean Golden Age Melodrama*, and is completing *The Intimate University: College and the Korean American Family*.

WANNI W. ANDERSON teaches anthropology and folklore at Brown University and is also a faculty member in the Ethnic Studies concentration. Her research includes the studies of Lao Americans, Thai Americans, Thai Muslims in southwestern Thailand, and the Iñupiaq Eskimo in northwest Alaska. Her most recent book is a bilingual Iñupiaq Eskimo and English textbook, *Folktales of the Riverine and Coastal Iñupiat*. She served on the editorial board of the journal *Play & Culture* and was associate director of the Center for the Study of Race and Ethnicity in America at Brown University from 1991 to 1996.

LOUIS-JACQUES DORAIS teaches anthropology at Université Laval, Quebec, Canada and had served as the editor of the journal *Etudes Inuit Studies*. Since the late 1970s, he has conducted research on various aspects of Vietnamese Canadian community organization. He has published edited books and articles on the Vietnamese Canadians, including *Exile in a Cold Land* and *Ten Years Later: Indochinese Communities in Canada*. He also specializes in questions of Inuit (Eskimo) language and identity.

EVELYN HU-DEHART is professor of history and director of the Center for the Study of Race and Ethnicity in America, Brown University. She also oversees the Ethnic Studies concentration within the center. She has conducted research and published on the Chinese in Mexico and Cuba, the Yaqui Indians in Mexico and

Arizona, and on women and minorities in higher education. Her most recent publication on Asians in the Americas is *Across the Pacific: Asian Americans and Globalization.*

WALTON LOOK LAI studied at Oxford University, England, and New York University in the United States. He is a lecturer in the History Department of the University of the West Indies in Trinidad. He is the author of *Indentured Labor, Caribbean Sugar: Chinese and Indian Migrants to the British West Indies 1838–1918* and *The Chinese in the West Indies: A Documentary History.* He is also a contributor to the volume *Coerced and Free Migration: Global Perspectives,* edited by David Eltis, for Stanford University Press, Making of Modern Freedom Series, as well as to the *Encyclopedia of the Chinese Overseas.*

CHRISTOPHER LEE received his B.A. from the University of British Columbia and is a doctoral candidate in English at Brown University. In 2002–2003 he studied at Tsinghua University at Beijing. He is currently writing his dissertation on Asian American literature and theories of the aesthetic.

ROBERT G. LEE is associate professor in the Department of American Civilization at Brown University. He is author of *Orientals: Asian Americans in Popular Culture* (best book in 1999 on the social construction of race from the American Political Science Association, honorable mention for the best book in American Studies in 1999 from the American Studies Association, and best book from the NE Popular Culture/American Culture Association), and editor of *Dear Miye, Letter Home from Japan* (special book award 1998, Association for Asian American Studies). He is currently at work on a book on Chinese American discourses of citizenship.

JEFFREY LESSER is professor and director of the Program in Latin American and Caribbean Studies at Emory University. His research focuses on ethnicity, immigration, and race, especially in Brazil. His *Negotiating National Identity: Immigrants, Minorities and the Struggle for Ethnicity in Brazil* was awarded the Best Book Prize, Latin American Studies Association, Brazil in Comparative Perspective Section. He is also author of *Welcoming the Undesirables: Brazil and the Jewish question,* winner of the best book prize from the New England Association of Latin American Studies, and is editor of *Searching for Home Abroad: Japanese-Brazilians and the Transnational Moment.*

BERNARD SCOTT LUCIOUS teaches literature and cultural studies at Morehouse College, Department of English. He has been a fellow-in-residence at the Princeton University Program in African American Studies, Virginia Tech, and University of Southern Maine. He received his Ph.D. in English at the University of Florida. Lucious is both Thai American and African American.

SUNAINA MAIRA is associate professor of Asian American Studies at the University of California, Davis. She is the author of *Desis in the House: Indian American Youth Culture in New York*, a study of second-generation Indian American youth and coeditor of *Contours of the Heart: South Asians Map North America*, which won the American Book Award in 1997. She is coeditor of *Youthscapes: Popular Culture, National Ideologies, Global Markets*, and is doing research on South Asian Muslim immigrant youth and the U.S. empire.

E. SAN JUAN JR. is visiting professor of English and fellow of the Center for the Humanities, Wesleyan University. He was previously chair of the Department of Comparative American Cultures, Washington State University, and visiting professor at Tamkang University, Taiwan, and University of Trento, Italy. His recent books are *Beyond Postcolonial Theory, After Postcolonialism* (winner of the 2001 Myers Center Outstanding Book Award), and *Racism and Cultural Studies*.

NINA GLICK SCHILLER, professor of anthropology and coordinator of the Race, Culture, and Power minor at the University of New Hampshire, has conducted research in Haiti, Germany, and the United States. The founding editor of the journal *Identities: Global Studies in Culture and Power*, she has written extensively on transnational migration and the questions of race, ethnicity, and migrant identity. She is a coauthor of *Nations Unbound Towards a Transnational Perspective on Migration*. Her most recent coauthored book is *Georges Woke Up Laughing: Long Distance Nationalism and the Search for Home*, coauthored with Georges Fouron.

K. SCOTT WONG is an associate professor of history at Williams College, where he teaches a variety of courses in Asian American history, comparative immigration history, the history of the American West, and American Studies. He is coeditor, with Sucheng Chan, of *Claiming America: Constructing Chinese American Identities during the Exclusion Era*, and will soon publish a book on the impact of the Second World War on Chinese Americans. When not teaching or writing, he fishes for trout and keeps trying to play like Mississippi John Hurt.

INDEX